CONTEMPORARY'S

American History 1

Matthew T. Downey

Wright Group

The McGraw·Hill Companies

Author
Matthew T. Downey received his Ph.D. in American History from Princeton University. He served as Director of the Clio Project in History-Social Science Education in the Graduate School of Education at the University of California, Berkeley. He also directed the U.C. Berkeley site of the California History-Social Science Project. He has taught at the University of Colorado, the University of California at Los Angeles, and at Louisiana State University. Currently, he directs the Social Science Program and the William E. Hewitt Institute for History and Social Science Education at the University of Northern Colorado.

Reading Consultant
Grace Sussman, Ed.D.
    University of Northern Colorado

Project Editor: Mitch Rosin
Executive Editor: Linda Kwil
Image Coordinator: Barbara Gamache
Cover Design: Tracy Sainz
Interior Design: Linda Chandler
Cartography and Graphics: Tim Piotrowski

Photo credits are on page 364.

Reviewers
Jeffrey J. Johll
    K–12 District Social Studies Supervisor
    Dubuque Community School District
    Dubuque, Iowa
Eleanor Nangle
    Social Studies Instructor
    Chicago, Illinois
Judy Novack-Hirsch
    Social Studies Instructor
    New York, New York
Brian Silva
    Social Studies Instructor
    Long Beach, California
Jill Smith
    Social Studies Instructor
    Giddings, Texas

About the Cover
The images on the cover include (from left to right): Ferdinand Magellan, Abigail Adams, Abraham Lincoln, Sequoya, Sojourner Truth, George Washington.

Wright Group

ISBN 0-07-704435-5 (Student Edition)
ISBN 0-07-704434-7 (Student Edition with DVD)
ISBN 0-07-704453-3 (Annotated Teacher's Edition)
ISBN 0-07-704436-3 (Teacher's Resource Binder)

Send all inquiries to:
Wright Group/McGraw-Hill
P.O. Box 812960
Chicago, IL 60681

Printed in the United States of America.

2 3 4 5 6 7 8 9 10 QUE/QUE 11 10 09 08 07 06 05

Contents

To the Instructor

This book is a survey of American history from prehistoric times to the Civil War. I have tried to make it as comprehensive in coverage as space permits. It includes important economic, social, and intellectual developments, as well as wars and political events. I also have tried to make the book broadly inclusive. It tells the story of ordinary Americans as well as of the rich and famous. It demonstrates that people of different ethnic groups, races, and cultures helped make American history.

The book also strives to be inclusive in another sense. I have tried to write a book that helps below-grade-level readers. Each chapter begins with a pre-reading activity. These help students find a purpose for reading or activate their prior knowledge by letting them anticipate what is to come. Many pages include comprehension strategies designed to help students better understand what they are reading. Each chapter ends with activities that sharpen students' understanding of what they have learned.

American history is the story of individuals as well as groups. To emphasize this, each chapter includes a brief biography of a person who left her or his mark on American life. Some of these people were rich and famous; others were ordinary folks. The chapters also include first-hand accounts by individuals who lived at the time. Among them are accounts by an English colonist, an African slave, and a frontier settler. Such accounts help give students a feel for the times.

This text tries to reach students who learn in different ways. Each chapter and virtually every page delivers historical information in multiple forms—text, visual images, maps, and charts. Many of the pictures are rich primary sources. The people included in this book shaped American society. My goal is to help your students understand that they, too, can shape the future of America.

Matthew T. Downey

About the Student Book

The Student Edition of *American History 1* was created for those students who need extra help in reading and comprehension. The text is written at a fifth- to eighth-grade reading level, but it contains the key concepts and basic facts necessary for the study of American history at the high school level. Key support is given with pre-reading activities that guide students through a preview of the text and illustrations.

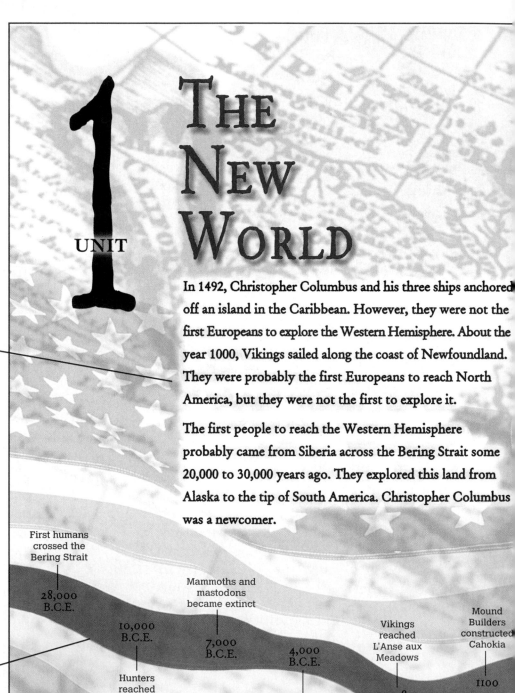

THE NEW WORLD

UNIT 1

In 1492, Christopher Columbus and his three ships anchored off an island in the Caribbean. However, they were not the first Europeans to explore the Western Hemisphere. About the year 1000, Vikings sailed along the coast of Newfoundland. They were probably the first Europeans to reach North America, but they were not the first to explore it.

The first people to reach the Western Hemisphere probably came from Siberia across the Bering Strait some 20,000 to 30,000 years ago. They explored this land from Alaska to the tip of South America. Christopher Columbus was a newcomer.

First humans crossed the Bering Strait

28,000 B.C.E.

10,000 B.C.E.

Hunters reached what is now United States

Mammoths and mastodons became extinct

7,000 B.C.E.

4,000 B.C.E.

Knowledge of farming spread to North America

Vikings reached L'Anse aux Meadows

998

Mound Builders constructed Cahokia

1100

2

Unit Opener

Units begin with a summary of the chapters included in the unit. Key concepts are identified and an overview of topics is introduced.

Timeline

Each unit presents a timeline. The timeline includes important events that are discussed in the chapters. The Annotated Teacher's Edition provides extension activities that relate to the timelines.

Pre-reading activities activate prior knowledge. Pre-reading questions and vocabulary focus the students' reading. Opportunity is given halfway through each lesson to stop and organize ideas, and again at the end of each lesson to summarize. Additional support is provided for remedial readers on the Student DVD, and with Blackline Masters and Overhead Transparencies in the Teacher's Resource Binder. Extra help for English Language Learners is provided on the Student DVD and on additional Blackline Masters on the Teacher's CD.

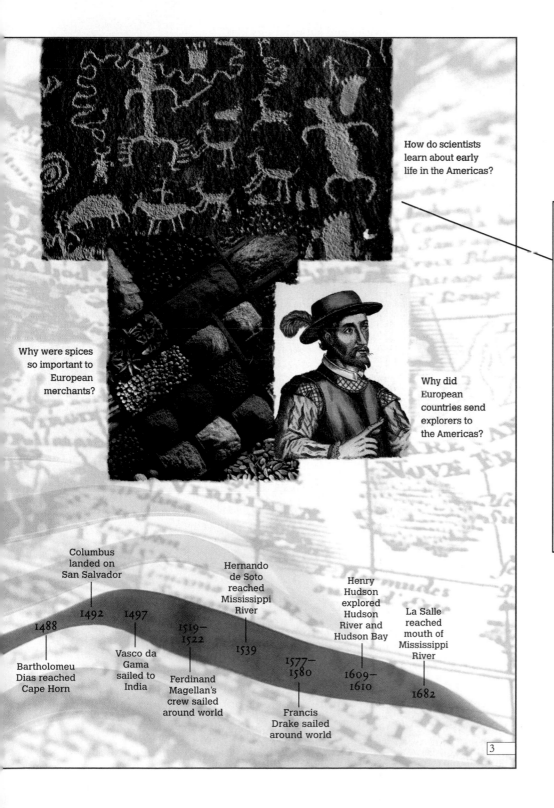

How do scientists learn about early life in the Americas?

Why were spices so important to European merchants?

Why did European countries send explorers to the Americas?

Collage

The collage of illustrations and accompanying questions should be used to generate a discussion about the chapters and develop students' prior knowledge about the topics covered. Each image represents a major event in the unit and provides information related to the question it accompanies.

1488 — Bartholomeu Dias reached Cape Horn

1492 — Columbus landed on San Salvador

1497 — Vasco da Gama sailed to India

1519–1522 — Ferdinand Magellan's crew sailed around world

1539 — Hernando de Soto reached Mississippi River

1577–1580 — Francis Drake sailed around world

1609–1610 — Henry Hudson explored Hudson River and Hudson Bay

1682 — La Salle reached mouth of Mississippi River

3

Getting Focused

The Getting Focused section of each chapter should be used as a pre-reading activity. Students are directed to read the lessons and subheadings, look at illustrations and read captions, examine maps, and review vocabulary words. Then students are asked to complete an activity in preparation for reading the chapter.

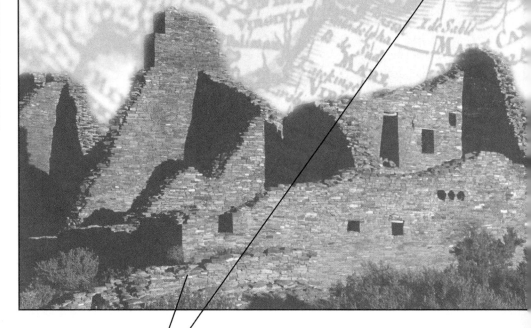

Chapter 1

EARLY PEOPLE AND CULTURES

Getting Focused

Skim this chapter to predict what you will be learning.

- Read the lesson titles and subheadings.
- Look at the illustrations and read the captions.
- Examine the maps.
- Review the vocabulary words and terms.

Think about what you already know about the early people and cultures of North America. Write the questions you have about the topic before reading the chapter. Discuss your questions with a partner.

Chapter Opener Images

Each chapter begins with one or two images. These images are explained in the Annotated Teacher's Edition and represent events discussed in the chapter. The images should be used to generate classroom discussion about the chapter topics. The images provide connections with key chapter concepts and help to further develop students' prior knowledge.

Early Hunters and Farmers

Thinking on Your Own

Read over the vocabulary. While you read, use each vocabulary word in a sentence of your own. Write the sentences in your notebook.

The first people to live in North America were big-game hunters. Many early settlers crossed the Bering Strait from Siberia around 20,000 to 30,000 years ago. They came to North America following herds of animals. Although the strait is now a body of water, during the last **Ice Age**, when portions of the oceans froze, it was a land bridge. The level of the Bering Sea was lower then because glaciers and ice sheets took up much of the world's water. In a few thousand years, descendents of these hunters occupied most of North and South America.

focus your reading

How did the first humans get to North America?

What animals did they hunt?

What kind of crops did early farmers raise?

vocabulary

Ice Age

archaeologists

hunters and gatherers

domesticate

Mound Builders

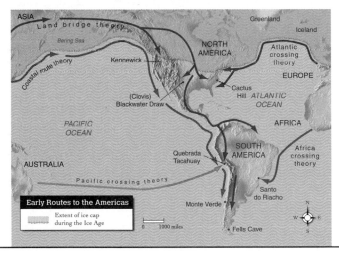

Early Routes to the Americas

Extent of ice cap during the Ice Age

0   1000 miles

5

Stop and Think

Stop and Think activities are designed to help students organize and interact with the material they have just read so that it can be remembered. The activity provides a stopping point midway through the lesson and encourages students to think about what they have read.

stop and think

In your notebook draw three interlocking circles with a common middle. Label the circles "Sebastian Cabot," "Martin Frobisher," and "Henry Hudson." In each circle write one interesting fact about that explorer. In the common middle write what the three had in common.

continent. He returned with his ship loaded with ore that looked like silver. It turned out to be worthless. In 1610, Henry Hudson thought he had found the Northwest Passage. It was only a large inland sea that later was named Hudson Bay.

Francis Drake's Voyage Around the World

The reign of Queen Elizabeth I (1558–1603) produced a new kind of English explorer. These English **"sea dogs" plundered**, or stole from, Spanish shipping while they explored new territory. The most daring of all was Francis Drake. Queen Elizabeth helped Drake outfit a fleet of ships for a voyage around the world. He crossed the Atlantic in 1577 and sailed through the Strait of Magellan. Then he sailed north to raid Spanish colonial towns along the Pacific coast of South America. After capturing a Spanish treasure ship near Panama, he sailed up the coast of Mexico and California. He was looking for a western entrance to the Northwest Passage. Drake arrived back in England in 1580. He spent nearly three years traveling 36,000 miles around the world, but did not find a shortcut to the Indies.

Putting It All Together

Sailors often told stories about their adventures at sea. Imagine that you are an English seaman who sailed with Martin Frobisher (1576) or Francis Drake (1577–1580). Write a story about your adventures. Include facts such as time of year, weather, conditions at sea.

Fra
Dra
the
dog

European Exp

Putting It All Together

A Putting It All Together activity appears at the end of each lesson. These activities tie together the key concepts of the lesson. They often involve using a graphic organizer or creating a piece of written work. They frequently ask students to work together or discuss ideas with a partner to expand their viewpoint or understanding. Students should be encouraged to incorporate key elements from each lesson into the Putting It All Together activities.

Biography

A Biography is included in each chapter. The biographies draw attention to individuals who lived during the time period discussed in the chapter.

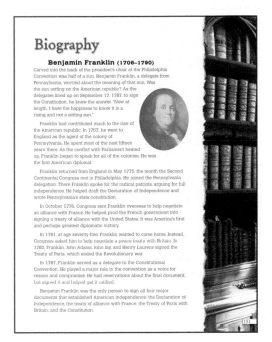

Biography

Benjamin Franklin (1706–1790)

Carved into the back of the president's chair at the Philadelphia Convention was half of a sun. Benjamin Franklin, a delegate from Pennsylvania, worried about the meaning of that sun. Was the sun setting on the American republic? As the delegates lined up on September 17, 1787, to sign the Constitution, he knew the answer. "Now at length, I have the happiness to know it is a rising and not a setting sun."

Franklin had contributed much to the rise of the American republic. In 1757, he went to England as the agent of the colony of Pennsylvania. He spent most of the next fifteen years there. As the conflict with Parliament heated up, Franklin began to speak for all of the colonies. He was the first American diplomat.

Franklin returned from England in May 1775, the month the Second Continental Congress met in Philadelphia. He joined the Pennsylvania delegation. There Franklin spoke for the radical patriots, arguing for full independence. He helped draft the Declaration of Independence and wrote Pennsylvania's state constitution.

In October 1776, Congress sent Franklin overseas to help negotiate an alliance with France. He helped prod the French government into signing a treaty of alliance with the United States. It was America's first and perhaps greatest diplomatic victory.

In 1781, at age seventy-five, Franklin wanted to come home. Instead, Congress asked him to help negotiate a peace treaty with Britain. In 1783, Franklin, John Adams, John Jay, and Henry Laurens signed the Treaty of Paris, which ended the Revolutionary war.

In 1787, Franklin served as a delegate to the Constitutional Convention. He played a major role in the convention as a voice for reason and compromise. He had reservations about the final document, but signed it and helped get it ratified.

Benjamin Franklin was the only person to sign all four major documents that established American independence: the Declaration of Independence, the treaty of alliance with France, the Treaty of Paris with Britain, and the Constitution.

151

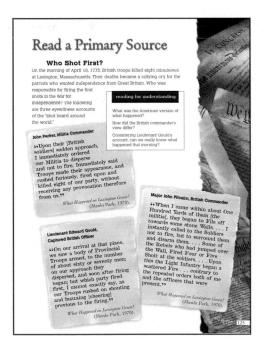

Read a Primary Source

Who Shot First?

On the morning of April 19, 1775, British troops killed eight minutemen at Lexington, Massachusetts. Their deaths became a rallying cry for the patriots who wanted independence from Great Britain. Who was responsible for firing the first shots in the War for Independence? The following are three eyewitness accounts of the "shot heard around the world."

reading for understanding

What was the American version of what happened?

How did the British commander's view differ?

Considering Lieutenant Gould's account, can we really know what happened that morning?

John Parker, Militia Commander

"Upon their [British soldiers] sudden approach, I immediately ordered our Militia to disperse and not to fire. Immediately said Troops made their appearance, and rushed furiously, fired upon and killed eight of our party, without receiving any provocation therefore from us."

What Happened on Lexington Green?
(Menlo Park, 1970).

Major John Pitcairn, British Commander

"When I came within about One Hundred Yards of them [the militia], they began to File off towards some stone Walls. . . . I instantly called to the Soldiers not to fire, but to surround them and disarm them. . . . Some of the Rebels who had jumped over the Wall, Fired Four or Five Shott at the soldiers. . . . Upon this the Light Infantry began a scattered Fire . . . contrary to the repeated orders both of me and the officers that were present."

What Happened on Lexington Green?
(Menlo Park, 1970).

Lieutenant Edward Gould, Captured British Officer

"On our arrival at that place, we saw a body of Provincial Troops armed, to the number of about sixty or seventy men; on our approach they dispersed, and soon after firing began; but which party fired first, I cannot exactly say, as our Troops rushed on shouting and huzzaing [cheering] previous to the firing."

What Happened on Lexington Green?
(Menlo Park, 1970).

125

Primary Source

Each chapter includes a Primary Source page. The documents enhance the content of the chapter.

Chapter Summary

By the 1840s, everyday life in the United States was
changing. Farm families who once raised most of their
own food and made their own clothing were now raising **cash
crops** and buying what they needed. Farmers who once cut
wheat with a **scythe** now used **mechanical reapers** that could
harvest more grain and make more money. Housework also
was changing. Women no longer had to weave their own cloth,
and the new cook stove made cooking easier.

The 1840s also saw more people living in towns and cities,
especially in the Northeast. Many people moved there to work
in **textile mills** and factories. In 1791, Samuel Slater built a
factory to make thread with **spinning machines**. Some of the
mills and factories were located in **company towns**, such as
Lowell, Massachusetts. American seaports grew as shipping
increased, and **wharves** were piled high with goods.

The factory and mill owners encouraged poor New England
families to move to the mill towns. As a result, many of the
new workers were children and teenage girls. They lived in
supervised **boardinghouses**. These children and "mill girls"
worked long hours under poor conditions for very little money.

Many **immigrant** workers were **peasant farmers** who fled
Ireland due to the **potato famine**. Unskilled and starving, they
gladly worked long hours for low wages. In time, they
replaced the young farm women in the textile mills.

Chapter Review

1 Create an ad for the mechanical reaper to distribute to
farmers in the 1840s.

2 Imagine that you are a young person who moved to the city
in the 1840s. Write a letter to your family back on the farm
about city life and work.

3 Organize a concept web with "Factory Workers" as the main
topic in the center circle. In lines going out from the circle,
add information related to the topic.

Chapter Summary

This is a summary of the events discussed in the
chapter. It includes vocabulary words and key
people.

Chapter Review

The questions at the end of the Chapter
Summary help to summarize the key events in
the chapter and provide a review of important
facts. Students are often asked to conduct
further research, to represent their ideas
visually, or to write about their opinions.

Skill Builder

Skill Builder pages address key skills necessary for successful mastery of social studies
concepts. Skills include:

Chapter 1: Primary and Secondary Sources
Chapter 2: Reading Maps
Chapter 3: Working with a Timeline
Chapter 4: Reading a Table
Chapter 5: Comparing Tables
Chapter 6: Reading a Bar Graph
Chapter 7: Identifying Propaganda
Chapter 8: Historical Works of Art
Chapter 9: Recognizing Persuasive Writing
Chapter 10: Reading a Historical Document
Chapter 11: Understanding Cause and Effect
Chapter 12: Diaries as Primary Sources
Chapter 13: Reading a Map
Chapter 14: Analyzing Political Cartoons
Chapter 15: Reading Graphs
Chapter 16: Critically Reading Primary Sources
Chapter 17: Mapping Change over Time
Chapter 18: Mapping Movement
Chapter 19: Reading a Presidential Election Map
Chapter 20: Interpreting Multiple Graphs

Skill Builder

Mapping Change over Time

Maps serve different purposes. All maps show where cities,
rivers, mountains, or other places are located. Maps also can
show change over time.

This map shows the growth of railroads in the Northeast,
Midwest, and South. Railroads that existed in 1850 are shown
in purple. Those built between 1850 and 1860 are shown in
orange. The locations of major cities are also shown.

Use the map to answer the following questions:

1 Which section
(Northeast, Midwest, or
South) had the most
railroads by 1850?

2 Which section
(Northeast, Midwest, or
South) added the most
railroads between 1850
and 1860?

3 Which section
(Northeast, Midwest, or
South) had the fewest
railroads by 1860?

4 Which cities were major
rail centers by 1860?

5 What advantage did the
Northeast have by 1860?

6 Why was New Orleans
at a disadvantage?

About the Student DVD

The Student DVD contains several instructional tools:

Student Book with Audio Files

The entire Student Edition is available on screen in PDF format. Next to each paragraph is an icon of a speaker. When the icon is clicked, the paragraph will be read aloud. Students with reading difficulties or English Language Learners will benefit from having the text read to them.

Spanish Introduction and Spanish Activity

Research has shown that English Language Learners benefit from verbally generating prior knowledge about a given topic in their first language prior to learning new concepts in English. Coupled with the generation of prior knowledge is a writing component. By writing about a concept in their first language, students increase comprehension and are better prepared for content acquisition in English. The last component is writing about acquired knowledge in English.

At the beginning of each chapter are two icons. The first icon is for a Spanish Introduction. This activity is designed to generate prior knowledge for Spanish speakers. It introduces the key concept of the chapter and presents lesson overviews. The second icon is for a Spanish Activity. This activity asks students to write about the key concept in Spanish. Students are instructed to revisit their Spanish paragraph after completing the chapter by completing an English writing activity that incorporates their prior knowledge with the new concepts learned. See pages xviii–xxxiii in this section for English translations of the Spanish Introductions and Activities.

Key Concepts Introduced in Spanish

Chapter 1: Culture

Chapter 2: Exploration

Chapter 3: Conquest

Chapter 4: Colonization

Chapter 5: Cash Crops

Chapter 6: Religious Freedom

Chapter 7: Protest and Resistance

Chapter 8: Revolution

Chapter 9: Political Organization

Chapter 10: The Constitution

Chapter 11: Democracy

Chapter 12: The War of 1812

Chapter 13: Expansion

Chapter 14: Displacement

Chapter 15: Slavery

Chapter 16: Tolerance

Chapter 17: Industrialization

Chapter 18: Manifest Destiny

Chapter 19: Compromise

Chapter 20: Civil War

Hot-linked Vocabulary Definitions

Vocabulary words at the beginning of each lesson are hot-linked to provide Glossary definitions. To access the Glossary definition of each word, students should click on the vocabulary word. A dialog box will then open that provides the Glossary definition.

Audio Captions

Captions for each photograph, painting, and cartoon are read aloud when the student clicks on the speaker icon.

Reading Comprehension and Vocabulary Reinforcement Activities

Each chapter is accompanied by four activities that reinforce reading comprehension and provide vocabulary reinforcement. They include: Fill in the Blank, Crossword Puzzle, eFlashcards, Multiple Choice, Text Identification, Concept Columns, Matching, and Vocabulary Concentration.

Interactive Timeline

The Interactive Timeline can be accessed by clicking on the timeline at the bottom of the Unit Opener pages. The Interactive Timeline provides additional information about events in American history, as well as additional images. This is a powerful tool for enhancing the curriculum and provides students with the opportunity to conduct research on the topics covered in the Student Edition.

Student Presentation Builder

The Student Presentation Builder utilizes PowerPoint technology and allows students to create presentations using images and maps from the chapters. An introductory lesson is included to teach students how to use this technology.

The Annotated Teacher's Edition

The Annotated Teacher's Edition provides answers to questions in the student text and extension activities to enhance the lessons. The extension activities are designed to help remedial students better understand the text material and to assist English Language Learners to develop a broader understanding of the text content.

Unit Objectives
Skills and concepts targeted in the two chapters in each unit are identified at the beginning of each unit.

Getting Started
Getting Started provides teachers with a method of introducing the unit to students. This section often includes an introduction to key vocabulary terms and concepts. Students are encouraged to read the unit introduction to generate prior knowledge.

Measuring Time

Measuring Time introduces the unit timeline. Questions are posed that will help students to better understand the period of history covered by the two chapters in the unit.

Timeline Extension

Understanding a timeline is an important social studies skill. Timeline Extensions provide additional information about the timelines at the beginning of each unit and questions that can be used to generate classroom discussion.

Collage Answers
The three illustrations that begin each unit, and the accompanying questions, should be used to generate students' prior knowledge about the topics covered in the unit. The Collage Extension activities can be used to enhance this instructional tool. Additional information is provided about the illustrations, and questions to the students are presented.

Related Transparencies

The Related Transparencies box lists the transparencies from the Teacher's Resource Binder that relate to the chapter.

Key Blacklines

Each chapter is accompanied by eight Blackline Masters from the Teacher's Resource Binder. These include: Biography, Primary Source, Reading Comprehension, Vocabulary Reinforcement, Map/Graphic Activity, Chapter Review, Chapter Activity, and Chapter Quiz. The topics of the Biography and the Primary Source are indicated in the Key Blacklines box.

DVD Extension

The Student DVD box is a reminder that students will benefit from the material presented on the DVD.

Pre-Reading Discussion

Pre-Reading Discussion is designed to provide questions and topics that generate prior knowledge among students. Students are asked to review specific sections of text, images, or charts within the chapter.

Bio Facts

Additional information about each person profiled on the Biography pages. This information adds to the background knowledge that teachers need to lead the class in a discussion about the person profiled on the Biography page.

Putting It All Together

Answers and/or suggestions are provided for the Putting It All Together activities that end each lesson.

Stop and Think

Answers and/or suggestions are provided for the Stop and Think activities that appear partway through each lesson.

Reading for Understanding

Each Primary Source page contains reading comprehension questions to guide students through the text. Answers to the Reading for Understanding questions will vary, but suggestions of key facts are provided.

Lesson Summary

Summaries are provided at the beginning of each lesson to help the teacher understand the overall themes and key concepts.

Lesson Objective

The Lesson Objective identifies the key goal for student learning.

Lesson Vocabulary

Vocabulary words and terms are explained at the beginning of each lesson. Teachers are provided with techniques to introduce each vocabulary word and a method of linking the terms to a key concept of the lesson.

Picturing History

The illustrations—photos, cartoons, graphs and charts, and paintings—in *American History 1* can be used to enhance students' understanding of the topics covered and to generate classroom discussion. Selected illustrations are identified in the Picturing History boxes, and additional information is presented about the illustrations.

Map Extension

Geography skills are an important component of social studies instruction. Map Extension activities are included with each map throughout the Student Edition. These activities target key skills students must have to ensure academic achievement in the social studies.

Biography Extension

The Student Edition contains one biography page per chapter. The Biography Extension box includes additional background information about the person highlighted in the Student Edition. The material can be used to supplement class discussion and to provide additional material for student research.

Novel Connections

At the end of each chapter is a list of supplemental reading materials for students. These books correlate to the concepts and topics of each chapter. The Thematic Strands of the National Council for the Social Studies are identified.

Classroom Discussion

The Classroom Discussion section provides teachers with questions to help wrap up the chapter. These questions incorporate key concepts from the chapter and guide students through making connections to related topics in American history.

The Teacher's Resource Binder

Blackline Masters

There are 160 Blackline Masters in the Teacher's Resource Binder. Each chapter contains one Blackline Master for each of the following topics: Biography, Primary Source, Reading Comprehension Activity, Vocabulary Reinforcement Activity, Map/Graphic Activity, Chapter Review, Chapter Activity, and Chapter Quiz. An Answer Key is included at the end of the Blackline Master section.

Overhead Transparencies

There are 20 Overhead Transparencies in the Teacher's Resource Binder. They include key maps that relate to the chapters, images that can be used to enhance classroom instruction, and graphic organizers: Concept Web, T-Chart, Venn Diagram, and a KWL Chart. Each Overhead Transparency is noted in the chapters where relevant, although many can be used repeatedly throughout the text.

CD

Included with the Teacher's Resource Binder is a CD. The CD contains the entire Annotated Teacher's Edition in PDF format, so it is not necessary to carry around the Annotated Teacher's Edition. Also on the CD are additional PDF Blackline Masters that can be printed. Included are: Vocabulary Reinforcement pages designed for ELL instruction, Reading Comprehension pages designed for ELL instruction, Chapter Puzzles, Chapter Assessments, Unit Assessments, and a Book Assessment.

On-Line Book Assessment Correlated to State Standards

Final book assessments are available on the McGraw-Hill/Contemporary website: www.mhcontemporary.com. This 50-question test assesses skills outlined by the state standards.

Spanish Introduction and Activities

Each chapter on the Student DVD is accompanied by an audio introduction in Spanish and an audio activity in Spanish. The introductions are designed to generate prior knowledge in the English Language Learner's first language. The activities are designed to link prior knowledge with the chapter being studied. The English and Spanish versions of each chapter's Introduction and Activity are provided below. They can also be used to assist non-English Language Learners.

English	Spanish
Chapter 1 – Spanish Introduction	
The lessons in this chapter are about the different groups of people who lived in North America many years ago, before the Europeans explored the continent. The key concept of this chapter is "culture." Culture is the way of life of a group of people and includes their customs, language, traditions, and beliefs. Lesson 1 introduces early hunters and gatherers. Lesson 2 discusses the daily life, food, and shelter of the Woodland People who lived in the eastern part of the current United States. Lesson 3 introduces the people who lived in the western section of what is now the United States.	Las lecciones en este capítulo detallan los diferentes grupos que vivieron en América del Norte hace muchos años, antes de que los europeos exploraran el continente. El concepto central de este capítulo es cultura. Cultura es el modo de vivir de un grupo de personas e incluye sus costumbres, su lenguaje, tradiciones y creencias. La lección 1 presenta a los cazadores y recolectores primitivos. La lección 2 discute la vida diaria, alimento y albergue de las gentes de Woodland que vivieron en el este de lo que es actualmente los Estados Unidos. La lección 3 presenta a la gente que vivió en el oeste de lo que ahora es los Estados Unidos.
Chapter 1 – Spanish Activity	
With a partner, discuss the concept of culture. What are some things that help define your culture? Make a bulleted list of ideas about your culture. (An example of a bulleted list can be found on page 35.) Use your notes to write a short paragraph in Spanish explaining your culture, including traditional foods, special clothing, and holiday celebrations. After you read the chapter, review your paragraph. Then write a second paragraph in English that describes one of the cultures you read about. Use the information from the chapter in your paragraph.	Con un compañero, discute el concepto de cultura. ¿Que define tu cultura? Haz una lista de tus ideas acerca de tu cultura. En la página 35 puedes encontrar un ejemplo de una lista Usa tu lista para escribir un párrafo breve en español acerca de tu cultura, incluyendo comidas tradicionales, ropa especial y celebraciones festivas. Después de leer el capítulo, revisa tu párrafo. Entonces, escribe otro párrafo en inglés que describa una de las culturas que leíste. Usa la información del capítulo en tu párrafo.

Chapter 2 – Spanish Introduction

The lessons in this chapter are about the Europeans who explored North America from the late 1400s until almost the end of the 1600s. The key concept in this chapter is "exploration." Exploration includes the discovery and examination of something new. In Lesson 1, you will learn about the earliest European explorers, the Portuguese and the Spanish who were looking for a new route to the Indies. Lesson 2 introduces the English explorers who searched for land for England while they looked for a new route to the Indies. Lesson 3 is about the French explorers who explored and claimed large portions of the North American continent for France.

Las lecciones en este capítulo son acerca de los europeos que exploraron Norte América desde el siglo XV a casi finales del siglo XVI. El concepto esencial en este capítulo es la exploración. La idea de exploración incluye el descubrimiento y la exploración de algo nuevo. En la lección 1, aprenderás acerca de los primeros exploradores europeos, portugueses y españoles que buscaban una ruta nueva para las Indias. La lección 2 introduce a los exploradores ingleses quienes mientras buscaban tierra nueva para Inglaterra buscaban una ruta nueva para las Indias. La lección 3 es acerca de los exploradores franceses que exploraron y reclamaron porciones grandes del continente norteamericano para Francia.

Chapter 2 – Spanish Activity

Think back to when you first arrived in the United States. How did you become familiar with your neighborhood? How did you figure out how to get to various places? Who were the people who helped you feel at home? Discuss this with a partner. Then write a short paragraph explaining how you felt when you first went somewhere all by yourself. After you read the chapter, choose one explorer that you read about in this chapter and imagine yourself as a member of his exploration party. Use the information from the chapter to write a short paragraph describing what you saw and how you felt.

Piensa acerca de cuando llegaste a los Estados Unidos por primera vez. ¿Cómo te familiarizaste con tu vecindario? ¿Cómo descubriste para llegar a varios lugares? ¿Quiénes fueron las personas que te ayudaron para que te sintieras como en casa? Discute esto con un compañero y luego escribe un párrafo breve explicando como te sentiste la primer vez que saliste a algún lugar solo o sola. Después de leer el capítulo, escoge uno de los exploradores e imagínate que eres un miembro de su equipo de exploración. Utiliza la información del capítulo para escribir un párrafo breve donde describas lo que viste y cómo te sentiste.

Chapter 3 – Spanish Introduction

The lessons in this chapter are about the European colonization of the Americas. The key concept in this chapter is "conquest." Conquest means "to take by force." Conquest comes from the verb "to conquer," which means "to overcome or subdue by force." In Lesson 1, you will learn how the Spanish established their first colonies on the Island of Hispaniola in 1493. The Spanish empire became the largest empire in the western world in less than one hundred years by conquering the Aztec in Mexico and defeating the Incas in Peru. In Lesson 2, you will read how the Spanish moved north to

Las lecciones en este capítulo son acerca de la colonización europea de las Américas. El concepto central de este capítulo es la "conquista." Conquista viene del verbo "conquistar," que quiere decir "someter por la fuerza." En la lección 1, vas a aprender como los españoles establecieron sus primeras colonias en la isla de la Española en 1493. El imperio español se volvió el más grande en el mundo occidental en menos de cien años después de conquistar a los aztecas en México y vencer a los incas en Perú. En la lección 2, vas a leer como los españoles avanzaron al norte de lo que es

Chapter 3 – Spanish Introduction, continued

the present-day United States to establish a colony in Florida and farms and missions in Arizona, New Mexico, and California. Lesson 3 is about the French colonization of southern Canada and the fur trade, as well as the Dutch colonies in the northeastern part of the present-day United States.

actualmente los Estados Unidos para establecer una colonia en Florida y granjas y misiones en Arizona, Nuevo México y California. La lección 3 es acerca de la colonización francesa en el sur de Canadá y del comercio de pieles, así como de la colonización holandesa en el nordeste de lo que es hoy los Estados Unidos.

Chapter 3 – Spanish Activity

Think about what you already know about the Spanish conquest of the Americas. How would you describe the colonization experience for the people who were already living there? Discuss this with a partner. After you read the chapter, imagine that you are trying to convince a Native American to settle near a mission and learn how to farm. What arguments would you use? Write a bulleted list in Spanish of the main points, and then discuss them with a partner. After you finish the chapter, review your Spanish notes and write a paragraph in English about the Spanish conquest.

Piensa acerca de lo que ya sabes de la conquista española de las Américas. ¿Cómo describirías la experiencia de colonización para la gente que vivía ahí? Discute con un compañero. Después de leer el capítulo, imagina que tú estas tratando de convencer a un nativo para que se establezca cerca una misión y aprenda a cultivar. ¿Que razones le darías? Escribe una lista de los puntos principales en español y discútela con un compañero. Después de completar el capítulo, revisa tus notas en español y escribe un párrafo en inglés acerca la conquista española.

Chapter 4 – Spanish Introduction

The lessons in this chapter are about how England established the most successful colonies in North America between 1587 and 1682. The key concept in this chapter is "colonization." Colonization means "to send settlers to live in a new area and to claim that area for the parent country." Lesson 1 is about the English colonies of Roanoke, Jamestown, Maryland, and South Carolina. Lesson 2 is about how important religious freedom was to the settlers of the first English colonies in New England, including Plymouth and the Massachusetts Bay. In Lesson 3, you will read how the English took land away from the Dutch to establish the colonies of New York and New Jersey. You will also learn about how the Quakers settled in Pennsylvania.

Las lecciones en este capítulo son acerca de cómo Inglaterra estableció las colonias más prósperas en América del Norte entre 1587 y 1682. El concepto central de este capítulo es "colonización." Colonización quiere decir enviar a colonos a vivir a un lugar nuevo y reclamar ese lugar para su propio país. La lección 1 es acerca de las colonias inglesas: Roanoke,, Jamestown, Maryland y Carolina del sur. La lección 2 es acerca de cómo la libertad religiosa fue muy importante para los colonizadores de las primeras colonias inglesas en Nueva Inglaterra, éstas incluyeron Plymouth y Bahía de Massachusetts. En la lección 3, vas a leer cómo los ingleses le quitaron tierra a los holandeses para establecer las colonias de Nueva York y Nueva Jersey. También aprenderás cómo los Cuáqueros se establecieron en Pennsylvania.

Chapter 4 – Spanish Activity

Think about what would make someone want to leave their homeland to live in a distant, unsettled land. In Spanish, make a list of five good reasons before discussing them with a partner. After you have read the chapter, select a colony described in the chapter. Write a short letter to a friend in English, listing your reasons for wanting to settle there.

Piensa qué motivaría a alguien a dejar su país para vivir en un lugar despoblado y lejano. Escribe una lista en español de cinco razones positivas antes de discutirlas con un compañero. Después de leer el capítulo, escoge una colonia de la cual leíste. Escribe una carta breve en inglés a un amigo explicando las razones por las que te gustaría vivir allí.

Chapter 5 – Spanish Introduction

This chapter describes how the Southern Colonies prospered and grew. It also explains the conflict with the Native Americans that resulted. The key concept of this chapter is "cash crops." Cash crops are plants or grains grown primarily for sale. In Lesson 1, you will learn about the people who settled in the South and their way of life. Lesson 2 is about the people who made up the labor force in the South—white servants and African slaves. Lesson 3 describes the conflicts that developed between the Native Americans and the settlers as the population of the colonies increased and they expanded their territories.

Este capítulo describe cómo las colonias del sur prosperaron y crecieron. También se explica el conflicto que se derivo con los indios americanos. El concepto general de este capítulo son las "cosechas comerciales." Las cosechas comerciales son plantas o granos cultivados principalmente para la venta. En la lección 1 vas aprender acerca de la gente que colonizó el sur y su modo de vida. La lección 2 es acerca de la gente que formó la fuerza de trabajo del sulos sirvientes europeos y los esclavos africanos. La lección 3 describe el conflicto que se desarrolló entre los indios americanos y los colonizadores al mismo tiempo que la población de las colonias aumentaba y los territorios se extendían.

Chapter 5 – Spanish Activity

Think about why it was necessary for the colonists to find a way to make some money. With a partner, discuss in Spanish what people do today to make extra money. Write a bulleted list of your ideas. After reading the chapter, imagine you are a farmer who needs to make extra money by raising cash crops. In English, write down your reasons for buying an African slave instead of hiring a white servant to help you. Use the ideas you created in your bulleted list.

Piensa porqué fue necesario que los colonizadores encontraran una forma de ganar dinero. Con un compañero, discute en español cómo la gente gana dinero extra en la época actual. Escribe una lista de tus ideas. Después de leer el capítulo, imagínate que eres un agricultor que necesita ganar dinero extra con el cultivo de granos y plantas. En inglés, escribe tus razones porqué comprarías un esclavo africano en lugar de contratar a un sirviente europeo para ayudarte. Utiliza la lista de ideas que creaste anteriormente.

Chapter 6 – Spanish Introduction

This chapter describes the lives of the settlers in the colonies from Delaware and Pennsylvania to New England, and the effects on the Native Americans of the same region. The key concept in this chapter is "religious freedom." Religious freedom means "the freedom to worship or practice one's religion without fear of retaliation." Lesson 1 describes the expansion of the New England Colonies, the importance of religion, and the impact of the expansion on the Native Americans. In Lesson 2, you will read how farming made the Middle Colonies prosperous and attracted many kinds of people. Lesson 3 describes the lives of the people who lived in the cities of New England and Middle Colonies.

Este capítulo describe la vida de la gente en las colonias de Delaware y Pennsylvania hasta Nueva Inglaterra y el efecto de esta colonización en los indios americanos de la misma región. El concepto principal en este capítulo es la "libertad religiosa." Libertad religiosa quiere decir la libertad de culto y práctica de religión sin miedo a represalias. La lección 1 describe la expansión de las colonias de Nueva Inglaterra, la importancia de la religión y el impacto de la expansión en los indios americanos. En la lección 2 vas a leer cómo la agricultura beneficio a las colonias del centro, las hizo más prósperas y atrajo gente de todo tipo. La lección 3 describe la vida de la gente que vivía en las ciudades de las colonias de Nueva Inglaterra y las colonias del centro.

Chapter 6 – Spanish Activity

With a partner, discuss in Spanish why religious freedom is an important idea. What makes religious freedom important today? Make a list of your ideas. After you have read the chapter, write a short paragraph in English explaining how religion affected the lives of the colonists.

Con un compañero, discute en español porqué la libertad religiosa es una idea importante. ¿Qué hace que la libertad religiosa sea importante hoy en día? Escribe una lista de tus ideas. Después de leer el capítulo, escribe un párrafobreve en ingles explicando cómo la religión afectó la vida de los colonos.

Chapter 7 – Spanish Introduction

The lessons in this chapter discuss how decisions about taxes and war that were made in England affected the British colonists. The key concepts in this chapter are "protests and resistance." In Lesson 1, you will learn how Britain more than doubled its territory in North America after the French and Indian War, how it tried to maintain peace with the Native Americans, and how this affected the colonists. Lesson 2 is about the British taxes on the colonists and the colonists' reaction. Lesson 3 explains how the tax on tea eventually led to the First Continental Congress and a list of rights that the colonists wanted Parliament in England to respect.

Las lecciones en este capítulo discuten cómo las decisiones hechas en Inglaterra acerca de los impuestos y de la guerra afectaron a los colonos británicos. Los conceptos centrales de este capítulo son "protestas y resistencia." En la lección 1, aprenderás como Gran Bretaña duplicó su territorio en América del Norte después de la guerra contra Francia y los indios, cómo trató de mantener la paz con los indios americanos, y cómo esto afectó a los colonos. La lección 2 es acerca de los impuestos británicos y la reacción de los colonos . La lección 3 explica cómo los impuestos al té promovieron la creación del Primer Congreso Continental y una lista de derechos que los colonos querían que el Parlamento en Inglaterra respetara.

Chapter 7 – Spanish Activity

Imagine that at your school students are told that they must contribute $1 for the purchase of a gift for the principal. Students who do not contribute will not be passed on to the next grade. How would you react and why? Discuss this in Spanish with a partner. After reading the chapter, write a paragraph in English explaining your understanding of "no taxation without representation."

Imagínate que en tu escuela se les dice a los estudiantes que todos tienen que contribuir con un $1 para comprar un regalo para el director y que los estudiantes que no contribuyan no pasaran al próximo grado. ¿Cuál sería tu reacción? ¿Porqué? Discute acerca de esto en español con un compañero. Después de leer el capítulo, escribe un párrafo breve en inglés explicando cómo entiendes "no impuestos sin representación."

Chapter 8 – Spanish Introduction

This chapter is about the war for independence fought against Great Britain by the colonies from 1775 to 1783. The key concept in this chapter is "revolution." Revolution means "the overthrow or replacement of a government or political system by those governed." In Lesson 1, you will read how Britain's reaction to the colonists' demand for certain rights led to the first violent encounters between the colonists and British soldiers. Lesson 2 is about the decision to declare independence and the writing of the Declaration of Independence. Lesson 3 describes several important battles of the war. It also introduces the Tories, who were loyal to the British king, and concludes with the Treaty of Paris in 1783 that officially ended the war.

Este capítulo es acerca de la guerra de independencia de los colonos contra Gran Bretaña que se llevo acabo de 1775 hasta 1783. El concepto principal en este capítulo es la "revolución." Revolución quiere decir el derrocamiento o sustitución de un gobierno o sistema político. En la lección 1, vas a leer acerca de cómo la reacción de Gran Bretaña ante la demanda de ciertos derechos por parte de los colonos provocó los primeros enfrentamientos violentos entre los colonos y los soldados británicos. La lección 2 es acerca de la declaración de independencia y de la redacción de la Declaración de Independencia. La lección 3 describe varias batallas importantes de la guerra. También introduce a los Tories quienes eran fieles al rey de Gran Bretaña, y concluye con el Tratado de París de 1783 que oficialmente termina con la guerra.

Chapter 8 – Spanish Activity

Think back to the list of rights that the First Continental Congress wanted the British Parliament to respect. What rights do you think were on that list? With a partner, discuss in Spanish what these rights might be. Then write a bulleted list of these rights in Spanish and why you think they are important. After reading the chapter, imagine that you are a Tory. What reasons would you give for wanting to stay under the rule of Great Britain? Write a list of reasons in English. Compare your list with a partner. Then, using your list, create a poster in English that urges readers to remain British subjects.

Piensa acerca de la lista de derechos que el Primer Congreso Continental quería que el Parlamento Británico respetara. ¿Cuales derechos crees que estaban en esa lista? Con un compañero discute en español cuáles derechospudieron haber sido. Entonces escribe una lista de estos derechos en español y las razones por las cuales piensas que eran importantes. Después de leer el capítulo, imagínate que eres un Tory. ¿Que razones darías para desear quedarte bajo el gobierno de Gran Bretaña? Escribe una lista de razones en inglés. Compara tu lista con un compañero. Entonces, utilizando tu lista, crea un anuncio en inglés exhortando a los demás a mantenerse bajo el régimen de Gran Bretaña.

Chapter 9 – Spanish Introduction

This chapter discusses how the first central government of the United States was organized and why it had to be changed to be more effective. The key concept in this chapter is "political organization." A political organization is a number of individuals who unite to influence government. In Lesson 1, you will learn how the newly independent colonies organized themselves into a confederation of powerful states and a weak central government. Lesson 2 is about how the problems with this type of organization led to a revision of the Articles of Confederation. Lesson 3 is about how representatives from each state except one worked to develop a constitution for the United States that provided for three branches of government: legislative, executive, and judiciary.

Este capítulo discute cómo el primer gobierno central de los Estados Unidos fue organizado y porqué tuvo que ser modificado para ser más efectivo. El concepto principal en este capítulo es la "organización política." Una organización política consiste en un grupo de individuos unidos para influenciar al gobierno. En la lección 1 aprenderás cómo los colonos, recientemente independientes, se organizaron en una confederación de estados poderosos y un gobierno central muy débil. La lección 2 es acerca de cómo los problemas con ese tipo de gobierno resultó en la necesidad de revisar los Artículos de la Confederación. La lección 3 es acerca de cómo representantes de cada estado, a excepción de uno, trabajaron para desarrollar una constitución para los Estados Unidos que determinaría las tres ramas de gobierno: legislativa, ejecutiva y judicial.

Chapter 9 – Spanish Activity

Think about what you have learned about a representative form of government. Now think about the student council in your school. With a partner, discuss in Spanish how you are represented on the student council. Write a short summary of your discussion in Spanish. After reading the chapter, draw a Venn diagram. In English, compare the Constitution to the Articles of Confederation. Using your diagram, write a short paragraph in English explaining why the Constitution was better than the Articles of Confederation.

Piensa acerca de lo que has aprendido acerca de una forma de gobierno representativo. Ahora piensa acerca del concilio estudiantil en tu escuela. ¿Cómo eres tu representado en el concilio estudiantil? Después de leer el capítulo, escribe un párrafo en ingles dando por lo menos 3 razones por las cuales la Constitución fue mejor que los Artículos de la Confederación.

Chapter 10 – Spanish Introduction

The lessons in this chapter are about the ideas that guided the writers of the Constitution of the United States. The key concept in this chapter is "constitution." A constitution is the written document that contains the basic principles and laws of a nation. This document determines the powers and duties of the government and guarantees certain rights to the people. Lesson 1 describes the powers unique to the federal government, the powers of the states, and the powers they share. Lesson 2 introduces the idea of

Las lecciones en este capítulo son acerca de las ideas que guiaron a los escritores de la Constitución de los Estados Unidos. El concepto principal en este capítulo es "constitución." Una constitución es un documento por escrito que contiene los principios básicos y las leyes de una nación que determinan los poderes y responsabilidades del gobierno y garantiza ciertos derechos para el pueblo . La lección 1 describe los poderes únicos del gobierno federal, los poderes de los estados, y los poderes que tienen en común. La

Chapter 10 – Spanish Introduction, continued

"checks and balances." You will learn why the writers of the Constitution made sure that the powers of the federal government were shared among the three branches of government. You will also learn how they ensured that no branch of government would become too powerful. Lesson 3 is about a group of ten amendments, known as the Bill of Rights, which were added to the Constitution after it was ratified.

lección 2 introduce la idea de "restricciones y equilibrios." Vas aprender porqué los escritores de la Constitución aseguraron que los poderes del gobierno federal fueran compartidos por las tres ramas del gobierno. También vas aprender cómo se aseguraron que ninguna rama del gobierno se hiciera demasiado poderosa. La lección 3 es acerca de un grupo de enmiendas, conocidas cómo la Declaración de Derechos, que fueron añadidas a la Constitución cuando ésta fue ratificada.

Chapter 10 – Spanish Activity

With a partner, discuss in Spanish what school would be like if students had no rights. Then write a list in Spanish of three rights you feel students should have in a public school in order to get a good education. Write a brief paragraph in Spanish explaining why these rights are important. After reading the chapter, think about how the need for school rules affects students' rights. Review your list. Then write a short paragraph in English about the relationship between students' rights and school rules.

Con un compañero discute en español cómo serian las escuelas si los estudiantes no tuvieran derechos. Entonces escribe en español una lista de tres derechos que tu consideras que los estudiantes deben de tener para obtener una buena educación. Escribe un párrafo breve en español explicando porqué estos derechos son importantes. Después de leer el capítulo, piensa cómo la necesidad de reglas escolares afecta los derechos estudiantiles. Revisa tu lista. Luego escribe un párrafobreve en inglés acerca la relación entre los derechos estudiantiles y las reglas de la escuela.

Chapter 11 – Spanish Introduction

This chapter is about the men who established the first U.S. government under the new Constitution. They were known as the Federalists because they had supported the new Constitution, which provided for shared power between the central government and the states. The key concept in this chapter is "democracy." A democracy is a government in which citizens have the power and exercise their power directly or indirectly through a system of representation. In Lesson 1, you will learn about the initial actions taken by the Federalists to govern the United States under the new Constitution. Lesson 2 describes the disagreements among the Federalists regarding how the government should deal with various issues and how the the Constitution should be interpreted. Lesson 3 describes some of the problems that resulted because of these disagreements among the Federalists.

Este capítulo es acerca de los hombres que establecieron el primer gobierno bajo la nueva Constitución. Eran reconocidos cómo los Federalistas porque habían apoyado la nueva Constitución que aseguraba un equilibrio del poder entre el gobierno central y los estados. El concepto principal en este capítulo es "democracia." Una democracia es un gobierno en el cual los ciudadanos tienen el poder y el poder de ejercerlo directamente o indirectamente a través de un sistema de representación. En la lección 1 vas aprender acerca de las primeras acciones que los Federalistas llevaron a cabo para gobernar los Estados Unidos baja la nueva Constitución. La lección 2 describe los desacuerdos entre los Federalistas con respecto a cómo el gobierno debetratar con varias situaciones y cómo la Constitución se debe interpretar. La lección 3 describe algunos de los problemas que resultaron a causa de estos desacuerdos entre los Federalistas.

Chapter 11 – Spanish Activity

At home, at school, and in sports there are rules we all must follow. Have you ever had a disagreement with an authority figure about how a rule should be interpreted? Discuss that disagreement with a partner in Spanish. Then write a list of three reasons in Spanish why you think people interpret rules in different ways. After reading the chapter, decide which position you would take: Federalist or Anti-Federalist. Write a list of reasons in English. Using that list, write a short paragraph in English explaining your reasons.

En el hogar, en la escuela, y en los deportes existen reglas que todos tenemos que seguir. ¿Has tenido alguna vez un desacuerdo con una autoridad acerca de cómo una regla se debe de interpretar? Discute ese desacuerdo con un compañero en español. Entonces en español escribe una lista de tres razones por las cuales la gente interpreta las reglas de diferente manera. Después de leer el capítulo, decide cuál posición tomarías : la federalista o la anti-federalista. Escribe una lista de razones. Utilizando tu lista, escribe un párrafo breve en inglés explicando tus razones.

Chapter 12 – Spanish Introduction

The lessons in this chapter are about government in the early 1800s. The key concept in this chapter is the "War of 1812." The War of 1812 was fought between Britain and the United States over issues of trade and defense. It has also been called the second American war for independence because the United States had to reassert its power against Britain. In Lesson 1, you will learn how Thomas Jefferson, with the Republicans in Congress, tried to simplify and limit the size of government during his eight years as president. Lesson 2 describes how the country grew and prospered in the early 1800s. It also describes how the United States faced threats from Britain and France, who were at war, because neither country respected the United States' neutral rights. Lesson 3 is about the events that led to the War of 1812 and how that war was resolved.

Las lecciones en este capítulo son acerca del gobierno a principios del siglo XIX . El concepto principal en este capítulo es la "Guerra de 1812. La Guerra de 1812 se llevó acabo entre Gran Bretaña y los Estados Unidos por cuestiones de comercio y defensa. A esta guerra se le ha denominado como la segunda guerra de independencia americana porque los Estados Unidos tuvieron que reafirmar su poder contra Gran Bretaña. En la lección 1 vas aprender cómo Thomas Jefferson, con su partido en el Congreso, trató de simplificar y limitar el tamaño del gobierno durante sus ocho años como presidente. La lección 2 describe cómo el país creció y prosperó durante los primeros años del siglo XIX. En éste también se describe cómo los Estados Unidos enfrentaron amenazas de parte de Gran Bretaña y de Francia que estaban en guerra porque ninguno respetaba el derecho de neutralidad de los Estados Unidos. La lección 3 es acerca de los eventos que llevaron a la Guerra de 1812 y cómo ésta guerra se resolvió.

Chapter 12 – Spanish Activity

The following statement has been attributed to Thomas Jefferson: "That government which governs least governs best." With a partner, discuss in Spanish what you think Jefferson meant by that statement. Write a short paragraph in Spanish explaining why you agree or disagree with that statement. After reading the chapter, imagine you are a farmer in the Ohio Valley in 1810. Write a short paragraph in English explaining why you think the country should go to war.

La siguiente declaración se ha atribuido a Thomas Jefferson: "El gobierno que gobierna menos gobierna mejor." Con un compañero, discute en español lo que piensas que Jefferson quiso decir con esa declaración. Escribe un párrafo breve en español explicando porqué estas de acuerdo o en desacuerdo con esa declaración. Después de leer el capítulo, imagínate que eres un agricultor en el valle de Ohio en 1810. Escribe un párrafo breve en inglés explicando porqué piensas que el país debe de ir a la guerra.

Chapter 13 – Spanish Introduction

The lessons in this chapter are about the country's expansion west after the War of 1812. The key concept in this chapter is "expansion." Expansion means "to increase." In Lesson 1, you will read how people traveled over land and water to settle new territories as far west as the Mississippi River. Lesson 2 describes the lives of the hunters and farmers who were the first to move west. It also describes the growth of towns and villages. Lesson 3 describes the settlements beyond the Mississippi River that included Texas. It also provides a description of how traders took supplies to new settlers in the Mexican town of Santa Fe.

Las lecciones en este capítulo son acerca de la expansión del país hacia el oeste después de la guerra de 1812. El concepto principal en este capítulo es "expansión." Expansión quiere decir aumentar. En la lección 1 vas a leer cómo la gente viajo por tierra y agua para establecerse en territorios nuevos tan lejos al oeste como hasta el río Mississippi. La lección 2 describe la vida de los cazadores y agricultores que fueron los primeros en mudarse al oeste. También se describe el desarrollo de pueblos y ciudades. La lección 3 describe las colonias más allá del río Mississippi que incluye Texas. También da una descripción de cómo comerciantes llevaron provisiones a los nuevos colonos en el pueblo mexicano de Santa Fe.

Chapter 13 – Spanish Activity

Pretend you are going camping for a year in the wilderness. You can take only what can be carried on horseback. Discuss this with a partner in Spanish. Then write a list in Spanish of what you would take. After reading the chapter, imagine you are a settler heading west in a wagon. Write a letter in English to a friend back home about what you are experiencing.

Imagina que vas a acampar en aislamiento por un año. Puedes traer solamente lo que se puede cargar en un caballo. Discute esto con un compañero en español. Entonces escribe una lista en español de lo que llevarías. Después de leer el capítulo, imagínate que eres un colono viajando al oeste en una carreta. Escribe una carta en inglés a un amigo en tu pueblo acerca de lo que estas viviendo.

Chapter 14 – Spanish Introduction

This chapter describes the events that began with the "Era of Good Feelings" in 1816 and ended with the depression of 1837. The key concept in this chapter is "displacement of people." In this chapter, displacement of people refers to the events that forced thousands of Native Americans to have to leave their homelands. In Lesson 1, you will learn how the U.S. government became stronger and how the country assumed a greater role in world affairs. You will also learn why this was a period of prosperity for the United States. Lesson 2 introduces the economic and political issues that began to trouble the country. Lesson 3 is about the presidency of Andrew Jackson. It describes some of the actions he took to shift more responsibility for government to the states and how he forced thousands of Cherokee from their homeland.

Este capítulo describe los eventos que comenzaron con la "era de buenos sentimientos" en 1816 y terminaron con la depresión económica de 1837. El concepto principal en este capítulo es "desplazamiento de gente." En este capítulo, "desplazamiento de gente" se refiere a los hechos que forzaron a miles de indios americanos a dejar su tierra. En la lección 1 vas aprender como el gobierno de los Estados Unidos se hizo más fuerte y como el país asumió un papel más importante en asuntos mundiales. También vas aprender porqué éste fue un periodo de prosperidad para los Estados Unidos. La lección 2 introduce las cuestiones económicas y políticas que comenzaron a preocupar al país. La lección 3 es acerca de la presidencia de Andrew Jackson. Describe algunas de las acciones que él tomó para dar más responsabilidad al gobierno de los estados y como él hizo que miles de Cherokees abandonaran su tierra.

Chapter 14 – Spanish Activity

The rights of Native Americans has been an issue since the first European settlers arrived in America. Why did the settlers think they could claim this land for their home country when the Native Americans were already living there? With a partner, discuss in Spanish the Native American issue and the concept of displacement. Then write a short paragraph in Spanish explaining your point of view. After reading the chapter, think about President Jackson's refusal to enforce the Supreme Court decision in favor of the Cherokee. Then write a short paragraph in English describing what you think this meant for the concept of "checks and balances."

Los derechos de los indios americanos han sido un punto de disputa desde que los colonos europeos llegaron a América. ¿Porqué los colonos pensaron que ellos podían reclamar esta tierra para su propio país cuando los indios americanos ya vivían allí? Con un compañero, discute en español la cuestión de los indios americanos y el concepto de desplazamiento. Entonces escribe un párrafo breve en español explicando tu punto de vista Después de leer el capítulo, piensa acerca del rechazo por parte del Presidente Jackson a hacer cumplir la decisión del tribunal supremo en favor de los Cherokees. Entonces escribe un párrafo breve en inglés describiendo lo que tu crees que esto significó con respecto al concepto de "restricciones y equilibri."

Chapter 15 – Spanish Introduction

The lessons in this chapter describe life in the South when cotton became a major cash crop. Plantation owners relied on slavery as a source of labor. The key concept in this chapter is "slavery." Slavery is the practice of keeping other people as property. In Lesson 1, you will read about how the invention of the cotton gin contributed to the growth and prosperity of the South. Lesson 2 describes the kind of work that slaves did and provides some examples of their resistance. Lesson 3 describes life in the slave community.

Las lecciones en este capítulo describen la vida en el sur cuando el algodón se volvió una cosecha comercial. Los dueños de las plantaciones dependían de la esclavitud como fuerza de trabajo . El concepto principal en este capítulo es "esclavitud." La esclavitud es la practica de tener gente como propiedad. En la lección 1 vas a leer acerca de cómo la invención de la desmotadora de algodón contribuyó al crecimiento y la prosperidad del sur. La lección 2 describe el trabajo que los esclavos hacían y da ejemplos de su resistencia. La lección 3 describe la vida en la comunidad de los esclavos.

Chapter 15 – Spanish Activity

In many Southern states, it was a crime to teach slaves how to read and write. With a partner, discuss in Spanish how the lack of education helped slavery to continue. Write a short paragraph in Spanish explaining how a slave knowing how to read and write would threaten his owner. After reading the chapter, write a list of ways in which the rights of slaves and the rights of women were similar. Then write a short paragraph in English explaining these similarities.

En muchos estados del sur, era un crimen enseñar a los esclavos a leer o a escribir. Con un compañero, discute en español cómo la falta de educación facilitaba la continuación de la esclavitud. Escribe un párrafo breve en español explicando porqué el hecho de que un esclavo supiera leer y escribir representaba una amenaza para su dueño. Después de leer el capítulo, escribe una lista de las similitudes de los derechos de los esclavos y de los derechos de las mujeres. Entonces escribe un párrafo en inglés explicándolas.

Chapter 16 – Spanish Introduction

This chapter is about the ideas that changed the way people thought about how they should live and work in the early 1800s. The key concept in this chapter is "tolerance." Tolerance is the acceptance of beliefs or practices that are different from one's own. Lesson 1 is about how a renewed interest in religion in the early 1800s led to efforts to reform society. In Lesson 2, you will read about the early efforts to free slaves and abolish slavery. You will also read about the early fight for the rights of women. Lesson 3 is about the emergence of a new American identity in literature and art during the first half of the 18th century.

Este capítulo es acerca de las ideas que cambiaron la manera de pensar de la gente acerca de cómo debían vivir y trabajar en los primeros años del siglo XVIII. El concepto principal en este capítulo es "tolerancia." Tolerancia es la aceptación de creencias o practicas que son diferentes de las propias. La lección 1 es acerca de cómo un nuevo interés en la religión en los primeros años del siglo XVIII resultó en esfuerzos para reformar la sociedad. En la lección 2 vas a leer acerca de los primeros esfuerzos para devolver la libertad a los esclavos y abolir la esclavitud. También vas a leer acerca de los primeros confrontamientos por los derechos de las mujeres. La lección 3 es acerca del surgimiento de una identidad nueva en la literatura y el arte americanos durante la primera parte del siglo XVIII.

Chapter 16 – Spanish Activity

Think about one major problem facing people in your community. Write a list in Spanish of ways to address this problem. Discuss these with a partner in Spanish. Select the best method and write a short paragraph in Spanish explaining what it is. After reading the chapter, imagine that you have been asked to paint a mural in the center of your neighborhood. The theme of the mural is "A Better Life for Us." Write a short paragraph in English describing what the mural would look like.

Piensa acerca de un problema importante que enfrenta la gente en tu comunidad. Escribe una lista en español de alternativas para resolver este problema. Discute estas alternativas con un compañero en español. Selecciona la mejor alternativa y escribe un párrafo breve en español explicando de lo que se trata. Después de leer el capítulo, imagínate que te han pedido que pintes un mural en el centro de tu vecindario. El tema del mural es "Una vida mejor para nosotros." Escribe un párrafo breve en inglés describiendo cómo se vería el mural.

Chapter 17 – Spanish Introduction

This chapter is about how the invention of machines that made work easier and quicker changed how and where people lived and worked. The key concept in this chapter is "industrialization." Industrialization is the transition from work done manually by individuals to work done by groups of people using machines. In Lesson 1, you will read how machines made life easier on American farms for both men and women and how this made farming more profitable. Lesson 2 is about several inventions that made it possible to produce goods faster and cheaper. As a result, these inventions contributed to the growth of cities and the expansion of the railroads. Lesson 3 describes the lives of the children and young women who worked long hours in factories for very low wages.

Este capítulo es acerca de cómo la invención de máquinas que hicieron el trabajo más fácil y más rápido repercutió en cómo y donde la gente vivía y trabajaba. El concepto principal en este capítulo es "industrialización." La industrialización es la transición del trabajo manual al trabajo colectivo hecho en máquinas. En la lección 1, vas a leer cómo las máquinas hicieron la vida más fácil en las granjas americanas para hombres y mujeres y cómo esto hizo que la agricultura fuera más lucrativa. La lección 2 es acerca de los inventos que hicieron que la producción de mercancías fuera más rápida y más barata. Como consecuencia, estos inventos contribuyeron al crecimiento de las ciudades y a la expansión de los ferrocarriles. La lección 3 describe la vida de niños y mujeres jóvenes que trabajaban largas horas en las fábricas por muy poco dinero.

Chapter 17 – Spanish Activity

Think about all the machines you rely on from the time you wake up until you go to bed. Discuss these in Spanish with a partner. Then write a short paragraph in Spanish describing how your life would be different if none of these machines existed. After reading the chapter, write a short paragraph in English explaining how your childhood was different from your grandfather's because of machines.

Piensa acerca de las máquinas de las cuales tu dependes desde que te levantas hasta que te vas a dormir. Discute esto con un compañero en español. Entonces escribe un párrafo breve en español describiendo cómo tu vida seria diferente si estas máquinas no existieran. Después de leer el capítulo, escribe un párrafo breve en inglés explicando cómo tu niñez fue diferente de la de tu abuelo por causa de las máquinas.

Chapter 18 – Spanish Introduction

The lessons in this chapter discuss the events that took place between the early 1830s and the late 1840s. The key concept in this chapter is "manifest destiny." Manifest destiny refers to the belief that white settlers were intended by God to extend the nation's boundaries to the Pacific Ocean. Lesson 1 describes the expansion west, beyond the Rocky Mountains. In Lesson 2, you will read about disputes between Mexico and the United States over territory in the southwest that led to war with Mexico in 1846. In Lesson 3, you will learn how the addition of new territory resulted in renewed concerns about the issue of slavery. You will also learn how the discovery of gold in California contributed to these concerns.

En las lecciones de este capítulo se discuten los eventos que se llevaron acabo entre 1830 y 1840. El concepto principal en este capítulo es "destino manifiesto." Destino manifiesto se refiere a la creencia de los colonos de que la expansión de la frontera americana hasta el océano Pacífico era predestinada por Dios. La lección 1 describe la expansión al oeste, más allá de las Montañas Rocosas. En la lección 2, vas a leer acerca de las disputas entre México y los Estados Unidos por el territorio en el sudoeste, trayendo consigo la guerra con México en 1846. En la lección 3, vas aprender cómo la adición de este territorio resultó en una reconsideración del asunto del problema de la esclavitud. También vas aprender cómo el descubrimiento de oro en California contribuyo a dicha reconsideración de la esclavitud.

Chapter 18 – Spanish Activity

Think about how the idea of "manifest destiny" could be used to justify moving Native Americans farther and farther west. Discuss this with a partner in Spanish. Then write a short paragraph in Spanish explaining reasons why white settlers would want Native Americans off the land. After reading the chapter, write a short paragraph in English explaining your understanding of the Treaty of Guadalupe.

Piensa acerca de cómo la idea del "destino manifiesto" pudo haber sido usado para justificar el movimiento de los indios americanos más allá del oeste. Discute esto con un compañero en español. Entonces escribe un párrafo breve en español dando razones por las cuales los colonos querían a los indios americanos fuera de su tierra. Después de leer el capítulo, escribe un párrafo breve en inglés explicando cómo entiendes el Trato de Guadalupe.

Chapter 19 – Spanish Introduction

This chapter is about various attempts to keep the issue of slavery from dividing the country. The key concept in this chapter is "compromise." Compromise refers to a settlement of differences reached when two parties each agree to give something up. In Lesson 1, you will read about the Compromise of 1850, which was an effort to maintain the balance of free and slave states in the country. Lesson 2 is about another compromise effort related to the issue of free and slave states—the Kansas-Nebraska Act. This lesson also introduces the idea of "popular sovereignty," which means that people in new territories had the right to choose to become a free or a slave state. Lesson 3 describes a Supreme Court case and an attack on a federal arsenal that were part of a series of events that led to seven Southern states seceding from the Union.

Este capítulo es acerca de varios intentos para prevenir que el asunto de la esclavitud no dividiera al país. El concepto principal en este capítulo es "compromiso." Compromiso se refiere a un arreglo de diferencias logrado por el acuerdo de dos partes a renunciar a algo. En la lección 1, vas a leer acerca del Compromiso de 1850 que fue un esfuerzo para mantener un equilibrio en el país de estados libres y estados con esclavitud. La lección 2 es acerca de otro esfuerzo de compromiso relacionado al asunto de estados libres y estados con esclavitud—el Acto de Kansas-Nebraska. Esta lección también introduce la idea de la "soberanía popular, " que quiere decir que la gente en territorios nuevos tenían el derecho de ser un estado libre o con esclavitud. La lección 3 describe un caso del tribunal supremo y un ataque a un arsenal federal que resultaron en la separación de siete estados sureños de los Estados Unidos.

Chapter 19 – Spanish Activity

Compromise is only possible when each side wants something. Think about a time when you disagreed with someone about something really important to you and you felt you lost the argument. With a partner, discuss this in Spanish. Then write a short paragraph in Spanish describing how this disagreement made you feel. After reading the chapter, write a short paragraph in English describing how it might have turned out if a compromise had been possible.

El compromiso es posible solamente cuando cada parte quiere algo. Piensa en alguna situación donde estuviste en desacuerdo con alguien acerca de algo muy importante y sentiste que perdiste el argumento. Con un compañero, discute esto en español. Entonces, escribe un párrafo breve en español describiendo cómo te sentiste. Después de leer el capítulo, escribe un párrafo breve en inglés describiendo cómo un compromiso pudo haber cambiado tu desacuerdo.

Chapter 20 – Spanish Introduction

The lessons in this chapter describe the American Civil War from 1861 to 1865. The key concept in this chapter is "civil war," which means a war between groups of citizens of the same country. In Lesson 1, you will read about President Lincoln's determination to defend the Union and about some of the early defeats for the Union side. Lesson 2 describes how the war affected the lives of people away from the battlefields. Lesson 3 describes how abolishing slavery became an important goal of the war and how the Union finally won the war in April of 1865.

Las lecciones en este capítulo describen la Guerra Civil Americana, de 1861 a 1865. El concepto principal en este capítulo es la "guerra civil" que quiere decir una guerra entre grupos de ciudadanos del mismo país. En la lección 1, vas a leer acerca de la determinación del presidente Lincoln de defender la Unión y acerca de algunas de sus primeras derrotas. La lección 2 describe cómo la guerra afectó la vida de la gente lejos del campo de batalla. La lección 3 describe cómo la abolición de la esclavitud se volvió un objetivo importante de la guerra y cómo la Unión ganó la guerra en abril de 1865.

Chapter 20 – Spanish Activity

In the American Civil War, some fathers, sons, and brothers disagreed about the issues that led to the war. Some even fought on opposing sides. Discuss with a partner in Spanish what you think about this situation. Then write a short paragraph in Spanish explaining why you think fighting between family members during the Civil War was right or wrong. After reading the chapter, write a short paragraph in English explaining the reasons for the Civil War.

En la Guerra Civil Americana, algunos padres, hijos y hermanos estaban en desacuerdo acerca de las cuestiones que llevaron a la guerra. Algunos hasta lucharon en lados opuestos. Discute con un compañero en español lo que piensas de esto. Entonces escribe un párrafo breve en español explicando porqué piensas que la lucha entre miembros de la familia durante la Guerra Civil fue correcta o incorrecta. Después de leer el capítulo, escribe un párrafo en inglés explicando las razones que llevaron a la Guerra Civil.

Unit Objectives

After studying this unit, students will be able to

- explain how scientists think the first humans arrived in the Americas

- compare and contrast ways of life before 1500 in various parts of what is now the United States

- identify why many Europeans came to the Americas in the early 1500s

- compare and contrast Spanish and Portuguese explorations with those of the English and French

Unit 1 describes the earliest arrivals to the Western Hemisphere (North and South America).

Chapter 1, Early People and Cultures, focuses on the ways of life that evolved in the Americas between the end of the last Ice Age and 1500.

Chapter 2, European Explorers, considers the impact of early Spanish, Portuguese, English, and French explorers on life in the Americas.

UNIT 1 THE NEW WORLD

In 1492, Christopher Columbus and his three ships anchored off an island in the Caribbean. However, they were not the first Europeans to explore the Western Hemisphere. About the year 1000, Vikings sailed along the coast of Newfoundland. They were probably the first Europeans to reach North America, but they were not the first to explore it.

The first people to reach the Western Hemisphere probably came from Siberia across the Bering Strait some 20,000 to 30,000 years ago. They explored this land from Alaska to the tip of South America. Christopher Columbus was a newcomer.

First humans crossed the Bering Strait
28,000 B.C.E.

Mammoths and mastodons became extinct
7,000 B.C.E.

10,000 B.C.E.
Hunters reached what is now United States

4,000 B.C.E.
Knowledge of farming spread to North America

Vikings reached L'Anse aux Meadows
998

Mound Builders constructed Cahokia
1100

2

Getting Started

Encourage students to keep track of unfamiliar words and ideas in a journal or notebook. They might begin by creating a working definition of the word *explore*. A working definition is one that grows as students read, reflect, and discuss ideas and events.

Ask students what the word *explore* means to them. Then read aloud the introduction on page 2, and discuss how the word is used in the two paragraphs. (As a verb, *explore* means *to search or travel for the purpose of discovery*.) As students continue reading, ask them to expand and revise their definitions. Also, discuss the meanings of related words—such as *explorer* and *exploration*.

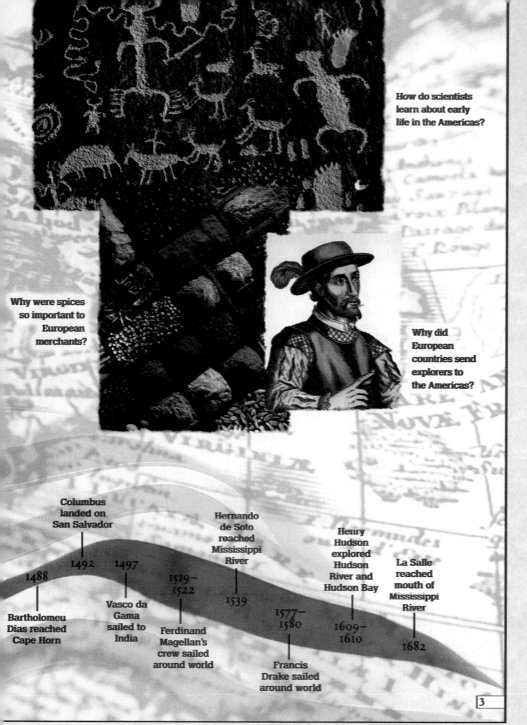

How do scientists learn about early life in the Americas?

Why were spices so important to European merchants?

Why did European countries send explorers to the Americas?

1488 — Bartholomeu Dias reached Cape Horn

1492 — Columbus landed on San Salvador

1497 — Vasco da Gama sailed to India

1519–1522 — Ferdinand Magellan's crew sailed around world

1539 — Hernando de Soto reached Mississippi River

1577–1580 — Francis Drake sailed around world

1609–1610 — Henry Hudson explored Hudson River and Hudson Bay

1682 — La Salle reached mouth of Mississippi River

3

Collage Answers

1 Scientists study the physical remains of ancient peoples — tools, weapons, skeletons, carvings.

2 Spices such as pepper, cinnamon, and nutmeg were in great demand. They were used to flavor foods and preserve meats in a time before refrigeration. They were also used in perfume, cosmetics, and medicine.

3 Europeans wanted to acquire spices, jewels, and gold from Asia without having to pay the cost of bringing those goods thousands of miles over land.

Collage Extensions

Use the images on page 3 to preview the unit. Discuss how the questions relate to the word *explore*. For example

- How might old tools or bits of pottery help scientists *explore* early life in the Americas?

- How might competition among European nations encourage *explorers* to sail to the Americas?

Measuring Time

Explain to students that a timeline shows the order in which key events took place. It begins with the earliest event and ends with the most recent.

Explain that events marked B.C.E. took place before the Common Era. For example, an event that took place in 7000 B.C.E. occurred about 9,000 years ago. (Add the 2,000+ years in the Common Era to the 7,000 years before the Common Era.)

Timeline Extensions

To preview Chapter 1, ask students what they know about each of the events on page 2 of the timeline and what they would like to know about those events. To review the chapter, have students tell what they learned about each event and its importance.

Chapter Summary
Refer to page 18 for a summary of Chapter 1.

Picturing History

The picture on page 4 shows the ruins of Pueblo Bonito in Chaco Canyon, New Mexico. Built around 850, the structure was originally four stories high and had 600 rooms and 40 kivas.

Pueblo Bonito is the largest of dozens of great houses built by the Chacoan People between 850 and 1250. Scientists think these buildings were used for ceremonies, meetings, and trade. Ask students what other things scientists might learn from these ruins.

Chapter 1 EARLY PEOPLE AND CULTURES

Getting Focused

Skim this chapter to predict what you will be learning.

- Read the lesson titles and subheadings.
- Look at the illustrations and read the captions.
- Examine the maps.
- Review the vocabulary words and terms.

Think about what you already know about the early people and cultures of North America. Write the questions you have about the topic before reading the chapter. Discuss your questions with a partner.

Pre-Reading Discussion

1 Use the chapter title to introduce the word *culture*. Explain that it is a way of life. It includes work, play, weapons, tools, housing, clothing, and food. Religion and art are a part of a culture.

2 Have students complete each bulleted direction on page 4. Discuss what students know about the early people of North America and their cultures. List their ideas on large sheets of paper. As students read and discuss the chapter, have them revise and expand the list.

DVD Extension

Encourage students to use the reading comprehension, vocabulary reinforcement, and interactive timeline activities on the student DVD

1 Early Hunters and Farmers

Thinking on Your Own

Read over the vocabulary. While you read, use each vocabulary word in a sentence of your own. Write the sentences in your notebook.

The first people to live in North America were big-game hunters. Many early settlers crossed the Bering Strait from Siberia around 20,000 to 30,000 years ago. They came to North America following herds of animals. Although the strait is now a body of water, during the last **Ice Age**, when portions of the oceans froze, it was a land bridge. The level of the Bering Sea was lower then because glaciers and ice sheets took up much of the world's water. In a few thousand years, descendants of these hunters occupied most of North and South America.

focus your reading

How did the first humans get to North America?

What animals did they hunt?

What kind of crops did early farmers raise?

vocabulary

Ice Age
archaeologists
hunters and gatherers
domesticate
Mound Builders

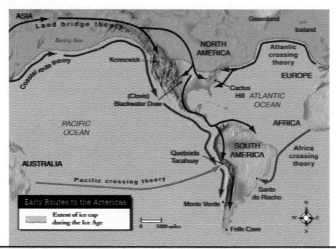

Early Routes to the Americas

Map Extensions

1 Explain to students that a map's title and legend are clues to the main idea of the map. Ask students to identify the main idea of the map on page 5 (**Map Transparency T-4**). (Humans may have come to the Americas by various routes.)

2 Help students locate the Bering Strait on the map. Explain that a *strait* is a narrow stretch of water that joins two bodies of water. What two bodies of water does the Bering Strait connect? (The Pacific and Arctic oceans)

3 What does the map suggest happened to the Bering Strait during the Ice Age? (As water in the strait froze, the sea level dropped, exposing a strip of land between Asia and North America.)

Lesson Summary

The first people to live in North America were hunters who crossed the Bering Strait during the last Ice Age. Their descendants spread out across North America. They lived as hunters and gatherers. About 5,000 years ago, some groups in what would become Mexico learned to domesticate wild plants. By about 2,000 years ago, knowledge of farming spread north to the area now known as the United States.

Lesson Objective

Students will learn how the first people reached North America and how life changed after the Ice Age ended.

Focus Your Reading Answers

1 The first humans either crossed a land bridge between eastern Asia and North America or followed one of the routes shown on the map.

2 The first humans hunted mammoths, mastodons, and giant bison.

3 Early farmers grew corn, beans, and squash.

Lesson Vocabulary

Discuss the meaning of each vocabulary word. Focus on the word *archaeologist*. Archaeologists try to learn about a culture by examining tools, weapons, skeletons, and other items.

- What clues may have helped *archaeologists* figure out when the *Ice Age* ended?

- How did they learn when and where wild plants were *domesticated*?

- What do they know about the lives of the *Mound Builders*?

Explain to students that each route on the map on page 5 is called a *theory*, because it is based on incomplete evidence. No one knows for sure how humans reached the Americas.

Each theory is based on evidence found at one or more sites in the Americas. Those sites are identified on the map. Ask students to research one or more of those sites and then present their findings to the class.

Also encourage students to use a globe to trace the various routes shown on the map. Globes can help students gain a better sense of the distances involved in the various journeys. For example, Japan is much closer to North America than it appears to be on a flat map.

Picturing History

The drawing on page 6 is based on the work of archaeologists. It shows how early people hunted mammoths. The animals stood 10 to 12 feet high and weighed between 6 and 8 tons (12,000 to 16,000 pounds). Ask students what weapons the hunters in the drawing are using. Discuss what dangers they may have faced.

Although many people came across the Bering Land Bridge, some scientists believe that people also came to the Americas from other parts of the world. Some scientists speculate that people came across the Pacific Ocean from Australia. Others believe groups of people came from Europe. Archaeological evidence even exists that shows some early settlers may have migrated from Africa.

Early people hunted mastodons with spears and rocks.

Hunters and Gatherers

Big-game hunters reached what is now the United States about 12,000 years ago. **Archaeologists**, scientists who study ancient people, have found stone spear points, or spear heads, in dozens of places. The points are mixed with the bones of mammoths, mastodons, and giant bison. In time, excessive hunting and climate changes wiped out these large animals. By about 9,000 years ago, the hunters had to rely mainly on elk, deer, and bison for meat. They were **hunters and gatherers**, as they also lived on the plants, roots, and seeds that they gathered.

Early North American spear heads

Early Farmers

About 5,000 years ago, hunters and gatherers in Mexico learned to **domesticate**, or regulate the growth of, wild plants. Their main crops were corn, squash, and beans. By 2,000 years ago, knowledge of farming had spread north to what is now the United States. The Hohokam people in Arizona and the Anasazi, or Ancestral Puebloans, in Colorado had learned to grow these plants. People who lived east of the Mississippi River also took up farming.

6 | Chapter 1

Ask students to research the giant bison, mastodons, or mammoths. Have each student prepare a presentation for the class. What modern-day animals do each of the three resemble? What do scientists think happened to the three animals?

The Hohokam planted crops for food.

Mound Builders

The people east of the Mississippi that scientists have learned the most about are the **Mound Builders**. They are named after the mounds of earth that they built. These people were hunters and gatherers who also farmed. Farming allowed them to produce surplus, or extra, food. This let some people become priests, governors, and mound builders. The Adena people (3,000 to 1,200 years ago) built the Great Serpent Mound in Ohio. This snake-shaped mound extends for a quarter of a mile along the Ohio River. Later, the Hopewell people (2,300 to 1,300 years ago) built even larger mounds shaped like snakes, birds, and humans. Some mounds were used as burial places.

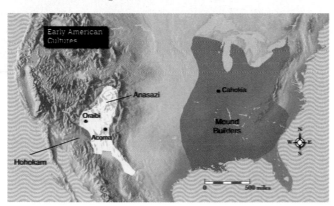

Early American Cultures

stop and think

On the basis of what you have read, write definitions for *Ice Age* and *archaeologist* in your own words. Then write one sentence about how these words are related to the topic of this chapter.

Stop and Think
Answers will vary. The definition of *Ice Age* and its use in a sentence should show an understanding that

- it was a time when the world was much colder than it is today

- glaciers (slow-moving masses of ice) and ice sheets covered large parts of Earth

The definition of *archaeologist* and its use in a sentence should reflect an understanding that an archaeologist is a scientist who studies ancient cultures by analyzing the things people left behind, such as tools, weapons, pottery, buildings, and bones.

Picturing History

Have students examine the drawing on page 7. Like the one on page 6, it is based on archaeologists' work. Ask students what they can learn from it about the culture of the Hohokam.

Map Extension

Have students use **Transparency T-1** (a political map of the United States) to identify the present-day states that were once home to the Hohokam and the Anasazi. (Arizona, New Mexico, California)

Putting It All Together

The timelines and the sentences explaining the timelines will vary, but should include the following facts:

- 20,000 years ago: Early settlers from Siberia crossed the Bering Strait into North America.

- 9,000 years ago: The mammoths, mastodons, and giant bison were gone; early North Americans were now hunting smaller animals and gathering plants, roots, and seeds.

- 5,000 years ago: People in northern Mexico domesticated wild plants.

- 2,000 years ago: People in what is now the United States knew how to farm.

- 900 years ago: The Mississippian people built entire cities around earthen mounds.

Picturing History

Have students trace the Great Serpent Mound shown in the photograph from its head to the end of its tail (1,300 feet in all). The mound, which is located in southern Ohio, is nearly the length of four football fields laid end to end. The mound averages four to five feet in height and 20 to 25 feet in width. Ask students to think about how long it would take to build such a structure using hand tools. How many people would be needed to complete the job?

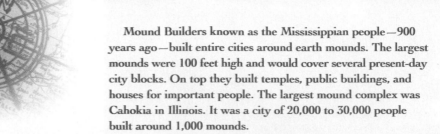

Mound Builders known as the Mississippian people—900 years ago—built entire cities around earth mounds. The largest mounds were 100 feet high and would cover several present-day city blocks. On top they built temples, public buildings, and houses for important people. The largest mound complex was Cahokia in Illinois. It was a city of 20,000 to 30,000 people built around 1,000 mounds.

The Great Serpent Mound in Ohio

Putting It All Together

In your notebook, make a timeline that includes the dates 20,000; 9,000; 5,000; 2,000; and 900 years ago. Below each date explain how the people of each era spent their time. Then write a sentence or two that explains the timeline.

8

Extension

Explain to students that scientists do not know why the Great Serpent Mound was built. Unlike other mounds, it was not used for burials. A similar mystery can be found along the coast of Peru in South America. Ancient people etched about 70 animals, birds, human forms, and other images into the landscape of a plain 37 miles long and 15 miles wide. They are known as the Nazca Lines. Ask students to find out more about these ancient people by researching them on the Internet using the key words "Nazca Lines." Ask students to present their findings to the class by using the Student Presentation Builder on the student DVD.

Biography

Ishi (1861?–1916)

In the summer of 1911, a lone Native American walked out of the hills of northern California. A crew of meat cutters working nearby saw him. They were puzzled, as they had not seen Native Americans in that part of the state for years.

When they asked the man what he wanted, they found that he did not speak English. The sheriff came and put him in handcuffs. He did not resist. "He had a big smile," one of the workmen remembered, "as much as to say, 'These are for me? Are you giving those to me?'"

The man in handcuffs was Ishi. He was believed to be the last Yahi person to survive in the backcountry of California. About fifty years old, Ishi was the last member of his family of four. The other three had recently died. Ishi could not survive on his own. He came out of the hills half-starved.

The Ishi story became front-page news. The local newspaper called him "the Wild Man of Deer Creek." The *San Francisco Examiner* described him as a "savage of the most primitive type." Alfred Kroeber, head of the University of California's Museum of Anthropology, offered Ishi a home.

Ishi spent the next five years living at the museum. He was amazed by light switches and other things most people took for granted. Getting used to large crowds took time. At a local bathing beach, he cried out, "Hansi salta!" or "So many white people!" Still, he adapted to civilized ways. He learned to eat at a table and sit on a chair. He liked doughnuts, ice cream sodas, and candy.

Although Ishi worked at the museum as a janitor, he also was a living museum exhibit. Visitors came to watch him make arrowheads and listen to him sing his native songs. He showed children how to catch birds with snares and trap fish by setting twigs close together in a stream bed. "He liked everybody, and everybody liked him," one of the professors said.

Ishi eventually became sick with tuberculosis. This was the leading killer disease of that time. He died of tuberculosis in 1916.

Bio Facts

- Born: circa 1861

- Grew up with an unknown number of other members of the Yahi-Yana in the tribe's traditional homeland in Tehama County. The group avoided contact with other Californians.

- Lived with three other Yahi survivors—a woman thought to be his mother, his sister, and an old man—until 1908, when surveyors disturbed their home. The three relatives probably died shortly after the encounter.

- Ishi left his homeland and traveled to Oroville, California, in 1911. After he was found at a slaughterhouse, he was placed in jail for his protection and released to T. T. Waterman, a University of California anthropologist.

- Ishi lived at the University of California Anthropology Museum from 1911–1916. He was employed as a janitor at the museum and gave demonstrations in archery, flint making, house construction, fire making, and other crafts. Worked with anthropologists to document Yahi-Yana culture and language.

- Died of tuberculosis on March 23, 1916. His body was cremated and placed with some possessions in Mt. Olivet Cemetery, Colma, California.

- Alfred Kroeber, head of the anthropology department at the University of California, had Ishi's brain preserved.

- The brain was repatriated to descendants of the Yahi-Yana and buried with Ishi's ashes on May 5, 1999.

Biography Extension

Have students find out what anthropologists learned from Ishi during his years at the University of California. Ask them to share their findings in poster format or by using Student Presentation Builder on the student DVD.

Lesson Summary

Many groups of people were living in the Eastern Woodlands of North America when Europeans arrived about 500 years ago. Most survived by eating the animals and plants in the forests. They also planted corn, beans, and squash. For the most part, they lived in villages. Their homes, known as wigwams, were made of poles, reeds, and tree bark. The Iroquois used similar materials to build longhouses that housed several families.

Lesson Objective

Students will learn how the people of the Eastern Woodland lived about 500 years ago.

Focus Your Reading Answers

1 The Woodland People went to war to protect their hunting groups, to prove their warriors' courage, and to replace losses during previous wars.

2 The Woodland People ate animals and plants of the forest, as well as corn, beans, and squash.

3 The Woodland People built wigwams made of poles, reeds, and tree bark. The Iroquois built longhouses with arched roofs.

Lesson Vocabulary

Discuss the meaning of each vocabulary word. Begin by locating the Eastern Woodlands on the map on page 12. Explain that Woodland People lived in forests. Many made their home in villages. *Palisades* are tall fences made of upright poles. Use the pictures on page 13 to help students distinguish between the *wigwams* built by most groups and the *longhouses* of the Iroquois.

Have students use the vocabulary words in a paragraph describing the villages of the Woodland People.

Woodland People

Thinking on Your Own

Read the Focus Your Reading questions. Make three columns in your notebook. Label them "Villages," "Food," and "Shelter." As you read, make notes in each column about what you learn about that topic.

When Europeans arrived 500 years ago, many cultures occupied North America. Many lived east of the Mississippi River in a region called the **Eastern Woodlands**. This was a vast region of forests, rivers, and lakes. The forests were broken by clearings and meadows where deer and other animals grazed. Wild plants, berries, and edible roots grew under the trees.

focus your reading

Why did Woodland People go to war?

What kind of food did they eat?

What kind of shelters did they build?

vocabulary

Eastern Woodlands

palisade

wigwams

longhouses

Groups and Villages

Several cultures lived in the Eastern Woodlands. The Iroquois were a powerful league, or confederation of groups, who lived in present-day New York State. The Powhatan Confederation occupied much of Virginia. The Miami, Shawnee, and smaller

The Iroquois used canoes as a means of travel.

Extension

The drawing on page 10 shows an Iroquois canoe. Like other Woodland People, the Iroquois used wood, birch bark, pitch, and other forest products to build these boats. Have students research how the Iroquois and other Woodland People constructed canoes. Ask students to present their findings to the class by using Student Presentation Builder on the student DVD.

groups hunted west of the Appalachian Mountains. Groups often were at war with one another. They fought to protect their hunting grounds and because warriors wanted to prove that they were brave. Sometimes war parties captured women and children, who were adopted into the tribe. The captives also helped replace losses a group had suffered during earlier raids.

The Woodland People lived in villages that usually were located along a creek or river. The streams provided water for everyday use and for canoe travel. Many villages were enclosed with a wall made of upright poles called a **palisade.** The wall helped protect the village from enemy raids.

stop and think

Discuss with a partner what Woodland People and people today have in common and what is different. Put your ideas on a chart labeled "Compare" and "Contrast." Write ideas for villages, food, and shelter.

Making a Living

The Woodland People lived mainly from the animals and plants of the forest. During the summer, women gathered seeds and berries. Men fished and left on hunting trips each autumn. The men hunted deer, bear, rabbits, and other small animals. Women did much of the work in the village. Each spring, they planted corn, beans, and squash known as "The Three Sisters." Women tended the fields and harvested the crops. They also cooked, made clothing, created pottery, and took care of young children.

Corn was a staple of the Woodland People's diet.

11

Use the map on page 12 (Map Transparency T-2) to discuss the cultures, or ways of life, in North America in 1500. Ask students to name the Eastern Woodland People. (Chippewa, Sauk, Fox, Kickapoo, Miami, Shawnee, Tuscarora, Powhatan Confederation, Iroquois League, Algonquin) What groups lived to the south of the Eastern Woodland? (Southeast Peoples) What groups lived to the west of the Eastern Woodland? (Plains Peoples) To the north of the Eastern Woodlands? (Cree and Inuit)

Clothing and Shelter

The Woodland People made clothing of woven grass or animal skins. Their clothing varied with the seasons. In summer, women wore wraparound skirts made of grass or deerskin. Men wore breechcloths fastened with a belt at their waists. During the winter, everyone wore robes made of animal skins.

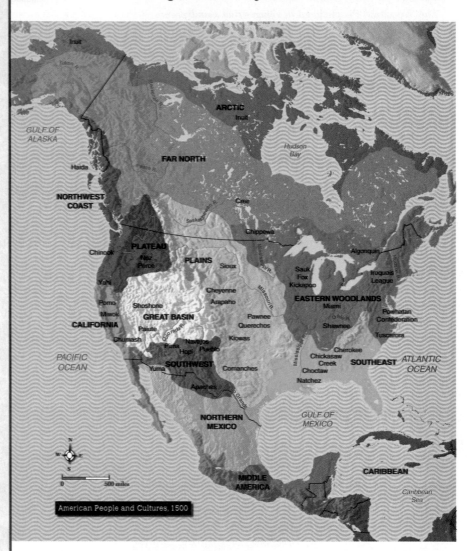

American People and Cultures, 1500

12 Chapter 1

Extension

Divide students into small groups, and ask each group to research one of the peoples identified on the map on page 12. One group might focus on a group that lived in the Eastern Woodland, while another gathers information about a Plains People, and yet another about a group that lived in the Southwest. Ask each group to share its findings by creating a poster that shows where the group lived, how its people made a living, what kind of clothing they wore, and what their houses were like. Use the posters to create a chart that compares and contrasts the various cultures.

The wigwam provided shelter.

The types of shelters varied from group to group. Most groups built **wigwams** made of poles, reeds, and tree bark. Some were cone shaped; others were shaped like domes. In warmer climates, people built circular houses with roofs made of thatched grass. The Iroquois built **longhouses** with arched roofs. Each longhouse was large enough to house several families.

Longhouses were home to many families.

Putting It All Together

In Thinking on Your Own, you created a three-column list. Use the information from your list to write a short paragraph about the lives of the Woodland People.

13

1 The Querechos used bison for food.

2 They lived in tents made of the hides of bison.

3 They used dogs to carry their belongings when they traveled.

Picturing History

Use the map on page 12 to locate the Querechos. In what geographic region did they live? (Plains) Have students study the painting on page 14. What does it suggest about the plains? (flat, treeless) Ask students to develop a working definition of the Plains. Encourage them to add more detail to that definition as they read Lesson 3.

Read a Primary Source

Coronado Describes the Querechos

In 1540, Spanish explorer Francisco Vásquez de Coronado marched north from Mexico with several hundred men. They were looking for the cities of gold that Indians said existed in the North. The following is his report about the Indians that he met on the plains in present-day Kansas.

reading for understanding

What did the Querechos use for food?

What kind of shelters did they live in?

How did they carry their belongings when they traveled?

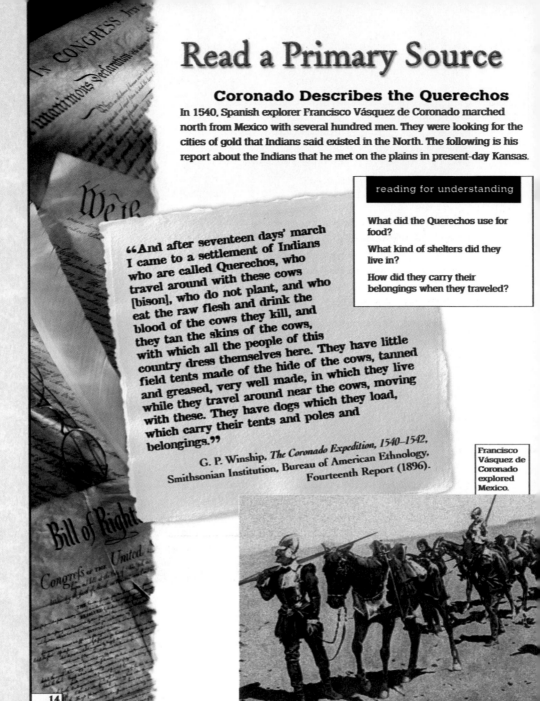

"And after seventeen days' march I came to a settlement of Indians who are called Querechos, who travel around with these cows [bison], who do not plant, and who eat the raw flesh and drink the blood of the cows they kill, and they tan the skins of the cows, with which all the people of this country dress themselves here. They have little field tents made of the hide of the cows, tanned and greased, very well made, in which they live while they travel around near the cows, moving with these. They have dogs which they load, which carry their tents and poles and belongings."

G. P. Winship, *The Coronado Expedition, 1540–1542*, Smithsonian Institution, Bureau of American Ethnology, Fourteenth Report (1896).

Francisco Vásquez de Coronado explored Mexico.

14

Extension

Have students research the lands described in this lesson—plains, mountains, deserts, Pacific Coast— by gathering photographs of each environment. Encourage them to share their pictures with the class. What resources did early peoples find in each place? How did they use those resources to build a unique way of life?

Cultures of the West

Thinking on Your Own

Read the Focus Your Reading questions. What image comes to mind for each question? In your notebook, predict the answers before you read. After reading the lesson, compare your predictions with what you learned.

The land west of the Mississippi River was more thinly settled than regions in the East. It was a region of mountains, deserts, and plains, with few woodlands. The people who lived there had to adapt to many different environments. As a result, they developed more diverse ways of life than the eastern cultures.

> **focus your reading**
>
> How did horses change the Plains People's way of life?
>
> How did people farm in the desert?
>
> What food was most important to the Coastal People?
>
> **vocabulary**
>
> nomadic   arid
>
> Southwest   adobe
>
> irrigate

Plains Cultures

In 1540, the Spanish explorer Francisco Vásquez de Coronado found bands of **nomadic** people on the plains. The groups followed the bison herds. It was a hard life, as killing bison on foot was difficult. Two hundred years later the Apaches, Comanches, and Kiowas also hunted bison on the plains. But they hunted on horseback.

With horses bought or stolen from the Spanish, the Plains People adapted their way of life to create a new culture. With fast horses they killed all the bison they needed. These animals provided them with food, hides to make clothing and shelter, and bones to make tools. They lived in teepees that were easy to move as they followed the bison herds.

Early People and Cultures | 15

Lesson Vocabulary

Discuss the meaning of each vocabulary word. Locate the Plains on the map on page 12. Explain that the Plains was home to huge herds of bison. The people of the Plains traveled from place to place following those herds. They were *nomadic*.

Next, have students locate the *Southwest* on the map on page 12. Explain that much of the Southwest is a desert—dry land with few trees. Deserts get less than 10 inches of rain per year. Southwest People made the most of their *arid* homeland. Some built permanent homes out of *adobe*. They dug canals to *irrigate* their fields.

Have students use the vocabulary words in a paragraph to contrast the cultures of Plains People with those of Southwest People.

Lesson Summary

The land west of the Mississippi River was home to people who adapted to many different environments. The Plains People followed herds of bison. Using horses brought to the Americas by the Spanish, the Plains People found that hunting on horseback was easier and safer than hunting on foot.

The oldest groups of people of the Southwest farmed in the deserts and river valleys. Later arrivals hunted and gathered or herded sheep.

Many people who lived in the Far West settled near the Pacific Coast. They depended on fish for much of their food supply.

Lesson Objective

Students will learn about the distinctive cultures developed by the peoples who lived west of the Mississippi River.

Focus Your Reading Answers

1 Horses eased some of the danger in hunting herds of bison. People no longer had to kill bison on foot.

2 Peoples in the Southwest were able to farm in the desert by irrigating, or bringing water to, their crops.

3 The food most important to the Coastal People was salmon and other fish.

Bison were a source of food on the Great Plains.

Peoples of the Southwest

The oldest people of the **Southwest** are the Pima, Yuma, and Pueblo. They lived in the deserts and river valleys of southern California, Arizona, and New Mexico. Like their ancestors, the Hohokam and the Anasazi, these people were farmers. They had to **irrigate**, or bring water to their fields, as they lived in an **arid**, or dry, climate.

The Apaches and Navajos were newcomers to the Southwest. They migrated from Alaska and Canada some 600 years ago. The Apaches lived by hunting and gathering; the Navajos hunted and herded sheep. The Navajos later became widely known for their brightly colored wool blankets.

Their houses varied from group to group. Some lived in shelters made of woven grass. The Pueblo built large houses made of stone and **adobe**, or sun-dried bricks. They used ladders to enter the rooms through the roof.

stop and think

Imagine that you are a Plains person hunting on foot. During the hunt, you see hunters from another group hunting on horseback. Go back to your village and explain why you, too, need horses. Write the heading "Why We Need Horses" and use a number for each point.

Picturing History

Have students compare and contrast the drawing on page 16 with the one on page 6. What advantages does a hunter on horseback have over those who hunt on foot? Why do you think hunters on horseback were able to kill more game?

Fishing for salmon provided food for the Chinook.

Cultures of the Far West

Several quite different groups lived in the Far West. The Piaute and Shoshone lived in the Great Basin, which is the desert country of Utah and Nevada. Most of the groups lived on or near the Pacific Coast. Among them were the Chinook, who lived in the forests near the mouth of the Columbia River. The Pomo and Chumash lived farther south along the California coast. Still other groups lived inland, such as the Miwok of the San Juaquin Valley of California.

The groups of the Far West lived quite different lives. The Coastal People depended heavily on fish. Salmon from the Columbia River was an important item in the Chinook diet. The groups farther south fished in the ocean with nets and gathered mussels and clams. Cultures living in the interior hunted deer and rabbits, and gathered acorns and grass seed.

The kinds of houses they built depended on local resources. The Chinook, who lived in the forests, built longhouses made of wooden planks. Each longhouse sheltered several families. The groups farther south lived in shelters made of thatched grass and reeds. Those living further inland and in the Great Basin also lived in reed huts and shelters covered with animal skins.

Putting It All Together

Create a Venn diagram with two interlocking circles. Label the circles "Southwest" and "Far West." Discuss the similarities and differences between the cultures with a partner. Then list differences in the outer circles and similarities in the overlapping area.

Putting It All Together

Similarities: Both groups were dependent on nearby resources for food, shelter, tools, and weapons; both built permanent homes. Differences: People in the Southwest farmed, hunted, and herded in a desert. They lived in homes made of woven grass or adobe. People who lived along the coast turned to the ocean for food and to the forests for building materials. Those who lived inland hunted deer and rabbits; gathered acorns and seeds; and lived in shelters made of grass, reeds, and animal skins.

Picturing History

The drawing on this page and the one on page 16 show hunters at work. Discuss similarities between the two drawings. What differences seem most striking?

Chapter Review

1 Answers will vary, but students should explain what ideas they held about early American peoples and cultures before reading the chapter and then how those ideas changed as a result of their reading.

2 Categories might include *places* (Eastern Woodland, Southwest); *ways people make a living* (archaeologists, hunters and gatherers); *things people build* (palisades, wigwams, longhouses, adobe); *words related to water* (irrigate, Ice Age, arid).

3 Answers will vary, but each chart should include facts from each lesson and each subheading within a lesson.

Extension

Ask students to locate their state on the map on page 12. What early American peoples lived there? Have students find out more about their cultures or ways of life. How are they similar to the way people live in the state today? What are the main differences?

Chapter Summary

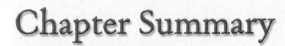

The first humans to live in North America arrived during the last **Ice Age**, some 20,000 to 30,000 years ago. They were **hunters and gatherers** who crossed a land bridge from Siberia. **Archaeologists** have discovered these hunters' stone spear points at dozens of places in the United States. About 5,000 years ago, these people learned how to **domesticate** plants. The early farmers who lived east of the Mississippi River are called the **Mound Builders**.

Many cultures lived in North America when Europeans arrived about 500 years ago. Most lived in the **Eastern Woodlands** east of the Mississippi River. Most groups built shelters called **wigwams** made of poles, reeds, and tree bark. The Iroquois built **longhouses** with arched roofs. They surrounded their shelters with **palisades**.

People also lived west of the Mississippi River. Some were **nomadic** bison hunters, but people of the **Southwest** were mostly farmers. Living in an **arid** desert climate, they had to **irrigate** their fields. The Pueblo lived in stone and **adobe** houses. Other tribes built shelters made of woven grass.

Most people of the Far West lived near the Pacific Coast. These coastal groups depended on fishing and hunting for food. Groups that were farther south lived in shelters made of thatched grass and reeds.

Chapter Review

1 In your notebook, explain how this chapter changed or confirmed your ideas about early American people and cultures.

2 Make a list of the vocabulary words for this chapter. Then arrange the words into categories. Label the categories. In two or three sentences explain why you chose these categories.

3 Create a two-column chart in your notebook. In the column on the left list the most important points made in this chapter. Use only one or two words for each. In the right-hand column write a brief explanation of each point.

Novel Connections

Below is a list of books that relate to the time period covered in this chapter. The numbers in parentheses indicate the related Thematic Strands of the National Council for the Social Studies (NCSS).

Raymond Bial. *The Navajo* (Lifeways series). Benchmark/Marshall Cavendish, 1998. (I, III)

Margaret Cooper. *Exploring the Ice Age.* Atheneum, 2001. (I, II, IX)

Jane Louise Curry. *Turtle Island: Tales of the Algonquian Nations.* Simon & Schuster, 2003. (I, II, V)

Mary Gunderson. *American Indian Cooking Before 1500.* Blue Earth Books, 2001. (I, II, III, V)

Georgia Lee. *A Day with a Chumash* (*A Day with . . .* series). Runestone/Lerner, 1999. (I, II, III)

Taylor Morrison. *The Great Unknown.* Houghton Mifflin, 2001. (III, V, VIII)

R. Gwinn Vivian and Margaret Anderson. *Chaco Canyon* (*Digging for the Past* series). Oxford University Press, 2002. (I, II, III)

Skill Builder

Primary and Secondary Sources

Historical writings consist of primary and secondary sources. A primary source is any firsthand account, document, artifact, photograph, or other piece of evidence created in the past. Secondary sources are accounts written later that are based on primary sources.

Coronado's Journey

In May 1541, Francisco Vásquez de Coronado led an army of Spanish explorers to the Great Plains. He kept a journal during the trip. An excerpt from this primary source is included on page 14.

In 1949, Herbert E. Bolton published a history of Coronado's journey, *Coronado: Knight of Pueblos and Plains*. To write this secondary source, Bolton relied heavily on Coronado's journal. The excerpt on the right is from Bolton's history.

> "Soon after reaching the great herd of buffaloes . . . [Coronado's men] first encountered the interesting people who, with their families and all their belongings, gypsy-like, followed the buffaloes for a living. . . . The life of these nomads, who were apparently a branch of the great Apache people so conspicuous in the same region at a later date, was graphically pictured by members of the expedition. These wandering natives, whose physique Coronado described as 'the best . . . of any I have seen in the Indies,' were Querechos. . . . They lived with and off the buffalo, and by this animal their whole life was regulated."
>
> Herbert E. Bolton, *Coronado: Knight of Pueblos and Plains* (New York: McGraw-Hill Book Company, Inc., 1949).

Compare the excerpt from Coronado's journal on page 14 with the one above from Bolton's history.

1 How do we know that Bolton read Coronado's journal?

2 To what extent is Bolton's conclusion in the last sentence based on the journal?

3 What information did Bolton add that was not part of Coronado's journal?

Skill Builder

1 Bolton quotes directly from Coronado's journal.

2 Coronado writes that the Querechos used the buffalo for food, clothing, and shelter. Bolton's conclusion summarizes the information in the journal.

3 Bolton adds information that Coronado did not have. For example, he describes the Querechos as a branch of the Apache people who were later well-known in the region. Bolton also quotes Coronado directly.

Extension

Have students bring to class examples of primary sources and secondary sources. Primary sources might include a letter, a photograph, a diary, or an eyewitness account in a newspaper. Secondary sources might include a newspaper or magazine article about an event, a chapter in a history textbook, or a biography. Discuss what can be learned from each type of account and the importance of knowing the difference between the two.

Classroom Discussion

Discuss with students some of the broader topics covered in this chapter.

- How do archaeologists explore the ways early peoples lived and worked in the Americas? What challenges do they face in uncovering ways of life thousands of years ago?

- How did the end of the Ice Age change life in the Americas? Why were those changes important?

- How did knowledge of farming change life in the Americas? Why were those changes important?

- What part did the land and the climate play in the ways people lived in North America 500 years ago? What part did local resources play? What part may contact with other peoples have played in shaping cultures?

- What factors shape a culture today? How are those factors like those that shaped cultures in North American 500 years ago? How do you account for the differences?

Related Transparencies

- **T-5** The World
- **T-8** European Exploration of North America
- **T-20** Venn Diagram

Key Blacklines

Biography
René Robert Cavelier, Sieur de La Salle

Primary Source
Jacques Cartier Claims Canada for France

DVD Extension

Encourage students to use the reading comprehension, vocabulary reinforcement, and interactive timeline activities on the student DVD.

Chapter
2 EUROPEAN EXPLORERS

Getting Focused

Skim this chapter to predict what you will be learning.

- Read the lesson titles and subheadings.
- Look at the illustrations and read the captions.
- Examine the maps.
- Review the vocabulary words and terms.

Some discoveries happen by accident. People find things while looking for something else. Recall a time when you found an item while searching for some other thing. Discuss this with a partner. Skim this chapter to see what that experience might have in common with European exploration. In your notebook, write one connection that you see.

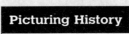

Picturing History

The picture on page 20 shows the ruins of a Viking settlement built in about 1000 at L'Anse aux Meadows in Newfoundland, Canada. Archaeologists have unearthed eight buildings and hundreds of tools and weapons at the site. They are proof that Europeans reached North America 500 years before Columbus's first voyage. Ask students to locate the Vikings' homeland on the map on page 22. How does it help explain why people in other parts of Europe knew nothing about the voyages the Vikings made or their settlement?

Pre-Reading Discussion

Have students complete each bulleted direction on page 20. Discuss how the word *discovery* is connected to the words *explore* and *surprise*. Ask students to name some ways their own discoveries have been surprising. What places or people in the Americas were likely to surprise European explorers?

Portuguese and Spanish Exploration

Thinking on Your Own

Read the Focus Your Reading questions. In your notebook write "Route to the Indies." As you read, make a list of all the explorers who looked for a route to the Indies.

In the late 1400s, Europeans searched for a new route to the **Indies**. The Indies, as East Asia and the islands of Indonesia were called, was the source of spices, gold, jewels, and perfume. They were known as the Spice Islands. The Arab merchants who controlled this trade charged high prices for their goods. Italian merchants bought the goods from the Arab merchants and shipped them to Europe. They also charged a fee for their service. People in Western Europe looked for ways to get these items at lower costs.

focus your reading

Why did Europeans look for a new route to the Indies?

What route did the Portuguese find?

Was Columbus's plan to sail west realistic?

vocabulary

Indies	cartographer
navigate	strait
caravel	

Marco Polo holpod establish the spice trade.

21

Picturing History

Marco Polo was a man from Venice who made a journey by land across Asia to China and Japan. He traveled with his father and uncle in the late 1200s. He wrote a book about the trip. That book inspired many explorers in Europe. It also inspired an unknown French artist to draw the picture on page 21. It shows Marco Polo with Asians gathering peppers. The artist created the picture from his imagination. What does it suggest about the way he and other Europeans saw themselves? about the way they viewed Asians?

Focus Your Reading Answers

1 Europeans wanted to find a less expensive way to get spices, gold, jewels, and perfume from the Indies.

2 The Portuguese found a route around Africa's Cape of Good Hope.

3 Answers will vary, but students are likely to point out that he had miscalculated the length of his voyage by over 7,000 miles.

Lesson Summary

In the late 1400s, Europeans were eager to find a new all-water route to the Indies. The first to set sail were the Portuguese. Bartholomeu Dias reached the southern tip of Africa in 1488. In 1496, Vasco da Gama retraced that route and sailed on to India. Christopher Columbus thought he could reach the Indies by sailing west across the Atlantic in 1492. Amerigo Vespucci was the first European to realize Columbus had reached a new continent. In 1513, Balboa found the ocean that separates the Americas from Asia—the Pacific Ocean. In 1519, Magellan and his crew sailed around the world.

Lesson Objective

Students will learn how Portugal's and Spain's search for an all-water route to the Indies resulted in the discovery of two continents new to Europeans.

Lesson Vocabulary

Discuss the meaning of each vocabulary word by focusing on the word *navigate*. Explain that it has several meanings— *to control the course of a ship; to sail;* and *to make one's way.*

- What route did Vasco da Gama *navigate* to the Indies?

- How might a *cartographer* have helped Christopher Columbus *navigate* on his voyage to the Indies?

- How far could one *navigate* in a Spanish *caravel*?

- How did Magellan *navigate* through the *straits* that were later named for him?

1 Ask students to use the map on page 22 to trace the route of each explorer. Which stayed close to the land? Which sailed farthest into the open sea?

2 Divide the class into small groups and ask each to trace the routes on a globe. Have students copy the globe's scale of miles onto a piece of string. Then ask them to use the string to measure the length of each voyage. Which explorers traveled the farthest distance? Which traveled the shortest?

Portuguese Explorers

The Portuguese were the first to set out to reach the Spice Islands by sailing around Africa's Cape of Good Hope. A Portuguese prince, Henry the Navigator, took the lead. He set up a school to help sea captains learn to **navigate** the African coast. In 1488, a Portuguese sea captain named Bartholomeu Dias reached the tip of Africa, known as the Cape of Good Hope. Nine years later, Vasco da Gama followed that route and sailed on to the west coast of India. In a short time, Portuguese ships reached Asia and the Spice Islands by sailing east. This was, however, a long and dangerous trip.

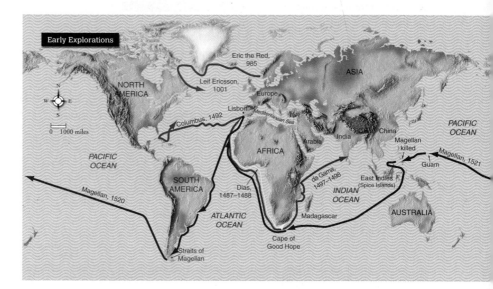

Christopher Columbus

A sea captain from Genoa, Italy, named Christopher Columbus thought he could reach the Indies by sailing west. This route had never been tried. He persuaded King Ferdinand and Queen Isabella of Spain to finance his voyage. In August 1492, Columbus sailed from Spain with three ships: the *Niña*, the *Pinta*, and the *Santa Maria*. By his calculations, the distance between Europe and Asia was about 2,500 miles. That was well within the sailing range of a Spanish **caravel**, his choice of

Extension

Sailors could not travel far from land until they had a way of charting their course on the open sea. One of the inventions that made long-distance voyages possible was the compass—a Chinese invention that found its way to the Middle East and then to Europe. Another was the astrolabe. Sailors used it to figure out the ship's approximate location. Ask students to research the history of the compass and the astrolabe and share their findings with the class. How did both inventions encourage voyages of discovery like those of da Gama and Columbus?

King Ferdinand
and Queen
Isabella of Spain

Picturing History

The drawing at the top of page 23 shows King Ferdinand and Queen Isabella of Spain. What does the drawing suggest about life in Europe in the late 1400s?

ship. In fact, the actual distance to Asia is about 10,000 miles. Columbus miscalculated the length of his voyage by thousands of miles.

After two months at sea, the crew demanded that Columbus sail for home. He agreed to do so, if they did not find land within three days. On the third day, October 12, 1492, a lookout sighted land. It was an island in the Caribbean Sea that Columbus named San Salvador. Columbus was certain that he had reached the Indies. Until this time, no European, other than the Vikings, had set foot on North and South America. Columbus called the people he met on San Salvador "Indios," a name that later became "Indians."

Columbus made a total of four trips to the Caribbean. He explored its islands and the coast of South America. Contrary to popular belief, he never touched the land of what is now the United States. He died in 1506, convinced that these lands were part of Asia instead of an unknown hemisphere.

Christopher
Columbus

He and his crew, however, were not the first Europeans to reach the Western Hemisphere. About the year 1000, a Viking named Leif Ericsson had sailed from Iceland to the coast of Newfoundland. The Vikings established a settlement at what is now the town of L'Anse aux Meadows, Newfoundland. Columbus knew nothing about that voyage or the Viking settlement.

Picturing History

Ferdinand, one of Columbus's sons, described his father as "a well-built man of more than medium height, long in his features with cheeks somewhat high, but neither fat nor thin. He had an aquiline nose and his eyes were light in color; his complexion too was light, but kindling to a vivid red. In youth his hair was blond, but when he came to his thirtieth year it all turned white."

Ask students to compare and contrast the written description with the painting. How are the two similar? What differences seem most striking?

Stop and Think

The statements will vary but should refer to the following events:

- Bartholomeu Dias reached the Cape of Good Hope in 1488.

- Vasco da Gama sailed around the Cape of Good Hope and on to the west coast of Asia in 1497.

- Christopher Columbus reached an island off the coast of the Americas in 1492.

- Amerigo Vespucci realized that Columbus had found a new continent after exploring the coast of South America in 1499.

- Vasco Nunez de Balboa was the first European to find the ocean that separates the Americas from Asia.

- In 1519, the crew led by Ferdinand Magellan became the first people to sail around the world.

Amerigo Vespucci and Vasco Nuñez de Balboa

Amerigo Vespucci was the first European to realize that Columbus had discovered a continent. He reached that conclusion in 1499, after exploring the coast of South America for Portugal. A **cartographer**, or mapmaker, later named the entire hemisphere America, after Amerigo Vespucci. Vasco Nuñez de Balboa, a Spanish explorer, was the first European to find the ocean that separates the Americas from Asia. In 1513, from the top of a hill in Panama, he saw the "South Sea." We know it today as the Pacific Ocean.

stop and think

In your notebook write a statement that describes each explorer's route to the Indies. Compare your statements with those of a partner.

Ferdinand Magellan

In 1519, Ferdinand Magellan set out to explore the Pacific Ocean. He crossed the Atlantic and sailed down the east coast of South America. At the tip of South America, known as Cape Horn, he discovered a **strait** that led to the Pacific. It is now called the Strait of Magellan. He sailed west to the Philippine Islands, where he was killed during a battle between two local groups. His crew sailed on to Asia. When they arrived in Spain in 1522, they were the first people to sail around the world.

Magellan's fleet off the tip of South America

24

Picturing History

The Spanish and the Portuguese explored the world on sailing ships powered by the wind. Magellan relied on small carracks—the ships shown in the drawing on page 24. They were more manageable than earlier sailing ships, had more cargo space, and were capable of long ocean voyages.

Extension

Ask students to research on the Internet the history of sailing ships used during the age of exploration. Then have them present their findings to the class by using Student Presentation Builder on the student DVD.

Spanish Exploration
of North America

Later Explorers

Thereafter, Spain sent other explorers to learn more about the Americas. Juan Ponce de León explored the coast of Florida. He also stopped to search for the Fountain of Youth, a story of legend. In 1539, Hernando de Soto set out from Florida with 600 men to explore what is now the southern United States. They were the first Europeans to reach the Mississippi River. Francisco Coronado later explored the American Southwest.

Putting It All Together

Columbus and other explorers made several mistakes in their calculations about getting to the Indies. Find three mistakes they made and write them in your notebook. Compare your list with a partner.

Hernando de Soto

Putting It All Together

Answers will vary, but students are likely to point to the following errors:

- Columbus miscalculated the distance between Europe and Asia.

- Columbus and other early Spanish explorers were certain they had reached Asia.

- Columbus and other early Spanish explorers did not realize there were two large continents west of Europe and east of Asia.

Map Extension

Ask students to use the map on page 25 to answer these questions:

- What parts of the present-day United States did Spain explore in the 1500s? (Southeast and Southwest)

- Which explorer traveled the farthest north? (Coronado)

- Who was the first to explore the Mississippi River? (de Soto)

Picturing History

Ask students to study the drawing on page 25. How do students think Native Americans responded to the tools and weapons de Soto and other explorers brought to the Americas?

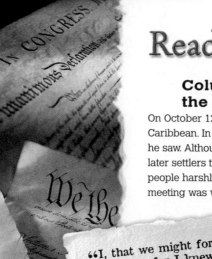

Reading for Understanding Answers

1 Columbus gave the people he encountered gifts to show friendship and to encourage them to convert to Christianity.

2 The people Columbus met took his trinkets and brought him gifts in return.

3 They had never seen European weapons and did not understand how dangerous they were.

Read a Primary Source

Columbus Describes the Caribbean People

On October 12, 1492, Christopher Columbus landed on an island in the Caribbean. In the following journal entry, he describes the first people that he saw. Although Columbus and later settlers treated the local people harshly, their first meeting was welcoming.

reading for understanding

Why did Columbus give the people gifts?

How did they respond?

How did they react to European weapons?

> "I, that we might form great friendship, for I knew that they were a people who could be more easily freed and converted to our holy faith by love than by force, gave to some of them red caps, and glass beads to put round their necks, and many other things of little value. . . .
>
> "They afterwards come to the ship's boats where we were, swimming and bringing us parrots, cotton threads in skeins, darts, and many other things. . . . In fine, they took all, and gave what they had with good will. . . .
>
> "They are very well made, with very handsome bodies, and very good countenances. . . . They neither carry nor know anything of arms, for I showed them swords, and they took them by the blade and cut themselves through ignorance."

J. Franklin Jameson, ed.,
*Original Narratives of Early
American History* (1909).

Picturing History

Many years after the event, an artist used accounts like Columbus's diary to imagine the explorer's meeting with Native Americans. How does the artist picture the Spanish? Native Americans? Why do you think Columbus is shown at the center of the picture? Ask students how the picture might change if it were drawn from a Native American's point of view.

26

LESSON **2**

The English Search for a Northwest Passage

Thinking on Your Own

Read the Focus Your Reading questions. Think about the term *northwest passage*. Imagine that you are an English explorer in 1500 looking out at the Atlantic Ocean. Where might a northwest passage be located? Why would finding it be important to you? Write the answers to these two questions in your notebook.

News that Columbus had reached the Indies quickly reached England. King Henry VII did not want England to be shut out of the Indies. The result was a series of English voyages of exploration.

John Cabot

John Cabot was the first explorer to sail in search of land for England. Cabot believed he could find a shorter route to the Indies by sailing directly west from England. Henry VII gave him a small ship and a crew of eighteen men. In 1497, Cabot sailed to Newfoundland, a land which he **claimed**, or took, for England. Highly pleased, the king sent Cabot out again in 1498. On this voyage, he explored the coast of North America as far south as Delaware. He, too, thought he had reached the coast of China.

> **focus your reading**
>
> Why were John Cabot's voyages important to England?
>
> What does the term *northwest passage* mean?
>
> How were the "sea dogs" a different kind of explorer?
>
> **vocabulary**
>
> claimed
> northwest passage
> sea dogs
> plundered

John Cabot

European Explorers 27

Picturing History

This painting is called "Cabot Leaves the Port of Bristol." It was painted by Ernest Board in 1906. The painting depicts John Cabot on May 2, 1497, as he prepared to sail on the *Matthew* from Bristol, England. He searched for a direct route to Asia and its exotic spices and silks. Who is pictured in the painting? What does the painting tell you about the importance of religion?

Lesson Vocabulary

Discuss the meaning of each vocabulary word. Begin by focusing on *northwest passage*. Use the map on page 28 to explain why explorers were unable to find such a route. Ask students how the search allowed the English to *claim* land in North America. By the late 1500s and early 1600s, some English sailors were *plundering*, or robbing, Spanish treasure ships as well as exploring new lands. They were known as *sea dogs*.

Lesson Summary

The English also wanted to find a route to Asia. In 1497, John Cabot claimed the coast of North America for England. He thought he had reached the Indies. Later explorers from England realized that they had reached a new continent. Many searched for an all-water route through North America to Asia. Later, English sea dogs robbed Spanish ships while they explored land in the Americas.

Lesson Objective

Students will learn how the search for a northwest passage to Asia helped England claim more and more land in North America.

Focus Your Reading Answers

1 John Cabot's voyages were important because they established England's claims in North America.

2 The term *northwest passage* refers to an all-water route through North America to Asia.

3 The main difference between "sea dogs" and other explorers is that "sea dogs" robbed Spanish ships while exploring.

European Explorers 27

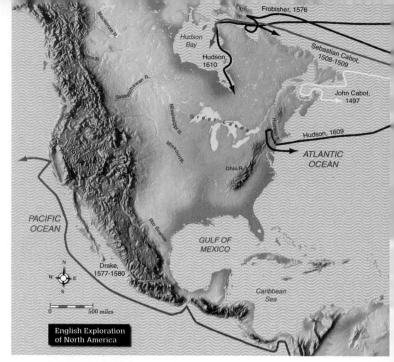

English Exploration
of North America

Map Extension

Explain to students that Magellan found a "southwest passage" to Asia around South America. Have students trace that voyage on the map on page 22. According to the map on page 28, why were the English unable to find a similar passage around North America? (North America extends too far north for ships to sail around the continent. Mountains in the west block any possibility of a river route through the continent.)

Searching for the Northwest Passage

Explorers searched for a northwest passage during the sixteenth century.

The next British explorers had a more definite purpose in mind. They knew that Columbus had not reached the Indies. They set out to find a **northwest passage**, a direct route to Asia through North America. In 1509, Sebastian Cabot, John Cabot's son, looked for it along the east coast of Canada. He claimed to have found the opening. Instead, he probably found the inlet to Hudson Bay. Later, in 1576, Martin Frobisher also searched in vain for a passage through the

28 Chapter 2

Picturing History

The map at the bottom of page 28 was created in the 1500s. What does it show? (North and South America) What parts of North America had been explored? (all but the northwest part of the continent) Do you think explorers would have continued their search for the northwest passage if they knew about the mountain ranges that lay along the Pacific Coast?

continent. He returned with his ship loaded with ore that looked like silver. It turned out to be worthless. In 1610, Henry Hudson thought he had found the Northwest Passage. It was only a large inland sea that later was named Hudson Bay.

Francis Drake's Voyage Around the World

The reign of Queen Elizabeth I (1558–1603) produced a new kind of English explorer. These English **"sea dogs" plundered**, or stole from, Spanish ships while exploring new territory. The most daring of all was Francis Drake. Queen Elizabeth helped Drake outfit a fleet of ships for a voyage around the world. He crossed the Atlantic in 1577 and sailed through the Strait of Magellan. Then he sailed north to raid Spanish colonial towns along the Pacific coast of South America. After capturing a Spanish treasure ship near Panama, he sailed up the coast of Mexico and California. He was looking for a western entrance to the Northwest Passage. Drake arrived back in England in 1580. He spent nearly three years traveling 36,000 miles around the world, but did not find a shortcut to the Indies.

Putting It All Together

Sailors often told stories about their adventures at sea. Imagine that you are an English seaman who sailed with Martin Frobisher (1576) or Francis Drake (1577–1580). Write a story about your adventures. Include facts such as time of year, weather, conditions at sea.

Francis Drake and the "sea dogs"

Stop and Think

The diagrams should show that all three explorers sailed for England and sought a northwest passage through North America. Differences might include the dates each explorer came to North America, the area each explored, and what each found.

Putting It All Together

Stories will vary, but students should focus on Frobisher's mistaken belief that he found silver, and the way Drake mixed plundering Spanish treasure ships with his search for a northwest passage.

Picturing History

On December 13, 1577, Francis Drake began his voyage around the world. He sailed on his ship *The Pelican*, later renamed the *Golden Hind*. This picture depicts Drake as he prepares to leave Plymouth, England. This image shows the style of dress during the late 16th century. How does Drake's clothing compare to others in the picture? Do his clothes tell you anything about his social status? What similarities are there between Drake's uniform and the uniforms worn in the U.S. Navy today?

Bio Facts

- Hudson was born in 1565, in Hertfordshire, about 17 miles northwest of London.

- Hudson may have sailed with John Davis in 1587 on his voyage to discover the Northwest Passage. Davis planned his 1585 trip in the home of Thomas Hudson, who may have been Henry's brother.

- As a young man, Hudson probably served in the offices of the Muscovy Company, a trading company in London. His family owned shares in the company.

- Little else is known about Hudson's life before 1607. Some sources say he took part in trade missions to the Mediterranean and Africa.

- In 1607 and again in 1608, Hudson searched for a northwest passage by sailing across the Arctic Ocean. Blocked by icebergs, both voyages failed.

- Hudson was then hired by the Dutch East India Company in 1609 to find the northwest passage. After sailing to Nova Scotia and then further south, he found what is now called the Hudson River.

- In 1610–1611, Hudson traveled through what is now called the Hudson Strait and into Hudson Bay. He died in 1611, after his crew mutinied and left him, his son, and seven crew members adrift in a small, open boat in Hudson Bay.

- Henry Hudson established claims in North America for two countries: the Netherlands, in what would become the New York area, and England, in northern Canada.

30

Biography

Henry Hudson (1565–1611)

Few names are as prominent on the map of North America as Hudson. The longest river in New York State is the Hudson River. Hudson Bay is North America's largest inland body of water. The 500-mile strait leading to it is called Hudson Strait. The name is there because of Henry Hudson's explorations to find a northwest passage to the Indies.

Little is known about Henry Hudson's youth. Hudson probably spent his earlier years as a cabin boy on a ship. Hudson's grandfather helped found the Muscovy Company. This company, made up of merchants in London, traded with Russia for furs, hides, and lumber.

In April 1607, the Muscovy Company sent Hudson to search for a passage to the Indies north of Greenland. He found polar bears, whales, and icebergs, but no ice-free route to the Indies.

The next year the company asked Hudson to look for a "Northeast Passage." He sailed north and east from England to the Barents Sea, searching for a way around Russia to China. Icebergs there forced him to turn back.

In 1609, Henry Hudson tried the northeast route again. This time his voyage was financed by Holland. Again, the icebergs stopped him. He took a long way home, crossing the Atlantic to explore the coast of North America. On this leg of the voyage, he sailed into a long waterway. What he hoped was the Northwest Passage turned out to be the Hudson River.

In 1610, London merchants again sent Hudson to search for the northwest passage. This time he sailed to the icy north coast of Canada. Hudson found a long waterway—now Hudson Strait—that led inland to a huge bay, today called Hudson Bay. Then the ice closed in, stranding the ship for the winter. In the spring, the starving crew refused to go further. They set Hudson, his son John, and seven others adrift in a small boat. The crew returned to England, leaving the men to die.

Biography Extension

Have students create a map showing all of the places in the United States and Canada named for Henry Hudson. What other places can students find in the United States that are named for explorers?

French Explorers in North America

Thinking on Your Own

Read the Focus Your Reading questions. Then look at the map and pictures included in this lesson. What clues do they give you about French explorers in North America? Write three predictions in your notebook. Compare your predictions with those of a partner.

As explorers of North America, the French were latecomers. In 1492, France, not Spain, was Europe's most powerful nation. The French kings kept their attention focused on Europe. For a hundred years they spent little time or money exploring new lands. When France finally did take an interest in North America, its explorers staked out a vast **empire**.

focus your reading
What did early English and French explorers have in common?
What was Champlain's goal as an explorer?
How did La Salle's explorations benefit France?

vocabulary
empire   missionary
trading posts   Louisiana

Verrazzano and Cartier

The first French explorers set out to find a water route to the Indies. Like the early English sea captains, they hoped to find a northwest passage. In 1523, Giovanni da Verrazzano, an Italian living in France, led the first expedition. He explored the coastline from North Carolina to Newfoundland, but found no passageway. From 1534 to 1541, Jacques Cartier made three voyages to North America. On his second voyage in 1535, he sailed up the St. Lawrence River. That journey established France's claim to eastern Canada. Cartier also failed in his attempt to find the Northwest Passage.

Giovanni da Verrazzano

31

Lesson Vocabulary

Explain the meaning of the word *empire*—a nation and the peoples and lands it rules. Locate *Louisiana* on the map on page 32, and explain that it was one of the lands included in France's North American empire in the 1600s. Tell students that France built its empire to gain wealth and much of that wealth came from furs purchased at *trading posts* throughout France's North American empire. Some of the explorers who built France's empire were *missionaries* who came to North America to convert Native Americans to Christianity.

Have students use the vocabulary words in a paragraph that describes how France built an empire in North America.

Lesson Summary

Like English explorers, French explorers also searched for a route to the Indies through North America. Jacques Cartier explored the St. Lawrence River and claimed the surrounding area for France. Samuel de Champlain set up trading posts to acquire furs to sell in Europe. The French were the first Europeans to explore the Ohio River valley. They also claimed the Mississippi River valley for France. They named the area Louisiana.

Lesson Objective

Students will learn how the French came to claim much of North America in the 1600s.

Focus Your Reading Answers

1 Both early English and French explorers wanted to find an all-water route through North America to Asia.

2 Champlain's goal as an explorer was to expand the trade in furs with Native Americans.

3 La Salle claimed the Ohio River valley for France.

Picturing History

Verrazzano was an Italian who sailed for France. In his search for the Northwest Passage, he explored every opening he saw along the eastern coast of North America. Ask students to use the map on page 32 to trace his voyage.

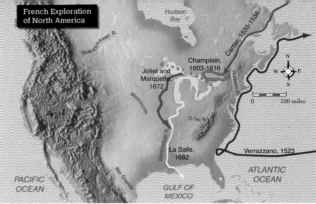

French Exploration of North America

Hudson Bay

Cartier, 1535-1536

Champlain, 1603-1616

Joliet and Marquette, 1672

La Salle, 1682

Verrazzano, 1523

PACIFIC OCEAN

ATLANTIC OCEAN

GULF OF MEXICO

0   500 miles

Stop and Think
Answers will vary, but students should show an understanding that life in North America offered opportunities for wealth, but French settlers lived far from home and had to overcome many obstacles.

Map Extension

Ask students what part of North America the French explored (lands mainly east of the Mississippi River). Which three river valleys did the French claim? (St. Lawrence, Ohio, and Mississippi) What do the explorations of La Salle and Joliet and Marquette have in common? (They established France's claim to the Mississippi River valley.)

Samuel de Champlain

The voyages of Samuel de Champlain opened a new chapter in French exploration. The main purpose of his eleven voyages (1603–1635) was to expand the fur trade with the people of America. The French exchanged brass kettles, iron pots, and knives for beaver, fox, bear, and wolf skins. Fur was used to make men's felt hats, to trim coats, and to make warm covers. Champlain explored the interior of Canada for places to set up **trading posts**. He also discovered a huge lake, which he named Lake Champlain.

Samuel de Champlain

stop and think

Create an ad for a French trading company that is trying to attract families to move to Canada. Include the advantages and rewards of making the move to Canada. You may have to do additional research to find specific information about different settlements.

Later French Explorers

Other French explorers followed Champlain's lead. Sieur de La Salle explored the Ohio River valley, claiming it for France. A French trader, Louis Joliet, and a **missionary** named Jacques Marquette traveled west to Lake Michigan. They also

Picturing History

Samuel de Champlain is often described as the founder of France's empire in North America. He started the first French colony. What does the picture suggest about the way he was viewed by both the French and the Native Americans?

Sieur de La Salle claimed land for France.

paddled down the Mississippi River to present-day Arkansas. In 1682, La Salle journeyed all the way down the Mississippi River, reaching the Gulf of Mexico. He claimed the entire Mississippi River valley for France, along with all the rivers that flowed into it. He named this vast area **Louisiana**, in honor of King Louis XIV.

Putting It All Together

With a partner review the sections describing the explorations of Verrazzano, Cartier, Champlain, and La Salle. Write questions about the explorers and quiz each other. Write the questions and the answers to them in your notebook.

Jacques Marquette

Putting It All Together

The questions will vary but should focus on main ideas. To help students find main ideas, explain that explorations were important news in the 1600s. Remind them that a good news story should answer the following questions:

- What happened?
- Who was involved?
- Where did it happen?
- When did it happen?
- Why did it happen?
- How did it happen?

Picturing History

Compare the two drawings on page 33. Both show explorers claiming land for France. How are the two pictures alike? What differences do you notice? Compare and contrast them with the drawing of De Soto on page 25 and the one of Columbus on page 26. How do you account for similarities?

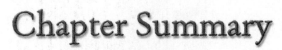

Chapter Review

1 Crossword puzzles will vary, but the clues should show the students' understanding of the chapter's key words and vocabulary.

2 Answers will vary, but should show an awareness that the French bartered for the furs. They traded pots, pans, and knives for beaver, fox, bear, and wolf skins.

3 The ads should reflect the high value placed on goods from the Indies.

Chapter Summary

In the late 1400s, Europeans tried to find a new route to the Indies. They wanted more control over the spice trade with that region. A Portuguese prince, Henry the Navigator, helped explorers learn to **navigate** around the tip of Africa. In 1492, Columbus sailed from Spain in three **caravels** to an island in the Caribbean Sea. He thought he had reached the Indies. In 1519, Ferdinand Magellan found a way to the Indies through the **strait** south of South America. These explorations helped **cartographers** map the hemisphere.

England also wanted to find a route to the Indies. In 1497, John Cabot **claimed** the coast of North America for England. He thought he had reached the Indies. The English explorers who came after him knew better. They searched for a **northwest passage** through North America to Asia. Later, English **"sea dogs" plundered** Spanish ships while exploring land in the Western Hemisphere.

French explorers also looked for a route to the Indies. Jacques Cartier explored the St. Lawrence River and claimed land for the French **empire**. Samuel de Champlain established **trading posts** to sell furs to help pay the cost of his journeys. The French were the first Europeans to explore the Ohio River valley. A **missionary** named Marquette explored part of the Mississippi River. Later, La Salle claimed the river valley for France, naming it **Louisiana** for King Louis XIV.

Chapter Review

1 Create a crossword puzzle using key words from this chapter. Connect the words horizontally and vertically where they share the same letters. Write definitions in your own words under the puzzle.

2 Imagine that you are listening to a conversation. Write several lines of dialogue between the French traders and Native Americans. Keep in mind what they exchanged for the furs.

3 Create a newspaper ad for a merchant who has various items from the Indies for sale.

Novel Connections

Below is a list of books that relate to the time period covered in this chapter. The numbers in parentheses indicate the related Thematic Strands of the National Council for the Social Studies (NCSS).

Joan Elizabeth Goodman. *Beyond the Sea of Ice: The Voyages of Henry Hudson.* (The Great Explorers series) Mikaya, 1999. (II, III)

_____. *Despite All Obstacles: LaSalle and the Conquest of the Mississippi.* (Great Explorers series) Mikaya Press, 2001. (II, VI, X)

Avery Hart. *Who Really Discovered America? Unraveling the Mystery and Solving the Puzzle.* (Kaleidoscope Kids series) Williamson Publishing 2001. (I, III, IX)

Virginia Schomp. *Around the World in . . . 1500.* (*Around the World In . . .* series). Benchmark Books, 2002. (I, III, V, VI)

Stuart Waldman. *We Asked for Nothing: The Remarkable Journey of Cabeza De Vaca.* (Great Explorers series) Mikaya Press, 2003. (I, II, V)

Skill Builder

Reading Maps

Maps link history to geography. They show where on the earth's surface past events and developments took place. Maps are valuable sources of information. However, to read the information one must understand the language and symbols of maps. These include the following:

- **Map Title.** It tells you what kind of information the map includes.

- **Map Labels.** They are words or names that identify places on the map.

- **Map Symbols.** The lines, arrows, dots, and icons present information.

- **Map Key or Legend.** The explanatory list, usually placed in a box, helps you interpret the information.

- **Compass Rose.** This indicator helps you find directions on the map.

- **Distance Scale.** It indicates the scale in miles on the map. Maps are drawn to different scales.

Use the map to answer the following questions:

1 What geographical area does this map include?

2 What part of North America did the first French explorer visit?

3 In what direction did Cartier sail when he explored the St. Lawrence River?

4 Who first explored the Mississippi River and in what year?

5 About how far did Joliet and Marquette travel down the Mississippi River?

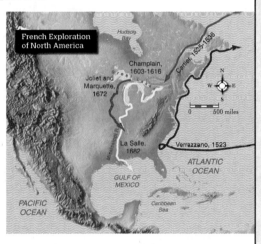

French Exploration of North America

Skill Builder

1 The map includes much of what is now the continental United States.

2 Verrazzano, the first explorer from France, visited the Atlantic Coast.

3 Cartier sailed south and west as he explored the St. Lawrence.

4 Joliet and Marquette were the first French explorers to travel down the Mississippi River in 1672.

5 Tracing the purple route of Joliet and Marquette, they traveled approximately 1,000 miles.

Map Extension

Ask students to use the maps on pages 25 and 28 to figure out what other nations claimed some of the land that France considered part of its empire. (Spain: Mississippi River valley; England: parts of Canada)

Classroom Discussion

Discuss with students some of the broader topics covered in this chapter.

- Compare and contrast explorers from Portugal, Spain, England, and France. In what ways are they alike? How do you account for differences among them?

- Why do many people believe that Columbus's voyage in 1492 changed the history of the world? In your opinion, what other explorers changed the world?

- In what ways do you think the lives of Native Americans were changed by the arrival of newcomers from Europe?

- How did each explorer build on what he and others learned from earlier explorers?

- What kinds of discoveries do people make today? How do they learn from those who have gone before them?

Unit Objectives

After studying this unit, students will be able to

- explain how Spain, France, England, and other European nations established colonies in the Americas

- compare and contrast life in various European colonies in the Americas

- discuss what brought many Europeans to the Americas in the 1600s and early 1700s

- analyze the impact of European colonies on Native Americans

Unit 2 focuses on the first colonies European nations established in North America.

Chapter 3, Spanish, French, and Dutch Colonies, describes the settlements each group of colonists built in the Americas.

Chapter 4, English Colonies, compares and contrasts the various settlements people from England started along the Atlantic coast.

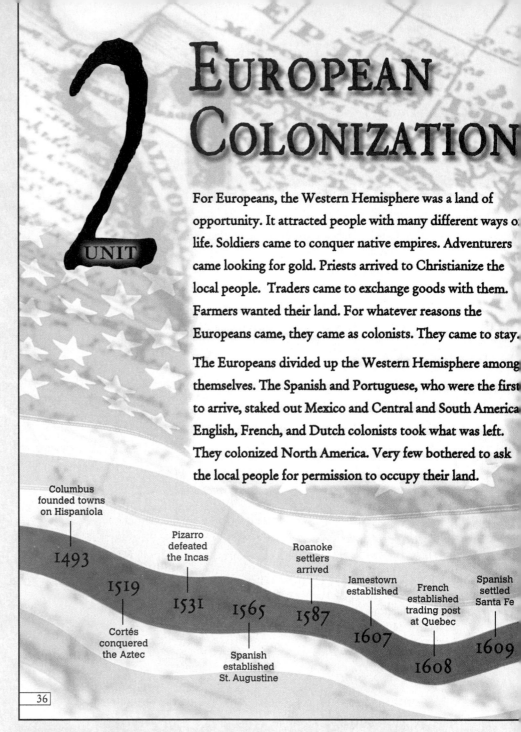

2 UNIT EUROPEAN COLONIZATION

For Europeans, the Western Hemisphere was a land of opportunity. It attracted people with many different ways of life. Soldiers came to conquer native empires. Adventurers came looking for gold. Priests arrived to Christianize the local people. Traders came to exchange goods with them. Farmers wanted their land. For whatever reasons the Europeans came, they came as colonists. They came to stay.

The Europeans divided up the Western Hemisphere among themselves. The Spanish and Portuguese, who were the first to arrive, staked out Mexico and Central and South America. English, French, and Dutch colonists took what was left. They colonized North America. Very few bothered to ask the local people for permission to occupy their land.

Columbus founded towns on Hispaniola
1493

Pizarro defeated the Incas
1531

Cortés conquered the Aztec
1519

Spanish established St. Augustine
1565

Roanoke settlers arrived
1587

Jamestown established
1607

French established trading post at Quebec
1608

Spanish settled Santa Fe
1609

36

What opportunities did the French and the Dutch find in North America?

How were the English colonies different from others?

What American empires did Spain conquer?

Timeline

The Netherlands set up Fort Nassau
1616

Pilgrims established Plymouth Colony
1620

Puritans founded Massachusetts Bay Colony
1630

English settled Maryland
1634

England founded Rhode Island
1636

England founded Connecticut
1662

French established New Orleans
1718

English settled Georgia
1733

37

Collage Answers

Ask students to copy the three questions on page 37 into their history notebooks. As they read the unit, have them record their answers to each question.

1 The French and the Dutch found opportunities for trade in the Americas—particularly for trade in furs.

2 England's colonies differed from those of Spain and France in that many English settlers came to North America in search of farmland and later, religious freedom.

3 Spain conquered the Aztec Empire in Mexico and the Inca Empire in Peru.

Collage Extensions

Ask students to examine the images on page 37.

- What do the pictures suggest about similarities and differences among the European colonies?

- What do the images suggest about the importance of resources like farmland, forests, or silver to the kind of colony each nation built?

- What other factors may have shaped the kind of colony each nation built?

Timeline Extensions

To preview the unit, ask students to use the timeline to answer these questions:

- Which country was the first to build colonies in the Americas? (Spain)

- In which century did Spain establish most of its American colonies? (1500s)

- Which country was the second to build colonies in the Americas? (England)

- How many years passed between the founding of a Spanish town on Hispaniola and England's first American settlement? (94 years)

Key Blacklines

Biography
Francisco Pizarro

Primary Source
Columbus's Colony at Navidad

DVD Extension

Encourage students to use the reading comprehension, vocabulary reinforcement, and interactive timeline activities on the student DVD.

Picturing History

The picture on page 38 shows San José de la Laguna Mission and Convent, in New Mexico. Built between 1699 and 1701, the mission has a large bell tower with two bells and is topped with a large cross.

Chapter

3 SPANISH, FRENCH, AND DUTCH COLONIES

Getting Focused

Skim this chapter to predict what you will be learning.

- Read the lesson titles and subheadings.
- Look at the illustrations and read the captions.
- Examine the maps.
- Review the vocabulary words and terms.

Pick a photo from this chapter that you find interesting and examine it closely. What questions does it raise about the Spanish, French, or Dutch colonies? Share your ideas with a partner. Write a sentence in your notebook summarizing your ideas.

Pre-Reading Discussion

1 Ask students to use the chapter title to predict what this chapter is about. Review the meaning of the word *colony*. (See page 36.)

2 After students complete each bulleted direction on page 38, discuss what students have learned about Spanish, French, and Dutch colonies from their preview of the chapter. To organize their ideas, have them divide a sheet of paper into three parts—Spanish colonies, French colonies, Dutch colonies. Next have them list the things they learned from their preview under the correct heading. As students read and discuss the chapter, encourage them to add information under each heading.

The Spanish Colonies

Thinking on Your Own

Read the Focus Your Reading questions. What do you expect to learn from this lesson? Write one sentence that predicts what you will learn. Then write the vocabulary words in your notebook. As you read each vocabulary word in the lesson, write a definition in your notebook.

Spain took the lead in establishing **colonies** in the Western Hemisphere. Columbus's discovery gave Spain a one-hundred-year head start. Its only rival was Portugal. Portugal established a colony in Brazil.

The Spanish in the Caribbean

focus your reading

How did Spanish colonists treat the Native Americans?

How did Spain gain control over Mexico and Peru?

How did American colonies make Spain a rich nation?

vocabulary

colonies   smallpox
founded

The first Spanish explorers set up colonies in the Caribbean. On his second voyage in 1493, Columbus brought 1,200 soldiers and colonists with him. They **founded**, or established, the towns of Isabela and Santo Domingo on the island of Hispaniola. Later explorers set up other colonies in the Caribbean.

Far from Europe, these first settlements struggled to survive. Most of the settlers were soldiers. They made slaves of the local people. The slaves did the hardest work. But the local people died by the thousands. They had no immunity to **smallpox** and other European diseases.

Diseases such as smallpox devastated many Native American groups.

39

Lesson Summary

Spain was the first European nation to build colonies in the Americas.

In 1519, the Spanish gained control of Mexico by conquering the Aztec people. Mexico made Spain rich.

In 1531, Spain conquered the Inca of Peru. Silver from Peru and Mexico made Spain one of the richest nations in Europe.

Lesson Objective

Students will learn how the Spanish built colonies in Mexico, South America, and the Caribbean.

Focus Your Reading Answers

1 Native Americans were treated as slaves.

2 Spain used armies to conquer both Mexico and Peru.

3 Spain became rich because its colonies had large supplies of silver.

Lesson Vocabulary

Discuss the meaning of each vocabulary word. Review earlier discussions of the word *colony* (pages 36 and 38). Then discuss the link between a *colony* and an *empire* by explaining that Spain used its colonies to build an empire.

Some students may confuse the word *founded* with the past tense of the word *find*. Explain that when people found a colony, they are building something new.

Smallpox is a highly contagious virus that can be deadly. People who have the disease generally run high fevers and feel weak. Their bodies are covered with raised bumps filled with pus.

Picturing History

An Aztec artist created the drawing on page 39 in the 1500s. It shows the impact of smallpox on a family in Mexico. What can we learn from the picture about smallpox and its effects on Native Americans? How does the artist seem to regard the disease?

Extension

The Spanish founded Isabela in 1493 on the north coast of the island of Hispaniola (today divided between the Dominican Republic and Haiti). They abandoned the town in 1498 after completing Santo Domingo, which became the center of Spanish government in the Americas. Encourage students to use the Internet to find out more about both towns and present their findings to the class.

Stop and Think

Answers will vary, but students are likely to mention that

- the first Spanish settlements were on the island of Hispaniola

- most Spanish settlers were soldiers

- the Spanish made slaves of local people in the Caribbean

- many local people died of smallpox

- Hernando Cortés conquered the Aztec Empire in Mexico and sent treasure ships loaded with gold and silver back to Spain

When Columbus arrived at Hispaniola in 1493, about 250,000 native people lived on the island. Only fifty years later, none were left. The Spanish settlers imported slaves from Africa to replace local laborers.

Spanish Colonies in Mexico

From its base in the Caribbean, Spain set out to gain control of Mexico. The powerful Aztec emperor, Montezuma, ruled Mexico. In 1519, Hernando Cortés invaded the mainland with an army of 500 men. He captured the city of Tenochtitlan with the help of groups opposed to the Aztecs. Montezuma was killed in the fighting. Cortés emptied the Aztec treasure houses and sent the gold and silver back to Spain.

stop and think

At this point, set your book aside. Tell a partner what you have learned about the Spanish in the Caribbean and in Mexico. Skim the section to check for accuracy. Then write two facts about this topic in your notebook.

Early Spanish Conquests
■ Areas and cities conquered by Spain

Map Extension

Explain to students that the map shows early Spanish conquests. Ask students to use the map to answer these questions:

- Where were the first Spanish colonies? (on islands in the Caribbean Sea)

- What part of the Americas did the Spanish take over next? (Central America)

- What role did the Caribbean Sea play in helping Spain build its empire in the Americas? (served as a highway between colonies)

- What parts of the Americas do you think the Spanish were likely to conquer next? (lands north of Mexico and south and east of Peru)

Hernando Cortés meeting Aztec leader Montezuma

Cortés's soldiers remained in Mexico as colonists. Spain gave individuals control over local villages. They put the local people to work as farmers. They raised cattle and mined silver. Spanish colonists in Mexico depended on the forced labor of local inhabitants.

The Spanish in South America

Spain next turned its attention to South America. In 1531, Francisco Pizarro led a Spanish army against the Incas. The Inca People controlled a large empire in Peru. Pizarro captured the Incan ruler, Atahualpa, and demanded gold and silver in exchange for his life. After collecting twenty tons of precious metal, Pizarro murdered Atahualpa. The Spanish then destroyed the empire and took all the wealth from its cities.

Spain sent colonists to settle in South America. They used the land for cattle ranches and took over the Incan silver mines. As in Mexico, the colonists forced the local people to do most of the work. In one silver mine in Peru, 58,000 locals worked as slaves. Silver shipped from Peru and Mexico made Spain the richest nation in Europe.

Putting It All Together

Create a three-column chart in your notebook. Label the columns "Spanish in the Caribbean," "Spanish in Mexico," and "Spanish in South America." In each column describe three or four things the Spanish did in each place.

Francisco Pizarro burning Incan chief Atahualpa

Spanish, French, and Dutch Colonies   41

Putting It All Together

Answers will vary, but students are likely to include the following under each column:

Spanish in the Caribbean

1 The Spanish founded Isabela and Santo Domingo on the island of Hispaniola.

2 Settlements struggled to survive.

3 They made slaves of local people.

4 Thousands of local people died of smallpox.

Spanish in Mexico

1 In 1519, Cortés conquered Mexico.

2 He had the help of groups that did not like the Aztec.

3 Cortés sent gold and silver back to Spain.

4 The Spanish raised cattle and mined silver in Mexico using Native Americans as forced labor.

Spanish in South America

1 In 1531, Pizarro conquered the Inca's empire in Peru.

2 He kidnapped the Inca ruler and demanded gold and silver for his life.

3 Spain destroyed the Inca's empire and took its wealth.

4 The Spanish forced the Inca to work in mines and on ranches.

Picturing History

The picture at the top of page 41 shows Cortés's initial meeting with Montezuma, the Aztec leader. It was the first time the Aztec saw horses or heard gunshots. How do you think they responded? Invite students to draw the picture from an Aztec point of view.

The picture at the bottom of page 41 shows Inca chief Atahualpa being burned at the stake by Francisco Pizarro. After being invited to meet with the newly arrived Spanish, Atahualpa was taken prisoner. In exchange for his release, the Incas provided Pizarro with vast quantities of gold. Once the ransom was paid, Pizarro had Atahualpa executed. On July 16, 1533, Atahualpa was burned at the stake. Why did Pizarro kill Atahualpa?

Biography

Hernando Cortés (1485?–1547)

In August 1519, Hernando Cortés marched into Mexico to attack the Aztec Empire. He brought with him about 500 Spanish soldiers, seventy-five sailors, sixteen horses, and a few small cannons. His goal seemed impossible. To reach the Aztec capital, Tenochtitlan, Cortés had to lead his men through 250 miles of unknown territory. Waiting for him were Montezuma, the Aztec emperor, and thousands of warriors. However, Cortés did not doubt for a moment that he would conquer the Aztec Empire. The only question was how.

Cortés was a risk taker. He had left Spain in 1504, at age nineteen, looking for adventure. He went to the Caribbean. There he helped conquer Cuba, receiving land and slaves as his reward. He discovered gold on his property, but he wanted more. On a voyage across the Gulf of Mexico, he found local people wearing gold jewelry. It came, they said, from the land of the Aztec. So, with men and ships provided by the governor of Cuba, Cortés was determined to conquer the Aztec.

On his march through the mountains, Cortés discovered how to do it. Groups that the Aztec had conquered were ready to rebel against them. The emperor Montezuma had taxed them heavily, taking their corn and gold. He also demanded people for human sacrifice. Cortés reached Tenochtitlan with thousands of native warriors at his side.

The emperor opened the city to Cortés, believing that he was the Aztec's white god, Quetzelcoatl. Once inside, Cortés took Montezuma prisoner. When the Aztec attacked, the Spaniards and their local allies destroyed the city. Montezuma died in the fighting. With Montezuma's gold, Cortés built a Spanish city, Mexico City, in its place. He stayed there as the new and very wealthy governor of Mexico.

42

Biography Extension

Have students find out more about Tenochtitlán, the city Cortés conquered in 1519. It was one of the largest and best-planned cities in the world in the 1500s. Over 100,000 people lived there at a time when most European cities were home to only a few thousand people. How was Cortés able to conquer such a large city with a small army? What advantages did he have? Ask students to share their findings with the class.

Spanish Settlements in North America

Thinking on Your Own

Spanish officials in Mexico thought of North America as a "borderland." What kind of borderlands exist today? Find the word in the Glossary and write a definition of *borderland* from your point of view.

N orth of Mexico were the **Spanish borderlands**. This vast area extended from Florida west to California. It was a poor country that had no gold or silver mines. Even so, Spanish officials in the late 1500s began to colonize this region. They needed to make a **barrier** in Florida against English and French settlers. They also wanted to bring Christianity to the native people who lived in this region.

focus your reading

Why did the Spanish set up a colony in Florida?

How did the Pueblo react to the Spanish settlements?

How were missions different from other settlements?

vocabulary

Spanish borderlands

barrier

imposed

missions

empire

The Spanish in Florida

In 1565, the Spanish built a fort and a town at St. Augustine on the Atlantic coast of Florida. It is the oldest continuous settlement in what is now the United States. The colony was a barrier in the east. French and British attacks upon the fort made it one of the most dangerous colonies. Not many farmers settled in St. Augustine. Spanish officials even had to import food for the soldiers at the fort.

St. Augustine was established by Spain in 1565.

43

Lesson Summary

The Spanish built settlements north of Mexico in a vast area that stretched from California to Florida. In Florida, they built a fort at St. Augustine. They also built farms and ranches in New Mexico and missions in what is now Arizona and California.

Lesson Objective

Students will learn about Spanish settlements north of Mexico, beginning in the late 1500s.

Focus Your Reading Answers

1 The Spanish set up a colony in Florida as a barrier to French and British attacks.

2 In 1680, the Pueblo reacted to Spanish settlements by killing several hundred colonists and driving the rest out of New Mexico.

3 Missions were founded by priests and used to convert Native Americans to Christianity and teach them Spanish ways of life.

Picturing History

St. Augustine was built as a fort. What does the drawing suggest about other roles the town played in Spanish Florida? (Students are likely to notice the church and the presence of women as well as men.)

Lesson Vocabulary

Introduce the vocabulary for this lesson by focusing on the word *empire*—a nation and the peoples and lands it rules. Explain that empires have *borders*. They are the outer edges of the land a nation rules. Most maps show borders as thin lines. Why might the Spanish have created a *borderland*—a large area of land that separated its holdings from those of other European nations?

The word *barrier* means anything that slows or stops free movement. To what extent were the Spanish borderlands a *barrier*? Whom did they slow or stop?

What role did *missions* play in the *empire* Spain built in the Americas? How did they act as *barriers*?

To *impose* is to force or compel someone to act in a certain way. How did the Spanish *impose* their rule over Native Americans?

Spanish Settlements in New Mexico

To protect Mexico's northern border and to Christianize the local people, Spanish officials decided to settle New Mexico. In 1598, Juan de Oñate led 400 settlers north from Mexico. They settled in present-day New Mexico and began farming. In 1609, Spanish officials founded the town of Santa Fe. From Santa Fe, colonial governors **imposed** Spanish rule over New Mexico's Pueblo Indians.

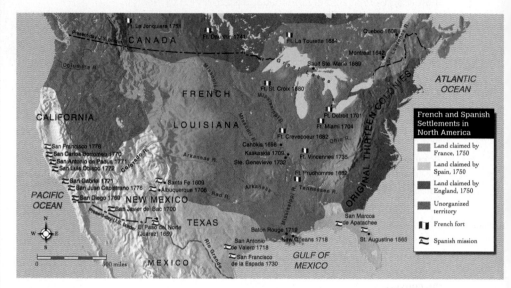

The early governors treated the Native Americans badly. They took away the Pueblo's corn to feed the settlers. They forced the Pueblo to weave cloth. Then, the governor sold the cloth and kept the money.

In 1680, the Pueblo rebelled. They killed several hundred Spanish colonists. They also drove the remaining colonists out of New Mexico. The Spanish returned in 1692. This time they stayed. They also realized that they had to treat the Pueblo more fairly.

stop and think

Make a list of the different kinds of Spanish settlements in North America. Add to the list as you read. Describe each in a sentence or two.

Spanish Missions in Arizona and California

The first Spanish settlers in present-day Arizona and California were Catholic priests. They built **missions** instead of towns. In 1687, Father Eusebio Kino founded eight missions in Arizona. Almost a hundred years later, Father Junipero Serra set up more than twenty missions in California. The Spanish also built mission churches in New Mexico and Texas.

Each mission included a church, living quarters for several priests and soldiers, and shelters for the Native Americans. The priests invited the local people to live at the mission. They tried to convert those who came to Christianity. They taught the converts how to farm and raise cattle. They wanted the Native Americans to live near the missions so they would not return to their old ways. The Spanish priests often sent soldiers out to bring back those who tried to escape.

By 1600, Spain's **empire** extended nearly eight thousand miles from California to the tip of South America. It was the largest empire in the western world since the Roman Empire.

Putting It All Together

Imagine that you are a Native American living in the Spanish borderlands during the 1680s. What would you say to a Spanish settler or priest about the Spaniards' treatment of your people? How would you feel about being converted to Christianity? Write your thoughts in your notebook.

Picturing History

Father Fermin Lasuen, the head of the chain of missions Spain built in California, founded Mission San Miguel Archangel in 1797. It was the 16th of 21 missions. Like the others, San Miguel was located a day's travel from its neighbors. Why did the Spanish build each mission a day's travel away from the next? (to provide a place for Spanish soldiers, traders, and other travelers to stay)

Putting It All Together

Answers will vary, but students should show some understanding that many Native Americans resented the way they were treated by both Spanish settlers and priests.

Extension

Invite students to research one or more of the California missions. Ask them to present their findings to the class by using Student Presentation Builder on the student DVD.

French and Dutch Colonies

Lesson Summary

France and the Netherlands were among the last to build colonies in North America. France's first colony was Quebec. Like most colonies in New France, Quebec served as a fur trading post and a mission. The Dutch also took part in the fur trade. They set up trading posts along the Hudson River in what is now New York. The Dutch called their colony New Netherland, and their largest city was New Amsterdam.

Lesson Objective

Students will learn about the colonies the French and the Dutch built in North America in the 1600s.

Focus Your Reading Answers

1 The French were late in establishing colonies because they were involved in European politics and wars. The Dutch were busy making money.

2 The chief purpose of French settlements was to promote the fur trade.

3 The Dutch established a colony along the Hudson River to get their share of the fur trade.

Extension

Point out that the fur trade brought wealth to both the French and the Dutch. Ask interested students to find out more about the fur trade and share their findings with the class. Why didn't the fur trade encourage large groups of settlers to come to North America? How did the fur trade change the way Native Americans lived and worked?

Thinking on Your Own

Read this section with a partner. Decide whether you will read aloud together, take turns, or read silently. At the end of each paragraph, each partner must ask a question, say a thought, or state an opinion about the French and Dutch colonies. Write one of your ideas in your notebook.

France and the Netherlands were latecomers in colonizing America. Both had focused their attention elsewhere. The French were involved in European politics and wars. The Dutch were busy making money. The Netherlands produced many wealthy merchant families. Most of the colonists that France and the Netherlands finally sent overseas were traders rather than farmers. The French also sent priests to spread Christianity to the local people.

focus your reading

Why were France and the Netherlands late in establishing colonies?

What was the chief purpose of French settlements?

Why did the Dutch establish colonies along the Hudson River?

vocabulary

New France

New Netherland

New Amsterdam

patroon

The French in Canada

French colonies in North America were closely linked to the fur trade. The first French settlements in Canada were at Quebec (1608) and Montreal (1611). These were missions and fur trading posts. The French government tried to attract farmers to Canada. Very few farmers came to the colonies. Canada had to import food from Europe. The pioneers of **New France** were fur traders and priests, not farmers.

Lesson Vocabulary

Locate France, the Netherlands, and Amsterdam on a world map. (There is a world map at the end of this book.) Then explain that in the Americas, Europeans built a *New* France, a *New* Netherland, and a *New* Amsterdam. Discuss what is *new* about each of the three places. How is each place linked to its counterpart in Europe?

Patroons were wealthy investors who, in exchange for large tracts of land, sent colonists to New Netherland and backed them financially. For example, the largest land owner in New Netherland was Kiliaen Van Rensselaer. He never saw his land holdings in North America. He sent Dutch farmers to New Netherland to work his land. They, in turn, sent him a share of their earnings.

Early French settlement of Montreal

French fur traders set out in their canoes each year for Algonquin and Huron villages. At times they helped those groups fight their enemy, the Iroquois. The traders spent the winter swapping trade goods for beaver, mink, and otter pelts. In the spring, they paddled back to Quebec or Montreal with canoes filled with furs.

The French in the Mississippi Valley

The French officials also wanted to control the Mississippi River valley. This region was rich in animal pelts. They also wanted to create a barrier to protect against Spain's northward expansion from Mexico. In 1682, Sieur de la Salle had claimed the entire valley for France. But words were not enough to stop the Spanish.

The French lined the Mississippi River with Catholic missions and forts. In 1699, they built Fort Detroit at the upper end of the Mississippi valley. They built a fort and missions in present-day Illinois. They also established forts near the mouth of the Mississippi. The largest settlement was the town of New Orleans. It was settled on the lower Mississippi River in 1718.

Quebec in the 17th century

stop and think

Write two or three sentences that describe New France. Include details about the early settlers.

Stop and Think

Answers will vary, but the sentences should show an understanding that New France included much of Canada and the Mississippi River Valley. French claims were based mainly on trading posts, missions, and forts built along major rivers. Few French farmers settled in New France.

Picturing History

The drawing at the top of page 47 shows Montreal in the 1700s. The French founded the city in 1642 as a combination fort and mission. Montreal grew slowly until the early 1700s, when it became an important center for fur traders and explorers heading west. Based on the drawing, what may have attracted people to the city?

Picturing History

The word *habitation* in the drawing at the bottom of page 47 refers to a place where a *habitant*, or French settler, lived. Champlain drew this picture of Quebec, using letters to name the parts of major buildings. For example, *C*, *D*, and *F* are rooms for workers. *H* marks Champlain's rooms. *Q* is the garden, and *R* is the St. Lawrence River.

New Netherland was settled in 1626.

The Dutch in New Netherland

The Dutch also wanted a share of the fur trade. Henry Hudson's voyage of 1609 gave the Netherlands a claim to present-day New York State and part of New Jersey. In 1616, the Dutch set up a trading post at Fort Nassau on the Hudson River. They used the fort to trade with the Iroquois. Located at the present site of Albany, New York, it became part of the Dutch colony of **New Netherland**.

In 1626, the Dutch founded a second settlement on Manhattan Island. Governor Peter Minuit bought the land from the local chiefs for about $24, paid in trade goods. He called the settlement **New Amsterdam**. In 1638, Peter Minuit helped Sweden set up a colony called New Sweden. It was located in present-day Delaware. The Dutch took it over in 1655.

The purchase of Manhattan Island

The Dutch worked hard to attract farmers to New Netherland. Anyone who brought over fifty families became a **patroon**. Patroons were landowners in New Netherland. The patroons were given large estates along the Hudson River in New York and New Jersey.

Putting It All Together

With your partner, make a list of words and phrases that best define or describe the French and Dutch colonies. Then try to agree on which are the three most important. Use each of the three terms in a sentence about colonization.

Read a Primary Source

A French Colonial Town

New Orleans was founded in 1718 as the capital of French Louisiana. In 1763, an early settler wrote the following description of the town.

reading for understanding

What was New Orleans' biggest advantage?

What are the town's main buildings?

What role did the Catholic Church play in early New Orleans?

"A better choice could not have been made, as the town [is] on the banks of the Mississippi, vessels, tho' of a thousand ton, may lay their sides close to the shore, even at low water. . . .

"The place of arms [parade ground] is in the middle of that part of the town which faces the river; in the middle of the ground of the place of arms stands the parish church, called St. Louis. . . . To the right stand the prison, or jail, and the guard-house. . . .

"The Governor's house stands in the middle of that part of the town, from which we go from the place of arms to the habitation of the Jesuits, which is near the town. . . . The House of the Ursilin Nuns is quite at the end of the town to the right; as is also the hospital of the sick, of which the Nuns have the inspection. . . . The greatest part of the houses is of brick: the rest are of timber and brick."

Le Page du Pratz, *The History of Louisiana 1* (London, 1763).

Reading for Understanding

1 New Orleans is located on the Mississippi River at a point where very large ships can come close to shore, even at low tide.

2 The town has a parade ground, church, prison, guard-house, governor's house, a place where Jesuit priests live, the House of the Ursilin Nuns, and a hospital.

3 The Catholic Church played a large role in the town as evidenced by the location of the parish church and the presence of both priests and nuns. The nuns seem to have run the hospital.

49

Chapter Review

1 Answers will vary, but the paragraphs should focus on similarities and differences among the colonies. Students may find it useful to use the charts they created to compare and contrast the colonies. (See Activity 2 under Pre-Reading Discussions on page 38.)

2 Answers will vary, but the flags should show an understanding of the location of each nation's colonies, key resources, and ways of earning a living.

3 Answers will vary, but students should show an understanding that

- many Native Americans died from diseases the Spanish unknowingly brought to the Americas

- many Native Americans were forced to adopt Spanish ways, including the Christian religion

- many Native Americans were enslaved by the Spanish

Chapter Summary

Spain took the lead in setting up **colonies** in the Western Hemisphere. Columbus **founded** towns on the island of Hispaniola. Many local people died of **smallpox** and other diseases brought from Europe. In 1519, Hernando Cortés invaded Mexico. Cortés's soldiers remained in Mexico as colonists. Francisco Pizarro defeated the Incan Empire in Peru.

The **Spanish borderlands** lay north of Mexico. They formed a **barrier** between the Spanish **empire** and the French and English colonies. In the late 1500s, Spanish officials began to colonize this region. They built a fort and the town of St. Augustine in Florida. Spanish farmers also settled in present-day New Mexico. Colonial governors **imposed** Spanish rule over local Native Americans. Spanish priests built **missions** in present-day Arizona and California.

France and the Netherlands were latecomers in colonizing America. France's first colony was Quebec. Like most colonies in **New France**, Quebec was a mission and fur trading post. The Dutch also wanted a share of the fur trade. They set up trading posts along the Hudson River. The largest was **New Amsterdam**. The Dutch called their colony **New Netherland**. They attracted farmers by giving large estates to **patroons** who brought other farmers to New Netherland.

Chapter Review

1 Write the first draft of a paragraph that summarizes what you have learned about the Spanish, French, and Dutch colonies. Include all the chapter's vocabulary words. Compare your draft with that of your partner. Then write a final draft.

2 Design banners to fly over the Spanish, French, and Dutch colonies. What key words would each banner have? What symbols best represent those colonies? What colors would you choose? Explain your reasons for each choice.

3 Write a description of Spanish colonization from a Native American's point of view.

Novel Connections

Below is a list of books that relate to the time period covered in this chapter. The numbers in parentheses indicate the related Thematic Strands of the National Council for the Social Studies (NCSS).

Imogen Dawson. *Clothes and Crafts in Aztec Times.* Silver Burdett, 2000. (I, II, VIII)

Mary Ann Fraser. *A Mission for the People: The Story of La Purisima.* Holt, 1998. (I, II, III)

Joan Elizabeth Goodman. *Despite All Obstacles: La Salle and the Conquest of the Mississippi.* (Great Explorers series). Mikaya Press, 2001. (I, II, III)

Sylvia A. Johnson. *Tomatoes, Potatoes, Corn, and Beans: How the Foods of the Americas Changed Eating Around the World.* Atheneum, 1997. (III, VII, IX)

Virginia Schomp. *Around the World in . . . 1500.* Benchmark Books, 2002. (I, III, V, VI)

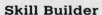

Skill Builder

Working with a Timeline

Chronology, the arrangement of events in time, is essential to understanding history. It tells when events took place and tells the sequence or order in which they happened. Knowing the sequence of events can also help us understand how they are related. Some events are caused by an earlier event.

A timeline is an easy way to show chronology. It is a visual tool that gives the dates of events and the sequence or order in which they happened. To show how events are related over time, timelines are divided into regular segments. The dates when events happened within each segment are clearly shown.

The timeline below shows major events in the European colonization of the Americas. Use the timeline to answer these questions:

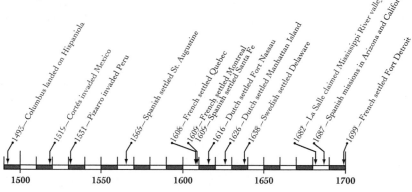

1 When was Santa Fe settled?

2 What was the first French settlement in Canada?

3 Which European nation took the lead in colonizing?

4 How much time passed between the first Spanish and French settlements?

5 Are any of the events on the timeline related to other events?

Skill Builder

1 Santa Fe was settled in 1609.

2 Quebec was the first French settlement in Canada.

3 Spain took the lead in colonizing.

4 Forty-three years passed between the settling of St. Augustine and the settling of Quebec.

5 All of the entries are related to invasion and/or colonization.

Extension

Explain to students that timelines can show trends or patterns. In what ways are the events in the 1500s similar to those in the 1600s? (Both show the establishment of colonies.)

In what ways are the events in the 1500s different from those in the 1600s? (There are fewer events in the 1500s, and all of the colonization is Spanish.)

Classroom Discussion

Discuss with students some of the broader topics covered in this chapter.

• How do you account for differences among the colonies built by Spain, France, and the Netherlands?

• How were Spanish, French, and Dutch colonists similar?

• In what kinds of places did Europeans choose to settle? What factors prompted them to build a town in one place rather than another?

• What effect did European colonization have on Native Americans?

• What attitudes and values shaped the way the newcomers regarded Native Americans?

Related Transparencies

- **T-7** The 13 Original Colonies
- **T-18** T-Chart
- **T-20** Venn diagram

Key Blacklines

Biography
Squanto

Primary Source
The First Thanksgiving

Picturing History

Jenney Grist Mill, in Plymouth, Massachusetts, is the oldest grist mill in America. It was operated by John Jenney from 1636 until his death in 1644. It was in continuous operation until 1847, when it was destroyed by fire. The mill was reconstructed in 1970.

DVD Extension

Encourage students to use the reading comprehension, vocabulary reinforcement, and interactive timeline activities on the student DVD.

Chapter 4 THE ENGLISH COLONIES

Getting Focused

Skim this chapter to predict what you will be learning.

- Read the lesson titles and subheadings.
- Look at the illustrations and read the captions.
- Examine the maps.
- Review the vocabulary words and terms.

The English colonists were strangers in a strange land. Think about a time when you were a stranger. How did you feel? How did those feelings affect your actions? Describe that situation in your notebook.

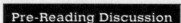

Pre-Reading Discussion

1 Have students complete each bulleted direction on page 52. Discuss the idea that English colonists were *strangers*. How do you learn to feel at home in a new place? What makes you feel welcome? What makes you feel like you belong? How do you think the English colonists learned to think of North America as home?

Have students list their ideas in their notebooks and share the list with a partner. Encourage them to add to the list as they read the chapter.

2 Explain to students that the English began colonizing the Americas during the late 1500s and early 1600s—at about the same time the Spanish, French, and Dutch were also founding colonies. Ask students to use what they know about these other groups of colonies to predict what the English colonies will be like. Encourage students to revise their predictions as they read the chapter.

The Southern Colonies

Thinking on Your Own

Read the Focus Your Reading questions. Then make two columns in your notebook. Label the first column "What England Wanted." As you read, fill in that column with what England wanted to get from the colonies. Label the second column "What the Colonies Produced." Fill it in with what products the colonies provided.

Why were there no English colonies in 1582, wondered Richard Hakluyt, an English geographer? Hakluyt believed that colonies would give England access to America's gold, slaves, fish, timber, furs, and sugar cane. Colonies would also provide a market for English goods. He urged the people of England to "advance the honor of our country" by "the possessing of those lands" not yet controlled by Spain.

---

focus your reading

Why did England want colonies in North America?

Why did the Roanoke Colony fail?

What did the English colonies export to England?

vocabulary

Spanish Armada

defeated

joint-stock company

indigo

The Roanoke Colony

Queen Elizabeth I followed Richard Hakluyt's advice. In 1584, she asked Sir Walter Raleigh to set up a colony in North America. Three years later, he sent 113 colonists to Roanoke Island. Roanoke Island is off the coast of present-day North Carolina. The ship that brought them went back to England for supplies. Before the ship could return, a war broke out.

The Roanoke Colony was a victim of bad timing. In 1588, the **Spanish Armada**, a fleet of 130 ships, attacked England. The queen outfitted every available ship for war. England **defeated** the armada, but it took Raleigh two years to find another supply ship. By the time the supply ship finally reached Roanoke in 1590, the settlers had vanished.

Lesson Summary

In 1587, Sir Walter Raleigh set up the first English colony in North America on Roanoke Island.

Nearly 20 years later, a joint-stock company founded Jamestown, Virginia. The colony floundered until settlers found a cash crop. People in Maryland, Carolina, and later Georgia found cash crops that allowed settlers to prosper.

Lesson Objective

Students will learn how England built its first successful colony in Virginia and how that success encouraged the founding of other colonies.

Focus Your Reading Answers

1 England wanted colonies in North America in order to have access to resources such as fish, timber, and furs, and to provide a market for English goods.

2 The Roanoke colony failed because a war with Spain made it impossible for a supply ship to reach the colony until the fighting ended.

3 English colonies exported tobacco, rice, and indigo to England.

Extension

Sir Walter Raleigh financed the colonists who came to Roanoke. When the colony failed, he lost a fortune. Joint-stock companies provided a way of financing a colony without risking a fortune. People who had a little money bought stock in the company. Then the companies hired colonists willing to work for the company for a certain number of years. Many joint-stock companies advertised for settlers.

Divide the class into small groups, and have each design an advertisement for people willing to start a colony in North America. Have each group share its ad with the class.

Lesson Vocabulary

Discuss the meaning of each vocabulary word. An *armada* is a fleet of ships. What, then, is a *Spanish Armada*? How did the *defeat* of the *Spanish Armada* affect the Roanoke colony?

A *joint-stock company* is a business owned by many people. Each person puts money into the company by buying stock—a part of the business. Stockowners share the costs of doing business. They also share the risks and the profits. What are the advantages of using a *joint-stock company* to found a colony?

Indigo is a dark blue dye obtained from a plant. It was used to dye the cloth used for military uniforms.

The word "Croatoah" was all that remained of the Roanoke colonists.

The drawing at the top of page 54 shows sailors searching for the whereabouts of the Roanoke settlers.

The portrait of Pocahontas at the bottom of page 54 was painted in

Picturing History

The drawing at the top of page 54 shows sailors searching for the whereabouts of the Roanoke settlers. They found only the word *Croatan* carved into a tree. The Croatan were a group of Native Americans who lived on a nearby island. Although the English searched the island, they found no sign of the colonists. To this day, no one knows what happened to them. Ask students what they think might have happened. What do their ideas suggest about the risks of being a colonist?

Success in Virginia

Nearly twenty years later, King James I gave the Virginia Company the right to establish a colony in North America. This **joint-stock company** expected to make a profit from the colony. The company was jointly owned by people who bought shares, or parts, of the company. They were known as shareholders.

In May 1607, the company sent three ships with 104 men and boys to Virginia. There they founded the settlement of Jamestown. The company forced the settlers to look for gold and silver instead of planting crops. That summer, almost half of the people died from malaria. The rest nearly starved.

The colony was saved by Captain John Smith. He asked the Powhatan People for food. They captured him and threatened to kill him. The chief's daughter, Pocahontas,

Pocahontas visited England.

Picturing History

The portrait of Pocahontas at the bottom of page 54 was painted in 1905 by Richard Norris Brooke. It is based on a painting made in England in 1616. At the time, Pocahontas was visiting London with her husband, John Rolfe, and their son, Thomas. Ask students why they think her visit sparked interest in Virginia and even led some people to move there. What can be learned by her style of dress?

Extension

Encourage students to find out more about Pocahontas's life and her visit to England, where she was reunited with Captain John Smith. Students can explore her death and burial in Gravesend, England. Ask them to share findings with the class by using Student Presentation Builder on the student DVD.

Tobacco was a major crop of the Southern Colonies.

persuaded her father to save Smith's life. The remaining colonists survived by trading with the Powhatan for food.

In the end, it was tobacco and not gold that made Virginia a profitable colony. A colonist named John Rolfe learned how to grow this plant. Tobacco became the colony's main export. John Rolfe later married Pocahontas.

> ## stop and think
>
> Imagine a newspaper headline announcing that an archaeologist has discovered a Roanoke colonist's diary. Discuss the living conditions in that English colony with a partner. Then write an entry that might have appeared in the colonist's diary.

Other Southern Colonies

Other English colonies were established in what is now the southern part of the United States. In 1634, Cecilius Calvert, an English Catholic, founded the Maryland Colony. The town of St. Mary's was its first settlement. This colony allowed settlers to have Catholic Church services, a practice that was outlawed in England.

Cecilius Calvert

55

James Oglethorpe landing in Georgia

Putting It All Together

The Venn diagrams will vary, but similarities should include

- the English founded both colonies

- both are located in what is now the southeastern part of the United States

- both depended on supplies from England

Differences may include

- Roanoke failed as a colony; its people disappeared

- Jamestown struggled to survive but eventually succeeded

- Jamestown had a strong leader in Captain John Smith

- settlers at Jamestown found a cash crop that allowed the colony to flourish

In 1670, more colonists settled in Carolina. They settled Charles Town—later Charleston. They traded with the native peoples for furs and grew rice and **indigo**. Indigo is a plant used for making dye.

The last Southern colony was Georgia. James Oglethorpe founded Georgia in 1733 to give poor people in England a new start in life. The colony also served to protect the colonies from Spanish settlements in Florida.

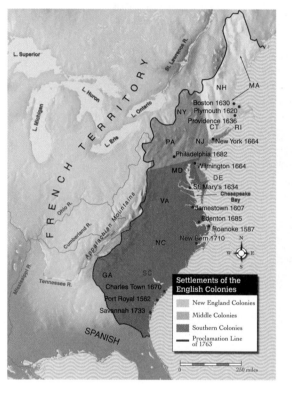

Settlements of the English Colonies

New England Colonies
Middle Colonies
Southern Colonies
Proclamation Line of 1763

0   250 miles

Putting It All Together

The Roanoke Colony vanished, but the Jamestown Colony survived. Create a Venn diagram with two overlapping circles. Label one circle "The Roanoke Colony" and the other "The Jamestown Colony." Discuss with a partner the similarities and differences between the two colonies. List the differences in the outer circles and list the similarities in the overlapping area.

Biography

John Smith (1580–1631)

In September 1607, the young colony at Jamestown was in trouble. Huddled inside a small fort, the settlers lived in constant fear of a Native American attack. No houses were built, no fields planted. Half the 104 settlers already had died of malaria. The survivors were giving up hope. Then John Smith took charge.

John Smith was at his best in difficult times. He had been shipwrecked at sea, robbed by Frenchmen, and captured by Turks. In 1602, Smith had joined a Christian army that tried to drive the Muslim Turks out of Europe. He killed three men in hand-to-hand combat, or so he claimed. When the Turks defeated the Christians, they captured Smith and sold him into slavery. He escaped by killing his Muslim overseer and fleeing to Christian Russia. From there he made his way back to England.

To rescue the colony, Smith made contact with the Powhatan. He began by trading hatchets and beads for food, which the colonists desperately needed. Then the Powhatan turned against the colonists, perhaps because they, too, were running out of food. They captured Smith and took him to the Powhatan chief. As the chief prepared to kill him, Smith was saved by Pocahontas, the chief's daughter. She went to Jamestown to live and later married a colonist, John Rolfe. Her friendship probably saved Jamestown.

In 1609, John Smith returned to England, but not for long. In March 1614, he again set sail for America, this time as an explorer. That summer, he explored the coastline north of Virginia and traded furs with the locals. He returned to England with the best map yet of that region, which he named New England.

John Smith spent the rest of his life promoting the settlement of New England. He hoped to found his own colony there, but he failed to get financial support. To advertise the region, he published his map as well as a book entitled *Description of New England*. He also published *General History of Virginia* and *True Travels*, an account of his early travels. He died in 1631, still yearning to return to New England.

57

Bio Facts

- Smith was born in England in 1580.

- He left home in 1596 at the age of 16 after his father died. He joined an army that fought for Dutch independence from Spain. He later worked on a merchant ship in the Mediterranean Sea. He also joined other European soldiers in a war against the Turks.

- In 1602, he was captured and sold as a slave to a Turk who sent him to Istanbul, the capital of the Ottoman Empire.

- Smith escaped Istanbul and returned to England in 1604.

- Smith invested in the joint-stock company that owned Virginia in 1606.

- In 1607, Smith sailed to Virginia as one of the members of the colony's governing council. While exploring, Smith fell into the hands of the Powhatan but was saved by Pocahontas.

- In 1608, Smith returned to Jamestown and became president of the Jamestown Council. He set a new policy for the colony: "He who does not work, will not eat."

- In 1609, Smith was injured in an explosion and returned to England. In London, he actively encouraged settlement in Virginia.

- In 1614, Smith visited Maine and the Massachusetts Bay. He named the region *New England*.

- In 1630, Smith wrote a book about his experiences in Virginia.

- Smith died in 1631 at the age of 51.

Reading for Understanding

1 When Richard speaks of being "in a most heavy case," he probably means that he is hungry and scared.

2 Richard's master allows him peas, a mixture of flour and water, a mouthful of bread, and beef.

3 The colonists probably did not get along well with the Native Americans, because Richard speaks of being afraid of them. He also says that he and others have fought with Native Americans and tried to enslave them.

Picturing History

This hand-colored woodcut depicts a Native American being sent into slavery by Virginia colonists in the 1600s.

Read a Primary Source

A Letter from Jamestown

In 1623, Richard Frethorne was a servant on a plantation near Jamestown. He described conditions there in this letter to his parents.

reading for understanding

What does Richard probably mean by being "in a most heavy case"?

What food does Richard's master allow him?

How well did the colonists get along with the Native Americans?

"Loving and kind father and mother . . . This is to let you understand that I, your child, am in a most heavy case, by reason of the nature of the country. . . . For since I came out of the ship, I never ate anything but peas, and loblollie (that is water gruel) [flour mixed with water]. As for deer or venison, I never saw any since I came into this land; there is indeed some fowl, but we are not allowed to go and get it, but must work hard both early and late for a mess of water gruel, and a mouthful of bread, and beef. . . . We live in fear of the enemy [Indians] every hour, yet we have had a combat with them . . . and took two alive and make slaves of them."

Richard Frethorne, "Letter to His Father and Mother, March 20, April 2 and 3, 1623," in Susan M. Kingsbury, ed., *The Records of the Virginia Company of London* (Vol. IV, Washington, D. C. Government Printing Office, 1935).

Picturing History

The Pilgrims sailed to North America on the *Mayflower*. The voyage took 66 days. Historians believe the ship was about 90–110 feet in length and about 25 feet wide.

To help students visualize the size of the ship, have them visit a baseball diamond. The distance from home plate to first base is 90 feet—the approximate length of the ship. The width of the ship was about 25 feet (less than half the distance from the pitcher's mound to home plate).

Ask students what it must have been like for over 120 people (102 passengers and about 20 crew members) to spend over two months in such cramped quarters.

New England Colonies

Thinking on Your Own

Make a list of the vocabulary words. With a partner, guess what each word means and write your definition next to the word. Check the Glossary to see how close you came. As you read each word in the lesson, write a sentence that summarizes what the word tells you about the founding of the New England colonies.

In 1534, King Henry VIII broke away from the Roman Catholic Church. He set up a Protestant church called the Church of England. Some English Protestants thought the English Church was still too Catholic. The **Puritans** wanted to purify it by simplifying its ceremonies and teachings. **Separatists** wanted to separate from it altogether. Both groups looked to North America to achieve their goals.

focus your reading

What was the Mayflower Compact?

Why did colonists settle in Massachusetts?

Why were other colonies founded in New England?

vocabulary

Puritans

Separatists

Pilgrims

Puritan commonwealth

The Plymouth Colony

In 1620, William Bradford and a group of Separatists sailed on the *Mayflower* from England. They wanted to get as far away as possible from the Church of England. While on the ship, the **Pilgrims** signed the Mayflower Compact. Pilgrims are people who take a journey for a religious purpose. The Mayflower Compact is a written agreement that set out the rules by which the Pilgrims would govern themselves.

Replica of the *Mayflower*

Lesson Vocabulary

Discuss the meaning of each vocabulary word. Begin by explaining that a *Puritan* was a person who wanted to *purify,* or cleanse, the English church. Tell students that in this context, the word *purify* means to reform or change.

A *separatist* was someone who wanted to separate or break away from the Church of England. Ask students what the difference is between a Puritan and a separatist. (The former wants to make the church better, and the latter plans to start a new church.)

A *pilgrim* is a person who makes a journey for religious reasons. To what extent were both the *Puritans* and the *separatists* pilgrims?

A *Puritan commonwealth* was a community in which the government was based on the Puritans' religious beliefs.

Lesson Summary

English Protestants founded the New England Colonies. In 1620, a group of Separatists arrived in what is now Massachusetts. They signed the Mayflower Compact.

In 1630, Puritans founded seven towns in Massachusetts, including Boston. The Massachusetts Bay Colony was a Puritan commonwealth. Roger Williams founded Providence in 1636, the first settlement in Rhode Island.

People from Massachusetts who needed more farmland founded other New England colonies. In 1662, those who settled in the Connecticut River Valley joined together to form the colony of Connecticut. In 1638, other Puritans settled in New Hampshire, which became a separate colony in 1680.

Lesson Objective

Students will learn how religious groups from England established colonies along the northeast coast of what is now the United States.

Focus Your Reading Answers

1 The Mayflower Compact was a written agreement that established rules for the new colony.

2 Colonists settled in Massachusetts to get as far away as possible from the Church of England. They wanted to practice their own religious beliefs.

3 Other colonies were founded in New England because settlers disagreed with the Puritan church or needed farmland.

Pilgrims landing at Plymouth Rock

The Separatists founded the town of Plymouth along the coast of Massachusetts. The first winter was difficult. The colonists ran out of food. The next spring, a Pawtucket named Squanto showed them how to plant corn and where to fish. Despite its early hardships, the Plymouth settlement survived.

The Massachusetts Bay Colony

In 1630, English Puritans sailed into Massachusetts Bay with seventeen ships and more than 1,000 people. They founded seven towns. The largest was the seaport of Boston. They had decided that the best way to purify the Church of England was to set up a church in New England to serve as a model. "We shall be as a city upon a hill," said John Winthrop, the colony's leader. "The eyes of the people are upon us."

The signing of the Mayflower Compact

John Winthrop and Puritans arrive in Massachusetts.

The Massachusetts Bay Colony grew rapidly, attracting thousands of English Puritans. It was a **Puritan commonwealth**, a community in which the government enforced the Puritans' religious beliefs. Only church members could vote. The Puritan leaders expelled, or sent away, anyone who disagreed with them.

stop and think

The Pilgrims made a compact with each other promising to live according to certain rules. Discuss with a partner a compact that you have made to follow rules.

Roger Williams

Rhode Island, Connecticut, and New Hampshire

Among those expelled by the Puritans was Roger Williams. Williams was a Separatist minister. He insisted that church and state should be separate. In 1636, he founded Providence, the first settlement in the colony of Rhode Island. It allowed freedom of religion. The Puritans also expelled Anne Hutchinson for her religious views. She, too, settled in Rhode Island.

Picturing History

John Winthrop was the first governor of Massachusetts. The Puritans named him as their leader before they left England in what became known as the "Great Migration." In 1630, more than 1,000 people sailed to Massachusetts on 11 ships. At the time, it was the largest single group ever to leave Europe for the Americas.

Stop and Think

Discussions will vary, but students should demonstrate their understanding of a *compact*.

Picturing History

The drawing shows Roger Williams with the Narragansett people. Unlike other colonial leaders, Williams paid Native Americans for their lands. Why do you think an artist considered that event important enough to draw a picture of it?

Picturing History

Anne Hutchinson is shown at her trial in the drawing at the top of page 62. The General Court of Massachusetts put her on trial for speaking out against Puritan beliefs.

The Court banished Hutchinson from the colony in 1637. Because the order was given in November and she was pregnant, the Court allowed her to stay in Massachusetts until the winter was over. In the spring of 1638, she, her husband, their 11 children, and 73 of their friends made their way to Rhode Island. There, Hutchinson helped found the town of Portsmouth. How was her journey similar to that of Roger Williams? What do their experiences suggest about what it was like to live in a Puritan commonwealth?

Putting It All Together

Letters will vary. Students should point out several complaints or issues that colonists faced, including religious freedom. Students may want to conduct additional research on the Internet or in the library to learn more about life in colonial Massachusetts.

Anne Hutchinson was expelled from Massachusetts Bay Colony.

Puritans who needed more farmland founded other New England colonies. In 1635, people from the Massachusetts Bay Colony began to settle in the Connecticut River valley. The settlements joined together to become the colony of Connecticut in 1662. Farmers who moved north from Massachusetts settled in New Hampshire in 1638. It became a separate colony in 1680.

Minister Hooker established Hartford on the Connecticut River in 1636.

Putting It All Together

Imagine that you are a dissatisfied Massachusetts Bay colonist. Write a letter to John Winthrop telling him why you are unhappy with life in Massachusetts Bay Colony. Explain alternatives to staying in the colony.

Picturing History

Most people who left Massachusetts to start a new community did not leave as individuals, or even as a family. Most left the colony with other members of their congregation. They were often led by their ministers. Thomas Hooker brought 100 followers from his congregation in what is now Newton, Massachusetts, to the Connecticut River Valley. In 1636, the group founded Hartford, Connecticut. How do you think settling in relatively large groups helped the newcomers survive?

3 The Middle Colonies

Thinking on Your Own

Think back to a time when you were not free to express yourself. As you read, write specific ways in which colonists in New York, New Jersey, and Pennsylvania were more free than people in the Massachusetts Bay Colony.

I n 1624, the Netherlands claimed what is now New York, New Jersey, and Pennsylvania. In 1638, they added the present-day state of Delaware by expelling the Swedish settlers who lived there. Many of the 8,000 people who lived in New Netherland were unhappy with Dutch rule. The government was unable to protect them from repeated Native American attacks. Besides that, Governor Peter Stuyvesant was a harsh governor.

focus your reading

How did New Netherland become New York?

Why were New York and New Jersey successful colonies?

Why did William Penn want a colony in North America?

vocabulary

proprietor   Quakers

New York and New Jersey

On August 29, 1664, a fleet of English ships sailed into the harbor at New Amsterdam. Its commander, Colonel Richard Nichols, demanded that the Dutch surrender. Governor Stuyvesant handed over the city without a fight. He had little choice, as many of the settlers were glad to see the British arrive.

The English take control of New Netherland.

63

Picturing History

In 1664, the King of England gave all of the land between the Connecticut and Delaware Rivers to his brother James, the Duke of York.

The duke could not ignore the fact that the Dutch had a prior claim to the rest of his territory. So he sent a fleet to take New Netherland. What does the picture suggest about the takeover? Ask students to imagine how people in the crowd may have felt as they watched the English enter their city.

Lesson Vocabulary

Explain that a *proprietor* is the owner of a business. In colonial times, a *proprietor* was also a person or group of people who had the right to rule a colony. The king or queen of England gave them that right. In a way, the *proprietor* or *proprietors* of a colony owned the colony.

Quakers are members of a religious group called the Society of Friends.

They are known as Quakers because they "quake," or tremble, before God. The Quakers think all people are equal. So they refuse to honor one person over another. They also refuse to go to war, even to defend themselves or their country. They believe no person has the right to take another's life. How did being the *proprietor* of Pennsylvania allow William Penn to help his fellow *Quakers*?

Lesson Summary

In 1664, England took over the Dutch colony of New Netherland and changed its name to New York. The colony's new proprietor sold part of the area to people who founded the colony of New Jersey. King Charles II gave another part of New Netherland to William Penn, a Quaker. He established a colony where Quakers were free to practice their religion.

Lesson Objective

Students will learn how the Middle Colonies were founded.

Focus Your Reading Answers

1 New Netherland became New York after a fleet of English sailed into the harbor of New Amsterdam. The commander demanded that the city surrender, and the governor handed it over without a fight.

2 New York and New Jersey were successful colonies because they were well-governed, offered religious freedom to almost everyone, and had rich soil that attracted settlers.

3 Penn wanted a colony so that his fellow Quakers would have a place where they could practice their religion.

Stop and Think

The scenes will vary, but should reflect the fact that most people in New Netherland were dissatisfied with Dutch rule. The government was unable to protect them from attacks by Native Americans.

As the new governor, Nichols changed the name of New Netherland to New York, in honor of the duke of York. The duke, King Charles II's brother, was the new **proprietor**, or owner, of the colony. The colony's main city of New Amsterdam became New York City.

The duke sold part of the area south of New York to two friends, Lord John Berkeley and Sir George Carteret. They became the proprietors of East and West Jersey, which later became the colony of New Jersey.

The colonies of New York and New Jersey did well and grew under English control. Both colonies were well governed. To avoid religious fights, the colonial governors granted freedom of religion to everyone. The rich soil of the region attracted settlers. New York City served as the seaport for both colonies.

Pennsylvania and Delaware

King Charles II gave William Penn part of what had been New Netherland. Penn was the son of an English admiral to whom the king owed money. He also was a member of a religious sect called the Society of Friends. The **Quakers**, as

stop and think

Imagine when Colonel Richard Nichols was sailing into New Amsterdam's harbor. From what you have read, how do you think the people reacted to Nichols? Why did they react that way? Describe the scene in your notebook. Include dialogue between the residents.

William Penn paying Native Americans for the land used to found Pennsylvania

Picturing History

The painting shows William Penn buying the land from Native Americans that he used to found his colony. Penn was a Quaker. How might his religious beliefs have influenced his decision to buy land from the Native Americans that the king had already given to him at no cost? Compare his relationship with the Native Americans to that of Roger Williams of Rhode Island.

they were called, refused to swear loyalty to the government or serve in the army. Thousands of Quakers had been thrown in jail because of their beliefs. Penn wanted to set up a colony where Quakers could practice their religion freely. By giving Penn land, the king paid off his debt and found a way to move the Quakers out of England. Later, he also gave Penn the area taken from the Dutch that became the colony of Delaware.

In 1681, William Penn founded the colony of Pennsylvania. The king named it in honor of Penn's father. The colony was a great success from the beginning. Penn avoided problems with the Native Americans by paying them for their land. He offered settlers farmland at prices they could afford. Since the colony tolerated all Christian beliefs, settlers began to arrive from throughout Europe. Philadelphia, established in 1682, became a prosperous seaport city.

The early settlement of Philadelphia

Putting It All Together

The Middle Colonies prospered and grew quickly. Make a two-column chart with "Problems" and "Solutions" as the headings. List the problems these colonies faced and the solutions the colonists used to address them.

Putting It All Together

The charts will vary, but the list of problems might include relations with Native Americans, religious quarrels, and the need to attract settlers. Penn addressed the potential for a problem with the Native Americans by purchasing land from them. The proprietors of Pennsylvania, New York, and New Jersey all provided religious freedom to avoid fights. They also used their colony's rich land to attract settlers.

Picturing History

This picture shows early settlers in Pennsylvania. William Penn secured the area for Quakers who quickly adapted to the new ways of life in the colony.

Chapter Review

1 Logos will vary, but should represent the students' understanding of the material, particularly the various reasons for settling each colony.

2 Lists will vary. Extend the activity by creating a class concept web on the board. Discuss how reasons for the settlement of various colonies were similar and different.

3 Answers will vary, but should reflect differences in why each group of colonies was founded, how settlers made their living, and their relations with Native Americans.

Chapter Summary

In 1587, Sir Walter Raleigh sent colonists to Roanoke Island. Although England **defeated** the **Spanish Armada**, a lack of supplies doomed the Roanoke Colony. Virginia was England's first successful colony. A **joint-stock company** expected to make a profit from the colony. Maryland, Carolina, and Georgia were other English colonies. The Southern Colonies prospered by exporting tobacco, rice, and **indigo**.

The New England Colonies were founded by **Separatists** and **Puritans**. In 1620, Separatists, also known as the **Pilgrims**, began the Plymouth Colony. The Puritans in 1630 founded the Massachusetts Bay Colony. That colony was a **Puritan commonwealth**, a community in which the settlers used the government to enforce their religious beliefs. They expelled people who disagreed with them.

In August 1664, England took over the Dutch colony of New Netherland. The English governor changed the name to New York. The colony's new **proprietor** sold part of the area to people who founded the colony of New Jersey. King Charles gave another part of New Netherland to William Penn, a **Quaker** who wanted to establish a colony where Quakers were free to practice their religion.

Chapter Review

1 Design a logo that represents the struggles and accomplishments of the English colonists. Review the vocabulary in this chapter for ideas.

2 Choose an event, person, or place that you found most interesting. Write a bulleted list of facts about your choice.

3 Create a three-column chart with the labels "Southern Colonies," "New England Colonies," and "Middle Colonies." Fill the columns with words or phrases that best describe each. Use the information to write a short paragraph about the English colonies.

Novel Connections

Below is a list of books that relate to the time period covered in this chapter. The numbers in parentheses indicate the related Thematic Strands of the National Council for the Social Studies (NCSS).

Joseph Bruchac. *Squanto's Journey: The Story of the First Thanksgiving.* Silver Whistle, 2000. (I, II, IV)

Kieran Doherty. *William Bradford: Rock of Plymouth.* Twenty-First Century/Millbrook, 1999. (II, V, IX)

Joyce Hansen and Gary McGowan. *Breaking Ground, Breaking Silence: The Story of New York's African Burial Ground.* Holt, 1997. (II, III, V)

James Haskins and Kathleen Benson. *Building a New Land: African Americans in Colonial America.* Amistad/Harper Collins Children's Books, 2001. (I, II, III)

Joy Masoff. *Colonial Times, 1600–1700.* Scholastic Reference, 2000. (I, II, III)

Marie Sewall. *James Towne: Struggle for Survival.* Atheneum Books, 2001. (III, V)

Kate Waters. *Giving Thanks: The 1621 Harvest.* Scholastic Press, 2001. (I, III, V)

Skill Builder

Reading a Table

Tables present different kinds of information in a small space. The information most often is presented in columns and rows.

The table below presents information about the English colonies in North America. It includes the names of the colonies organized by region (New England, Middle, Southern), when they were founded, and why they were founded.

Use the table to answer these questions:

1 In which region was the first colony founded?

2 In which region were the colonies most often founded for religious reasons?

3 What was the most common reason for English settlement?

4 Which region did England take the longest period of time to settle?

The Founding of the English Colonies

	Colonies	Date Founded or Claimed by England	Reason for Founding

New England	Massachusetts
	   Plymouth
	   Massachusetts Bay
	Connecticut
	Rhode Island
	New Hampshire
		
		1620
		1630
		1635
		1636
		1638
			
			Religious freedom, farming, trade
			Puritan commonwealth, farming, trade
			Farming, trade
			Religious freedom, farming, trade
			Farming, trade

Middle	New York New Jersey Pennsylvania Delaware	1664 (Dutch 1624) 1664 (Dutch 1629) 1681 1701 (Dutch 1638)	Trade, farming Farming, trade Farming, trade Farming, trade
Southern	Virginia Maryland Carolina° Georgia	1607 1634 1670 1733	Search for gold, farming Religious freedom, farming, trade Trade, farming Refuge for poor, farming, buffer from Spanish Florida

°Divided into North Carolina and South Carolina by King George II in 1729

Classroom Discussion

Discuss with students some of the broader topics covered in this chapter.

- Compare and contrast Southern, Middle, and New England Colonies. In what ways were they similar? How do you account for differences among them?

- How were the people who settled in English colonies different from those who settled in Spanish colonies? How did those differences shape the kinds of colonies the English built?

- What role did religion play in the English colonies? Why did religion divide some colonies and unite others?

- Suppose you lived in the 1600s. Which colony would you have liked to live in? For what reason?

Skill Builder

1 Virginia, the first successful English colony, was founded in the Southern region in 1607.

2 The New England colonies were most often founded for religious reasons.

3 The most common reasons for English settlement were farming and trade.

4 England took the longest period of time to settle the Southern region—from 1607–1733.

Extension

Ask students to use the table to practice their skills.

- In which region did England take the shortest period of time to settle? (New England)

- In which region did England take over land owned by another European nation? (Many of the Middle Colonies were claimed by the Dutch.)

- What do Connecticut and Carolina have in common? (Both were settled for farming and trade.)

- How did the reasons for settling Georgia differ from those of the other colonies? (Georgia was settled as a refuge for the poor and as a buffer from Spanish Florida).

Unit Objectives

After studying this unit, students will be able to

- explain why the English colonies grew rapidly in the early 1700s

- compare and contrast life in the South with life in the New England and the Middle Colonies

- discuss how English colonists developed unique cultures, distinct from European ways of life

Unit 3 focuses on English colonial life in North America.

Chapter 5, Life in the Southern Colonies, describes the distinctive culture created by people of European, Native American, and African descent.

Chapter 6, Life in the New England and Middle Colonies, examines life in the two regions in the late 1600s and early 1700s.

UNIT 3

COLONIAL SOCIETIES

By 1700, the English settlements in North America were solidly established. They had survived their first struggling years. Most of the 250,000 English colonists lived in villages and farms close to the Atlantic coast. They had stronger ties to England than to their neighbors north or south.

The English colonies expanded rapidly during the next fifty years. By 1750, the population had increased to nearly two million. Three distinct societies emerged. The people of New England, the Middle Colonies, and the South had very different ways of life. They also had less in common with their cousins overseas.

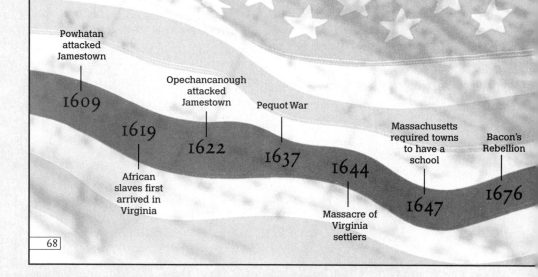

Powhatan attacked Jamestown
1609

1619
African slaves first arrived in Virginia

Opechancanough attacked Jamestown
1622

Pequot War
1637

1644
Massacre of Virginia settlers

Massachusetts required towns to have a school
1647

Bacon's Rebellion
1676

68

Getting Started

Write the word *culture* on the board and remind students that it was defined in Chapter 1 as "a way of life." By 1700, English people had lived in North America for nearly 100 years. Over the years, they and their neighbors developed distinctive ways of life.

Ask a student to read aloud the introduction on page 68, and then have students study the pictures in Chapters 5 and 6. What do the pictures suggest about similarities and differences in the ways of life that developed in each group of colonies?

Measuring Time

Explain to students that the timeline covers both chapters in this unit. Chapters 5 and 6 include events that took place between 1609 and 1740.

Why did the
South use
slave labor?

Why were the Middle Colonies
called the breadbasket?

How did religion
shape life in New
England?

King Philip's War

1675–1677   1681

Pennsylvania
Colony
founded

1692

Salem
witch trials

Tuscarora
defeated in
North
Carolina

1712

1715

Yamasee
Border War

Great
Awakening
began

1740

69

Collage Answers

Ask students to copy the three questions on page 69 into their notebooks. As they read the unit, have them record their answers to each question.

1 English colonists in the South used enslaved workers because their crops were labor intensive, and they could not find enough free workers.

2 The Middle Colonies were known as the breadbasket because wheat was the main cash crop.

3 Religion shaped who could live in some New England colonies and what rights individuals had.

Timeline Extension

To preview Unit 3, ask students to use the timeline to answer these questions:

- What does the timeline suggest about relations between colonists and Native Americans? (The timeline includes references to several wars with Native American groups.)

- When did Africans arrive in Virginia? (1619)

- What signs of cultural and religious change do you notice on the timeline? (Likely answers include a Massachusetts law requiring towns to have schools, Salem's witch trials, and the Great Awakening.)

Collage Extension

Ask students to examine the images on page 69.

- What do the images suggest about the resources important to each group of colonies?

- What other factors may have shaped the cultures that developed in each region?

Chapter Summary
Refer to page 84 for a summary of Chapter 5.

Related Transparencies

T-7 The 13 Original Colonies

T-18 T-Chart Graphic Organizer

T-20 Venn Diagram

Key Blacklines

Biography
Pocahontas

Primary Source
An Indentured Servant

Picturing History

The picture on page 70 shows a large tobacco field located on a Southern plantation.

Pre-Reading Discussion

1 Ask students to read aloud the chapter title and locate the five Southern Colonies on the map on page 73.

2 After students complete each bulleted direction on page 70, review the first lesson in Chapter 5 by discussing what the Southern Colonies were like in the early 1600s. Ask students to predict how those colonies might have changed over the years. Focus on kinds of settlements, work, and relations with Native Americans. As students begin to read and discuss the chapter, encourage them to revise or correct their predictions.

Getting Focused

Skim this chapter to predict what you will be learning.

- Read the lesson titles and subheadings.
- Look at the illustrations and read the captions.
- Examine the maps.
- Review the vocabulary words and terms.

In your notebook write a statement predicting what you will learn about life in the Southern colonies. Explain why you think so to a partner. Then copy the vocabulary words into your notebook. As you read each vocabulary word in the lesson, write a sentence using the word.

Picturing History

Like many plantations, the one shown on page 71 is located on a river. Ask students why most planters built their plantations along rivers. What does the photograph suggest about the life of a planter?

Extensions

1 Ask students to find out how cash crops like tobacco and rice a grown today. Where in the United States are these crops grown How are the methods similar to those popular in the 1600s? How do they differ? Encourage students to present their findings to the class by using the Student Presentation Builder on the student DVD.

2 Explain that indigo is still an important dye. Americans use today to dye denim for blue jeans. However, nearly all of the indigo used today is synthetic. Have students find out more about the dye and its importance in the 1600s and 1700s. Ask them to share their findings by creating a poster on the histor of indigo.

Settling the South

Thinking on Your Own

Read the Focus Your Reading questions. As you read, write answers in your notebook.

By 1630, the future of the Virginia Colony looked bright. It had survived the early years when three out of four colonists died of disease, starvation, or Native American attacks. The colony had a **cash crop** that provided a steady income. John Rolfe learned how to grow and cure a mild variety of West Indian tobacco. It sold very well in London. A single crop, it was said, could pay for a Virginia plantation.

focus your reading

Why did tobacco growers want large plantations?

Where were small farms located?

Why did few people live in cities?

vocabulary

cash crop   frontier

plantations   homespun

Southern Plantations

Englishmen with money to invest went to Virginia or Maryland in large numbers. Later, many people went to North Carolina and Georgia. They laid out **plantations**, or large farms, along the rivers. Tobacco planters needed more land than they could use in any year, because the plants robbed the soil of its nutrients. New fields had to be cleared every two or three years. Planters settled along the river

Many plantations were located along rivers.

71

Lesson Summary

By 1630, the South had cash crops that provided a steady income. The profitability of tobacco and later rice and indigo encouraged wealthy settlers to build plantations along the many rivers in the region.

Most settlers, however, owned just a few acres of land. These people raised, grew, or made most of what they needed. Very few people settled in towns or cities.

Lesson Objective

Students will learn about life in the Southern Colonies in the late 1600s and early 1700s.

Lesson Vocabulary

Discuss the meaning of each vocabulary word. Begin by focusing on the connection between *cash crops* and *plantations*. A *cash crop* is a crop that is grown to sell for money rather than for a farmer's use. Explain that a *plantation* is a large farm on which *cash crops* are grown.

A *frontier* is a borderland. It marks the place where settlements end and the wilderness begins. Many English families farmed on the frontier. They grew or made most of the things they needed, including cloth. *Homespun* is the name given to homemade cloth. People used spinning wheels to turn raw wool or cotton into yarn, and then they wove the yarn into cloth.

Focus Your Reading Answers

1 Tobacco growers wanted large plantations because the more they grew, the more money they made. They also knew that tobacco plants rob the soil of nutrients, so new fields had to be cleared every two or three years.

2 Small farms were located inland from the rivers or on the frontier where land was cheap.

3 Few people lived in cities because most people farmed for a living, and large plantations served many of the purposes of towns.

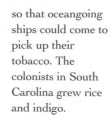

Picturing History

Have students study the drawing on page 72. How is the plantation similar to a village? What differences do you notice?

Picturing History

The photograph at the bottom of page 72 shows a re-creation of a log cabin on a tenant farm. Ask students how it differs from the home of the planter shown in the drawing at the top of the page.

DVD Extension

Encourage students to use the reading comprehension, vocabulary reinforcement, and interactive timeline activities on the student DVD.

so that oceangoing ships could come to pick up their tobacco. The colonists in South Carolina grew rice and indigo.

In the Southern Colonies, the planters were the upper class. They built large frame or brick houses with columns in front. The planters could afford to import fine furniture and beautiful clothes from England.

Plantations consisted of many buildings and fields for planting.

Colonial Farms

The majority of settlers in the Southern Colonies owned small farms. Arriving with little or no money, they worked as servants or rented land. In time, many of them bought a few acres inland from the rivers. Some settled on the **frontier**—the western edge of settlement. Land was cheap on the frontier.

Tenant farms included small houses and plots of land for growing crops.

72

Extension

Swedish colonists, who settled in Delaware in 1638, brought with them the idea of building houses entirely out of logs. The idea quickly caught on.

Most log cabins consisted of a single room about 15 by 20 feet in size. Many also had a loft reached by a ladder. The children often slept in the loft and their parents in the large room below.

Ask students to research the log cabin and other colonial houses and then share their findings with the class. They can build three-dimensional models using cardboard or poster board.

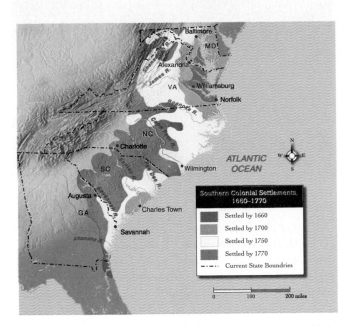

They raised, grew, or made most of what they needed. A small patch of tobacco provided cash to buy what they could not make for themselves.

Small farmers made up the middle class in the Southern Colonies. They lived in frame houses of three or four rooms. Frontier farmers often lived in log cabins. Most farmers wore clothes made of **homespun**, or homemade, cloth. They could not afford luxuries.

Towns and Cities

Few people settled in towns or cities, as hardly any towns existed. In the Southern Colonies, plantations served many of the purposes of towns. The planters acted as merchants. They shipped their tobacco, as well as crops grown by their poorer neighbors, from their wharves. They ordered manufactured goods directly from England. The planters did not need townspeople

> **stop and think**
>
> In your notebook, write three facts about where and how people lived in the Southern Colonies.

Ask students to use the map on page 73 to answer the following questions:

- What does dark blue mean on this map? (shows the parts of the Southern Colonies that were settled by 1660)

- What does pink show? (areas settled by 1770)

- Which colony was largely settled by 1700? (Maryland)

- Which colony was largely settled by 1750? (Virginia)

Stop and Think

Answers will vary, but students are likely to mention the following:

- The planters lived along the rivers near the coast.

- Most settlers who owned small farms lived inland from the rivers or on the frontier.

- Few settlers lived in cities or towns.

- Almost everyone in the Southern Colonies farmed for a living.

- Planters grew mainly cash crops.

- Small farmers raised, grew, or made most of the things they needed.

Extension

Ask students to find out more about such Southern cities as Williamsburg, Annapolis, Charles Town, or Savannah and share their findings with the class. Who lived in these cities? What kinds of jobs did city dwellers have? In what ways were the cities important to planters? How were cities important to farmers on the frontier?

Slave labor was used for growing, drying, and packing tobacco.

Picturing History

The slaves in the drawing at the top of page 74 are shown packing dried tobacco leaves into barrels called hogsheads for the long ocean voyage to England. How did the artist choose to portray the slaves? How do they compare to the slaves in the illustration at the bottom of page 74?

such as carpenters, wagon-makers, and blacksmiths. They had skilled slaves to do that work.

Most of the towns and small cities that did exist were centers of colonial government. These included Annapolis, the capital of the Maryland Colony. In 1699, Williamsburg replaced the little village of Jamestown as Virginia's capital. Savannah was both the capital and main port city of Georgia. The largest city was Charles Town, South Carolina, which had a population of 7,000 people by 1750.

Many of the wealthier rice and indigo planters kept homes in seacoast cities. These homes were used to escape the heat and humidity of the interior. While in the city, wealthy planters socialized and established themselves as community leaders.

Putting It All Together

The tables should show the following:

- *Plantation Owners*: grew cash crops; owned slaves; lived in large brick or frame houses; imported furniture and clothes from England

- *Small Farmers*: raised or grew most of what their families needed; did their own farm work; lived in log cabins or frame houses; made their own furniture and clothes

Large port cities provided access to ships.

Putting It All Together

Discuss your Focus Your Reading answers with a partner. Then work together to create a table labeled "Plantation Owners" and "Small Farmers." Compare their ways of life.

74 Chapter 5

Picturing History

Cities such as Charles Town served as ports for shipping goods to England. What can be learned from this image about businessmen and slaves?

Biography

Eliza Lucas Pinckney (1722–1793)

Early in 1740, Colonel George Lucas wrote a letter to his eighteen-year-old daughter, Eliza. Lucas was on duty with the British army in the Caribbean. Eliza was at home in South Carolina. Colonel Lucas suggested that it was time for Eliza to think about marriage. He proposed two men as suitable husbands, one an elderly gentleman with money. "I beg leave to say to you," she quickly replied, "that the riches of Peru and Chile, if he had them put together, could not purchase a sufficient esteem for him to make him my husband." Her father said nothing more on that subject.

Eliza Lucas was a determined young woman. In 1738, she moved from England with her family to South Carolina, where her father had bought three plantations. In his absence, and with her mother in ill health, she managed one plantation by herself. She supervised the overseers at the other two. She also read for two hours each day, practiced music two hours, did needlework for an hour, and helped her younger sister learn to read and write.

Eliza Lucas also experimented with indigo, a plant used to make blue dye. Her father sent her indigo seeds, convinced that this Caribbean plant could be a moneymaker for South Carolina. Frost killed the first crop. The plants came up the next year, but the dye maker ruined the dye. The next crop was a complete failure. Finally, in 1744, Eliza Lucas's patience paid off. She grew the colony's first successful crop of indigo. Three years later, South Carolina exported 135,000 pounds of the blue dye. Production increased thereafter.

In 1744, Eliza married Charles Pinckney, a husband of her own choosing. They had four children. The eldest, Charles Cotesworth Pinckney, was a general in the Revolutionary War. Their youngest son, Thomas, became governor of South Carolina. Eliza Lucas Pinckney died of cancer in 1793 at age seventy. President George Washington asked to be a pallbearer at her funeral.

Bio Facts

- Eliza Lucas was born in 1722 in Antigua, an island in the West Indies, to George and Anne Lucas. Her father was the lieutenant governor of Antigua, then a British colony.

- Educated at a school in England, she took classes in botany—the study of plant life.

- In 1738, the Lucas family moved to a South Carolina plantation on Wappoo Creek—one of three plantations the family owned.

- When her father returned to duty in the British Army, Eliza managed the plantations. She was just sixteen years old. In her father's absence, she taught her younger sister and several enslaved children how to read and write, studied music and art, and learned enough law to draft legal wills for neighbors.

- After three years of experiments with ginger, cotton, indigo, and alfalfa plants, Eliza succeeded in marketing North America's first indigo crop. Indigo was in demand because it was used to dye the cloth for military uniforms.

- On her husband's plantation, she cultivated the silkworms used to make silk cloth.

- When her husband died in 1758, Eliza took over the management of the family plantation.

- She died in 1793 in Philadelphia, Pennsylvania.

75

Biography Extension

The first English women arrived in Virginia in 1619, 12 years after the colony was founded. Of the 144 women who came that year, just 35 were still alive six years later. Yet what amazed many men in the Southern Colonies was not the number of early deaths, but the number of women who thrived in the colonies.

Encourage students to find out more about the lives of women in the Southern Colonies. Some may want to research Margaret Brent of Maryland, the first woman lawyer in North America. Like Eliza Pinckney, she also ran her own plantation.

Have students use the Student Presentation Builder on the DVD to share their findings with the class.

Lesson Summary

Tobacco, rice, and indigo require lots of work, and the colonies had very few workers. Some planters tried to solve the problem with indentured servants or redemptioners. By 1700, however, most planters were relying on enslaved Africans for most jobs. At first, they were treated much like European workers, but as their numbers increased, they were formally enslaved.

Lesson Objective

Students will learn how the planters in the Southern Colonies found the workers they needed for their farms and plantations.

Focus Your Reading Answers

1 The Southern Colonies were always in need of workers because tobacco, rice, and indigo are crops that require constant care.

2 Indentured servants signed a labor contract before leaving England, promising to work without pay for four to seven years in return for the cost of their voyage to North America. At the end of that time, servants often received a few acres of farmland.

3 Planters replaced European workers with African slaves because many white servants ran away. Even those who completed the terms of their indenture left once they were free. Many planters decided that relying on slave labor was less costly in the long run.

LESSON **2** Servants and Slaves

Thinking on Your Own

Read the Focus Your Reading questions and vocabulary. What do they tell you about who did most of the work in the Southern Colonies? Talk about your ideas with a partner. Then write a short paragraph summarizing your main points.

The Southern Colonies always needed farm workers. Tobacco, rice, and indigo were **labor-intensive** crops. Growing, harvesting, and shipping these crops to market required long hours of manual labor. The servants and slaves who did this work made up the lower classes in the Southern Colonies.

focus your reading

Why were the Southern Colonies always in need of workers?

How did indentured servants get to the colonies?

Why did African slaves replace white servants?

vocabulary

labor-intensive

redemptioners

indentured servants

triangle trade

slave codes

Unfree Servants

In the early years of colonization, planters solved the labor problem by importing unfree white workers. Some were convicts shipped to the colonies to work out their prison terms. Others were **redemptioners**, people in the colonies who sold their labor. The buyer owned the person's services for a fixed period in return for food, clothing, and shelter. Most unfree workers came to the colonies as **indentured servants**.

At least half of the white settlers in the English colonies were indentured servants. These workers signed a labor contract before leaving England. The contractor paid their passage to America and provided them with food and clothing. In return, the servant agreed to work in the colonies for a period of four to seven years. At the end of the time period, most servants received a few acres of farmland as freedom dues.

Lesson Vocabulary

Introduce each vocabulary word by focusing on the term *labor intensive*. Growing cash crops in the Southern Colonies was *labor intensive*, that is, these crops required constant care. Planters tried to overcome the shortage of workers by contracting with *redemptioners*.

Redemptioners made a deal with the captain of a ship traveling to North America. He lent them the money for the voyage in exchange for a promise to repay, or *redeem*, that loan shortly after arrival in the colonies. If they could not pay off the loan in that time, and most could not, the captain would sell the loan to the highest bidder. The passengers were then required to pay off the cost of their voyage by working for a certain number of years.

Indentured servants had a similar arrangement. Unlike redemptioners, they agreed to the terms of indenture before they left home. Explain that even though these

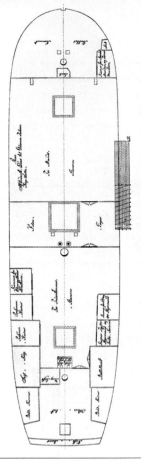

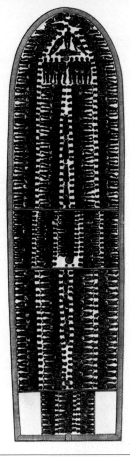

Slaves were brought to America in tightly packed slave ships.

Picturing History

This plan of a slave ship was created in England in the late 1700s to show the evils of slavery. The plan reveals how 482 slaves could be packed on board a single ship, the *Brookes of Liverpool,* for a 6- to 8-week voyage between Africa and the West Indies. The *Brookes,* which was about the same size as the *Mayflower,* actually carried as many as 609 slaves on a single voyage. Ask students to write a brief description of a slave ship using the plan, the drawings on page 79, and the primary source account on page 80.

Being a servant was a hard life. Most worked in the fields or cleared new farmland. They could not leave the farm or plantation without permission. Single people needed permission to marry. Servants had to make up any time that was lost due to illness or absence. Many tried to run away, often successfully.

stop and think

Think about how owning land and social class relate to each other. Write two or three sentences that explain the relationship. Discuss your answer with a partner or the class.

Stop and Think

Answers will vary, but students should show an understanding that social class in the Southern Colonies was linked to land ownership. The more land a person or family owned, the higher their standing in society. Planters and their families were considered upper class. Farmers who owned small farms or businesses made up the middle class. People who owned no land at all were the lower class.

Lesson Vocabulary, continued

workers were not free to leave until their contracts had been fulfilled, they were not *slaves.*

Slavery had no end, and slaves had few rights. Explain that a code is a set of laws. The *slave codes* were colonial laws that enslaved Africans, their children, and their children's children. The buying and selling of slaves was an international trade. Ask students to use the map on page 78 to explain why that trade was known as the *triangle trade.*

Extension

Between 1680 and 1700, about 300,000 people were shipped from Africa to North America on English ships. About one in five died on the journey.

Have students work in small groups to find out more about the slave ships and the Middle Passage as shown on the map on page 78. Ask each group to create a poster illustrating its findings.

Picturing History

Explain to students that during colonial times, the letter "s" was often written as "f." Therefore, the word "forts" is read as "sorts," and the word "Houfe" is read as "House."

What does the newspaper ad at the top of page 78 reveal about slavery in the Southern Colonies?

Extension

Share with students the following advertisement that appeared in the *Virginia Gazette* in August of 1751. Discuss what it adds to our understanding of slavery and the slave trade.

"RAN away from the Subscriber, a short Negroe Fellow, named Stepney; he has a Sailor's and Negroe's Dress, a large Scar on his Temple, occasioned by a Burn, speaks thick and stutters; he may pretend to be a free Negroe, having been with me in England, Scotland, Ireland, New and Old Spain, Portugal, and the West-Indies; he was my Cabin-Boy at first. Whoever brings him to me, shall have Two Pistoles Reward, besides what the Law allows. Thomas Dansie. N.B. All Masters of Vessels are strictly forbid carrying him out of the Country."

Additional ads can be found on-line as part of the University of Virginia's Geography of Slavery in Virginia Project.

African Slaves

In 1619, a Dutch slave trader sold the first African slaves in Virginia. The number of slaves grew slowly. It was cheaper for a planter to import a servant than to buy a slave. However, servants who ran away were difficult to recover. They blended into the white population. Every five years or so, planters had to train new workers. In time, they decided that slaves cost less in the long run.

Many of the slave traders followed a route that became known as the **triangle trade**. This is because the routes formed the shape of a triangle. On one leg, traders brought sugar and molasses from the West Indies to the colonies. These products were used to make rum, which was shipped to Africa and traded for slaves. The slaves were then shipped to the West Indies and the colonies. Many other goods were also shipped across the Atlantic, such as indigo, wood, and iron.

TO BE SOLD,
A Likely negro Man, his Wife and Child; the negro Man capable of doing all forts of Plantation Work, and a good Miller: The Woman exceeding fit for a Farmer, being capable of doing any Work, belonging to a Houfe in the Country, at reasonable Rates, inquire of the Printer hereof.

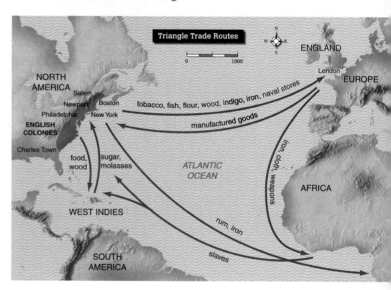

Map Extension

Ask students to use the map to answer the following questions:

- What products did Boston merchants ship to London? (tobacco, fish, flour, wood, indigo, iron, and naval stores)

- What did London merchants ship to West Africa? (iron, cloth, weapons)

- What did those merchants ship from Africa to North America? (slaves)

- Who seemed to control the triangle trade? (merchants in London, New York, Boston, Philadelphia, Salem, and Newport)

Conditions on the slave ship were terrible.

By 1700, African slaves were common throughout the Southern Colonies. Virginia had approximately 10,000 African slaves by that time. At first, African slaves and English servants were treated in a similar way. As the number of slaves increased, that changed. The colonies enacted **slave codes**. These laws enslaved Africans and their descendants for as long as they lived. The slave codes also controlled every aspect of a slave's life.

Putting It All Together

Create a two-column chart in your notebook. Label the first column "Unfree Servants" and the second "Slaves." Using information from the chapter, describe each type of labor in the appropriate column.

Slaves arriving at Jamestown

Putting It All Together

Answers will vary, but students should include the following:

Unfree Servants: redemptioners and indentured servants; worked to pay off the cost of their passage to the colonies; most worked four to seven years; had no freedom; often treated harshly

Slaves: Africans; they and their descendents were enslaved for life; no freedom as slave codes controlled every aspect of their lives; often treated harshly

Picturing History

The two drawings on page 79 show two parts of the slave trade. The top picture reveals conditions on the ship, and the picture at the bottom of the page shows the Africans' arrival in the colonies and preparations for their sale. Discuss with students what each picture adds to their understanding of the slave trade.

1 A ship could hold 220–250 slaves.

2 The slaves were separated into four groups: men, women, boys, and the sick.

3 The slaves were kept from moving around by leg irons.

Extension

Have students use this primary source account to write a newspaper story about the slave ships. Remind students that a good news story answers the following questions:

- Who is the story about?
- What happened?
- Where did it happen?
- When did it happen?
- Why did it happen?
- How did it happen?
- Why is it important?

80

Read a Primary Source

A Tightly Packed Slave Ship

Slave ship captains disagreed on how tightly to pack their human cargo. The "loose-packers" argued that slaves arrived in better condition and brought higher prices if allowed some additional space. The "tight-packers" replied that the larger the cargo, the greater the profits, even if more slaves died on the voyage. The following is a firsthand description of a tightly packed ship.

reading for understanding

How many slaves could a ship hold?

How were they separated into groups?

What kept the slaves from moving around?

"The cargo of a vessel of a hundred tons or a little more is calculated to purchase from 220 to 250 slaves. Their lodging rooms below the deck which are three (for the men, the boys and the women) besides a place for the sick, are sometimes more than five feet high and sometimes less; and this height is divided toward the middle for the slaves to lie in two rows, one above the other, on each side of the ship, close to each other like books upon a shelf. I have known them so close that the shelf would not easily contain one more.

The poor creatures, thus cramped, are likewise in irons for the most part which makes it difficult for them to turn or move or attempt to rise or to lie down without hurting themselves or each other. Every morning, perhaps, more instances than one are found of the living and the dead fastened together."

Quoted in Daniel P. Mannix in collaboration with Malcolm Cowley,
Black Cargoes: A History of the Atlantic Slave Trade, 1518–1865.

Map Extension

There are many native groups shown on the map on page 81 that are not discussed in the lesson. Have students select one of the groups and research their history. Students can then present their information to the class.

Settlers and Native Americans

Thinking on Your Own

Read the Focus Your Reading questions with a partner. Together, discuss possible answers. Write a possible answer for each question in your notebook.

The growing number of farms and plantations caused serious problems for the native people. Entire villages died from diseases brought by explorers and settlers. By clearing fields in the forests, the settlers destroyed native hunting grounds. Settlers' dogs also chased the deer away. The colonial settlements succeeded, but only at the expense of the Native Americans.

focus your reading

How did the Powhatan chiefs react to the English settlement of Virginia?

Why did angry frontier settlers attack and burn Jamestown?

What did white settlers in the Carolinas do to the Native Americans besides taking their land?

vocabulary

Bacon's Rebellion

Yamasee Border War

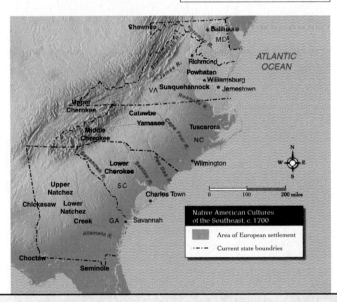

Native American Cultures of the Southeast, c. 1700

▨ Area of European settlement
-·-·- Current state boundries

81

Focus Your Reading Answers

1 The Powhatan chiefs reacted to the English settlement of Virginia by declaring war against the newcomers.

2 Angry frontier settlers attacked and burned Jamestown because the governor refused to protect them from attacks by Native Americans.

3 White settlers in the Carolinas took land from Native Americans and tried to enslave them.

Lesson Summary

As the Southern Colonies grew, many native groups were pushed farther and farther west. Others died from diseases brought by the settlers.

From the beginning, Native Americans fought back. They were almost constantly at war with the colonists in eastern Virginia. By 1676, the conflict had shifted to the frontier. When the governor of Virginia refused to send troops to protect settlers, Nathaniel Bacon and 400 armed men marched to Jamestown and set it on fire to show their anger. In 1712, fighting broke out in North Carolina after the colonists took land from the Tuscarora and tried to enslave them. In 1715, the Yamasee Border War began in South Carolina. The violence continued until most Native Americans had been killed or forced out of the Carolinas.

Lesson Objective

Students will learn how the growth of the Southern Colonies affected Native Americans in the late 1600s and early 1700s.

Lesson Vocabulary

Explain that a *rebellion* is an uprising against the government. *Bacon's Rebellion* was an uprising against the governor of Virginia, who refused to protect frontier settlements from attacks by Native Americans. The leader was Nathaniel Bacon.

The *Yamasee Border War* was a war fought between the Yamasee People and colonists in South Carolina. It took place between 1715 and 1718. When the fighting ended, most of the Yamasee had been pushed out of the Carolinas.

Stop and Think

Answers will vary, but the facts should show an understanding that in *Virginia* and the *Carolinas*, Native Americans fought to protect their lands but eventually were forced out. In the *Carolinas*, the colonists tried to take over the Native Americans' land and enslave them. In *Virginia*, the conflict began in the eastern part of the colony and eventually shifted to the frontier.

Uprisings in Virginia

Powhatan, the chief of the Powhatan Confederation, kept waiting for the English to leave Jamestown. He did not want them to stay forever. Instead of leaving, however, the settlers kept coming. In 1609, Powhatan declared war against the settlers. Fighting continued for the next four years. Opechancanough, the next chief, tried to drive the colonists out once and for all. A surprise attack in 1622 killed at least 347 settlers. In 1664, another 500 colonists died in a second

stop and think

Make a Venn diagram to describe what happened to Native Americans in the Southern Colonies. Label one circle "Virginia" and the other "The Carolinas." In the overlapping area, write words that describe what they experienced in common. In the other circles describe how they were treated differently.

Jamestown was burned during Bacon's Rebellion.

Picturing History

Ask students to write a brief description of Bacon's arrival in Jamestown from various points of view, using information provided in the picture on page 82 and the text on page 83. One group might describe the event from the governor's point of view, a second from the vantage point of one of Bacon's followers, and a third might express the views of a resident of Jamestown. Ask each group to read aloud its paragraph and discuss similarities and differences.

uprising. Each time, the colonists hit back, destroying every native village they could find. In the end, the colonists drove the native people out of eastern Virginia.

Bacon's Rebellion

The conflict then shifted to the Virginia frontier. In 1676, fighting broke out between settlers and the Susquehannock. Led by Nathaniel Bacon, the settlers asked Governor William Berkeley to send troops. Berkeley refused because he wanted to protect his business of trading furs with the locals. Bacon led 400 armed men to Jamestown. The farmers burned the town because they were angry at Berkeley. This uprising, known as **Bacon's Rebellion**, ended when Bacon fell ill and died. His followers either surrendered or were captured. Twenty-three participants in the uprising were convicted and hanged. Conflict on the frontier continued until the settlers drove the native population completely out of Virginia.

Conflict in the Carolinas

Fighting between settlers and native people broke out next in North and South Carolina. The colonists not only took land, but they also enslaved the local people. In 1712, the Tuscarora of North Carolina attacked and killed 130 slave traders. The survivors burned a Tuscarora fort, killing over 150 Native Americans. The **Yamasee Border War** broke out in 1715 in South Carolina. The Yamasee killed more than 400 settlers. Most of the Yamasee were tracked down and killed or sold as slaves. The violence continued until 1718, when the remaining Native Americans left the Carolinas.

Some colonists found themselves in conflict with Native American groups.

Putting It All Together

Return to the answers you wrote earlier for the Focus Your Reading questions. Revise or expand your answers based on what you have read. Share your answers with a partner or the class.

Putting It All Together
Students should expand their answers to the Focus Your Reading questions. The revised answers should include information that was not known to the students at the beginning of the lesson. Have students work in pairs to further develop their understanding of the lesson's concepts.

Picturing History

The picture on page 83 shows the conflict between the colonists and Native Americans. What is the artist's view of the conflict? How does he seem to regard Native Americans? How does he view the colonists? If you wanted to show the conflict from a different point of view, what changes would you make in the picture?

Chapter Review

1 The posters will vary but should show an understanding that a plantation is larger than a farm and is devoted to a *cash crop*. Additionally, there were few cities in the Southern Colonies and most were capitals.

2 Dialogue will vary, but the conversation should show an understanding of the similarities and differences between indentured servants and slaves.

3 The articles should focus on the complicated relationship between the colonists and Native Americans. Students may want to conduct additional research on the Internet or in the library to enhance their background knowledge.

4 Answers will vary.

Chapter Summary

Tobacco provided Virginia and its neighboring colonies with a **cash crop**. The tobacco planters had large **plantations**. They needed a great deal of land because tobacco drained the soil of nutrients. Families who owned small farms made up the middle class. They settled inland from the rivers, or on the **frontier**. They grew, raised, or made most of what they needed, including **homespun** clothing.

Tobacco, rice, and indigo were **labor-intensive** crops. Planters tried to solve their labor problem by hiring white servants called **redemptioners** and **indentured servants**. Both sold their labor for a period of four to seven years.

By 1700, African slaves were common throughout the Southern Colonies. The **triangle trade** routes brought many slaves to the colonies. At first, they were treated much like white servants, but that did not last long. As their number increased, the colonies enacted **slave codes**. These laws enslaved Africans and their children forever.

As colonial settlement grew, Native Americans were pushed off their land. The Powhatan fought with the Virginia colonists many times. In 1676, **Bacon's Rebellion** increased tension with native groups. Later, in 1715, the **Yamasee Border War** resulted in the deaths of more than 400 colonists.

Chapter Review

1 Create a poster that describes plantation, farm, and city life in the Southern Colonies.

2 Imagine a conversation between a white indentured servant and an African slave about their lives. Write their pretend dialogue.

3 Write an article for a London newspaper about life in colonial Virginia. Include information about and possible quotes from Chief Powhatan and John Rolfe.

4 Read over the vocabulary. Choose five words that are the least familiar to you and invent a way to remember their definitions. Use symbols, word games, pictures, or rhymes.

Novel Connections

Below is a list of books that relate to the time period covered in this chapter. The numbers in parentheses indicate the related Thematic Strands of the National Council for the Social Studies (NCSS).

Linda Jacobs Altman. *Slavery and Abolition in American History.* (In American History series) Enslow, 1999. (III)

James Bial. *The Strength of These Arms: Life in the Slave Quarters.* Houghton Mifflin, 2000. (V)

Sylviane A. Diouf. *Growing Up in Slavery.* Milbrook Press, 2001. (I, II, III)

James Haskins and Kathleen Benson. *Building a New Land: African Americans in Colonial America.* Amistad/Harper Collins Children's Books, 2001. (I, II, III)

Joy Masoff. *Colonial Times, 1600–1700.* Scholastic Reference, 2000. (I, II, III)

Richard Watkins. *Slavery: Bondage Through History.* Houghton Mifflin, 2001. (I, II, III)

Skill Builder

Comparing Tables

Tables present different kinds of information. Both tables below contain information about the growth of slavery in England's North American colonies. But the information is not the same. The first step in using a table is to see what kind of information it contains. It also is important to compare tables if more than one is available. A second table may provide valuable information that the first does not include.

Use the two tables to answer the following questions:

1 Both tables have a "Total" column. How are they different?

2 Which table tells you the number of slaves in the New England and Middle Colonies in 1700? What is the answer?

3 Which table would you use to find out what percentage of slaves lived in the South in 1740? What was the percentage?

4 In what year did the slave population exceed 10 percent of the total population? Which table includes that information?

5 In what decade—a period of ten years—did the total colonial population grow the fastest? In what decade did the slave population grow the fastest?

Slave Population, 1650–1760

Year	North	South	Total
1650	880	720	1,600
1660	1,162	1,758	2,920
1670	1,125	3,410	4,535
1680	1,895	5,076	6,971
1690	3,340	13,389	16,729
1700	5,206	22,611	27,817
1710	8,303	36,563	44,866
1720	14,091	54,748	68,839
1730	17,323	73,698	91,021
1740	23,958	126,066	150,024
1750	30,222	206,198	236,420
1760	40,033	285,773	325,806

Colonial Population, 1650–1760

Year	Total population	% Black
1650	50,368	3%
1660	75,058	3%
1670	111,935	4%
1680	151,507	5%
1690	210,372	7%
1700	250,888	11%
1710	331,711	13%
1720	466,185	14%
1730	629,445	14%
1740	905,563	16%
1750	1,170,760	20%
1760	1,593,625	20%

Skill Builder

1 The "Total" column in the Slave Population table shows the total number of slaves in England's North American colonies for each year between 1650 and 1760. The "Total" column in the Colonial Population table shows the total number of people living in the colonies, including slaves for the same period.

2 The Slave Population table tells the number of slaves in the North (New England and the Middle Colonies) in 1700. That year, there were 5,206 slaves in the North.

3 The Slave Population table allows you to figure out what percentage of slaves lived in the South in 1740. The percentage was about 84 percent. (Divide the number of slaves in the South by the total slave population in 1740.)

4 According to the tables, the slave population exceeded 10 percent of the total population in 1700. Both tables are required to solve this question.

5 The total population grew fastest between 1750 and 1760; the slave population grew fastest in that same decade.

Classroom Discussion

Discuss with students some of the broader topics covered in this chapter.

- How did the shortage of workers affect the way redemptioners and indentured servants were treated? How did the shortage affect the growth of slavery?

- How were the lives of indentured servants and slaves similar? What differences were most striking?

- How did the triangle trade link the Southern Colonies to other English colonies? to England? to Africa?

- Why were there so many wars between Native Americans and colonists in the late 1600s and early 1700s? What was the outcome of these wars?

Chapter

6 LIFE IN THE NEW ENGLAND AND MIDDLE COLONIES

Getting Focused

Skim this chapter to predict what you will be learning.

- Read the lesson titles and subheadings.
- Look at the illustrations and read the captions.
- Examine the maps.
- Review the vocabulary words and terms.

Compare the topics covered in Chapter 5 with those in Chapter 6 by examining the vocabulary words in each chapter. Write three predictions in your notebook about what you will learn in Chapter 6.

Lesson Vocabulary

Discuss the meaning of each vocabulary word. Help students find the word *migrant* in the word *immigrants*. A migrant is someone who moves, or *migrates*, from place to place. An immigrant is someone who moves, or migrates, *to* another country. Both immigrants and migrants contributed to the expansion of New England.

Ask students to use context clues to figure out the meaning of the word *meetinghouse*. What kind of gatherings might take place there?

Explain to students that the *Great Awakening* was a revival, or renewal, of religious enthusiasm. It began in the late 1730s and lasted until the 1760s. Ministers preaching fiery sermons traveled through not only the New England colonies but also the

The Expansion of New England

Thinking on Your Own

Make a three-column chart in your notebook. Label the columns "Reasons for Villages," "Reasons for Native American Conflict," and "Reasons for Schools." As you read, make notes in each column concerning these topics.

During the 1600s, the New England Colonies attracted thousands of Puritan **immigrants**. The eight towns that existed in 1630 increased to thirty-three by 1647. Fifty years later, Puritan settlements lined the coast from Maine to Rhode Island. They extended west into central Massachusetts and Connecticut.

focus your reading

Why did New England colonists settle in villages?

What caused King Philip's War?

What was the Great Awakening?

vocabulary

immigrants

meetinghouse

Great Awakening

grammar schools

Latin schools

Farm and Fishing Villages

Most New England colonists settled in farm villages. They cleared fields in the forest and divided the land for planting. The first homes of the settlement were built close together in the village. The houses were clustered around the **meetinghouse.** This central location made it easy to attend religious services and other events.

The fireplace was the center of life in the New England home

87

Lesson Vocabulary, continued

Middle and Southern Colonies. They attracted huge audiences that wept with despair for their sins, but also cried for joy at the thought of being saved. The movement offered fellowship, comfort, and emotional release to people who were enduring many hardships.

New Englanders built two kinds of schools—*grammar schools* and *Latin schools*. *Grammar schools* taught reading and writing. What else might they teach? *Latin schools* prepared boys for college. Most colleges at the time, including Harvard College, trained young men to become ministers. Why might boys preparing for college study Latin?

Lesson Summary

During the 1600s, thousands of newcomers settled in the New England Colonies. Before long, Puritan villages lined the Atlantic Coast and stretched west into central Massachusetts and Connecticut.

As New England's population grew, conflicts with Native Americans increased. In 1675, a war between the Puritans and the Wampanoag virtually wiped out most Native Americans in eastern Massachusetts.

As conflict with Native Americans heightened tensions in the region, many colonists turned to religion for answers. New Englanders experienced a religious revival in the 1740s.

Lesson Objective

Students will learn about life in the New England Colonies and consider why these colonies grew so rapidly in the late 1600s and 1700s.

Focus Your Reading Answers

1 New England colonists settled in villages for protection, to make it easier to attend religious services and other events, and to educate their children.

2 The colonists declared war after the Wampanoag attacked Puritan towns in 1675.

3 The Great Awakening was a revival of religious enthusiasm in the 1740s.

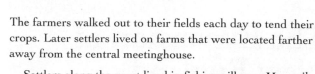

The farmers walked out to their fields each day to tend their crops. Later settlers lived on farms that were located farther away from the central meetinghouse.

Settlers along the coast lived in fishing villages. Men sailed out to catch codfish off the coast of Newfoundland. After salting or drying their catch, they shipped the best fish to Europe. The less tasty fish were sent to Virginia or to the West Indies to feed the slaves. Fish was New England's most valuable export.

New England towns were built around a central meetinghouse.

Relations with Native Cultures

The expanding Puritan settlements caused conflict with the native people. The colonists wanted more land for farming and settlement. The settlers continued to clear land, ruining Native American hunting grounds.
The settlers' pigs uprooted the unfenced cornfields of the local people. Trying to preserve their way of life, angry Pequot attacked a Connecticut village in 1637. In response, the colony formed an army made up of settlers and attacked the natives. The colonists slaughtered most of the Pequot.

stop and think

Imagine that you are planning a new settlement in New England. Create a flyer that describes the settlement to attract new settlers.

Stop and Think

Flyers will vary, but students should stress nearby resources, the availability of farmland, relations with Native Americans, and ties to other settlements.

Extension

Ask students to compare and contrast the drawing of the New England town with the drawing of a Southern plantation and the picture of a frontier farm on page 72. Which differences seem most striking?

DVD Extension

Encourage students to use the reading comprehension, vocabulary reinforcement, and interactive timeline activities on the student DVD.

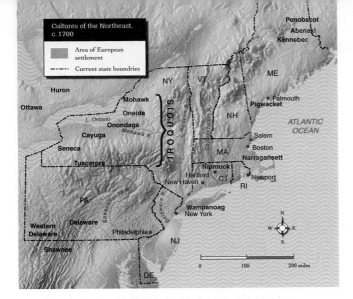

Cultures of the Northeast.
c. 1700

- Area of European settlement
- Current state boundries

Huron
Ottawa
Mohawk
Oneida
Onondaga
Cayuga
Seneca
Tuscarora
IROQUOIS
L. Ontario
Mohawk R.
Hudson R.
NY
VT
ME
Penobscot
Abenaki
Kennebec
Falmouth
Pigwacket
NH
ATLANTIC
OCEAN
Salem
Boston
Narragansett
Nipmuck
Hartford
New Haven
CT
Newport
RI
MA
PA
Delaware R.
Susquehanna R.
Wampanoag
New York
Western
Delaware
Delaware
Philadelphia
NJ
Shawnee
DE

N
W E
S

0   100   200 miles

In 1675, the Wampanoag attacked Puritan towns in Massachusetts. Their leader was Chief Metacomet. The Puritans called him King Philip. The colony declared war against the Wampanoag and their native allies. An army of colonists attacked the Native Americans. They killed Chief Metacomet and most of his warriors. King Philip's War, as the colonists called it, virtually wiped out the native people of eastern Massachusetts.

Tensions between the Wampanoag and the Puritan settlers resulted in King Philip's War.

Map Extension

The colonists who moved to the New England Colonies were surrounded by various Native American groups. Have students research one group named on the map and present their findings to the class.

Picturing History

Pictures often reflect the artist's point of view. How does the artist of the picture on page 89 view Native Americans? How does the artist regard English colonists? What emotions does the picture evoke?

Accusations of witchcraft led to the Salem witch trials.

Picturing History

In the 1600s, even educated people believed in witches, and many countries, including England, executed people for practicing witchcraft.

In 1692, a few girls in Salem Village (now Danvers, Massachusetts) began to accuse older people of being witches. Each accusation led to a trial and often to more accusations. Before the trials finally ended, 165 people had been formally charged with being witches, and 20 of them had been killed. What does the drawing suggest about the atmosphere at the trials? the role the girls played?

Extension

The Salem witch trials came to an end soon after the girls accused the wife of the new governor of being a witch. The accusation led ministers to question the charges and the kind of evidence used at the trials. In October 1682, the governor stopped all new arrests for witchcraft and in 1693, released all remaining prisoners. He also issued a general pardon. Ask students to find out more about the Salem witch trials. What prompted the girls to accuse their neighbors? Why did so many people go along with those accusations? Have students share their findings with the class.

Religion and Education

Religion was a strong force in Puritan life. In Salem Village in 1692, several people began acting strangely. The bizarre behavior was thought to be the work of the devil. A court tried and executed twenty people for practicing witchcraft and being possessed by the devil.

New England's increasing wealth also alarmed Puritan ministers. In the 1740s, Jonathan Edwards and George Whitefield helped bring about a revival of religious enthusiasm known as the **Great Awakening**. They warned people at revival meetings that they would burn in hell if they neglected religion.

Reading and writing were required in Massachusetts Bay Colony.

Picturing History

Ask students to use the picture at the bottom of the page to imagine what it was like to attend school in the Massachusetts Bay Colony. The children, who varied in age, usually met in the home of their teacher, often a young woman in the community. There, they studied the alphabet, learned to read a few words, and practiced writing Roman numerals.

The Puritans also placed great emphasis on education. Everyone, they believed, should be able to read the Bible. In 1647, the Massachusetts Bay Colony required each town of fifty families or more to open a school. **Grammar schools** taught reading and writing. **Latin schools** prepared boys for college. The Puritans established Harvard and other colleges to prepare young men to become ministers.

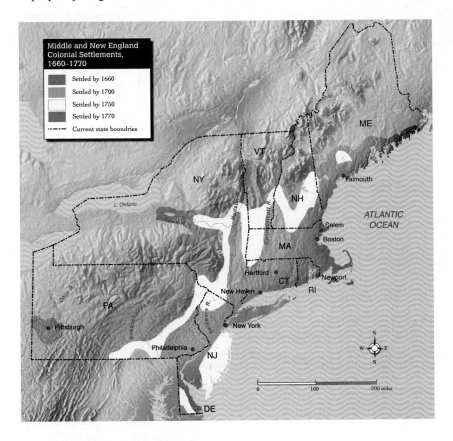

Putting It All Together

Paragraphs will vary but should contain some of the following information:

- Villages were easier to defend than isolated farms and plantations. Villagers benefited by working together to build houses and clear land. They were also able to help each other in times of trouble.

- As colonists settled more land, they took over more and more land that belonged to Native Americans. The Pequot and other groups responded by attacking settlements. The colonists eventually wiped out most of the native people.

- Colonists in Massachusetts wanted schools to teach their children how to read the Bible, prepare some boys for college, and train future ministers.

Putting It All Together

Go back to the three-column chart that you created. Use the information from your chart to write a short paragraph about the expansion of New England.

Life in the New England and Middle Colonies | 91 |

Map Extension

Ask students to use the map to answer the following questions:

- Name the New England Colonies. (New Hampshire, Massachusetts, Rhode Island, Connecticut)

- Name the Middle Colonies. (New York, New Jersey, Pennsylvania, Delaware)

- By what year was nearly all of Massachusetts settled? (1750)

- If you were hoping to found a new settlement in 1770, where might you find lots of open land? (Western New York and Pennsylvania; most of what is now Maine)

1 The attack took place at
sunrise.

2 The writer says the attack
was in retaliation for the
way the Pequot murdered
30 English people.

3 Underhill believes the
Puritans were in the right
because they had God on their
side. He quotes from the
Scriptures to support his view.

Picturing History

Ask students to study the
drawing on page 92 and
read the primary source
to develop a working
definition of the word
massacre. What
distinguishes a massacre
from other attacks?

Read a Primary Source

The Pequot Massacre

In his last will and testament, John Underhill described the 1637
massacre of Pequot at Mystic River. The account also helps to explain
the mindset of the Puritans who killed about 500 Pequot that day.

reading for understanding

At what time of day did the attack
take place?

What reasons did the writer give
for the attack?

Why was Underhill convinced the
Puritans were in the right?

> "Drawing near to the fort, we yielded up
> ourselves to God and entreated His
> assistance in so weighty an enterprise. . . .
>
> "We could not but admire at the
> providence of God in it, that soldiers
> so unexpert in the use of their arms,
> should give so complete a volley, as
> though the finger of God had touched
> both match and flint. Which volley
> being given at break of day, and
> themselves fast asleep for the most part, bred in
> them such a terror, that they brake forth
> into a most doleful cry; so as if God had
> not fitted the hearts of men for the
> service, it would have bred in them a
> commiseration toward them. But every
> man being bereaved of pity, fell upon the
> work without compassion, considering the
> blood they [the Pequots] had shed of our
> native countrymen, and how barbarously
> they had dealt with them, and slain, first
> and last, about thirty persons. . . .
>
> "It may be demanded, Why should you
> be so furious (as some have said)?
> Should not Christians have more mercy
> and compassion? But I would refer you
> to [King] David's war. . . . Sometimes
> the Scripture declareth women and
> children must perish with their parents.
> Sometimes the case alters; but we will
> not dispute it now. We have sufficient
> light from the Word of God for our
> proceedings."

From Charles M. Segal and David C. Stineback, *Puritans, Indians,
and Manifest Destiny* (New York: Putnam's, 1977).

Extension

Briefly explain to students the details of the massacre and its outcome. Then ask
students why some historians consider the Pequot Massacre a turning point in
relations between the colonists and Native Americans.

In the spring of 1637, a few hundred colonists attacked the Pequots' main
settlement on the Mystic River in Connecticut. The massacre Underhill describes
resulted in the murder of more than half of the native population—including women
and children. After the massacre, many Pequot were captured and sold into slavery.
The native group itself was disbanded, and the survivors were adopted by
neighboring Native Americans. The colonists' victory gave them control of the
Connecticut River valley.

Growth of the Middle Colonies

Thinking on Your Own

Imagine you live in a region that people call a "breadbasket." What characteristics do you think give the region this name? Write three characteristics in your notebook.

The Middle Colonies grew more rapidly than England's other colonies. The fertile soil of New York, New Jersey, Pennsylvania, and Delaware attracted tens of thousands of settlers. These colonies also welcomed people of all religious beliefs, so long as they were Christians. As the most **tolerant**, or open-minded, of England's colonies, they attracted the most diverse group of settlers.

focus your reading

Who did farmers depend upon for farm labor?

Why were the Middle Colonies more diverse than New England?

How did William Penn treat the native people of Pennsylvania?

vocabulary

tolerant

breadbasket

haven

Pennsylvania Dutch

Scots-Irish

Farming in the Middle Colonies

By founding Pennsylvania in 1682, William Penn opened a floodgate of immigration. Four thousand immigrants arrived the first year. Immigrants kept coming to the colonies. Some settled in Philadelphia. Most went inland to buy farms. The farms were larger than those in New England but smaller than Virginia plantations. Immigrants also settled on farms in New York, New Jersey, and Delaware.

The Middle Colonies were England's **breadbasket** colonies. Wheat was the main cash crop. From the wheat came flour and bread. The colonies also produced corn, vegetables, and livestock.

Life in the New England and Middle Colonies 93

Lesson Summary

The Middle Colonies grew even faster than New England. The region's fertile soil attracted newcomers. With wheat as the main cash crop, the region quickly became England's breadbasket.

Pennsylvania was also a haven for religious minorities. It drew the Pennsylvania Dutch and the Scots-Irish. These settlers had fewer conflicts with Native Americans than did other colonies.

Lesson Objective

Students will learn about life in the Middle Colonies and why they were a haven for many religious and ethnic groups.

Focus Your Reading Answers

1 Farmers mainly depended on their family for labor. For extra help, they hired workers or bought the time of indentured servants.

2 The Middle Colonies were more diverse than New England because they were more tolerant of religious differences.

3 William Penn won the friendship of native people by paying them a fair price for their land.

Lesson Vocabulary

Discuss the meaning of each vocabulary word. Begin by explaining that a *breadbasket* is a geographic region that produces lots of grain. The grain produced by the Middle Colonies was wheat.

A *haven* is a place of safety. From whom were religious minorities like the Quakers seeking safety? Among the religious minorities that settled in Pennsylvania was a group known as the *Pennsylvania Dutch*. They got their name from the German word *Deutch*, which means "German." They were Lutherans from what is now Germany. The Scots-Irish were also a religious minority. They were Protestants who lived in Northern Ireland. They got their name because their ancestors went to Ireland from Scotland.

The Middle Colonies became known as the breadbasket because of the rich soil.

Picturing History

Ask students to compare the drawing at the top of page 94 with illustrations of plantations in the Southern Colonies (Chapter 5). What is the biggest difference? (In the Middle Colonies, farmers depended on their family for labor.) How do you think that difference shaped life in the Middle Colonies?

Extension

New York City was one of the most diverse cities in North America in the late 1600s and early 1700s. Over 18 languages were spoken there, including French, Spanish, Portuguese, Dutch, German, Swedish, and various African languages. Settlers also followed different religions. The colony was home to Jews, Catholics, and a wide variety of Protestant sects. Ask students to gather information about why the city was so diverse and how that diversity shaped life there.

These colonies had relatively few slaves. Farmers mainly depended on their families for labor. For extra help, they hired farm laborers or bought the time of indentured servants. About half of North America's indentured servants lived in Pennsylvania.

Social Diversity

The Middle Colonies had the most diverse population in colonial America. Under the rule of both the Dutch and the English, New York tolerated most religious groups. Pennsylvania was a **haven** for religious minorities, including Quakers and Mennonites. About one-third of the settlers were German Lutherans, also known as the **Pennsylvania Dutch**. The term *Dutch* comes from the German word *deutsch*, which simply means *German*. Cheap land on the frontier attracted large numbers of poor **Scots-Irish** immigrants from Northern Ireland.

Folk art designs, such as the one painted on this pie dish, became popular among the Pennsylvania Dutch.

Picturing History

The Pennsylvania Dutch painted bird and floral designs not only on pie dishes, but also on birth and marriage certificates, family Bibles, and even on furniture. Many also decorated their barns with colorful geometric patterns, including six-pointed star designs. In explaining these designs, the newcomers referred to them as "sechs," the German word for *six*. To their English-speaking neighbors, it sounded as if they were saying the word "hex." In time, all of the patterns the Pennsylvania Dutch created became known as hex signs. Ask students to research some of these patterns and share them with the class by creating a poster.

Colonists and Native People

The settlers of the Middle Colonies had fewer conflicts with the Native Americans than most colonists. English officials in New York made peace with the powerful Iroquois Confederation. The English colonists wanted to profit from the fur trade, which the Iroquois controlled. In Pennsylvania, William Penn won the friendship of the Delaware People. He insisted on paying them a fair price for their land.

William Penn's sons, Thomas and John Penn, did not continue that policy. After inheriting the colony, they signed a new treaty that cheated the Delaware out of much of the land that remained. The Penns called on the Iroquois, the Delaware's enemy, to help enforce the treaty. Together, they pushed the Delaware out of Pennsylvania.

stop and think

Create a concept web for the Middle Colonies with "Keys to Success" in the middle. On lines extending out from the center, write words or terms that help explain the success of these colonies.

William Penn treated the native cultures fairly, which helped to ease tensions.

Putting It All Together

In your notebook, summarize in one paragraph why the Middle Colonies attracted more settlers than other colonies during the 1700s.

Life in the New England and Middle Colonies 95

Stop and Think

Concept webs will vary but should use words or terms such as breadbasket, diverse, tolerate, haven, fur trade, and friendship.

Putting It All Together

Encourage students to use their concept webs to help them write their paragraphs. The paragraphs will vary but should include the following ideas:

- The Middle Colonies were England's breadbasket colonies.

- The Middle Colonies had the most diverse population in North America.

- Settlers in the Middle Colonies had fewer conflicts with Native Americans than did other colonists.

Picturing History

Explain that in the drawing on page 95, William Penn is shown shaking hands with a Native American. What does that gesture suggest about their relationship?

- Wheatley was born in Senegal, West Africa, in about 1753.

- John Wheatley, a Boston merchant, and his wife, Susanna, purchased the child at a slave auction. The Wheatleys were impressed with how quickly Phillis learned to speak English and read the Bible and English poetry. They encouraged her to write.

- At age seventeen, Phillis wrote a poem about the death of Reverend George Whitefield, one of the preachers who inspired the Great Awakening. The poem made her famous.

- The Countess of Huntingdon, a friend of Whitefield, was so moved by the poem that she invited Wheatley to England in 1773. There, the Countess helped Wheatley publish a book of poetry entitled *Poems on Various Subjects, Religious and Moral*. After her book of poems was published, the Wheatleys gave Phillis her freedom.

- The book helped Wheatley become famous in Europe as well as in North America. She was celebrated as the first African-American poet.

- In 1776, she wrote a poem dedicated to George Washington that brought her more acclaim.

- In 1778, Wheatley married John Peters, a free African American.

"May Whitefield's Virtues flourish with his Fame,

And Ages yet unborn record his Name.

All Praise and Glory be to God on High,

Whose dread Command is, That we all must die.

To live to Life eternal, may we emulate

The worthy Man that's gone, e'er tis too late."

96

Biography

Phillis Wheatley (1753?–1784)

In March 1776, George Washington wrote Phillis Wheatley a letter. He thanked her for a poem she had written. Her poem praised him for taking command of the colonial army.

"If you should ever come to Cambridge, or near headquarters," he replied, "I shall be happy to see a person so favored by the muses." The man who became the father of his country wrote this compliment to an African-born slave.

Phillis Wheatley was born about 1753 in Africa. At age seven, she was captured by slave traders. A frail, little girl, Phillis barely survived the voyage to Boston.

Susanna Wheatley, the wife of a Boston merchant, bought Phillis. She needed a girl to train as a maid. She placed her daughter, Mary, in charge of Phillis's education. Before she could explain the household duties, Mary had to teach Phillis to speak English. A quick learner, Phillis also mastered the alphabet. Within two years, Phyllis could read the Bible. Then she learned how to write. Most of all, she liked to read and write poetry.

Phillis published her first poem at age fourteen. Among her best-known poetry was the elegy or funeral poem that she wrote at age seventeen for the preacher George Whitefield.

When the poem was published in 1770, Phillis was in poor health. She was only able to do light housework and to write poems.

In 1773, Phillis sailed for London. The Wheatleys' doctor thought the sea air would do her good. She became very popular in England, where people called her the "African poetess." That year, she published a book of poems, and the Wheatleys gave Phillis her freedom.

Susanna Wheatley died shortly after Phillis returned from England. Phillis left the Wheatley household in 1778 upon the death of John Wheatley. That year, she married John Peters, also a free African American. Her health grew steadily worse. Phillis Wheatley Peters, the first African American to publish a book of poetry, died in December 1784 at age thirty-one.

Biography Extension

Have students think about why people in both Europe and North America were so astonished by Wheatley's poetry. Based on the discussion of slavery in Chapter 5, how did Europeans in Wheatley's day seem to regard Africans? What questions might her success have raised about those views? What questions might her success have raised about the right of one person to hold another in slavery?

LESSON 3 Cities of the Northeast

Thinking on Your Own

Create two columns in your notebook titled "Ship Owners, Merchants, and Shopkeepers" and "Craftspeople and Laborers." As you read, fill in the columns with key information about each group.

Towns and cities played an important role in the New England and Middle Colonies. They provided a market for the products of colonial farms and forests. Their workshops and stores sold goods that the colonists could not make themselves. They also provided education, entertainment, and music.

> **focus your reading**
>
> Why did the New England and Middle Colonies need cities?
>
> What items did city merchants import?
>
> What products did colonial cities export?
>
> **vocabulary**
>
> farm produce
> forest products
> craftspeople

Ship Owners, Merchants, and Shopkeepers

The largest cities of the Northeast were seaports. Merchants imported cloth, hardware, books, tea, and other items from England. They exported grain, meat, and other **farm produce**. They also exported **forest products** such as ships' masts and roof shingles.

The ship owners of New England were involved in a three-sided, or triangular, trade. That is, they shipped rum to Africa to exchange for slaves. They sold the slaves in the West Indies, where they bought sugar. They sold the sugar in Boston to distillers who made the rum.

Wealthy merchants and ship owners were the cities' upper class. These families lived in big houses in the center of town and wore fine clothes. Below them in status were shopkeepers, whose homes were smaller and less well furnished. They also dressed more plainly.

Life in the New England and Middle Colonies 97

Lesson Summary

Towns and cities were important places in both the New England and Middle Colonies. Wealthy merchants imported goods from England and exported wheat and other farm products, fish, timber, and other forest products. The docks were busy places.

Colonial cities were also home to many craftspeople. They made shoes, silverware, clothing, and other goods.

By the 1700s, cities were centers of culture. They were places where people could see a play, hear a concert, and even borrow books from a lending library.

Lesson Objective

Students will learn what life was like in the cities of the Northeast in the 1700s.

Focus Your Reading Answers

1 Cities in the New England and Middle Colonies provided a market for the products of colonial farms and forests. They also sold goods that the colonists could not make themselves. In addition, the cities became educational and cultural centers.

2 City merchants imported cloth, hardware, books, tea, and other items from England.

3 Colonial cities exported farm products and forest products.

Lesson Vocabulary

The word *produce* has several meanings. As a verb, it means to create or manufacture something. The items a person *produces* are known as *products*. Colonists *produced* ship's masts and roof shingles from wood they found in the forests. These items are *forest products*. Explain that as a noun, *farm produce* refers to fresh fruits and vegetables.

A *craft* is an occupation or trade that requires specific skills. Shoemaking is a craft. So is sewing, printing, and carpentry. People who have these skills are *craftspeople*. What products did craftspeople *produce*?

New York skyline during the early eighteenth century

Picturing History

Ask students what the picture at the top of page 98 suggests about what New York City was like in the early 1700s. Ask why the largest city in every colony was a seaport.

Stop and Think

The scenes and bulleted lists will vary but should reflect economic, social, and cultural aspects of city life. Encourage students to use the Internet or the library to gather information about the city they chose.

Craftspeople and Laborers

Cities were also places for work. Boston's meatpackers slaughtered cattle and pigs, pickled the meat, and packed it in barrels. Millers in New York and Philadelphia ground wheat into flour. Every large city had a printer, such as Benjamin Franklin in Philadelphia. **Craftspeople**, or skilled workers, made shoes, silverware, and clothing. Unskilled laborers loaded and unloaded ships and kept the streets in repair.

Skilled workers and their families occupied the bottom half of society. The craftspeople usually worked at home. They often turned the front room of their home into a shop. Unskilled workers were the poorest of all. They lived in shacks on the edge of the city.

stop and think

Create a movie in your mind about a day in a colonial city. Illustrate three scenes in the movie. Use a bulleted list to make notes of details for each scene.

Printers contributed to the economic development of the colonies.

98   Chapter 6

Picturing History

By the early 1700s, nearly 50 printers lived in the colonies, mostly in large cities. They printed books, newspapers, pamphlets, almanacs, and posters. Ask students to think about how print shops like the one shown at the bottom of page 98 helped unite a colony or group of colonies.

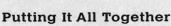

Centers of Culture

City people were more likely than others to write books, open libraries, hold concerts, and put on plays. Most books, especially in New England, had religious themes. Boston produced two widely read women poets—Phillis Wheatley and Anne Bradstreet. Wheatley, a slave, was the first African American woman to have her work published.

In Philadelphia in 1731, Benjamin Franklin set up the colonies' first lending library. Music lovers in Boston and New York City could attend classical music concerts by the 1750s. By then, every colonial city had a theater. People especially liked to watch plays by William Shakespeare.

The wealthy often gathered to listen to classical music.

Putting It All Together

Look through Lesson 3. Find three kinds of connections with what you have read: 1) how it relates to something else you have read; 2) how it relates to something in your own life; and 3) how it relates to something you know about. Choose the strongest connection and write a paragraph about it in your notebook.

Putting It All Together
Paragraphs will vary but should show an understanding of various aspects of city life in the New England and Middle Colonies.

Picturing History

What does the picture on page 99 suggest about the kinds of goods wealthy city dwellers purchased from England? What does the picture suggest about the changes that took place in the colonies between Boston's founding in 1630 and the early 1700s?

Chapter Review

1 Questions and answers will vary but should show an understanding of both rural and urban life in the New England and Middle Colonies.

2 In evaluating sentences, look for signs that students understand not only the meaning of each word but also how it relates to life in the New England and/or Middle Colonies.

3 Paragraphs will vary but should reflect an understanding that there were more conflicts with Native Americans in New England than in the Middle Colonies. Answers should also show an understanding that as both groups of colonies expanded, Native Americans were forced out.

Chapter Summary

During the 1600s, the New England Colonies attracted thousands of **immigrants**. Most New England colonists settled in farm villages with homes clustered around the **meetinghouse**. The expanding settlements caused conflict with the native people.

In the 1740s, New England Puritan ministers led a religious revival called the **Great Awakening**. Education was also important. The Puritans set up **grammar schools** to teach reading and writing and **Latin schools** to prepare boys for college.

The Middle Colonies also grew rapidly. The fertile soil of New York, New Jersey, Pennsylvania, and Delaware attracted tens of thousands of settlers. Because wheat was their main cash crop, these colonies were called England's **breadbasket**.

Pennsylvania was a **haven** for religious minorities. Because the colony was **tolerant**, it attracted **Pennsylvania Dutch** and **Scots-Irish** immigrants. These settlers had fewer conflicts with native people than other colonies had.

Towns and cities played an important role in the New England and Middle Colonies. Wealthy merchants imported goods from England, and exported **farm produce** and **forest products**. **Craftspeople** made shoes, silverware, and clothing. Laborers worked on the docks.

Chapter Review

1 Imagine that you are a newspaper reporter interviewing colonists from the New England and Middle Colonies about life in those regions. Write questions that could be asked of a city resident and a village resident. Then write answers that explain the benefits of each region.

2 Use each vocabulary word in a sentence. Relate each word to life in the colonies.

3 Write a paragraph describing English colonization in the New England and Middle Colonies from the point of view of the native people of those areas.

Novel Connections

Below is a list of books that relate to the time period covered in this chapter. The numbers in parentheses indicate the related Thematic Strands of the National Council for the Social Studies (NCSS).

David A. Adler. *B. Franklin, Printer*. Holiday House, 2001. (III, V, VI)

Marc Aronson. *Witch-Hunt: Mysteries of the Salem Witch Trials*. Atheneum Books, 2003. (II, V, VI)

Kathryn Lasky. *A Voice of Her Own: The Story of Phillis Wheatley, Slave Poet*. Candlewick Press, 2003. (V, VI).

Joyce Hansen and Gary McGowan. *Breaking Ground, Breaking Silence: The Story of New York's African Burial Ground*. Holt, 1997. (II, III, V)

Mark Kurlansky. *The Cod's Tale*. G. P. Putnam's Sons, 2001. (II, VII)

Joy Masoff. *Colonial Times, 1600–1700*. Scholastic Reference, 2000. (I, II, III)

Christina Mierau. *Accept No Substitutes: The History of American Advertising*. (People's History series) Lerner, 2000. (I, VII)

Skill Builder

Reading a Bar Graph

Information presented in graph form is easy to visualize. The bars or lines on a graph also make it easy to compare information. Bar graphs present information in vertical or horizontal bars, as on the population graph below. That graph compares the populations of five colonial cities at three periods in time.

Use the population bar graph to answer the following questions:

1 Which was the largest city in 1730?

2 Which city experienced the most rapid growth between 1730 and 1760?

3 In what year did the population of New York City exceed that of Boston?

4 Which city grew at the slowest rate between 1700 and 1760?

5 What is the difference in population between the largest and smallest city in 1700? in 1730? in 1760?

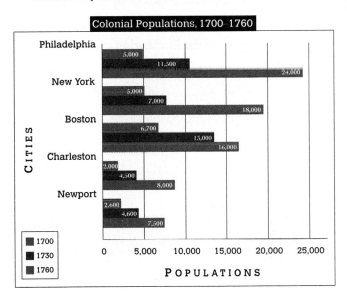

Colonial Populations, 1700-1760

Philadelphia: 5,000 / 11,500 / 24,000
New York: 5,000 / 7,000 / 18,000
Boston: 6,700 / 13,000 / 16,000
Charleston: 2,000 / 4,500 / 8,000
Newport: 2,600 / 4,600 / 7,500

CITIES

□ 1700
■ 1730
■ 1760

0   5,000   10,000   15,000   20,000   25,000

POPULATIONS

1 The largest city in 1730 was Boston.

2 Philadelphia was the city that experienced the most rapid growth between 1730 and 1760.

3 The population of New York City exceeded that of Boston in 1760.

4 Newport grew at the slowest rate between 1700 and 1760.

5 In 1700, the difference in population between the largest city (Boston) and the smallest city (Charleston) was 4,700; in 1730, the difference between Boston and Charleston was 8,500; in 1760, the difference between Philadelphia and Newport was 16,500.

Extension

Ask students to use the bar graph to answer the following questions:

- Which cities more than doubled their population between 1700 and 1730? (Philadelphia and Charleston)

- Which city nearly doubled its population between 1700 and 1730? (Boston)

- Which two cities more than doubled their population between 1730 and 1760? (Philadelphia and New York)

Classroom Discussion

Discuss with students some of the broader topics covered in this chapter.

- What changes took place in the New England and Middle Colonies between the early 1600s and the early 1700s?

- Why do you think cities grew so rapidly in the New England and Middle Colonies during the early 1700s? What effect did that growth have on life in both groups of colonies?

- How did colonists in the early 1700s build on the experiences of earlier settlers?

- What did the Great Awakening suggest about the tensions of life in the colonies in the late 1600s and early 1700s?

- Why do you think every large city in the colonies in the 1700s was a seaport? How did overseas trade shape both sets of colonies?

Unit Objectives

After studying this unit, students will be able to

- describe clashes between the British and their colonists in North America over a wide range of issues

- explain why the colonists declared their independence from Britain in 1776

- describe how the colonists won their freedom from the British

Unit 4 focuses on the conflict between England and its thirteen American colonies.

Chapter 7, Conflict with Britain, describes the growing number of disagreements between Great Britain and its colonies.

Chapter 8, The War for Independence, details how the colonists won their freedom from Britain.

UNIT 4 THE AMERICAN REVOLUTION

The American Revolution was a process that required twenty years to complete. At the end of the French and Indian War in 1763, American colonists were loyal subjects of Great Britain. By 1783, they were free and independent citizens of the United States of America.

The War for Independence began as a change in the hearts and minds of the people. Laws passed by Parliament and regulations approved by the king threatened liberties they had long enjoyed. Bonds of affection turned into chains meant to enslave them. The revolution in the colonists' feelings led to the Declaration of Independence. The War for Independence established the United States of America.

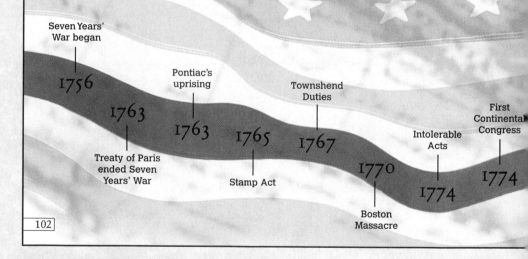

Seven Years' War began
1756

Pontiac's uprising
1763

1763
Treaty of Paris ended Seven Years' War

1765
Stamp Act

Townshend Duties
1767

1770
Boston Massacre

Intolerable Acts
1774

First Continental Congress
1774

102

Getting Started

Introduce the word *revolution* by reading aloud the title of Unit 4. Explain that the word *revolution* can describe a single and complete turn—for example, the *revolution* of Earth around the sun. The word can also mean a complete and far-reaching change in government or in ways of thinking and behaving. Consider why the election of a new leader is not a revolution, but the replacement of a king or queen by an elected leader is a revolution. Discuss with students other political revolutions with which they are familiar.

Ask a volunteer to read aloud the two paragraphs on page 102. Which meaning of the word *revolution* is used in the two paragraphs? When did the *revolution* described in this unit begin? When did it end?

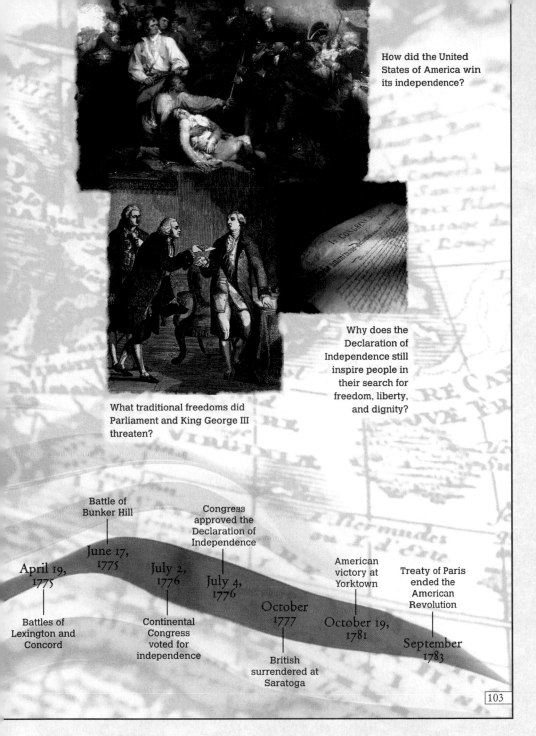

How did the United States of America win its independence?

Why does the Declaration of Independence still inspire people in their search for freedom, liberty, and dignity?

What traditional freedoms did Parliament and King George III threaten?

Battle of Bunker Hill

Congress approved the Declaration of Independence

April 19, 1775

June 17, 1775

July 2, 1776

July 4, 1776

October 1777

American victory at Yorktown

Treaty of Paris ended the American Revolution

October 19, 1781

September 1783

Battles of Lexington and Concord

Continental Congress voted for independence

British surrendered at Saratoga

103

Collage Answers

Ask students to copy the three questions on page 103 into their history notebooks. As they read the unit, have them record their answers to each question.

1 The United States won its independence by defeating Great Britain in a war.

2 Parliament and King George III threatened such traditional freedoms as the right of the colonists to be taxed only by their elected representatives.

3 The Declaration of Independence inspires people in their search for freedom, liberty, and dignity, because it is based on broad principles that apply to all people. It defends every person's right to get rid of an oppressive government.

Timeline Extension

To preview Unit 4, ask students to use the timeline to answer these questions:

- What does the timeline suggest about relations between colonists and England? (The timeline includes references to a massacre and several battles, suggesting a hostile relationship.)

- In what year did Congress declare independence? (1776)

- Based on events on the timeline, how did Britain respond to the Declaration of Independence? (with war)

- In what year did Americans officially gain their independence? (1783)

Measuring Time

Explain to students that the timeline covers both chapters in this unit. Chapter 7 focuses on events from 1756 to 1774. Chapter 8 describes events from 1775 to 1783. According to the two paragraphs describing Unit 4, what events marked the beginning and end of the American Revolution? (end of French and Indian War in 1763 and the Treaty of Paris in 1783) Explain to students that in Europe, the war was called the Seven Years War, but in the colonies it was known as the French and Indian War.

7 CONFLICT WITH BRITAIN

Chapter Summary

Refer to page 118 in the student book for a summary of Chapter 7.

Related Transparencies

T-5 The World

T-7 The 13 Original Colonies

Key Blacklines

Biography
Samuel Adams

Primary Source
The Boston Massacre: A British Account

Picturing History

The picture on page 104 shows the Boston Tea Party in 1770. It shows colonists disguised as Native Americans dumping boxes of tea into the harbor to protest a British tax on tea. What does the drawing suggest about relations between Britain and the colonists?

DVD Extension

Encourage students to use the reading comprehension, vocabulary reinforcement, and interactive timeline activities on the student DVD.

Getting Focused

Skim this chapter to predict what you will be learning.

- Read the lesson titles and subheadings.
- Look at the illustrations and read the captions.
- Examine the maps.
- Review the vocabulary words and terms.

Sometimes disputes over property and rights cause people to set strict limits: This is mine, and that is yours. As you read, look for signs of limits that led to conflict and how the conflicts were resolved. Take notes in your notebook.

Pre-Reading Discussion

1 Ask students to read the chapter title aloud and discuss its meaning. What do the pictures in the chapter suggest about who is in conflict with Britain? (the French initially and then the colonists)

2 After students complete each bulleted direction on page 104, ask students to read aloud the last paragraph on page 104. What does it suggest about the causes of the conflicts discussed in the chapter and the outcomes of those conflicts? Ask students to record their ideas in their journal. As students read and discuss the chapter, encourage them to revise or correct their ideas.

The Expanding Empire

Thinking on Your Own

Read the Focus Your Reading questions and discuss possible answers with a partner. Skim through this lesson looking for clues. In your notebook, predict answers for each question.

In the 1750s, **Great Britain** and France clashed over control of the Ohio Valley. The Virginia Colony granted land there to companies. Farmers wanted to buy farms and settle there. The French were determined to keep control of the Ohio Valley because of its valuable fur trade. French officials in Canada and their Native American allies tried to stop British settlement.

> **focus your reading**
>
> How did the French try to block British expansion?
>
> How did the Treaty of Paris change the map of North America?
>
> Why did Parliament pass the Stamp Act?
>
> **vocabulary**
>
> Great Britain   proclamation
> militia   Parliament

Frontier Fighting

To block British expansion, the French built Fort Duquesne on the Ohio River. In 1754, the governor of Virginia sent Colonel George Washington and forty **militia**, or volunteer, soldiers to destroy the fort. A much larger force of French troops and their Native American allies attacked Washington's small army. The Virginians surrendered and returned home.

George Washington in the Ohio Valley

Lesson Summary

In the 1750s, Britain and France competed for control of the Ohio Valley. By 1754, the two nations were at war in North America. Britain won that war and greatly increased not only the size of its American empire but also its debts. To pay for the war and keep the peace with Native Americans, the British passed a Stamp Act and tried to keep colonists east of the Appalachian Mountains.

Lesson Objective

Students will learn about how Britain's victory in the French and Indian War led to conflict with colonists in North America.

Focus Your Reading Answers

1 The French tried to block British expansion by building Fort Duquesne on the Ohio River.

2 The Treaty of Paris changed the map of North America by turning over to Britain all of France's territory in North America east of the Mississippi River, except New Orleans. France also gave up its claims to Canada.

3 Parliament passed the Stamp Act, because it insisted that the colonists pay part of the cost of defending the colonies.

Lesson Vocabulary

Discuss the meaning of each vocabulary word. Begin by focusing on the term *Great Britain*. Explain that in the early 1600s, the term *Great Britain* referred to England and Scotland. Both were ruled by the same king. In 1707, the two kingdoms were joined into a "United Kingdom" known as the "Kingdom of Great Britain."

In the 1700s, *Great Britain* was governed by not only a king but also a *Parliament*. *Parliament* was the group that made laws in Great Britain. It was divided into two parts: an elected House of Commons and a House of Lords.

Parliament could not only make laws but also issue *proclamations*. A *proclamation* is an official public announcement.

In North America, Great Britain relied on not only the British army to protect colonists but also a colonial *militia*. A *militia* is an army made up of ordinary citizens. Discuss related words such as *military* (related to the armed forces) and *militant* (warlike).

Picturing History

The painting at the top of page 106 shows the results of a surprise attack by the French and the Native Americans on General Edward Braddock and his troops. Braddock is the man in the red uniform on the ground. He was injured in the battle and died soon after of his wounds. Why did the uniforms worn by the British soldiers make them easy targets for a surprise attack? Why did the colonists call the British "lobsterbacks"?

Picturing History

The illustration at the bottom of page 106 shows the British capture of Quebec. The French thought the city was impossible to capture, because it was built on high, steep cliffs. They did not expect the British to land a few miles north of the city and scale the cliffs at night along an unguarded path. The British then moved west of the city to the Plains of Abraham where they faced the French in battle.

Ask students to compare the two surprise attacks—one by the French and the other by the British. What similarities do they notice? How do they account for differences?

When news of Washington's defeat reached Britain, the government sent General Edward Braddock with a larger army to Virginia. Joined by Virginia militiamen, Braddock's troops set out early in 1755 for Fort Duquesne. They were attacked by surprise. Shooting from behind trees and boulders, the French and Native American fighters nearly wiped out the British. General Braddock died on the battlefield.

General Braddock's troops were ambushed in 1755.

The French and Indian War

Braddock's defeat triggered a full-scale war between England and France. They fought in Europe as well as in the colonies. Determined to drive their rival out of North America, the British attacked the French in Canada. They captured Quebec in 1758. That year, British and colonial forces also seized control of Fort Duquesne, which they renamed Fort Pitt— present-day Pittsburgh. In 1760, the British captured Montreal, Canada's second major city. That brought the fighting in North America to an end.

The British captured Quebec in 1758.

106

In Europe, the war was known as the Seven Years' War (1756–1763). Fighting there ended three years later. In the peace treaty signed in Paris, France gave up its claim to Canada.

Extension

General Edward Braddock was a professional soldier. He led an army of 1,400 British soldiers and 450 Virginia volunteers against French soldiers and Native American warriors. Braddock only knew the European ways of waging a war. Neither he nor his soldiers had ever been taught to take advantage of the forest in a battle. Ask a group of students to gather information about the style of fighting used by the French and their Native American allies. How did they use the forests to their advantage? Invite a second group of students to gather information about the way the British waged war. Encourage both groups to share with the class the advantages and disadvantages of both approaches to war.

The Treaty of Paris also turned over to Britain all of France's territory east of the Mississippi, except the town of New Orleans.

Defending the British Empire

The war with France greatly increased Britain's territory in North America. It also created problems. The war nearly doubled Britain's national debt. Although nearly broke, Britain had to pay for additional soldiers to defend the new territory. The Native Americans also were of concern. In 1763, Pontiac, an Ottawa chief, led an uprising of native groups in the West. They burned British forts and attacked colonists who settled on Native American land.

stop and think

Turn over the book and discuss with a partner what you have learned about 1) events that led to the Treaty of Paris, and 2) how the treaty changed the map of North America. Write a three-sentence summary of your discussion in your notebook.

Stop and Think

The three-sentence summaries should reflect an understanding that the capture of Quebec, Fort Duquesne, and Montreal by the British led to the Treaty of Paris of 1763. Because of those British victories, France gave up its claims to Canada and the Ohio Valley.

Map Extension

Ask students to use the map on page 107 to answer the following questions:

- What does green mean on this map? (shows the original 13 colonies)

- What does orange show? (other British territory)

- Why do you think the mapmakers did not show all British territory in a single color? (They wanted to highlight the territory the British won during the war and now set aside for Native Americans.)

- What does blue indicate on this map? (Spanish territory)

- Why is the red line important? (It shows the Proclamation Line of 1763.)

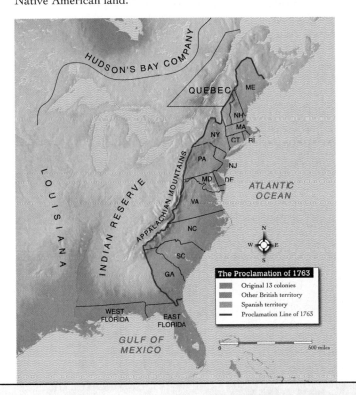

The Proclamation of 1763
- Original 13 colonies
- Other British territory
- Spanish territory
- — Proclamation Line of 1763

0   500 miles

107

Extension

Ask students why most of the land west of the Appalachian Mountains is labeled "Indian Reserve." A *reserve* is land set aside for a particular purpose. For what purpose was the land west of the Appalachians set aside? (Native Americans)

Chief Pontiac met with British Major Gladwyn in 1763 to discuss peace.

The British government acted quickly. To restore peace with the native people, King George III issued the **Proclamation** of 1763. It prohibited colonists from settling on Native American land west of the Appalachian Mountains. The British government insisted that the colonists should help keep the peace and pay part of the cost of defense. The colonists were forced to pay the salaries of soldiers, feed them, and provide them with housing. In 1764, the British **Parliament**, or legislature, passed the Sugar Act. It placed import duties, or fees, on sugar and other products shipped into the colonies. The Stamp Act of 1765 taxed legal documents and other printed matter.

Stamps were required on many taxed items.

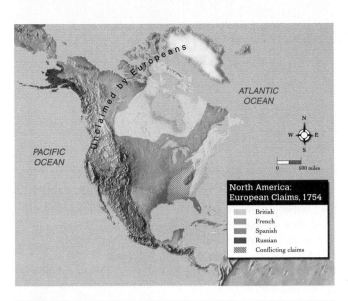

North America:
European Claims, 1754

- British
- French
- Spanish
- Russian
- Conflicting claims

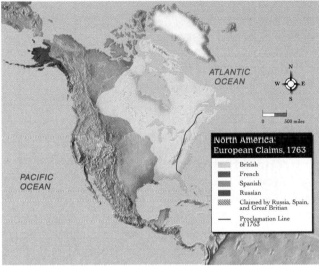

North America:
European Claims, 1763

- British
- French
- Spanish
- Russian
- Claimed by Russia, Spain, and Great Britian
- Proclamation Line of 1763

Putting It All Together

Review the predictions you made for the Focus Your Reading
questions. Make changes, if needed, based on what you now
know. Write your answers in your notebook.

Map Extension

Ask students to use the two
maps on page 109 to answer
the following questions:

- Which European
  countries claimed land in
  North America in 1754?
  (Britain, France, Spain,
  Russia)

- Which European
  countries claimed land in
  North America in 1763?
  (Britain, Spain, Russia)

- What part of the
  continent was claimed by
  more than one nation in
  1754? (Ohio Valley)

- What part of the
  continent was claimed by
  more than one nation in
  1763? (the northwest
  part of the continent—
  excluding Alaska)

- What European nations
  made the greatest gains
  in territory between 1754
  and 1763? (Britain and
  Spain)

Map Extension

Have students use the two maps on this page and a political map of the United States
today to answer the following questions:

- In 1754, which European country claimed what is now your state?

- In 1763, which European country claimed your state?

- Based on information provided on the maps, to what extent did the outcome of the
  French and Indian War affect your state?

Lesson Summary

After the French and Indian War, policies that seemed reasonable to the British provoked anger in the colonies. The first large protest was over the Stamp Act. Parliament repealed the law in 1766, but insisted on its right to tax the colonies. In 1767, Parliament passed new taxes and once again the colonists protested. Feelings ran so high in Boston that the British government sent troops to maintain order. On March 5, 1770, a mob attacked the soldiers with clubs and snowballs. In the confusion, five colonists were killed. The riot came to be known as the Boston Massacre.

Lesson Objective

Students will learn how and why the colonists increasingly opposed British policies.

Focus Your Reading Answers

1 The colonists opposed the Stamp Act because it threatened their right to be taxed only by elected representatives to colonial assemblies.

2 Charles Townshend proposed a tax on such imports as glass, lead, paint, paper, and tea.

3 The British tried to restore order in Boston by sending 4,000 troops to the city.

LESSON **2**

No Taxation Without Representation

Thinking on Your Own

Read the vocabulary words. As you read this lesson, use each word in a sentence of your own. Make sure that your sentences show the meaning of each word. Write your sentences in your notebook.

Policies that seemed reasonable to the king and Parliament outraged the colonists. The Proclamation of 1763 angered those who wanted land in the Ohio Valley. Parliament had required importers to pay duties before, but the laws were seldom enforced. This time Parliament intended to collect the duties. It cracked down on **smuggling**—importing goods without paying duties. That reduced the profits of certain merchants. Most troubling of all was the Stamp Act.

focus your reading

Why did the colonists oppose the Stamp Act?

What was Charles Townshend's new tax plan?

How did Britain try to restore order in Boston?

vocabulary

smuggling   boycott

assemblies   repeal

Resistance to the Stamp Act was strong among merchants.

The Stamp Act Crisis

The tax imposed by the Parliament in the Stamp Act threatened a basic right. Until then, the colonists were taxed only by representatives they elected to their colonial **assemblies**, or legislatures. This time, they were taxed by Parliament, where they had no representatives.

Picturing History

Explain to students that the drawing on page 110 shows a protest over the Stamp Act. It was one of many demonstrations in the colonies.

What does the picture suggest about the way the colonists showed their anger with government? What does it suggest about which colonists took part in the protests?

Lesson Vocabulary

Introduce each vocabulary word. Point out that *smuggling* and *boycotts* were ways the colonists protested British policies. Colonists guilty of *smuggling* were secretly bringing into North America illegal goods or goods on which a tax must be paid. A *boycott* is an attempt to influence a government or business to make a change by refusing to buy certain goods or services.

The word *assembly* has many meanings. In this lesson, it refers to colonial legislatures. Members of a colonial *assembly* made laws for a colony. Parliaments and *assemblies* can not only make laws but also *repeal* them. *Repeal* means to overturn or get rid of a law.

The colonists protested against the Stamp Act. "No taxation without representation," they insisted. In Boston, a mob ruined the house of the lieutenant governor, who supported the act. Nine colonies sent delegates to a Stamp Act Congress in New York City. The Stamp Act Congress sent a declaration to Parliament defending the colonists' right to tax themselves. The colonists also agreed to **boycott**, or refuse to buy, English goods.

Stamp Act protestors in Boston wrecked the lieutenant governor's house.

Under pressure from British merchants, Parliament decided to **repeal** the Stamp Act in March 1766. However, it still insisted that it had the right to tax the colonies. The issue was far from settled.

The Townshend Duties

In 1767, Charles Townshend, the British finance minister, came up with a new tax plan. He noticed that the colonists did not object to duties collected at the port. They opposed only direct, or internal, taxes. Townshend asked Parliament to place import duties on more goods being shipped to the colonies. The new Townshend Revenue Act included duties on glass, lead, paint, paper, and tea.

The colonists saw this as just another attempt to tax them. This time they objected to any kind of taxes by Parliament. Once again the colonists stopped buying British goods. Instead, they bought smuggled goods. British officials accused John Hancock, a Boston merchant, of smuggling. They seized one of his ships. In protest, people in Boston rioted in the streets.

stop and think

Imagine that you hear an argument over the Stamp Act between a British member of Parliament and an American colonist. Write four or five lines of dialogue that you overheard.

Picturing History

The drawing on page 111 shows Stamp Act protestors in Boston. How is this drawing similar to the one on page 110? What differences do you notice?

Stop and Think

Dialogues should reflect the basic disagreement between Parliament and the colonists. The colonists maintained that only representatives elected to their colonial assembly could tax them. Parliament insisted that it represented all British citizens and therefore it had the right to tax the colonies.

Extension

Ask students to find out more about the Stamp Act Congress. Then have students use the information they gather to assume the role of one of the 27 delegates to the meeting in New York City. Encourage each participant to express his or her views in a brief speech to members of the Congress.

Crispus Attucks was killed in the Boston Massacre.

The Boston Massacre

To restore law and order, the British government sent troops to Boston. By late 1769, approximately 4,000 troops had arrived in a city that had only 15,000 residents. That created tension. Off-duty soldiers competed with citizens for jobs. Fights broke out. On March 5, 1770, a Boston mob attacked a detachment of troops with clubs and snowballs.

In the confusion, the troops fired into the crowd. Five rioters were killed, including Crispus Attucks, a former African American slave. Although little is known about Crispus Attucks, many people believe that he was the first death of the Revolutionary War.

Colonists rushed to Boston from nearby towns to protest the Boston Massacre, as it was called. Colonial officials restored order by arresting the soldiers accused of firing the shots. They were promised a fair trial in Boston. Britain withdrew the remainder of the troops from the city.

Putting It All Together

At the beginning of this chapter, you looked for the strict limits, or boundaries, set by the colonists and Parliament as signs of conflict. Write a paragraph describing the limits set by each side over taxes and import duties.

Extension

John Adams, a lawyer (and later the second president of the United States), helped win acquittal for six of the British soldiers, even though he shared the views of the protestors. Sam Adams disagreed with his cousin John's stand. He called the incident a "plot to massacre the inhabitants of Boston" and used it to encourage further protests.

Ask half of the class to find out more about John Adams and why he agreed to represent the British soldiers. Ask the other half to gather information about Sam Adams and the stand he took. Have both groups of students share their findings by debating one another as to whether the Boston Massacre was really a massacre.

Read a Primary Source

The Boston Massacre: An American Account

On the night of March 5, 1770, British troops fired into a Boston crowd, killing five people and wounding others. The following is an account of what happened. It was published in Boston shortly after the event. The author was not present, however, he interviewed people who were there that night.

reading for understanding

According to this writer, who began the fight?

How did the crowd respond?

What orders did Preston give the soldiers?

66 . . . the ringing of the meetinghouse bell brought out a number of the inhabitants, who . . . were naturally led to King Street . . . [where they joined] a number of boys, round the sentry at the Custom House. . . . There was much foul language between them, and some of them, in consequence of his pushing at them with his bayonet, threw snowballs at him. . . .

"The officer on guard was Captain Preston, who with seven or eight soldiers, with firearms and charged bayonets, issued from the guardhouse, and in great haste posted himself and his soldiers in front of the Custom House. . . . In passing to this station the soldiers pushed several persons with their bayonets. . . . This occasioned some snowballs to be thrown at them, which seems to have been the only provocation that was given. . . .

"Captain Preston is said to have ordered them to fire, and to have repeated that order. One gun was first; then others in succession, and with deliberation, till ten or a dozen guns were fired. . . . By which means eleven persons were killed or wounded. . . ."

From *A Short Narrative of the Horrid Massacre in Boston,* (Boston, 1770).

Reading for Understanding

1 The British prompted the fight by pushing several persons with their bayonets.

2 The crowd responded with snowballs and foul language.

3 Captain Preston ordered the soldiers to fire several times.

113

Extension

Have students use this primary source account and the drawing on page 112 to write a news story about the Boston Massacre. A good news story answers the following questions:

- Who is the story about?
- What happened?
- Where did it happen?
- When did it happen?

- Why did it happen?
- How did it happen?
- Why was it important?

In Defense of Liberty

Lesson Summary

The conflict between the British and the colonists died down after the violence in Boston. Parliament repealed several laws and softened its stand on the Proclamation of 1763. Then, in 1773, Parliament passed a new tax law, this time a tax on tea. Bostonians responded by dumping the tea into the harbor. Parliament then passed a series of laws to punish the people of Boston. To protest those laws, the colonies sent delegates to a Continental Congress in Philadelphia. The Congress voted to boycott goods from Britain.

Lesson Objective

Students will learn how and why new protests between 1773 and 1774 further divided Britain and the colonists.

Focus Your Reading Answers

1 The colonists opposed the Tea Act because they believed it was Parliament's way of tricking them into paying the tax.

2 The Intolerable Acts were laws Parliament passed to punish Boston and Massachusetts Colony.

3 The colonists responded to the Intolerable Acts by rallying behind Massachusetts. They organized a Continental Congress to decide what to do next. The Congress agreed to boycott British goods and to defend themselves against future attacks by the British Army.

Thinking on Your Own

Divide one page in your notebook into top, middle, and bottom sections. Entitle the sections "Tea Act," "Intolerable Acts," and "Continental Congress." As you read this lesson, write two questions that you have about each topic.

A period of calm followed the violence in Boston. Parliament repealed the Townshend Duties, except for the tax on tea. It softened the Proclamation of 1763, allowing settlers to move into eastern Tennessee and Kentucky. For many colonists, this was too little, too late. They refused to pay the tax on English tea, smuggling in Dutch tea instead. Leaders in each colony set up Committees of Correspondence to keep in touch with other colonies. One misstep by Parliament could start a new round of protest.

focus your reading

Why did the colonists oppose the Tea Act?

What were the Intolerable Acts?

How did the colonists respond to those acts?

vocabulary

Intolerable Acts

delegates

Samuel Adams founded the Committees of Correspondence.

The Tea Act

A misstep came in 1773, when Parliament passed the Tea Act. This act helped the East India Company, a British trading company in India, cut its costs. The act allowed the company to sell directly to the colonies. It no longer had to ship the tea to London, where merchants charged a handling fee. The company could undersell smugglers, even after the colonists had paid the tea tax.

Lesson Vocabulary

Explain that the word *act* is used in this lesson as a synonym for the word *law*. The word *intolerable* means unbearable, impossible, even painful. Discuss what kind of a law would be considered *intolerable*. Ask students who is more likely to call a law intolerable—those who enact the law or those who are the target of the law.

A *delegate* is a person appointed or elected to represent others. Each *delegate* to the Continental Congress represented a particular colony at the meeting.

Dressed as Native Americans, protestors dumped tea into Boston Harbor.

Many colonists believed the Tea Act was Parliament's way of tricking them into paying that tax. When the company's ships arrived, they refused to unload the tea. In Boston, the protestors took more direct action. On December 16, 1773, they boarded the ship and dumped the tea into the harbor. They called it the Boston Tea Party.

The Intolerable Acts

For Parliament, dumping the tea was the last straw. It moved quickly to punish Boston and the Massachusetts Colony. It wanted to set an example that would keep other colonies in line. Parliament passed a set of laws that the colonists called the **Intolerable Acts**. These laws

- closed the port of Boston until the tea was paid for
- allowed Boston to hold only one town meeting each year
- permitted any British official accused of a crime to be sent to England for trial
- required Massachusetts to house British troops in empty houses, barns, or buildings at the colony's expense

stop and think

Do you agree or disagree with the patriots that the term "Intolerable Acts" is a good description of those acts of Parliament? Why? Discuss your reason with a partner.

Stop and Think

Responses will vary but should show an understanding that the Intolerable Acts were meant to punish the people of Massachusetts.

Extensions

1 Explain that the colonists who opposed British policies called themselves *patriots*. A patriot is someone who loves and defends his or her country. What name might the British use to describe those who opposed their policies? (traitors)

2 Why do you think people in Virginia, New York, Pennsylvania, and other colonies came to Boston's aid? What does your answer suggest about the changes that were taking place in the colonies in the 1760s and early 1770s? Were those changes revolutionary?

Extension

In the days before telegrams, telephones, radio, television, or the Internet, people got their news from handwritten letters carried aboard ships or by horseback. If colonists in Massachusetts wanted their neighbors to know what the British were doing in Boston, they had to write letters to the other colonies. As the conflict between Britain and the colonies grew, the colonists organized special groups known as Committees of Correspondence to keep in touch with like-minded people in other colonies. Samuel Adams organized the first formal committee in Boston in 1764.

Ask students to use the Internet or the library to find out how these committees got out the news and rallied opposition to British laws. Have students share their findings with the class. How was the method used by the committees in the 1770s similar to the use of the Internet by political parties and political action groups today? How do you account for differences?

At the same time, Parliament passed the Quebec Act. This law shifted control of land in the Ohio Valley to Britain's new colony in Quebec. That angered colonists in Pennsylvania and Virginia, who wanted that land for farms.

The Continental Congress

The punishment of Massachusetts did not have the effect that Parliament wanted. The other colonies rallied behind Massachusetts. Each colony agreed to send **delegates**, or representatives, to a Continental Congress to decide what to do next. Patrick Henry, a delegate from Virginia, said he went to the meeting "not as a Virginian, but as an American."

Patrick Henry represented Virginia at the First Continental Congress.

Meeting in Philadelphia in 1774, the Continental Congress drew up a list of rights that Parliament should respect. The delegates also agreed to a new boycott against British-made goods. But they were not ready to cut their ties to Britain. They declared their loyalty to the king, but they refused to obey Parliament. They also agreed to defend themselves from any future attack by the British army.

Putting It All Together

With a partner, compare the questions you wrote about the Tea Act, the Intolerable Acts, and the Continental Congress. Together write possible answers to each question.

Biography

Patrick Henry (1736–1799)

On March 23, 1775, Patrick Henry addressed the Virginia Assembly. He urged the reluctant delegates to prepare for war against Britain. "Gentlemen may cry, peace, peace—but there is no peace. The war is actually begun. . . . Is life so dear, or peace so sweet, as to be purchased at the price of chains and slavery? Forbid it, Almighty God! I know not what course others may take; but as for me, give me liberty or give me death!" His motion to create a Virginia militia won by a solid majority.

Patrick Henry was born in western Virginia in 1736. He received little formal education and barely passed his law exam. He learned about the power of the human voice by listening to revival preachers. His magic with words made him a very successful trial lawyer and a vote-getting politician. Elected to the Virginia Assembly in 1764, he represented the common people of western Virginia. In the assembly, he became a thorn in the side of Virginia's aristocratic planters.

Patrick Henry realized earlier than most Virginians that Parliament posed a serious threat to the colonies. In 1765, he led the opposition to the Stamp Act. He persuaded the Virginia Assembly to defy the law. He stepped forward again in 1774 to protest against the Intolerable Acts. He went to Philadelphia with George Washington and other Virginian delegates to serve in the Continental Congress. There he became good friends with Sam and John Adams, who shared his views about the likelihood of war. He returned from Philadelphia to give his famous "Liberty or Death" speech.

Patrick Henry spent the remainder of his life serving Virginia. He commanded the Virginia militia in 1775, and in 1776 was elected the first governor of the State of Virginia. In 1787, he opposed the U.S. Constitution on the grounds that it took too much power away from Virginia and other states. He died on June 6, 1799, active in Virginia politics to the end.

117

Biography Extension

Ask a volunteer to read aloud a part of Patrick Henry's famous "Liberty or Death" speech. Discuss how Henry's words rallied support against the British. Which words or phrases in the speech are most memorable? For what reasons?

Bio Facts

- Born May 29, 1736, in Hanover County, Virginia.

- Was educated at home by his father who taught him to read Latin.

- Patrick Henry studied law on his own and in 1760 took his attorney's examination in Williamsburg before a committee of lawyers.

- In 1763, in arguing a case in Hanover County, Henry proclaimed that a king who would veto a law made by a locally elected assembly was "a tyrant who forfeits the allegiance of his subjects."

- A year after his election to the Virginia assembly in 1764, Henry spoke against the Stamp Act.

- In 1774, Henry protested the Intolerable Acts and attended the First Continental Congress.

- In March 1775, he urged his fellow Virginians to arm in self-defense, with the words: "I know not what course others may take; but as for me, give me liberty or give me death."

- In 1775, Henry commanded the Virginia militia.

- Henry was a member of the Virginia Committee of Correspondence, a delegate to the Virginia Convention, and a delegate to the convention in 1776 that wrote a new constitution for Virginia as an independent state.

- He was the first governor of the commonwealth of Virginia under its new constitution. He served three terms as governor of Virginia.

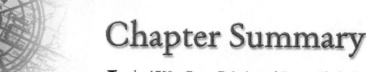

Chapter Summary

Chapter Review

1 Paragraphs will vary but should reflect an understanding that the arguments against the Stamp Act were arguments that reappeared in various forms throughout the late 1760s and early 1770s.

2 Editorials will vary, but they should show an understanding that the Proclamation of 1763 was unpopular with the colonists.

3 Points at which the British set limits include the Proclamation of 1763, the Stamp Act, the Townshend Duties, the Tea Act, and the Intolerable Acts. Points at which the colonists set limits include the Stamp Act protests and the Stamp Act Congress, the Boston Massacre, the Boston Tea Party, and the Continental Congress.

4 Answers will vary.

In the 1750s, **Great Britain** and France clashed over control of the Ohio Valley. France defeated a Virginia **militia** led by Colonel George Washington. This led to the French and Indian War. The Treaty of Paris gave Canada and most of France's territory east of the Mississippi to the British. The **Proclamation** of 1763 prohibited colonists from settling west of the Appalachian Mountains. To raise money, the British **Parliament** taxed the colonists.

The colonists insisted that only their elected **assemblies** had the right to tax them. In protest, they agreed to **boycott** British goods. Under pressure from British merchants, Parliament chose to **repeal** the Stamp Act. To raise money, it placed new import duties on goods shipped to the colonies. It also cracked down on **smuggling** in Boston.

In 1773, many colonists saw the Tea Act as Parliament's way to trick them into paying a tax. When tea arrived in Boston, protestors held the Boston Tea Party. Parliament passed the **Intolerable Acts** to punish the people of Massachusetts. To protest these acts, the colonies sent **delegates** to a Continental Congress in Philadelphia. The colonists boycotted British goods.

Chapter Review

1 Go back to the argument over the Stamp Act that you overheard in Stop and Think for Lesson 2. Knowing what happened in the years following that act, write a paragraph defending one of the positions.

2 The Proclamation of 1763 set limits on where colonists could live. Write an editorial arguing against this law.

3 Describe at least three times when Britain and the colonies set limits with each other between 1763 and 1774.

4 Do any of your questions from Putting It All Together for Lesson 3 remain unanswered? If so, work with a partner to compile a list of possible resources that you can use to answer these questions. Find the answers to the questions.

Novel Connections

Below is a list of books that relate to the time period covered in this chapter. The numbers in parentheses indicate the related Thematic Strands of the National Council for the Social Studies (NCSS).

David A. Adler. *B. Franklin, Printer.* Holiday House, 2002. (III, V, VI)

Natalie S. Bober. *Countdown to Independence: A Revolution of Ideas in England and Her American Colonies: 1760–1776.* Atheneum Books, 2001. (II, VI, X)

Russell Freedman. *Give Me Liberty!: The Story of the Declaration of Independence.* Holiday House, 2002. (VI, X)

Betsy Maestro. *Struggle for a Continent: The French and Indian Wars, 1689–1763* (The American Story series). HarperCollins, 2000. (I, II, IV)

Ann Rinaldi. *Or Give Me Death: A Novel of Patrick Henry's Family* (Great Episodes series). Gulliver Books/Harcourt Children's Books, 2003. (I, IV, X)

Skill Builder

Identifying Propaganda

Information presented in a way to win people over to a point of view is called propaganda. Propaganda may include untrue or biased statements. It may also present the truth, but not the whole truth. When looking at words or images, keep in mind the following questions:

- What is the intent of the author?
- Is the author presenting opinion as fact?
- Does the article, book, or picture present both sides of the issue?
- Does the style appeal more to emotions than to reason?

Paul Revere made this engraving of the clash in Boston on March 5, 1770, between British soldiers and townspeople. The engraving is entitled *The Bloody Massacre*. It shows a British officer ordering his troops to fire into the crowd. The poem printed at the bottom of the engraving begins:

Analyze Revere's print for its propaganda value by answering the following questions:

1 What was Revere trying to accomplish with this engraving?

2 Does the engraving appeal primarily to emotion or reason?

3 How is Crispus Attuchs portrayed in this image? How does this differ from the image on page 112? How is this propoganda?

4 Do the title and poem try to win over the reader to a particular point of view? Which view?

Unhappy Boston! See thy sons deplore,

Thy hallowe'd Walks besmear'd with guiltless Gore;

While faithless P[resto]n, and his savage Bands

With murd'rous Rancour stretch their bloody hands;

Like fierce Babarians grinning o'er their Prey,

Approve the Carnage, and enjoy the Day.

Skill Builder

1 Revere was trying to rally opposition to British policies.

2 The engraving appeals primarily to emotion.

3 The engraving shows Attucks as a white man. The image on page 112 shows him as an African American.

4 The title and the poem try to persuade the viewer that the British were in the wrong.

Extension

Ask students how a British soldier might have changed the engraving to represent his point of view.

Classroom Discussion

Discuss with students some of the broader topics covered in this chapter by focusing on causes and effects of the events described.

- What were the causes of the French and Indian War? What were its effects?

- What were the causes of the Proclamation of 1763? What were its effects?

- What were the causes of the tax laws the British passed in the late 1760s and early 1770s? What were their effects?

- How did each of these events bring Britain and its colonies closer to armed conflict?

Chapter Summary

Refer to page 134 in the student book for a summary of Chapter 8.

Picturing History

The photograph on page 120 shows men today reenacting a battle in the War for Independence. They are dressed in uniforms similar to those worn by soldiers in the Continental army. What does the picture suggest about the conflict between Britain and its American colonies in the mid-1700s? (It was becoming increasingly violent.)

Chapter

8 THE WAR FOR INDEPENDENCE

Getting Focused

Skim this chapter to predict what you will be learning.

- Read the lesson titles and subheadings.
- Look at the illustrations and read the captions.
- Examine the maps.
- Review the vocabulary words and terms.

Think about the consequences of not being able to resolve a conflict peacefully. In your notebook write three questions that you have about the War for Independence.

Pre-Reading Discussion

1 Have students complete each bulleted direction on page 120. Remind them that Chapter 7 focused on a growing conflict between the British and their American colonies. As students read Chapter 8, ask them to look for reasons the protests turned to war in the mid-1700s.

2 Explain to students that the word *independence* means freedom from outside control. Ask them to write a definition of a "war for independence." What does the term suggest about the reasons for the war? What does it suggest about the consequences of a victory? Have students record their ideas in their journal and revise their answers as they read the chapter.

From Peaceful Protest to Violence

Thinking on Your Own

Create a two-column chart in your notebook. On one side write the three Focus Your Reading questions. As you read, fill in the other side with the answers. Use the vocabulary in your answers.

In their struggle with Parliament, the colonists looked to King George III for help. The king, however, chose to side with Parliament. He considered the colonists to be in rebellion. "Blows must decide whether they are to be subject to the Country or Independent," he told a British official. The king demanded that rebel leaders in Massachusetts be arrested. He appointed General Thomas Gage as the colony's new governor.

focus your reading

Why did British troops march to Concord?

Who did the Continental Congress ask for help?

Why did the British leave Boston?

vocabulary

patriots

minutemen

redcoats

Olive Branch Petition

Continental army

Paul Revere raised the alarm of approaching British troops.

121

Lesson Vocabulary

Discuss the meaning of each vocabulary word. Explain that a *patriot* is someone who loves his or her country and is willing to defend it. The colonists called themselves *patriots*. Would the British agree?

Remind students that a militia is a volunteer army—an army made up of ordinary citizens. Members of the Massachusetts militia called themselves *minutemen* because they boasted that they could be ready to fight at a minute's notice.

Ask students why the Americans called British soldiers *redcoats*. (The jackets of their uniforms were bright red.)

Explain that when someone "holds out an olive branch," he or she is trying to make peace with a rival. The idea dates back to ancient Greece. A petition is a formal request to a ruler or government official. Ask students what they think the term *Olive Branch Petition* means. Who might have written it? To whom might it be addressed?

The army the colonists organized in 1775 is known as the *Continental army*, because it included soldiers from almost every colony in British North America.

Lesson Summary

King George III believed that the colonists were engaged in a rebellion and ordered the arrest of rebel leaders in Massachusetts. That order led to the Battles of Lexington and Concord in April of 1775. In May, the Second Continental Congress tried to avoid a war by declaring their loyalty to the king, but members also organized an army. In June, the patriots fought a second battle against the British, this time in Boston.

Lesson Objective

Students will learn how Americans turned from relatively peaceful protests to violence in a growing conflict with Britain.

Focus Your Reading Answers

1 British troops marched to Concord to capture the leaders of the patriots and destroy their military supplies.

2 The Continental Congress asked King George III for help.

3 The British left Boston because General Washington mounted cannons on the hills above the place where the British army was stationed.

DVD Extension

Encourage students to use the reading comprehension, vocabulary reinforcement, and interactive timeline activities on the student DVD.

Picturing History

The British had hoped to surprise the minutemen by reaching Lexington before dawn. They arrived as planned, but the minutemen were waiting for them. The British commander ordered the minutemen to go home, but they stood their ground. Suddenly a shot rang out and the British responded by opening fire. They killed eight colonists and wounded ten more. Why do you think that first shot has become known as "the shot heard 'round the world"?

Picturing History

The British had hoped to surprise the minutemen by reaching Lexington before dawn. They arrived as planned, but the minutemen were waiting for them. The British commander ordered the minutemen to go home, but they stood their ground. Suddenly a shot rang out and the British responded by opening fire. They killed eight colonists and wounded ten more. Why do you think that first shot has become known as "the shot heard 'round the world"?

Picturing History

Captain John Parker was a farmer elected by his neighbors to lead the minutemen in Lexington. The words he said on the morning of the battle are carved on the monument: "Stand your ground. Don't fire unless fired upon, but if they mean to have a war, let it begin here." Ask students what Parker's words suggest about the way he and his men viewed the conflict with Britain.

Lexington and Concord

In Boston, General Gage ordered British troops to capture the leaders of the **patriots**, those who favored independence, and to destroy their military supplies. Gage believed that the patriots were hiding supplies in the town of Concord. The soldiers set out

A monument recalls the words of Captain John Parker at the Battle of Lexington.

for Concord on the morning of April 19, 1775. Paul Revere, who learned of their plans, rode ahead with Dr. Samuel Prescott and William Dawes to warn the patriots.

At Lexington, the British troops fired on the **minutemen**, or colonial militia, gathered there. They killed eight men. At Concord, they burned the supplies the colonists had not managed to remove. By then, hundreds of militia armed with muskets had set out for Concord. They killed seventy-three **redcoats**—the nickname given the British soldiers—and wounded dozens more as the patriots marched back to Boston.

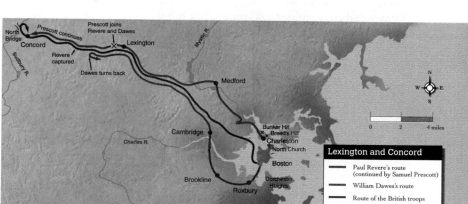

Lexington and Concord

— Paul Revere's route (continued by Samuel Prescott)
— William Dawes's route
— Route of the British troops

Map Extension

Ask students to use the map on page 122 to answer the following questions:

- Whose route is shown in blue? (the route followed by Paul Revere and continued by Samuel Prescott)

- Whose route is shown in purple? (the route followed by William Dawes)

- Where did Dawes and Revere meet? (west of Lexington)

- What happened at that meeting? (Prescott joined Revere and Dawes.)

- Which of the three men reached Concord? (Prescott) What happened to the other two men? (Revere was captured and Dawes turned back.)

Patriots and British troops skirmished at Concord's North Bridge.

When the British reached Concord, they found that most of the town's military supplies had been carted away. The town was quiet. On their way out of Concord, the British found a few minutemen waiting for them at North Bridge. The picture shows the Battle of Concord, which lasted about five minutes. At its end, two minutemen and three British soldiers were dead.

The British decided to return to Boston. Based on their encounter at the bridge, what do you think their trip was like? (Americans shot at the British all along the route—from windows and trees and from behind stone walls.)

The Olive Branch Petition

In May 1775, delegates met again in Philadelphia. This Second Continental Congress sent George III an **Olive Branch Petition**, or peace petition. It again declared the colonies' loyalty to the king and asked for his help in their struggle against Parliament. The majority of colonists still hoped for a peaceful settlement. Nevertheless, Congress created a **Continental army**, made George Washington its commander, and printed money to support the troops. Unlike each colony's militia, the Continental army enlisted soldiers from several colonies.

> **stop and think**
>
> Discuss with a partner the arguments the Second Continental Congress probably made in the Olive Branch Petition. Write two or three sentences in your notebook that summarize your discussion. If needed, find more information in the library or the Internet.

Battle of Bunker Hill

After Lexington and Concord, militia soldiers gathered on the hills around Boston. They surrounded the British army in the city. On June 17, 1775, General Gage led an attack against Breed's Hill. The British finally captured the hill, but at a terrible price. At the Battle of Bunker Hill—actually Breed's Hill—the British suffered 1,000 casualties. Patriot losses were less than half of British losses. The minutemen proved they had the courage to stand and fight.

The War for Independence 123

Stop and Think

Answers will vary but students are likely to suggest that those who wanted a peaceful settlement suggested turning to the king rather than the Parliament for help. They probably stressed the importance of their relationship with Britain. Those who favored independence probably focused on the importance of liberty and the rights of a free people.

Extension

Ask volunteers to read aloud two poems that recall the Battles of Lexington and Concord: "Paul Revere's Ride" by Henry Wadsworth Longfellow and "Concord Hymn" by Ralph Waldo Emerson. Explain that neither poet was alive in 1775. Each wrote his poem to inspire patriotic feelings rather than to give an accurate account of the events of April 19, 1775. How does each poem make you feel about men like Paul Revere? How does each poem make you feel about the War for Independence?

After retreating from Lexington, the British army occupied Boston. In response to anti-British feelings in the city, the British decided to fortify the Charlestown peninsula. When Americans learned of the plan, they decided to get there first. On June 16, 1775, they secretly constructed a dugout fort on Breed's Hill. From there they could look down on the British.

The next morning, the British set out to destroy the fort. As they marched up the hill, the Americans opened fire and forced back the British. A second try to take the hill also failed. The third attack succeeded only because the Americans ran out of ammunition. In the end, they were forced to retreat to nearby Bunker Hill (after which the battle was named).

The British won the battle, but their losses were so great (of the 2,400 British soldiers in Howe's command, 1,054 men were killed or wounded) that it was not much of a victory. Although the Americans lost the battle, it gave many of them hope. It showed them that Americans could defeat the British army in battle.

Scene from Battle of Bunker Hill

General Washington arrived two weeks later. He took command of the militia and enlisted them into the Continental army. That winter, he had cannons brought down from a fort captured from the British on Lake Champlain. With cannons mounted on the hills above them, the British army was forced to withdraw from Boston. They sailed to Nova Scotia in March 1776, taking 1,000 Loyalists with them.

Militiamen fire on British troops.

Putting It All Together

On a page in your notebook, write the heading "Successful Moves by the Minutemen." Under the heading, list at least three of those successes.

The picture at the bottom of page 124 shows how the minutemen attacked the British army. Compare and contrast their style of warfare with that of the French and Native Americans during the French and Indian War. (See Chapter 7, page 106). What similarities do you notice? How do you account for differences?

Putting It All Together

Lists should include the Battles of Lexington and Concord, the Battle of Bunker Hill, and the removal of the British army from Boston.

Read a Primary Source

Who Shot First?

On the morning of April 19, 1775, British troops killed eight minutemen at Lexington, Massachusetts. Their deaths became a rallying cry for the patriots who wanted independence from Great Britain. Who was responsible for firing the first shots in the War for Independence? The following are three eyewitness accounts of the "shot heard around the world."

reading for understanding

What was the American version of what happened?

How did the British commander's view differ?

Considering Lieutenant Gould's account, can we really know what happened that morning?

John Parker, Militia Commander

"Upon their [British soldiers] sudden approach, I immediately ordered our Militia to disperse and not to fire. Immediately said Troops made their appearance, and rushed furiously, fired upon and killed eight of our party, without receiving any provocation therefore from us."

What Happened on Lexington Green?
(Menlo Park, 1970).

Lieutenant Edward Gould, Captured British Officer

"On our arrival at that place, we saw a body of Provincial Troops armed, to the number of about sixty or seventy men; on our approach they dispersed, and soon after firing began; but which party fired first, I cannot exactly say, as our Troops rushed on shouting and huzzaing [cheering] previous to the firing."

What Happened on Lexington Green?
(Menlo Park, 1970).

Major John Pitcairn, British Commander

"When I came within about One Hundred Yards of them [the militia], they began to File off towards some stone Walls. . . . I instantly called to the Soldiers not to fire, but to surround them and disarm them. . . . Some of the Rebels who had jumped over the Wall, Fired Four or Five Shott at the soldiers. . . . Upon this the Light Infantry began a scattered Fire . . . contrary to the repeated orders both of me and the officers that were present."

What Happened on Lexington Green?
(Menlo Park, 1970).

Reading for Understanding

1 John Parker, the American militia commander, claimed that the British rushed the Americans and opened fire.

2 One British officer, Lieutenant Edward Gould, claimed he could not tell who fired first. The other, Major John Pitcairn, claimed that the rebels jumped over the wall and fired four or five shots at his men.

3 Answers will vary, but it seems likely that no one will ever know exactly what happened that morning.

Extension

The American writer Ralph Waldo Emerson was the first to call the first shot at Lexington "the shot heard 'round the world." Ask students to list some of the ways that shot was heard throughout the colonies, Britain, and other European nations. Encourage students to add to their list as they continue to read the chapter. Also discuss how "the shot" may have inspired wars for independence in other parts of the Americas as well as in Asia and Africa in the 1800s and 1900s.

Lesson Summary

In November 1775, the delegates to the Second Continental Congress learned that the king had rejected their Olive Branch Petition. He also called for a blockade of the colonies. The group had to decide what to do next. Thomas Paine suggested that they declare independence. On July 4, 1776, Congress approved a declaration of independence. It explained why the colonists were cutting off their ties to Great Britain.

Lesson Objective

Students will learn why the colonists decided to declare their independence from Britain.

Focus Your Reading Answers

1 The delegates concluded they could not rely on the king after he rejected their Olive Branch Petition and called the colonists "open and avowed enemies."

2 The pamphlet *Common Sense* called on Americans to declare their independence from Britain. The Second Continental Congress did just that by issuing the Declaration of Independence. The document reflects much of Thomas Paine's argument for independence.

3 Jefferson made the Declaration of Independence a statement about human rights by basing the document on broad principles that apply to all people.

LESSON **2**

Moving Toward Independence

Thinking on Your Own

Read the Focus Your Reading questions. With a partner, discuss what you know about the Declaration of Independence. In your notebook, write one sentence summarizing what you know.

In November 1775, the delegates at Philadelphia learned that the king had rejected the Olive Branch Petition and declared the colonists "open and avowed enemies." They soon learned that he had also blocked all trade with the colonies. A British fleet was on its way to enforce the **blockade**. The members of the Continental Congress had to choose between submitting to the king and Parliament or declaring independence.

King George III

focus your reading

Why did the delegates conclude that they could not rely on the king?

How are the pamphlet *Common Sense* and the Declaration of Independence related?

How did Jefferson make the Declaration of Independence a statement about human rights?

vocabulary

blockade   human rights
tyranny

Common Sense

The publication of *Common Sense* in January 1776, made that choice easier. Offering "simple facts, plain arguments, and common sense," this pamphlet was a slashing attack against King George III. Its author, Thomas Paine, called the king "a royal brute" who ruled by force. He insisted that the king had lost any claim to the colonists' loyalty. Paine urged the colonists to declare independence from Britain.

Common Sense was published in 1776.

Lesson Vocabulary

Discuss the meaning of each vocabulary word. Begin by explaining that a *blockade* is a measure or act that *blocks* entry to or exit from an area.

When people speak of *rights*, they are referring to the powers or privileges that individuals or groups hold in a society. *Human rights* are rights that all people share. The Declaration of Independence refers to such human rights as the right to life, liberty, and the pursuit of happiness. These rights do not belong just to Americans or people from Britain; they belong to all people everywhere.

The word *tyranny* is related to the word *tyrant*. A tyrant is a ruler who has no legal right to rule. He or she rules by oppressing or putting down the people. A *tyranny* is a government headed by a tyrant. In the Declaration of Independence, George III is viewed as a tyrant.

Thomas Paine put into words what many colonists were thinking. Few dared to say it so bluntly. *Common Sense* became a bestseller. It sold 120,000 copies in three months. Paine's message also had a political impact. One by one, the colonies instructed their delegates at Philadelphia to vote for independence.

stop and think

Imagine that you are listening to a discussion among colonists who have just read *Common Sense*. In your notebook, write four or five lines of dialogue from that conversation.

Congress Votes for Independence

In June 1776, the Second Continental Congress created a committee to write a draft for a declaration of independence. The committee asked Thomas Jefferson, one of its members, to write a draft. After making a few changes, the committee sent Jefferson's document to Congress.

On July 2, the Continental Congress voted in favor of independence. "Yesterday," John Adams wrote on July 3, "the greatest question was decided, which ever was debated in America." On July 4, Congress voted to approve Jefferson's Declaration of Independence. It announced to the world that the thirteen former British colonies had become the free and independent United States of America.

Thomas Jefferson drafted the Declaration of Independence in 1776.

Stop and Think

Answers will vary but the dialogue should show an understanding that Paine put into words what many colonists were thinking—that perhaps the time had come to break away from Britain.

Picturing History

In the illustration on page 127, Thomas Jefferson is shown standing. Seated are Benjamin Franklin of Pennsylvania and John Adams of Massachusetts. The three were members of a group chosen to draft a declaration of independence. The two members not shown in the painting are Roger Sherman of Connecticut and Robert R. Livingston of New York. What do the crumbled papers on the floor suggest about the difficulties the committee faced in drafting the document?

Extension

Before Thomas Jefferson died, he asked that only three of his accomplishments be listed on his tombstone: author of the Declaration of American Independence, author of the Virginia Statute for Religious Freedom, and father of the University of Virginia. Ask students to find out more about Jefferson's life and then discuss what these three accomplishments suggest about Jefferson and the things he valued and believed in.

The Declaration of Independence was signed on July 4, 1776.

Putting It All Together

The concept maps will vary but should reflect some of the following ideas:

- All men are created equal and have unalienable rights—including life, liberty, and the pursuit of happiness.

- Governments get their power from the people.

- People should not change their governments lightly, but when the government denies basic rights, people have a responsibility to overthrow such a government and create a new one.

The Declaration of Independence

In the Declaration, Jefferson took care to explain why the colonists cut their ties with Great Britain. People, he wrote, "are endowed by their Creator with certain unalienable Rights." Among them are the right to "Life, Liberty, and the pursuit of Happiness." All people, he said, are justified in getting rid of any government that abuses those rights. He then included a long list of abuses by King George III, who tried to establish "an absolute **Tyranny** over these States." Tyranny is a government in which one person has absolute power.

By basing the Declaration on broad principles that apply to all people, Jefferson made the document a declaration of

The Declaration was publicly read to soldiers.

human rights. He defended everyone's right to get rid of an oppressive government. This has made the Declaration a timeless, living document. It continues to inspire people in their search for freedom, liberty, and dignity.

Putting It All Together

Create a concept map with "Declaration of Independence" in the middle circle. Then read the copy of the Declaration of Independence included in this book. As you read, list on lines extending out from the circle the major points made in the Declaration.

Biography

Abigail Smith Adams (1744–1818)

In March 1776, Abigail Adams wrote to her husband, John Adams, who was attending the Continental Congress. She hoped that Congress would soon declare independence and create a "Code of Laws" for the new nation. When that time came, she added, "I desire you would Remember the Ladies, and be more generous and favourable to them than your ancestors. Do not put such unlimited power into the hands of the Husbands."

Abigail Adams was ahead of her time. The delegates who gathered in Philadelphia in 1776 were not there to grant rights to women. Their wives

had no legal rights and could not vote, hold office, or take part in town meetings. That was fine with John Adams and his friends. Even Abigail Adams did not expect to see much change in her lifetime. But she could not resist reminding her husband that King George III was not the world's only tyrant.

Abigail Adams was subordinate to her husband in every way but one. John always admitted that his wife was intellectually his equal. He fell in love with his "Miss Adorable" partly because of her "habit of Reading, Writing, and Thinking." She loved poetry and memorized page after page of William Shakespeare and Alexander Pope. They married in 1764 when John, a rising young lawyer, was twenty-nine and she was almost twenty.

During the coming years, Abigail became more independent than most women of her time. She raised four children largely by herself. One of their children—John Quincy Adams—became the sixth president of the United States. She managed the family farm when John Adams served as a delegate to the Continental Congress and as a diplomat in Europe. She called herself "Mrs. Delegate" because he had left so much work for her at home.

In time, Abigail shared John Adams's public life. In 1785, she joined her husband in London, where he was the first United States minister to Great Britain. She helped him represent the United States at diplomatic events. As wife of the first vice president of the United States (1789–1797) and as first lady during her husband's administration (1797–1801), she entertained official guests at the nation's capital. In 1801, Abigail and John Adams returned to Massachusetts. She died there in 1818.

129

Bio Facts

- Abigail Smith was born in Weymouth, Massachusetts, in 1744.

- Like other women of the time, Smith lacked a formal education but read avidly.

- Abigail Smith married John Adams in 1764. The young couple lived in Braintree on a small farm and in Boston where he practiced law.

- Abigail Adams had three sons and two daughters. She looked after the children and the family business while her husband traveled as circuit judge.

- In 1784, Abigail Adams joined her husband in Paris. After 1785, they moved to London where he served as the first United States Minister to Great Britain.

- As wife of the first vice president (1789–1797) and the second president (1797–1801), Abigail Adams drew on her experiences abroad for her new roles in the nation.

- In 1800, the Adams family became the first to live in the barely completed President's House, now known as the White House.

- The Adamses retired to Quincy, Massachusetts, in 1801.

- Abigail Adams died in 1818. Her son John Quincy Adams became the nation's sixth president in 1825, seven years after his mother's death.

Biography Extension

In many of her letters, Abigail Adams wrote passionately about women's need for education. In 1776, she wrote, "If we mean to have heroes, statesmen, and philosophers, we should have learned women."

Abigail Adams regretted her own lack of education. While living in England during the late 1780s, she attended a series of lectures on science—her first classroom experience. She later wrote of the lectures, "It was like going into a beautiful country, which I never saw before, a country which our American females are not permitted to visit or inspect."

Encourage students to find out more about education for both men and women in the colonies and later the new United States. Why was education so important to Americans like Abigail Adams?

130 Chapter 8

Lesson Summary

Britain tried repeatedly to put down the colonial rebellion and failed. Outnumbered by British troops, Washington withdrew his army from New York to New Jersey. In 1777, the British captured Philadelphia but failed once again to destroy Washington's army.

In 1780, the British concentrated on the South. The following year, the Americans and their French allies won a major victory at the Battle of Yorktown. In 1783, the British signed a treaty recognizing the independence of the new United States. The war was over.

Lesson Objective

Students will learn how the Americans managed to win a war against one of the most powerful nations in the world.

Focus Your Reading Answers

1 The British attacked from Canada in an effort to isolate and occupy New England but failed.

2 The Tories were people who remained loyal to Britain.

3 There were more Tories (Loyalists) in the South, and the British thought they would help them.

4 France provided the United States with military supplies as well as an army and a fleet of ships.

Winning Independence

Thinking on Your Own

Read the Focus Your Reading questions. Divide a page in your notebook into two columns, one headed "Militia/Continental Army," the other "British Army." As you read, list the battles won by each side in the conflict.

A colonial soldier

Britain focused on putting down the rebellion in the New England and Middle Colonies. The patriots there seemed to be the biggest troublemakers. In August 1776, British General William Howe landed 32,000 **troops** near New York City. Facing him was General Washington's Continental army of 13,000 men. Howe won battles at Brooklyn Heights and White Plains, but failed to destroy Washington's army. Washington won victories that winter in New Jersey at Trenton and Princeton. These victories lifted the patriots' spirits.

focus your reading

What did the British try to accomplish in the North?

Who were the Tories?

Why did the British expect to do better in the South?

How did France help the Americans win their independence?

vocabulary

troops ally

Tories

The War in the North

In 1777, the British unleashed a major attack from Canada. They hoped to isolate and occupy New England. Instead, American militia troops defeated the British at the Battles of Saratoga and Oriskany in New York.

The winter at Valley Forge was brutal, and the troops suffered greatly.

That summer, General Howe attacked the Continental army in Pennsylvania. Washington lost battles at Brandywine Creek and Germantown, but again saved his army. The army

130

Lesson Vocabulary

Explain that the word *troops* refers to soldiers as a group. The name may have come from the way soldiers *troop*, or march, onto the battlefield.

An *ally* is a country, person, or group that joins with another or others for a common purpose. During the War for Independence, France became an *ally* of the Americans.

Tories are people who remained loyal to Great Britain. They are named for a political party in Britain. The British Tories were conservatives—people who did not like change.

spent the winter camped at Valley Forge. Howe occupied Philadelphia, but withdrew the next summer. The British accomplished little from their attacks in the north.

The War on the Frontier

On the frontier, the results were no better. There the British fought American militia soldiers for control of the frontier. In 1777, the Americans defeated the British and their Iroquois allies in western New York. The British and the Shawnee then

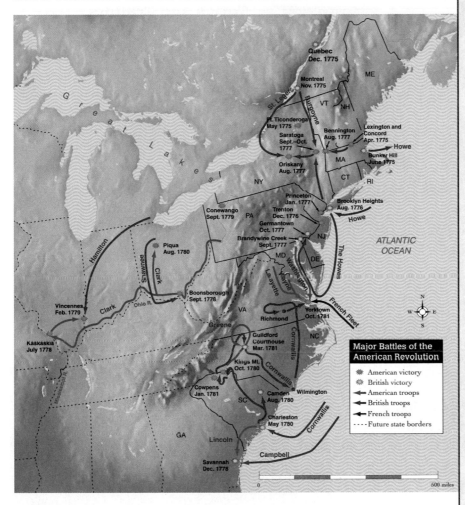

Major Battles of the American Revolution

- ✹ American victory
- ✸ British victory
- ← American troops
- ← British troops
- ← French troops
- ---- Future state borders

Ask students to use the map on page 131 and its key to answer the following questions:

- When were most of the battles fought in New England? (1775–1777)

- When were most of the battles fought in the Middle Colonies? (1776–1777)

- When were most of the battles in the South fought? (1780–1781)

- When were most of the battles fought in the West? (1777–1779)

- In which part of the country were the French of most help? (along the Virginia coast)

Extension

Ask students to gather information about one of the battles shown on the map and report their findings to the class. Their reports should include

- who led the soldiers on both sides

- when the battle took place

- where the battle was fought

- what happened during the battle and who won

- why the battle was important

Picturing History

The two pictures on page 130 show soldiers in the Continental army. The picture at the bottom of the page shows George Washington and his soldiers at Valley Forge, Pennsylvania. In December 1777, Washington brought 11,000 troops to Valley Forge to spend the winter. What does the painting suggest about conditions in the camp?

Europeans who came to Valley Forge to meet with Washington were dismayed by what they saw there. A young French nobleman, the Marquis de Lafayette, later wrote, "The unfortunate soldiers were in want of everything. They had neither coats, hats, shirts, nor shoes, their feet and legs froze till they became black, and it was often necessary to amputate them."

Despite these harsh conditions, few soldiers deserted the army that winter. Instead, they prepared for the spring. Another nobleman, Baron Friedrich von Steuben, spent the winter showing them how to use their muskets and bayonets and how to obey orders. He turned a rag-tag band of farmers, shopkeepers, clerks, students, lawyers, and teachers into an army.

attacked American settlers in Kentucky. George Rogers Clark led Virginia militia troops to drive the British out of the Ohio Valley. They captured British forts at Kaskaskia and Vincennes. These Battles of the Old Northwest gave the United States a strong claim to the Ohio Valley at the end of the war.

Tories were harrassed in the colonies

stop and think

During most of the war, General George Washington lost more battles than he won. What did he do that caused people to consider him a great military leader? Write a brief answer to this question in your notebook and compare it with that of a partner.

Tories and Traitors

The patriots' most hated enemies were Americans who were loyal to Britain. Some 20 percent of the population was made up of **Tories**, or Loyalists. Patriots forced suspected Loyalists to sign oaths of loyalty to the United States. Many Tories lost their homes and property. In fact, not all patriots could be trusted. American General Benedict Arnold tried to turn over the fort at West Point to the British.

The War in the South

In 1780, the British decided to concentrate their efforts in the South, which had more Loyalists. They captured Charleston, South Carolina. With Loyalist help, an army under Lord Cornwallis also defeated the Americans at Camden. Then the tide turned. The patriots defeated Tory armies at Kings Mountain and at Cowpens. Losing Tory support, the British army withdrew to Yorktown, Virginia, in 1781.

Molly Pitcher and other women fought for independence from Britain.

132 | Chapter 8

Daniel Morgan at the
Battle of Cowpens

The British move to Yorktown was a mistake. Yorktown placed the British within striking distance of Washington's army. By then, the United States had a powerful **ally**—or partner. France agreed to provide the United States with military supplies. It also sent an army and a fleet to help the Americans. The combined armies surrounded Yorktown by land. The French fleet prevented the British from escaping by sea and provided the support needed to achieve victory.

The fighting ended when General Cornwallis surrendered on October 19, 1781. The Treaty of Paris officially ended the war in November 1783. The treaty recognized American independence and made the Mississippi River the western boundary of the United States.

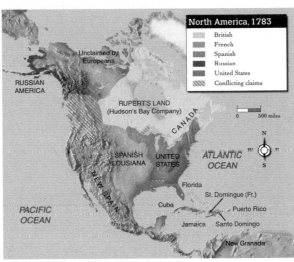

North America, 1783

- British
- French
- Spanish
- Russian
- United States
- Conflicting claims

RUSSIAN AMERICA

RUPERT'S LAND (Hudson's Bay Company)

CANADA

Unclaimed by Europeans

0   500 miles

N

SPANISH LOUISIANA

UNITED STATES

ATLANTIC OCEAN

NEW SPAIN

PACIFIC OCEAN

Florida

St. Domingue (Fr.)

Cuba

Puerto Rico

Jamaica   Santo Domingo

New Granada

Putting It All Together

Why did the Americans win the War for Independence? List three reasons in your notebook. Rank these in order of importance. Compare your reasons with those of other students.

Chapter Review

1 Sentences will vary but each should show an understanding of the word's meaning.

2 In evaluating the flags students create, focus on the appropriateness of the symbols students chose and their reasons for making those choices.

3 Answers will vary but should reflect an understanding of the chapter as a whole.

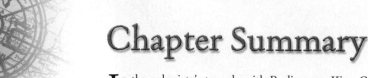

Chapter Summary

In the colonists' struggle with Parliament, King George III sided with Parliament. He demanded that the **patriot** leaders be arrested. On April 19, 1775, British soldiers killed eight **minutemen** at Lexington. The colonial militia killed seventy-three **redcoats** as the troops marched back to Boston. In May, delegates meeting in Philadelphia sent the **Olive Branch Petition** to the king. They also appointed George Washington as commander of the **Continental army**.

In November 1775, the delegates at Philadelphia learned that the king had rejected their Olive Branch Petition. He also established a **blockade** of the colonies. On July 4, 1776, Congress approved the Declaration of Independence. It accused King George of trying to establish a **tyranny** over the colonies. It also was a declaration of **human rights**.

Britain tried to put down the rebellion. General Washington, outnumbered by British **troops**, moved his army to New Jersey. In 1777, British General Howe captured Philadelphia, but again failed to destroy Washington's army.

In 1780, the British concentrated their efforts in the South—a region with more **Tories**. The next year, the Americans and their French **ally** won a major victory at the Battle of Yorktown. The Treaty of Paris recognized the United States as an independent nation and ended the war in 1783.

Chapter Review

1 Review the vocabulary words. Write a sentence related to this chapter for each word.

2 Create a flag for the new United States of America of 1776 that does not include stars and stripes. Research other flags and think of symbols that represent the United States and what it stood for. Write a paragraph explaining why you chose those symbols for your flag.

3 Return to the questions that you wrote at the beginning of the chapter. Write answers for them based on your reading.

Novel Connections

Below is a list of books that relate to the time period covered in this chapter. The numbers in parentheses indicate the related Thematic Strands of the National Council for the Social Studies (NCSS).

Marsha Amstel. *Sybil Ludington's Midnight Ride* (On My Own History series). Carolrhoda, 2000. (III, IV, VI)

Natalie S. Bober. *Countdown to Independence: A Revolution of Ideas in England and Her American Colonies: 1760–1776.* Atheneum Books, 2001. (II, VI, X)

Clinton Cox. *Come All You Brave Soldiers: Blacks in the Revolutionary War.* Scholastic Press, 1999. (IV, V)

Jean Fritz. *Why Not Lafayette?* Putnam/Penguin, 1999. (II, V, IX)

Milton Meltzer, ed. *Hour of Freedom: American History in Poetry.* Wordsong/Boyds Mills Press, 2003. (I, II, X)

Sarah L. Thomson. *Stars and Stripes: The Story of the American Flag.* HarperCollins, 2003. (II, X)

Skill Builder

Historical Works of Art

Paintings, portraits, and other works of art can be useful tools for learning history. They help us visualize what events, people, or everyday life was like in the past. However, like other historical source materials, they must be used critically. To view a historical work of art critically means asking at least the following questions:

- Is the artist biased?
- Does the piece of art favor one person or point of view?
- Does it take sides in a controversy?
- Is it faithful to known historical facts?
- How far removed was the artist from the subject or time period?

The painting below is one artist's interpretation of the Battle of Lexington on April 19, 1775. Look at the painting critically by answering the following questions:

1 Does the artist show a bias toward the colonists or the British soldiers?

2 Is the painting faithful to the known facts about the Battle of Lexington?

3 How does this artist's view of the battle compare with the illustration on page 122?

Use the information presented in this chapter, including primary sources and illustrations, to answer the above questions. Then write a critical review of the painting in your notebook.

1 The artist shows a bias toward the colonists. The British did not charge into the colonists on their horses.

2 No, there are different versions of what actually happened at the Battle of Lexington. Students should include what the various primary sources reported about the battle.

3 The artist shows the militia with guns raised, ready to fire. The illustration on page 122 does not.

Classroom Discussion

Discuss with students some of the broader topics covered in this chapter.

- How important was the Declaration of Independence to the struggle for independence?

- Why do you think countries like France were willing to help the Americans?

- Why do you think that most people expected the British to defeat the patriots in the War for Independence? How were the Americans able to win?

- As the British turned over their guns to the Americans after the Battle of Yorktown, a military band played a song called "The World Turned Upside Down." Why was it a good choice for the occasion?

- Who do you think were the heroes in the War for Independence? For what reasons?

- To what extent did the War for Independence turn the colonists into Americans?

Unit Objectives

After studying this unit, students will be able to

- describe the nation's first state and central governments and identify their strengths and weaknesses

- explain why Americans needed a stronger central government in the late 1780s and how they came to write the Constitution

- describe the division of powers created by the U.S. Constitution

Unit 5 focuses on the efforts of the newly independent United States to build a strong central government.

Chapter 9, The Confederation Period, describes the nation's first state and national governments.

Chapter 10, The Constitution, examines the government created by the Constitution of the United States.

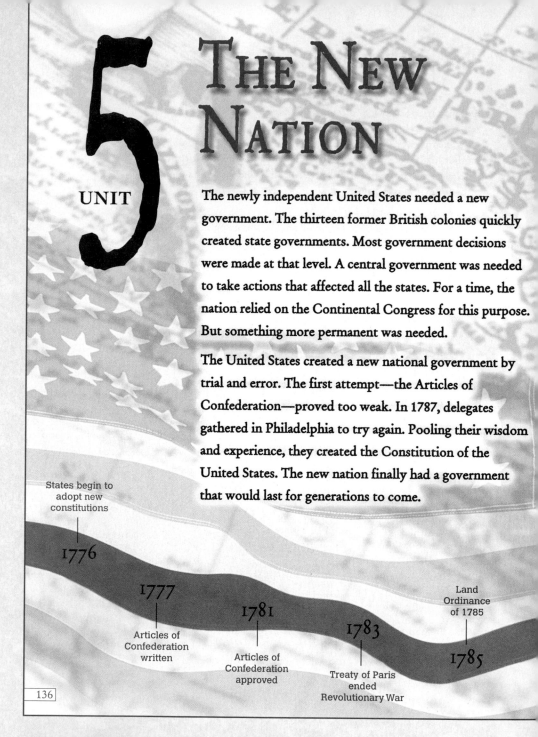

UNIT 5

THE NEW NATION

The newly independent United States needed a new government. The thirteen former British colonies quickly created state governments. Most government decisions were made at that level. A central government was needed to take actions that affected all the states. For a time, the nation relied on the Continental Congress for this purpose. But something more permanent was needed.

The United States created a new national government by trial and error. The first attempt—the Articles of Confederation—proved too weak. In 1787, delegates gathered in Philadelphia to try again. Pooling their wisdom and experience, they created the Constitution of the United States. The new nation finally had a government that would last for generations to come.

States begin to adopt new constitutions

1776

1777
Articles of Confederation written

1781
Articles of Confederation approved

1783
Treaty of Paris ended Revolutionary War

Land Ordinance of 1785

1785

136

Getting Started

Introduce the word *government* by asking students to read aloud the two paragraphs on page 136. Explain that this unit focuses on *government*—a system that people create to make and enforce laws or rules for a community, a state, or a nation.

Explain to students that as soon as Americans declared their independence, they had to create new governments to replace the ones established by the British. What do the two paragraphs suggest about the governments Americans created after 1776? Then have students examine the pictures in Chapters 9 and 10. What do they suggest about the people who created the new governments?

Why did the
Articles of
Confederation
fail?

Why did the
Constitution succeed?

What kind of governments
did the states create?

Annapolis
Convention

1786

1786

Shays's
Rebellion

Philadelphia
Convention

1787

Constitution
ratified

1787

Northwest
Ordinance

1788

Collage Answers

1 The Articles of Confederation failed because the document did not provide for a central government strong enough to deal with the nation's problems, such as shipping and exports.

2 The states created republics—governments that get their power from the people.

3 The Constitution succeeded because it established a new central government that was stronger than one created by the Articles of Confederation. The new document also protected both the rights of the states and those of the American people.

Collage Extension

Use the images and questions on page 137 to preview the unit. Discuss how the questions relate to the word *government*.

Measuring Time

Explain to students that the timeline focuses on events described in Chapter 9. Chapter 10 examines the system of government created by the Constitution.

Timeline Extension

To preview Unit 5, ask students to use the timeline to answer these questions:

- When did the states begin to adopt new constitutions? (1776)

- In what year were the Articles of Confederation written? (1777) How long did it take before they were approved? (four years)

- For how many years did Americans live under the Articles of Confederation? (seven years, 1781–1788)

- How long did it take for Americans to approve, or ratify, the Constitution? (one year)

Chapter Summary

Refer to page 152 in the student book for a summary of Chapter 9.

Related Transparencies

T-17 Concept Web

T-18 T-Chart

Key Blacklines

Biography
James Madison

Primary Source
Putting Down Shays's Rebellion

Picturing History

The picture on page 138 shows Independence Hall in Philadelphia. From 1775 to 1783 (except for the winter of 1777–1778 when the British army occupied the city), the building was the meeting place for the Second Continental Congress. It is where the Declaration of Independence was adopted. It is also the place where the first American flag was approved, the Articles of Confederation were drafted, and the U.S. Constitution was written. Ask students how these events may explain why Independence Hall is often called the "cradle of liberty."

Getting Focused

Skim this chapter to predict what you will be learning.

- Read the lesson titles and subheadings.
- Look at the illustrations and read the captions.
- Examine the maps.
- Review the vocabulary words and terms.

There are many different styles of government around the world. Make a list of the words and phrases that come to mind when you hear the word *government*. After reviewing the lesson, add more words to the list in your notebook.

Pre-Reading Discussion

1 Ask students to read aloud the chapter title, and explain that it refers to the years Americans lived under the Articles of Confederation. Have a volunteer use the timeline on pages 136–137 to identify those years. (1781–1788) What do the pictures in the chapter suggest about life in the new United States during those years?

2 After students complete each bulleted direction on page 138, ask them to read aloud the last paragraph on page 138 and then brainstorm a list of words or phrases related to government. As students read and discuss the chapter, have them expand their lists.

Governing the New Nation

Thinking on Your Own

Read the Focus Your Reading questions and the vocabulary words. Write the vocabulary words in your notebook. Discuss the possible meanings of the words with a partner.

During the War for Independence, Americans set up new governments. They replaced their old colonial charters with new state **constitutions**. A constitution is a document that outlines a plan of government. The old charters gave the colonists only limited power. This power came from the king. The Declaration of Independence swept that aside. The nation also created a new government to replace the Continental Congress.

focus your reading

How were the state constitutions and the colonial charters different?

Why was the first central government called a confederation?

What did the Confederation Congress accomplish?

vocabulary

constitutions

republic

bill of rights

confederation

Northwest Territory

State Governments

Early in 1776, the Continental Congress asked the individual colonies to form new governments. Most quickly adopted written constitutions. After July 4, 1776, these constitutions provided the basis for new state governments.

The Virginia state legislature met in the House of Burgess's capitol building.

The Confederation Period 139

Lesson Summary

During the Revolutionary War, Americans replaced their colonial charters with new state constitutions. Most included a bill of rights. Americans also adopted the Articles of Confederation, the nation's first central government. Although the Confederation was a weak government, it did open the Northwest Territory for settlement.

Lesson Objective

Students will learn about the first state and central governments Americans established after they declared their independence.

Focus Your Reading Answers

1 State constitutions derived their power from the people and colonial charters derived their power from British rulers.

2 The first central government was called a confederation because it was a loose alliance of the states.

3 The Confederation Congress negotiated the peace treaty that ended the war with Britain and it also opened the Northwest Territory to settlement.

DVD Extension

Encourage students to use the reading comprehension, vocabulary reinforcement, and interactive timeline activities on the student DVD.

Lesson Vocabulary

Each of the vocabulary words in this lesson relates to the governments Americans were organizing in the late 1700s. Every state wrote a *constitution*. A *constitution* is a plan for a government. It spells out how a government will be organized, who holds what jobs, and what government officials can and cannot do.

A *republic* is a government that gets its power from the people. Americans replaced a monarchy with a *republic* in 1776. Many states included a *bill of rights* in their constitution. It is a list of the rights that all people in that state have. These are rights and liberties that the government cannot take away.

The 13 states banded together to form a loose *confederation*, or union. The *confederation* opened the *Northwest Territory* for settlement. Have students locate it on the map on page 141. (the area north of the Ohio River) Explain that a *territory* is a part of the United States that has a government but is not yet a state. Discuss why the area was called the *Northwest Territory*.

Picturing History

The photograph shows the opening page of the Articles of Confederation. Ask students to use the map on page 141 to identify the states that belonged to the Confederation. (New Hampshire, Massachusetts, Rhode Island, Connecticut, New York, New Jersey, Pennsylvania, Delaware, Maryland, Virginia, North Carolina, South Carolina, and Georgia)

The new governments had much in common. Each was a **republic**, or a government that derives its power from the people. Within the republics, people elected representatives to make and enforce the laws. The new constitutions placed most of the power in the elected assemblies. Because of this, the states had weak governors.

Most of the constitutions included a **bill of rights**. These were "natural rights" that no government should be allowed to violate. They included the right to hold property, to a trial by jury, freedom of the press, and freedom of speech and assembly.

The Articles of Confederation

The Continental Congress also created a plan for a central government. Called the Articles of Confederation, it created a **confederation**, or a loose alliance, of states. A dispute over western lands delayed the states' approval of the Articles. Some states claimed land in the Ohio Valley. Landless states opposed these claims. The states finally agreed to turn over all western land claims to Congress. The states approved the Articles of Confederation in 1781.

The Articles of Confederation were adopted in 1781.

ARTICLES
OF
Confederation
AND
Perpetual Union
BETWEEN THE
STATES
OF

New Hampshire, Massachusetts Bay, Rhode Island, and Providence Plantations, Connecticut, New York, New Jersey, Pennsylvania, Delaware, Maryland, Virginia, North Carolina, South Carolina, and Georgia.

WILLIAMSBURG,
Printed by ALEXANDER PURDIE.

stop and think

Make sentences of the vocabulary words that you have found so far. For each word, write a sentence in your notebook using the word in context.

The Articles of Confederation provided for a congress similar to the Continental Congress. There was no president or national system of courts. Congress had the power to declare war, make peace, coin and borrow money, and regulate Native American affairs. The states retained many important powers of government. They alone had the power to enforce laws, regulate trade, and impose taxes. Each state had one vote in Congress, and nine votes were required to pass a law. The Articles reflected the American people's fear of a strong central government.

Extension

Article II of the Articles of Confederation reads, "Each state retains its sovereignty, freedom, and independence, and every power, jurisdiction, and right, which is not by this Confederation expressly delegated to the United States, in Congress assembled." Article III describes the Confederation as a "firm league of friendship." What do the two articles suggest about the role of the states in the Confederation and the role of Congress? (Congress gets its power from the states.) Which is more powerful? (The states are more powerful.)

CANADA

ME

VT

NH

NY and NH
statehood 1791

MA

NY

CT

RI

PA

NJ

Virginia 1784

Conn.
1800

Virginia 1784
Massachusetts 1785

Ohio R.

MD

DE

Virginia 1784
Connecticut 1786

ATLANTIC
OCEAN

Virginia 1784
New York 1782

VA

Virginia 1789
New York 1782

NC

North Carolina 1790
New York 1782

SC

South Carolina 1787
Georgia 1802
New York 1782

GA

Georgia 1802

Spain 1795
Georgia 1802

SPANISH FLORIDA

SPANISH LOUISIANA

Missouri R.

N
W E
S

Western Land Claims and Cessions

- States
- Land claimed by states
- Boundary of the Northwest Territory

0   500 miles

Successes of Congress

Although its power was limited, the Confederation Congress did accomplish important things. It negotiated the peace treaty that ended the war with Britain. The Treaty of Paris (1783) was more favorable to the United States than most people had expected. The boundaries to which Britain agreed created a nation ten times the size of Great Britain and four times larger than France.

Benjamin West's unfinished portrait of the American representatives drafting the Treaty of Paris. The British delegates refused to sit for the painting.

141

Map Extension

Explain to students that the dates on the map indicate the years the land was given to the new government. Once ceded, the land was open for settlement and could become a territory.

Ask students to use the map on page 141 to answer the following questions:

- What does yellow mean on this map? (It shows the original 13 states.)

- What does brown show? (land claimed by two or more states or nations)

- What does green show? (land claimed by other countries)

- What states are "landless" in the West, according to this map? (Rhode Island, New Jersey, Delaware, Pennsylvania, Maine, New Hampshire, and Maryland)

- What state was the last to give up its claims to land in the West? (Georgia in 1802)

Picturing History

The painting by Benjamin West shows, from left to right, John Jay of New York, John Adams of Massachusetts, Benjamin Franklin of Pennsylvania, Henry Laurens of South Carolina, and Franklin's grandson, William Temple Franklin. William Temple Franklin served as secretary to the American delegation. Have students consider why the British representatives might have refused to sit for the painting.

Extension

Benjamin West was an American artist who lived in Britain. When he started the painting of the diplomats who drafted the Treaty of Paris (1783), he assumed that both sides would pose for him. Ask students to find out why West was so confident of the cooperation of both the British and the Americans. (He was a noted artist in London with close ties to Americans. He was also a friend of George III, who commissioned several paintings from him.)

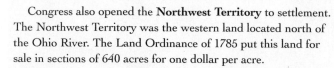

Putting It All Together

Answers will vary, but students are likely to include on their webs such words and phrases as *republic, bill of rights, elected assemblies, weak governors, power to enforce laws, regulate trade,* and *impose taxes.*

Map Extensions

1 Ask students to use the map on page 142 to answer the following questions:

- Which was first state to enter the United States from the Northwest Territory? (Ohio, in 1803)

- How many years passed before a second state entered the United States? (13 years until Indiana entered in 1816)

- Which state was last to enter the United States from the Northwest Territory? (Wisconsin, in 1848)

- How many years did it take to create five states from land in the Northwest Territory? (45 years)

2 Point out to students that the map shows two new states just south of the Northwest Territory: Kentucky and Tennessee. In what year did they become states? (Kentucky in 1792 and Tennessee in 1796) Ask students to find out why they were ready for statehood before any part of the Northwest Territory. (Americans had been settling in Kentucky and Tennessee since the 1750s.)

Congress also opened the **Northwest Territory** to settlement. The Northwest Territory was the western land located north of the Ohio River. The Land Ordinance of 1785 put this land for sale in sections of 640 acres for one dollar per acre.

The Northwest Ordinance of 1787 created a way to admit new states into the confederation. It allowed settlers to create territorial governments. The ordinance also outlawed slavery in these future territories.

Once a region had 5,000 adult white males, it could elect a legislature and send a nonvoting member to Congress. When the region reached 60,000 people, it could draft a constitution and become a state. Five states emerged from the Northwest Territory.

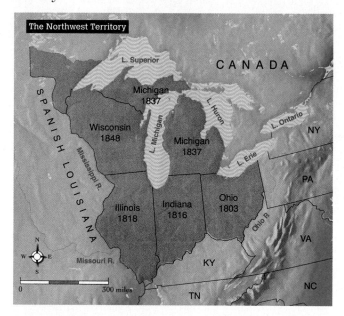

The Northwest Territory

Putting It All Together

In your notebook write "State Governments" in the middle of a concept web. Go back and gather notes from the paragraphs related to the states. On lines coming from the circle, add words that describe the responsibilities of the state governments.

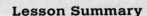

LESSON 2 Problems of the Confederation

Thinking on Your Own

Read the Focus Your Reading questions. Create a chart in your notebook labeled "The Nation's Problems." List the major problems as you read about them. Include the vocabulary words that are related to the problems.

The confederation period (1781–1789) was a difficult time for the new nation. Congress faced many problems that it could not solve. It could not pay the nation's debts because it had no power to tax. It could not remove British troops from western forts. It failed to persuade Spain to let Americans trade at New Orleans. To make matters worse, the new nation faced economic hard times. Congress could do even less about that.

focus your reading
What problems did the nation face during the confederation period?
Why did some members of Congress want to change the Articles of Confederation?
How are Shays's Rebellion and the Philadelphia Convention related?

vocabulary
national debt
convention
Shays's Rebellion

Difficult Times

During the war, the Continental Congress had borrowed millions of dollars from foreign governments and banks. This debt had to be paid. Britain demanded payment of prewar debts owed to its merchants. It refused to withdraw its troops from western forts until these debts were paid. Exports had slumped because Britain closed its ports to American ships. Crop prices were down, and workmen were out of work. Yet the states kept raising taxes to pay their debts.

Lesson Summary

The years under the Articles of Confederation were economically difficult for the new nation. Congress faced a large national debt but did not have the power to raise money through taxes. A number of leaders in Congress wanted to create a stronger national government, but the states refused to consider the idea. Then in 1786, Congress was unable to put down an uprising led by Daniel Shays in Massachusetts. The incident touched off lawlessness in other states. As a result, Congress agreed to call a convention to strengthen the Articles of Confederation.

Lesson Objective

Students will learn about the challenges faced by the Confederation between 1781 and 1789.

Focus Your Reading Answers

1 During the confederation period, the nation faced economic hard times. It could not pay its debts or remove British troops from forts in the West. Furthermore, the nation was unable to persuade Spain to let Americans trade at New Orleans.

2 Some members of Congress wanted to change the Articles of Confederation to create a stronger central government.

3 Concerns over the lawlessness touched off by Shays's Rebellion persuaded Congress to call a convention in Philadelphia to revise the Articles of Confederation.

Vocabulary

Introduce each vocabulary word. Ask a volunteer to define the word *debt* (money owed). Have students then explain what a *national debt* is and how it differs from a *personal debt*. (A national debt is money owed by a national government. A personal debt is money owed by an individual.)

Explain that the word *convention* has several meanings. In this chapter, it refers to a formal assembly or meeting. It comes from a Latin word meaning "to meet."

Remind students that a *rebellion* is an uprising against the government. *Shays's Rebellion* was an uprising against the state of Massachusetts.

During the 1780s, American ships were prohibited from entering British ports.

Congress could do little to solve these problems. Lacking the power to tax, it could not pay off the **national debt**. It lacked an army to drive British troops out of western forts. It could not make new trade agreements, as only states could regulate, or control, trade. The states further restricted trade by placing import duties on goods made in other states.

Calls for Change

Several leaders in Congress wanted a stronger central government. Among them were James Madison of Virginia and Alexander Hamilton of New York. In 1781, they tried to change the Articles of Confederation to give Congress the power to tax. Twelve states agreed, but Rhode Island voted against the proposed change. To change the Articles, all thirteen states had to agree. On two occasions Congress asked the states to give it the power to regulate trade. Each time they refused.

Robert Morris proposed the Capitol National Bank in 1781, which helped to stabilize the economy.

In 1786, Virginia invited other states to a **convention**—or a meeting of delegates—at Annapolis, Maryland, to consider ways to regulate trade. Because representatives from only five states came, the meeting accomplished little. Before they left for home, the delegates asked Congress to call another convention to meet in Philadelphia in 1787.

Shays's Rebellion

In 1786, an armed uprising in western Massachusetts shocked the nation. Angry farmers attacked the county courts. The courts were seizing, or taking, their farms for nonpayment of debts and taxes. Leading a mob of 1,000 farmers, Daniel Shays tried to capture muskets from a state arsenal. The Confederation Congress was powerless. It could create an army only in case of Native American attack. Massachusetts finally put down the rebellion by creating a private army of 4,000 men.

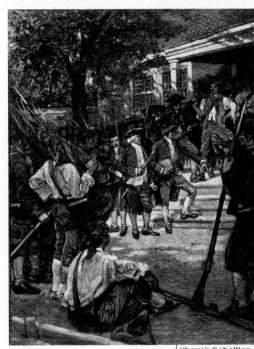

Shays's Rebellion helped Congress realize the weaknesses in the Articles of Confederation.

Shays's Rebellion touched off attacks against courts and tax collectors in other states. This frightened many Americans. "We are fast verging on anarchy and confusion," George Washington wrote. Fearing more lawlessness, Congress agreed to call a convention to revise the Articles of Confederation.

Putting It All Together

Compare and contrast the powers of the state governments and those of Congress. Compare your ideas with a partner and write a brief paragraph about this topic.

Putting It All Together

Answers will vary, but students should note that state governments had the power to tax, to raise an army, and to regulate trade. Congress lacked these powers.

Picturing History

On August 29, 1786, rebels led by Daniel Shays stormed the courthouse in Northampton, Massachusetts, to keep the judges from entering the building. They wanted to stop the courts from trying and imprisoning debtors. How does the artist seem to regard the rebels?

Extension

Encourage students to compare and contrast Bacon's Rebellion (Chapter 5) with Shays's Rebellion. Begin by having students answer the following questions:

- Who participated in each event?

- What happened at the event?

- Where did the event take place?

- When did the event take place?

- Why did the event take place?

- Why is the event important?

Have students use their answers to identify key similarities and major differences between the two events.

Extension

Have students find out more about Shays's Rebellion and Daniel Shays. Then ask them to use the information they gathered to explain what Baron Friedrich von Steuben (the German who trained Washington's troops at Valley Forge) meant when he said of the rebellion, "When a whole people complains something must be wrong."

Reading for Understanding

1 Abigail Adams regarded the leaders of the rebellion as "ignorant, restless desperadoes, without conscience or principles."

2 Jefferson sees periodic unrest ("turbulence") like the rebellion as the major disadvantage of a republican government.

3 The benefits of the "turbulence" are that it prevents corruption ("degeneracy of government") and encourages government attention to public affairs.

Abigail Adams and Thomas Jefferson on Shays's Rebellion

Thomas Jefferson, the United States minister to France, asked Abigail Adams for information about Shays's Rebellion. In her response, Abigail Adams told Jefferson what she thought about the riots. She was living in London, where her husband, John Adams, was the United States minister to Great Britain. Jefferson then shared his thoughts about the rebellion with his friend James Madison.

reading for understanding

What did Abigail Adams think of the leaders of the rebellion?

What does Jefferson see as the major disadvantage of republican government?

What benefits does this disadvantage produce?

"With regard to the tumults in my native state which you inquire about, I wish I could say that report had exaggerated them. It is too true, sir, that they have been carried to so alarming a height as to stop the courts of justice in several counties. Ignorant, restless desperadoes, without conscience or principles, have led a deluded multitude to follow their standard, under pretense of grievances which have no existence but in their imaginations."

Abigail Adams to Thomas Jefferson, January 2, 1787; Julian P. Boyd, ed., *Jefferson Papers* (Princeton, 1955).

"I am impatient to learn your sentiments on the late troubles in the Eastern states. . . . This uneasiness has produced [violent] acts absolutely unjustifiable: but I hope they will provoke no severities from their governments. . . . [Republican government] has its evils too: the principal of which is the turbulence to which it is subject. . . . Even this evil is productive of good. It prevents the degeneracy of government and nourishes a general attention to the public affairs. I hold that a little rebellion now and then is a good thing, and as necessary in the political world as storms in the physical. . . . An observation of this truth should render honest republican governors so mild in their punishments of rebellions, as not to discourage them too much. It is a medicine necessary for the sound health of government."

Thomas Jefferson to James Madison, January 30, 1787; Paul L. Ford, ed., *The Writings of Thomas Jefferson* (New York, 1894).

146

Extension

A laborer in Massachusetts named William Manning tried to explain Shays's Rebellion in 1789. Ask students to compare his views with those of Abigail Adams and Thomas Jefferson. How do they account for differences in points of view?

"Taxes were extremely high. Some counties were two or three years behind. And with the prices of labor and produce falling very fast, creditors began calling for old debts and saying that they would not take payment in paper money. Those who had money demanded forty or fifty percent [interest] for it. . . . Property was selling almost every day by execution for less than half its value. The jails were crowded with debtors."

Making the Constitution

Thinking on Your Own

Write the Focus Your Reading questions in your notebook. As you read, write answers for each question. Compare your answers with those of a partner and rewrite if necessary.

In May 1787, fifty-five delegates arrived in Philadelphia. They came from every state but Rhode Island, which refused to participate. The delegates agreed that the United States needed a stronger central government. The question was whether the Articles should be revised or replaced with something new.

focus your reading

How were the Virginia and New Jersey Plans different?

What role did compromise play in creating the Constitution of the United States?

Why did many Americans oppose the Constitution?

vocabulary

legislature

executive

judiciary

Great Compromise

ratify

Federalists

Anti-Federalists

Opening Moves

The Virginia delegates arrived with a bold proposal for a new national government. Prepared by James Madison, it included a two-house **legislature**, or assembly. The Virginia Plan also called for an **executive**, or president, and a **judiciary**, or court system. The number of representatives in the legislature would be determined by a state's population. Delegates from the larger states liked this plan.

Those who wanted to revise, but not replace, the Articles of Confederation introduced an alternative plan. The New Jersey Plan was introduced by William

---

Lesson Vocabulary

Explain that the vocabulary words in this lesson relate to the word *government*. The delegates to the Philadelphia Convention created a *legislature* (Congress) to make laws, an *executive* (the president) to enforce those laws, and a *judiciary* (judges) to determine how those laws apply to particular cases.

Explain to students that a *compromise* is a settlement in which each side gives up some of its demands. The *Great Compromise* settled a disagreement. The small states, like Connecticut, wanted every state to have the same number of votes in Congress. The large states believed that the more people a state has, the more votes it should have in Congress. The compromise was the division of Congress into two houses: a Senate in which every state has the same number of votes and a House of Representatives in which representation is based on population.

After the Constitution was written, it was sent to the states to be *ratified*, or approved. The people who supported the Constitution were known as *Federalists* and those who were against it as *Anti-Federalists*. The word *federal* refers to a national government that shares power with the states.

Lesson Summary

In May 1787, delegates from twelve states met in Philadelphia. Some favored the Virginia Plan, which would replace the Articles of Confederation with a new national government. Others supported the New Jersey Plan, which would revise but not replace the Articles of Confederation. In the end, the delegates decided to use the Virginia Plan as the basis for a new government.

Once all of the compromises had been made, the convention submitted the new Constitution to the states for their approval. By August 1788, nine states had ratified the document.

Lesson Objective

Students will learn how and why delegates from twelve states wrote a new constitution for the United States.

Focus Your Reading Answers

1 The Virginia Plan was a proposal for a new national government; the New Jersey Plan was an attempt to revise but not replace the existing national government.

2 The delegates used compromises to resolve differing points of view in that each side agreed to give up a part of its demands.

3 Many Americans opposed the Constitution because they thought it gave too much power to the central government.

Stop and Think

The main characteristics of the Virginia Plan: a new national government with a two-house legislature, an executive, and a judiciary; representation determined by a state's population.

Main characteristics of the New Jersey Plan: a revision of the Articles of Confederation that gave Congress the power to tax and regulate trade but kept a one-house legislature and a weak executive appointed by Congress; each state had the same number of representatives.

Picturing History

Fifty-five delegates from 12 states (Rhode Island did not send delegates) attended the Philadelphia Convention. The oldest person at the Convention was Benjamin Franklin, at 81. The youngest, at 26, was Jonathan Dayton of New Jersey. At a time when few men had more than an elementary school education, 26 of the delegates had college degrees.

George Washington, shown standing to the right, was president of the convention. As president, he could not make speeches, but he was allowed to vote as a delegate from Virginia.

Patterson of New Jersey. The plan gave Congress the power to tax and to regulate trade. It kept the Articles of Confederation's one-house legislature. It would have a weak executive branch appointed by Congress. This plan appealed to delegates from the smaller states, as each state would have only one vote in Congress.

A Product of Compromise

The delegates voted to use the Virginia Plan as the basis for a new constitution. However, the small-state delegates insisted on changes. The result was a set of compromises.

The Constitutional Convention met in 1787 to revise the Articles of Confederation.

A Connecticut delegate, Roger Sherman, proposed that representation in one house of the legislature should be determined by population. States should be equally represented in the other. The convention delegates adopted this Connecticut Compromise, also known as the **Great Compromise**.

Slavery was another issue at the convention. The delegates from the South wanted to count slaves when determining a state's representation, but not when

stop and think

Make a two-column chart with the titles "Virginia Plan" and "New Jersey Plan." List the main characteristics of each.

Extension

Explain to students that sometimes what has been left out of a picture is as important as what is in the picture. What individuals or groups seem to be missing from the picture on page 148? (women, African Americans, Native Americans) Ask students to find out how these Americans were affected by the Constitution and share their findings with the class.

determining its share of taxes. Northern delegates took the opposite view. The Three-Fifths Compromise ended this deadlock. The South was allowed to count three-fifths of the slaves for both purposes.

The convention appointed a committee to prepare a final draft of the Constitution. The result was a document limited to "essential principles only," as one member described it. This framework allowed each generation to interpret and apply the document to changing times.

Ratification

The Confederation Congress sent the Constitution to the states to be **ratified**, or formally approved. In most states, ratification was a hard-fought contest. In Virginia, George Washington and James Madison led the **Federalists** who supported the Constitution. Patrick Henry, Sam Adams, and other **Anti-Federalists** opposed it. They thought the Constitution gave too much power to the central government.

New York City celebrated ratification of the Constitution in 1788.

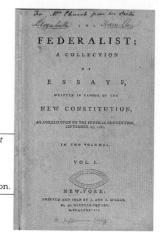

The Federalist Papers were published to support the ratification of the Constitution.

John Jay

The Federalists won over some opponents by promising to add a bill of rights to the Constitution as soon as the new Congress met. James Madison, Alexander Hamilton, and John Jay helped persuade voters by writing a series of essays known today as *The Federalist Papers*.

The eighty-five *Federalist Papers* were written between 1787 and 1788. It is believed that Hamilton wrote fifty-two papers, Madison wrote twenty-eight papers, and Jay wrote the remaining five papers. The papers were published in New York. Each of the authors went on to become an important figure in the new government. James Madison became president, John Jay became the first chief justice of the Supreme Court, and Alexander Hamilton served in the cabinet.

By August 1788, eleven states had ratified the Constitution. During the next two years, North Carolina and Rhode Island also gave their approval.

Putting It all Together

In your notebook write the heading "The Constitution as a Product of Compromise." Using bulleted notes, make a list of the major compromises that led to ratification of the Constitution.

Dates of Ratification of the Constitution

State	Date
Delaware	December 7, 1787
Pennsylvania	December 12, 1787
New Jersey	December 18, 1787
Georgia	January 2, 1788
Connecticut	January 9, 1788
Massachusetts	February 6, 1788
Maryland	April 28, 1788
South Carolina	May 23, 1788
New Hampshire	June 21, 1788
Virginia	June 25, 1788
New York	July 26, 1788
North Carolina	November 21, 1789
Rhode Island	May 29, 1790

Table Extension

Ask students to use the table on page 150 to answer the following questions:

- How many states ratified the Constitution in 1787? (three—Delaware, Pennsylvania, and New Jersey)

- Nine states had to ratify the Constitution before it went into effect. Which state was the ninth to ratify? (New Hampshire)

- The two largest states in the 1780s were Virginia and New York. When did they ratify the Constitution? (June 25 and July 26, 1788)

- Which states ratified after George Washington was elected the nation's first president in April 1789? (North Carolina and Rhode Island)

Biography

Benjamin Franklin (1706–1790)

Carved into the back of the president's chair at the Philadelphia Convention was half of a sun. Benjamin Franklin, a delegate from Pennsylvania, worried about the meaning of that sun. Was the sun setting on the American republic? As the delegates lined up on September 17, 1787, to sign the Constitution, he knew the answer. "Now at length, I have the happiness to know it is a rising and not a setting sun."

Franklin had contributed much to the rise of the American republic. In 1757, he went to England as the agent of the colony of Pennsylvania. He spent most of the next fifteen years there. As the conflict with Parliament heated up, Franklin began to speak for all of the colonies. He was the first American diplomat.

Franklin returned from England in May 1775, the month the Second Continental Congress met in Philadelphia. He joined the Pennsylvania delegation. There Franklin spoke for the radical patriots, arguing for full independence. He helped draft the Declaration of Independence and wrote Pennsylvania's state constitution.

In October 1776, Congress sent Franklin overseas to help negotiate an alliance with France. He helped prod the French government into signing a treaty of alliance with the United States. It was America's first and perhaps greatest diplomatic victory.

In 1781, at age seventy-five, Franklin wanted to come home. Instead, Congress asked him to help negotiate a peace treaty with Britain. In 1783, Franklin, John Adams, John Jay, and Henry Laurens signed the Treaty of Paris, which ended the Revolutionary war.

In 1787, Franklin served as a delegate to the Constitutional Convention. He played a major role in the convention as a voice for reason and compromise. He had reservations about the final document, but signed it and helped get it ratified.

Benjamin Franklin was the only person to sign all four major documents that established American independence: the Declaration of Independence, the treaty of alliance with France, the Treaty of Paris with Britain, and the Constitution.

Bio Facts

- Born on January 17, 1706, in Boston. He was the tenth son of soap maker Josiah Franklin. Benjamin's mother was Abiah Folger, Josiah's second wife. In all, Josiah would father 17 children.

- Opened his own print shop in Philadelphia in 1728 and became the publisher of the *Pennsylvania Gazette* the following year.

- Married Deborah Read Rogers in 1730. The couple had three children.

- Founded the first circulating library in 1731.

- Began publication of *Poor Richard: An Almanack* in 1732.

- Began writing about his experiments with electricity in 1747.

- Performed his famous kite experiment in 1752. That year he also founded the first American fire insurance company.

- Elected to Continental Congress in 1775 and signed the Declaration of Independence the following year. He then traveled to France to negotiate an alliance.

- Appointed Minister to France in 1779.

- Along with John Adams and John Jay, negotiated the Treaty of Paris with Great Britain in 1782.

- Elected president of the Pennsylvania Society for Promoting the Abolition of Slavery in 1787; served as delegate to the Constitutional Convention.

- Died at age eighty-four in Philadelphia on April 17, 1790.

Biography Extension

Almanacs were one of the most widely read books in the American colonies. Published each year, an almanac gave calendar information sprinkled with advice on farming and personal living. The most popular was Franklin's *Poor Richard's Almanack*. Challenge students to rewrite in their own words each of the following sayings from the almanac:

- Early to bed and early to rise, makes a man healthy, wealthy, and wise.

- Laws too gentle are seldom obeyed; too severe, seldom executed.

- A fool and his money are soon parted.

- No gains without pains.

- Well done is twice done.

- Strive to be the greatest man in your country, and you may be disappointed; Strive to be the best, and you may succeed.

- A good example is the best sermon.

- God helps them that help themselves.

Chapter Review

1 Answers will vary but should reflect an understanding of the arguments in favor of a strong central government.

2 Answers will vary, but paragraphs should show an understanding that Americans were trying to organize a government strong enough to protect the nation and its interests without destroying individual freedoms.

Chapter Summary

During the Revolutionary War, new state **constitutions** replaced old colonial charters. The new state governments were **republics**. Most of the constitutions included a **bill of rights**. The Articles of Confederation created a **confederation** of states. Although weak, the Confederation Congress opened the **Northwest Territory** to settlement.

The Confederation period was difficult as Congress could not pay off the **national debt**. It lacked the power to tax. Several leaders in Congress wanted a stronger central government. When the states refused, Congress invited delegates to a **convention** to revise the Articles of Confederation.

In 1786, Daniel Shays led an uprising in Massachusetts. Congress lacked the power to restore order. **Shays's Rebellion** showed that the United States government needed to be stronger.

In May 1787, delegates from twelve states met to review the Virginia Plan that included a **legislature**, an **executive**, and a **judiciary**. A state's population would determine the number of its representatives in Congress. It gave Congress more power, but each state had an equal vote.

The **Great Compromise** made population the basis of representation in the House of Representatives. It gave each state an equal vote in the Senate. The convention submitted the new Constitution of the United States to the states to be **ratified**. The **Federalists** supported the new constitution. The **Anti-Federalists** opposed it. By August 1788, the necessary nine states had ratified the Constitution.

Chapter Review

1 Imagine that you are a friend of Patrick Henry and that you favor the new Constitution. Write a letter to him explaining why he should change his mind and support the Constitution.

2 Revise your list of the words and phrases that are associated with the word *government*. Use them in a paragraph that describes the new nation's struggle to organize an effective government.

Novel Connections

Below is a list of books that relate to the time period covered in this chapter. The numbers in parentheses indicate the related Thematic Strands of the National Council for the Social Studies (NCSS).

Deborah Chandra and Madeleine Comora. *George Washington's Teeth.* Farrar, Straus and Giroux, 2003. (I, III, X)

Candace Fleming. *Ben Franklin's Almanac: Being a True Account of the Good Gentleman's Life.* Anne Schwartz Book/Atheneum Books, 2003. (I, IV, X)

James Cross Giblin. *The Amazing Life of Benjamin Franklin.* Scholastic Press, 2000. (III, VI, X)

Milton Meltzer, ed. *Hour of Freedom: American History in Poetry.* Wordsong/Boyds Mills Press, 2003. (I, II, X)

Sarah L. Thomson. *Stars and Stripes: The Story of the American Flag.* HarperCollins, 2003. (II, X)

Skill Builder

Recognizing Persuasive Writing

People use persuasion to win other people over to their point of view. Persuasion is neither good nor bad in itself, but it is a special kind of speech or writing. It typically presents only one point of view. It tends to appeal to the reader or listener's emotions. A critical reader or listener must be able to recognize persuasion.

In 1788, James Madison, Alexander Hamilton, and John Jay wrote a series of persuasive essays entitled *The Federalist Papers*. They were trying to persuade delegates to state conventions to ratify the Constitution. The following is an excerpt from one of Alexander Hamilton's *Federalist* essays (No. 15).

As you read, answer the following questions:

1 How does Hamilton appeal to patriotism in his argument for a stronger government?

2 How does he try to make his readers feel ashamed, weak, or defenseless due to the lack of a strong government?

3 What evidence is Hamilton not presenting about the present state of affairs?

"We may indeed . . . be said to have reached almost the last stage of national humiliation. There is scarcely any thing that can wound the pride or degrade the character of an independent nation which we do not experience. . . . Do we owe debts to foreigners and to our own citizens? . . . These remain without any proper or satisfactory provision for their discharge. Have we valuable territories and important posts in the possession of a foreign power which . . . ought long since to have been surrendered? These are still retained. . . . Are we in a condition to resent or to repel the aggression? We have neither troops, nor treasury, nor government."

Skill Builder

1 Hamilton appeals to patriotism by listing the humiliations Americans have experienced as a result of the weaknesses of the Articles of Confederation.

2 He tries to make his readers feel ashamed by reminding them of the humiliations the nation has experienced due to the lack of a strong government.

3 The last sentence indicates the American people did not have troops, a treasury, or a government. This is not completely true since there was an army, the government had a small treasury, and the Articles of Confederation did provide for a government. Hamilton chose his words to exaggerate the need for the Constitution's ratification.

Extensions

1 Point out to students how Hamilton uses questions to make his case. What do the questions have in common? (They all pinpoint a weakness in the existing government.) How do his answers underscore that weakness? (by repeating it)

2 Imagine you lived in 1787. Write a letter to a newspaper editor for or against ratification of the Constitution. Be sure to make your argument as persuasive as possible.

Classroom Discussion

Discuss with students some of the broader topics covered in this chapter.

- In what ways were the new state governments similar to the colonial governments? How did they differ?

- To what extent did the attitudes of Americans toward the British government affect their first state constitutions and the Articles of Confederation?

- How might Shays's Rebellion have affected the decisions delegates made about the executive branch of government?

- What were the advantages of the Constitutional Convention being held in secret? What were the disadvantages?

- To what extent does the Constitution carry out the ideas expressed in the Declaration of Independence?

Getting Focused

Skim this chapter to predict what you will be learning.

- **Read the lesson titles and subheadings.**
- **Look at the illustrations and read the captions.**
- **Examine the maps.**
- **Review the vocabulary words and terms.**

The Constitution of the United States places limits on the power of government. Look over the major headings, tables, and charts for clues about how this was accomplished. List these clues in your notebook.

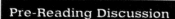

Pre-Reading Discussion

1 Have students complete each bulleted direction on page 154. Remind them that Chapter 9 focused on the events that led to the creation of the Constitution. Chapter 10 focuses on the document itself.

2 Remind students that a *constitution* is a plan for a government. The plan spells out how a group plans to divide power. Have students look over major headings, tables, and charts in this chapter for clues that suggest how the Constitution will divide the powers of government. Have students record their ideas in their journal and then revise their answers as they read the chapter.

The Federal Government

Thinking on Your Own

Read the Focus Your Reading questions and the vocabulary words. Create a two-column chart in your notebook. Write the vocabulary words on one side. As you read, define the words on the other side.

The Constitution of the United States created a **federal government**. That means that the national and state governments share power. The new central government was stronger than the Confederation Congress that it replaced. But it was not all-powerful. Some powers are shared with the states; others belong only to the states.

focus your reading

Why do we call the United States government a federal government?

What is the difference between Congress's enumerated and implied powers?

What powers are reserved for the states?

vocabulary

federal government

enumerated powers

implied powers

concurrent powers

Powers of the National Government

The Constitution created a central, or national, government with three branches, or divisions. Article I of the Constitution describes and lists the powers of the legislative branch. The Congress—or legislature—consists of the Senate and the House of Representatives. Its **enumerated powers**, or stated powers, include the power to tax, regulate trade, and declare war.

Congress maintains the nation's armed forces, can coin and borrow money, and can make immigrants citizens. The Constitution also allows Congress to pass any law "necessary and proper" to carrying out its powers. This "elastic clause" gives the Congress **implied powers** not specifically stated in the Constitution.

The Constitution 155

Lesson Vocabulary

Explain that a *federal government* is one that shares power with state governments. *Federal* comes from a Latin word that means "league or union." The words *federation* and *confederation* come from the same root.

In the new Constitution, some powers are *enumerated*, or listed. For example, the Constitution says that Congress has the power to "raise and support armies" and "provide and maintain a Navy." It does not mention an air force. The power of Congress to raise an air force is an *implied* power.

Concurrent means simultaneous. *Concurrent powers* are held by both the states and the national government. For example, both have the power to enforce laws, borrow money, and establish courts.

Lesson Summary

The Constitution created a federal government, one that shares power with state governments. The document enumerates the powers specifically given to Congress, the legislative branch of government. Congress also has implied powers not mentioned in the Constitution. Other powers are given to the executive and judicial branches of government. The national and state governments share some powers. For example, both can levy taxes and borrow money. All powers not specifically granted to the national government belong to the states.

Lesson Objective

Students will learn how the Constitution divides power between the national and state governments.

Focus Your Reading Answers

1 The United States government is called a federal government because it shares power with state governments.

2 Congress's enumerated powers are spelled out in Article I of the Constitution. Its implied powers are not specifically stated in the Constitution. They are understood because the document says that Congress may pass any law "necessary and proper" to carry out its powers.

3 The powers reserved for the states are those not specifically granted to Congress.

The powers of the executive branch—the presidency—are listed in Article II. The president acts as commander-in-chief of the armed forces, makes treaties, and appoints ambassadors, judges, and other officials. Article III set up the judicial branch, which consists of the Supreme Court and other federal courts.

Comparison of the Articles of Confederation with the Constitution

The Articles	The Constitution
The Executive Branch	
• Congress has exclusive power to govern • Executive Committee acts for Congress when it is not in session • No executive branch to enforce legislation	• President administers and enforces federal laws • President chosen by electors who have been chosen by the states
The Legislative Branch	
• A one-house legislature • Each state has one vote • Nine votes needed to pass legislation	• A two-house legislature • Each state has equal number of representatives in the Senate • Representation in the House determined by state population • Simple majority required to enact legislation
The Judicial Branch	
• No national court system • Congress can establish temporary courts to hear cases of piracy	• National court system directed by the Supreme Court • Courts hear cases related to national laws, treaties, the Constitution; cases between states, between citizens of different states, or between a state and citizens of another state
Other Provisions	
• Admission to the confederation requires nine votes • Amendment of the Articles must be unanimous	• Congress to admit new states • All states must have a republican form of government • Amendment of the Constitution by two-thirds vote of both houses of Congress, or by a national convention, and ratified by three-fourths of the states

State Governments' Powers

The Constitution places limits on the power of the national government. Powers not specifically granted to Congress, or implied under the necessary and proper clause, are reserved to the states. The Tenth Amendment states this clearly. States alone can set up town, city, or county governments. State legislatures have the power to set up business corporations and regulate trade within the state. Only states can create a police force, establish schools, and pass marriage laws. The Constitution also places limits on the powers of the states (Article IV) and places federal law above state law (Article VI).

stop and think

With a partner, discuss what you have read about the powers of the states. Then check the accuracy of your information by reviewing the lesson. Write a paragraph describing the powers of the states.

Concurrent Powers

The Constitution allows the federal government and the states to exercise some nearly identical powers. Both governments can make and enforce similar laws. For example, states make laws regulating state elections, while the federal government controls congressional and presidential elections. Both state legislatures and Congress can levy taxes, charter banks, and borrow money.

States have court systems to administer justice, including a supreme court. So does the national government. Powers that exist at both levels of government are called **concurrent powers**.

The Federal System: Division of Powers

Powers Delegated to the Federal Government	Powers Shared by the Federal and State Governments	Powers Reserved to the States
• Declare war • Regulate interstate and foreign trade • Coin money • Establish post offices • Set standards for weights and measurements • Admit new states • Establish foreign policy • Establish laws for citizenship • Regulate patents and copyrights • Pass laws necessary for carrying out its powers	• Enforce laws • Borrow money • Levy taxes • Charter banks • Establish courts • Provide for general welfare	• Establish local governments • Regulate commerce within a state • Provide for public safety • Create corporation laws • Establish schools • Make marriage laws • Assume all the powers not granted to the federal government or prohibited by the Constitution

Putting It All Together

Draw three boxes. Label them "National Government Powers," "State Government Powers," and "Concurrent Powers." Write at least three powers of government in each box.

Stop and Think

Answers will vary but paragraphs should show an understanding that states share some powers with the federal government, while other powers are reserved to the states.

Putting It All Together

Answers will vary but students should list under "National Government Powers" at least three of the powers that appear under the heading "Powers Delegated to the Federal Government" in the table on page 157; under "State Government Powers," they should list three powers that appear under the heading "Powers Reserved to the States;" and under "Concurrent Powers," they should list three powers that appear under the heading "Powers Shared by the Federal and State Governments."

Table Extension

Ask students to use the table on page 157 to answer the following questions:

- Who has the power to establish foreign policy? (federal government)

- Who is in charge of schools? (state governments)

- Who has the power to levy taxes? (both)

- Who has all powers not granted to the federal government or outlawed by the Constitution? (state governments)

Separation of Powers

Lesson Summary
The Constitution divides power within the federal government. The legislative branch has the power to make laws, the executive branch to enforce laws, and the judicial branch to interpret the laws. To keep any branch from becoming too powerful, the Constitution sets up a system of checks and balances—a system in which each branch needs the approval of another branch for certain acts. No one branch of government has complete authority.

Lesson Objective
Students will learn why the writers of the Constitution established the system of checks and balances and how the system works.

Focus Your Reading Answers

1 The Constitution divides the government into three branches because the delegates did not want the new central government to become too powerful.

2 Checks and balances prevent any one branch of government from gaining too much power.

3 The veto gives the president the power to overturn an act of Congress. However, it also limits that power by allowing Congress to override a veto. Thus, the two branches check and balance each other.

Thinking on Your Own

The major concept in this lesson is "checks and balances." As you read, make notes that describe the checks and balances built into the Constitution.

The men who created the Constitution of the United States did not trust governments with unlimited power. As colonists, they had experienced the abuse of power by Parliament and King George III. The delegates wanted a stronger central government, but not one that would become tyrannical.

focus your reading

Why does the Constitution divide the government into three branches?

What purpose do checks and balances serve?

Why is the veto power a good example of checks and balances?

vocabulary

checks and balances

impeach

veto

A Division of Power

The writers of the Constitution took care to divide power within the central government. The "accumulation of all powers, legislative, executive, and judiciary in the same hands," wrote James Madison, is "the very definition of tyranny." The delegates at Philadelphia divided the powers of the new government among three branches of government.

They gave the legislative branch—or Congress—the power to make laws and do certain other things. They divided those powers, in turn, between the House of Representatives and the Senate. The House has the sole power to initiate and write tax bills and budgets. Only the Senate can ratify treaties and approve the appointment of top officials.

The Constitution created an executive branch to enforce the laws passed by Congress. It consists of the president, vice

Lesson Vocabulary

Explain that each word in this lesson relates to the idea that the power of government should be limited. Use the diagram on page 160 to illustrate how the system of *checks and balances* keeps each branch of government from becoming too powerful.

The word *impeach* means to place a public official on trial for misconduct. Discuss how the power of Congress to impeach can check the executive and judicial branches.

Veto is a Latin word that means "I forbid." In issuing a *veto*, a president is refusing to allow an act of Congress to become law. How is the president checking the power of Congress? When Congress overrides a president's *veto*, how is it checking the power of the executive branch?

Division of Powers		
Executive Branch	Legislative Branch	Judicial Branch
President • Enforces the laws • Acts as commander-in-chief of the armed forces • Appoints ambassadors, judges, and other officials • Makes treaties with other nations	**Congress** • Writes the laws • Raises troops for armed forces • Decides how much money may be spent on government programs	**Supreme Court** • Interprets the laws • Reviews court decisions

president, and officials in the executive departments. The president's cabinet is part of the executive branch. The executive branch also has the power to conduct war, sign treaties, and nominate people for federal office.

The judiciary is the third branch of the government. The Constitution gives it the power to decide conflicts between states and between individuals in different states. It includes the Supreme Court and any other federal courts that Congress deems necessary.

stop and think

Think about what you have just read concerning the separation of powers. Write three sentences in your notebook to explain this concept.

Checks and Balances

The delegates in Philadelphia created **checks and balances** to prevent any branch of the government from gaining too much power. The Constitution requires treaties signed by the executive branch to be ratified, or approved, by the Senate. The Senate also must approve top-level appointments made by the president, including justices of the Supreme Court. Congress also has the power to **impeach** the president or judges. Impeachment means to bring a public official to trial for misconduct.

Congress can pass legislation by a simple majority. The Constitution gives the president power to **veto**—or refuse to approve—this act of Congress. However, it also limits this power by allowing Congress to override a veto. A vetoed bill

The Constitution 159

Extension

Ask students to find out how many representatives their state sends to the House of Representatives. Who is the representative from their district? When is he or she up for reelection? How many U.S. senators does their state have? What are their names? When are they up for reelection?

Table Extension

Review the definition of the word *tyranny*. (See Chapter 8.) Then ask students to use the table to explain what James Madison meant when he said that "the accumulation (gathering) of all powers, legislative, executive, and judiciary in the same hands is the very definition of tyranny."

Putting It All Together

The paragraphs should show an understanding that each branch of government has the power to check or balance the power of the other two branches.

can become law if passed again in both houses by a two-thirds majority. This allows the two branches to check and balance each other. The president checks the judiciary by having the power to appoint federal judges and to pardon persons convicted in federal courts.

The Supreme Court plays a major role in the system of checks and balances. It can overturn acts of Congress and actions of the president if it finds that they violate the Constitution. The Supreme Court first exerted these powers in its decisions in the cases of *Marbury v. Madison* (1803) and *Ex parte Milligan* (1866). The only check given the Court in the Constitution is the power of the chief justice to preside over the impeachment trial of the president.

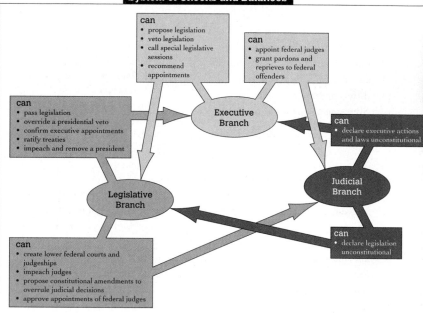

System of Checks and Balances

can
- propose legislation
- veto legislation
- call special legislative sessions
- recommend appointments

can
- appoint federal judges
- grant pardons and reprieves to federal offenders

can
- pass legislation
- override a presidential veto
- confirm executive appointments
- ratify treaties
- impeach and remove a president

can
- declare executive actions and laws unconstitutional

Executive Branch

Judicial Branch

Legislative Branch

can
- create lower federal courts and judgeships
- impeach judges
- propose constitutional amendments to overrule judicial decisions
- approve appointments of federal judges

can
- declare legislation unconstitutional

Putting It All Together

Using your notes about checks and balances, write a paragraph about the concept. Include information about each of the three branches.

Chart Extension

Ask students to use the diagram on page 160 to answer the following questions:

- Name one way the legislative branch can check the power of the president.

- Name one way the executive branch can check the power of Congress.

- Name one way the judicial branch can check the power of Congress.

- Name one way the executive branch can check the power of the courts.

Biography

Roger Sherman (1721–1793)

Roger Sherman attended the Constitutional Convention in 1787 as a delegate from Connecticut. He was the most awkward person John Adams had ever seen. "When he moves a hand . . . it is stiffness and awkwardness itself, rigid as starched linen." Adams and his college-educated friends could barely keep from laughing at Sherman's back-country language. A delegate from Georgia called him "unaccountably strange in his manner."

Roger Sherman was an odd but honest man. The people of Connecticut trusted him. They trusted him as a young man to make a good pair of shoes at an honest price. When he was twenty-four, they chose the young cobbler to be county surveyor. They could depend on him to settle boundary disputes fairly. They elected him to Connecticut's colonial assembly ten years later. By then, the honest surveyor had become a large landowner and successful merchant.

Like most colonial merchants, Roger Sherman opposed Parliament's taxes on imports. In 1774, the Connecticut assembly sent him to the Continental Congress to protest against parliamentary taxation. Sherman spent the next eight years as a member of Congress. There he took charge of military supplies, planning, and finance. War contractors dreaded doing business with the tight-fisted Sherman. He kept trying to cut costs.

Despite his odd ways and rough manners, Roger Sherman was a good politician. He knew when to stand firm and when to compromise. At the Constitutional Convention, Sherman put this ability to good use. He favored the New Jersey Plan, which gave each state an equal vote in Congress. Most delegates wanted representation based on population. Sherman proposed a compromise—give the states equal representation in the Senate, but base representation in the House of Representatives on population.

The Connecticut Compromise—known as the Great Compomise—was Sherman's greatest contribution to the new republic. It saved the Philadelphia Convention, which almost broke up over this issue. Roger Sherman died in New Haven, Connecticut, on July 23, 1793, at the age of seventy-two.

161

Bio Facts

- Born in Newton, Massachusetts, on April 19, 1721.

- Two years after his father's death in 1741, he moved to New Milford, Connecticut, where his older brother lived.

- Became the surveyor of New Haven County in 1745.

- Married Elizabeth Hartwell of Stoughton in 1749; they had seven children.

- Studied law and was admitted to the bar in 1754.

- Served as a member of the Connecticut assembly and as justice of the peace for Litchfield County.

- Moved to New Haven, Connecticut, in 1761, where he became a justice of the peace and later a judge.

- Served as a member of the Continental Congress in 1774–1781 and 1784.

- Served on the committee that drafted the Declaration of Independence; later signed the document.

- Helped prepare the Articles of Confederation.

- Served as a delegate to the Constitutional Convention at Philadelphia in 1787.

- Served as mayor of New Haven from 1784 until his death.

- Elected to the first Congress (March 4, 1789–March 3, 1791).

- Elected to the United States Senate and served from 1791 until his death in 1793.

Biography Extension

Roger Sherman and Richard Morris were the only Americans to sign the Declaration of Independence, the Articles of Confederation, and the U.S. Constitution. (Sherman also signed the Declaration of 1774.) Four other signers of the Declaration of Independence—George Clymer, Benjamin Franklin, George Read, and James Wilson—also signed the Constitution. Encourage students to find out more about the life of one of these delegates and then compare and contrast his life with that of Roger Sherman.

The Bill of Rights

Thinking on Your Own

Read the Focus Your Reading questions and the vocabulary words. In your notebook, write two questions that you have about the Bill of Rights.

In 1787, many Americans opposed the Constitution despite its separation of powers and system of checks and balances. They worried that Congress or the president would misuse the power and abuse the rights of the people. To win support for ratification, the Federalists agreed to add a **bill of rights**, or list of rights.

Amending the Constitution

The delegates in Philadelphia tried to make the Constitution a timeless document. With that in mind, they made it possible to add **amendments**, or make changes. "In framing a system which we wish to last for all ages," James Madison said, "we should not lose sight of the changes which ages will produce."

According to Article V, Congress or the state legislatures, by

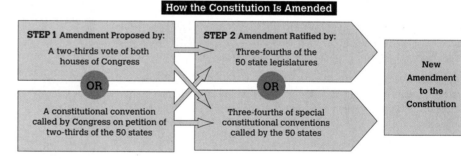

How the Constitution Is Amended

STEP 1 Amendment Proposed by:
A two-thirds vote of both houses of Congress

OR

A constitutional convention called by Congress on petition of two-thirds of the 50 states

STEP 2 Amendment Ratified by:
Three-fourths of the 50 state legislatures

OR

Three-fourths of special constitutional conventions called by the 50 states

New Amendment to the Constitution

Chart Extension

Ask students to use the flow chart on page 162 to answer the following questions:

- What is the first step in amending the Constitution? (winning approval of the proposed amendment by a two-thirds vote of both houses of Congress or a constitutional convention called by Congress on petition of two-thirds of the states)

- What is the second step? (ratification by three-fourths of the state legislatures or three-fourths of special constitutional conventions called by the states)

- Why do you think the delegates to the Constitutional Convention did not make it easier to amend the Constitution? (They wanted the document to be changed only when it was necessary to do so.)

a two-thirds vote, can propose an amendment. It can be ratified by a vote of three-fourths of the legislatures or conventions called by the states for that purpose. To date, twenty-seven amendments have been added to the Constitution.

stop and think

Discuss with a partner how the men who wrote the Constitution planned to make it last "for all ages." Write two sentences in your notebook summarizing your points.

Adding the Bill of Rights

During its first session, Congress took up the question of a bill of rights. The states had submitted dozens of proposals. James Madison organized them into nineteen amendments. Congress approved twelve and sent them to the states for ratification. The states, in turn, ratified ten of them. An amendment related to representation in Congress was never approved. The other amendment, concerning congressional pay, was ratified in 1992 as the Twenty-Seventh Amendment.

The Bill of Rights

The Bill of Rights addresses several of the American people's most important concerns. The first four amendments protect basic rights that Britain violated during the protest over taxes and tea. These include freedom of speech, press, assembly and religion; the right of people's militias to keep and bear arms; the right not to have troops quartered, or live, in a person's house; and freedom from unreasonable searches and seizures of property. The next four amendments protect Americans against unfair court procedures, trials, and convictions. The Ninth Amendment protects rights not

The Bill of Rights	
1	Guarantees freedom of religion, speech, assembly, and press, and the right of people to petition the government
2	Protects the rights of states to maintain a militia and of citizens to bear arms
3	Restricts quartering of troops in private homes
4	Protects against unreasonable searches and seizures
5	Assures the right not to be deprived of life, liberty, or property without due process of law
6	Guarantees the right to a speedy and public trial by an impartial jury
7	Assures the right to a jury trial in cases involving the common law—the law established by previous court decisions
8	Protects against excessive bail, or cruel and unusual punishment
9	Provides that people's rights are not restricted to those specified in the first eight Amendments
10	Restates the Constitution's principle of federalism by providing that powers not granted to the national government nor prohibited to the states are reserved to the states and to the people

Stop and Think

Answers will vary but should reflect the idea that the framers recognized that changes would be necessary from time to time, but those changes should not be made casually or lightly.

Table Extension

Ask students to use the table on page 163 to answer the following questions:

• Which amendment protects protesters? (first amendment)

• Which amendment protects an individual's right to worship as he or she pleases? (first amendment)

• What do the fifth, sixth, seventh, and eighth amendments have in common? (They protect individuals from practices that would make it difficult or impossible to have a fair trial.)

• Why is the ninth amendment important? (It says that even rights not listed in the first eight amendments are protected.)

Putting It All Together

Answers will vary. Students may find more information about the Bill of Rights by reading the first ten amendments to the Constitution on pages 339–340, by reading civics or government books, or by gathering information from the Internet or the public library.

specifically mentioned in the Constitution. The Tenth Amendment is another "catchall" amendment. It reserves to the states any powers not delegated to the central government or prohibited by the Constitution.

Putting It All Together

Review the questions that you had before reading this lesson. Did you find the answers? What other questions do you have now? In your notebook, make a list of places where you can find more information about the Bill of Rights.

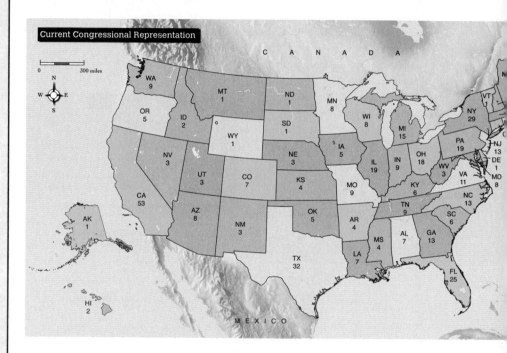

Current Congressional Representation

Map Extension

Ask students to use the map on page 164 to answer the following questions:

- What do Vermont, Delaware, North Dakota, South Dakota, Alaska, Montana, and Wyoming have in common? (Each has one representative in the House of Representatives.)

- Which state has the most representatives? (California)

- What determines how many representatives a state has in the House of Representatives: size or population? (population)

Read a Primary Source

Sam Adams Against the Constitution

At first, Sam Adams opposed ratifying the Constitution. He eventually supported it after the Federalists promised to add a bill of rights.

reading for understanding

Why did Adams describe the Constitution as a "national" government?

What problem did he foresee from such a government?

Why did he prefer a confederation of sovereign states?

"I [find the Constitution to be] a national government, instead of a federal union of sovereign states. I am not able to conceive why the wisdom of the Convention led them to give the preference to the former before the latter. If the several states in the union are to become one entire nation, under one legislature, the powers of which shall extend to every subject of legislation . . . can this national legislature be competent to make laws for the free internal government of one people, living in climates so remote and whose 'Habits & particular Interests' are and probably always will be so different?

Should we continue distinct sovereign states, confederated for the purposes of mutual safety and happiness . . . the people would govern themselves more easily, the laws of each state being well adapted to its own genius and circumstances, and the liberties of the United States would be more secure than they can be, as I humbly conceive, under the proposed new constitution."

Letter from Sam Adams to Richard Henry Lee, December 3, 1787; in William V. Wells, *The Life and Public Services of Samuel Adams, III* (Boston, 1866).

Reading for Understanding

1 Adams described the Constitution as a "national" government because the new government was no longer a confederation of sovereign states.

2 Adams believed that a "national government" would not be competent to make laws for people scattered across such a large area with differences in habits and interests.

3 He preferred a confederation of sovereign states because it allowed people to govern themselves more easily and adapt their laws to their own unique circumstances.

165

Extension

Ask students to use a search engine like Google to look for news stories that feature the Bill of Rights. Which rights are featured in these stories? What do the stories suggest about the Constitution as a timeless document?

Extension

Ask students to reread the Bill of Rights on page 163 and use that information to decide which amendments addressed Sam Adams's concerns. Have them share their answers with the class.

Chapter Review

1 Logos will vary but should reflect the right or rights to which each logo refers.

2 Categories will vary but might include powers of government (enumerated powers, implied powers, and concurrent powers) and limits on government (federal government, checks and balances, impeachment, veto, bill of rights, amendments).

3 Answers will vary but should reflect an understanding that each branch of government checks and is checked by the other two branches.

Chapter Summary

The Constitution of the United States created a **federal government**. Congress has **enumerated powers**, which include the power to tax, regulate trade, and declare war. The Constitution also gives Congress **implied powers** not mentioned in the Constitution. The Constitution leaves to the states all powers not granted to Congress or implied under the necessary and proper clause. The national and state governments share some powers, such as the power to tax and borrow money. These are called **concurrent powers**.

The Constitution divides power within the national government. The legislative branch has the power to make laws. The executive branch enforces the laws. The judicial branch interprets the laws. To prevent any branch from gaining too much power, the Constitution includes **checks and balances**. For example, the president has the power to **veto** an act of Congress, but Congress can override his veto. Congress can **impeach** the president, but the Supreme Court oversees the trial.

To win support for ratification, the Federalists promised to add a **bill of rights**. This was possible by adding **amendments**. During its first session, Congress approved the first ten amendments—the Bill of Rights. They protected basic rights and guarded against unfair trials and court proceedings.

Chapter Review

1 Design a poster about the Bill of Rights. Include logos that would match the different rights that it protects.

2 Look over the vocabulary words. Work with a partner to organize the words into categories. Write the categories in your notebook. Then explain in writing why you chose these categories.

3 Imagine that you are a newspaper reporter in 1788 writing an article about the Constitution's system of checks and balances. What major points would you include in your article?

Novel Connections

Below is a list of books that relate to the time period covered in this chapter. The numbers in parentheses indicate the related Thematic Strands of the National Council for the Social Studies (NCSS).

Eileen Christelow. *Vote!* Clarion Books, 2003. (V, VI, X)

Lynn Curlee. *Capital.* Atheneum Books, 2003. (III, X)

Russell Freedman. *In Defense of Liberty: The Story of America's Bill of Rights.* Holiday House 2003. (VI, X)

Skill Builder

Reading a Historical Document:
The Constitution of the United States

Historical documents from early periods can pose problems for modern readers. They often use words that are no longer in everyday use. Words may be arranged in ways that now sound odd. The document may be divided into sections or parts for reasons that are not obvious. The following are useful guidelines for reading historical documents:

- Find out who wrote the document.
- Check when it was written.
- Read the introduction to learn what the document is about.
- Read the subtitles to determine how the document is organized.
- Read the document one section at a time.
- Try to define unknown words by using context clues.

Apply the above guidelines to the Constitution of the United States by answering the following questions. The Constitution can be found at the back of this book.

1 Where are the names of the delegates to the Philadelphia Convention listed?

2 On what date did these men sign the Constitution?

3 What does the Preamble—Introduction—indicate this document is about?

4 Into how many articles—subsections—is the Constitution divided, and what is each about?

5 Why are some articles divided into sections?

6 Read one article carefully. In your own words, explain what it is about.

7 What unfamiliar words did you learn the meaning of by using context clues?

Classroom Discussion

Discuss with students some of the broader topics covered in this chapter.

- How did the authors of the Constitution try to correct the weaknesses of the Articles of Confederation?

- Why do you think the Constitution gave Congress both enumerated and implied powers?

- What are the advantages of a system of checks and balances? What are the disadvantages?

- How many amendments have been added to the Constitution? Why do you think the framers of the Constitution included a method for changing the document?

Skill Builder

1 The names of the delegates are listed at the end of the main portion of the Constitution and before the list of amendments.

2 The delegates signed the Constitution on September 17, 1787.

3 The Preamble says that this document was created by the people of the United States in order to bind the states more closely together and establish a just government—one that keeps the peace, protects the nation, promotes prosperity, and secures freedom not only for Americans in 1787 but also for generations to come.

4 The Constitution is divided into seven articles. Article 1 describes the legislative branch; Article 2, the executive branch; Article 3, the judicial branch; Article 4, relations between the states and the nation; Article 5, how to amend the Constitution; Article 6, the Constitution as the supreme law of the land; Article 7, how the Constitution will be ratified.

5 Some articles are divided into sections because they include a variety of subtopics.

6 Answers will vary but should reflect the main idea of the article.

7 Answers will vary.

Unit Objectives

After studying this unit, students will be able to

- describe the first national government established under the Constitution

- explain how and why Americans formed political parties

- outline the changes that took place in the United States in the early 1800s

Unit 6 focuses on the nation's first national government under the Constitution.

- **Chapter 11, The Federalists in Power,** describes the Federalists' approach to the nation's problems in the late 1700s.

- **Chapter 12, The Republican Era,** examines changes of the new United States in the early 1800s.

Getting Started

Introduce the word *republic* by asking students to read aloud the two paragraphs on page 168. Remind students that a *republic* is a government that gets its power from the people.

The Constitution created a republic. What do the two paragraphs suggest about the challenges the young republic faced? Ask students to examine the pictures in Chapters 11 and 12. What do they add to students' understanding of those challenges?

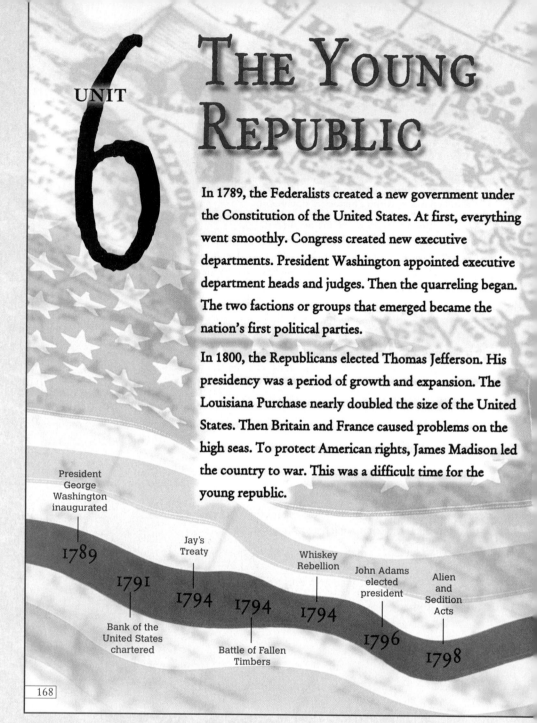

UNIT 6

THE YOUNG REPUBLIC

In 1789, the Federalists created a new government under the Constitution of the United States. At first, everything went smoothly. Congress created new executive departments. President Washington appointed executive department heads and judges. Then the quarreling began. The two factions or groups that emerged became the nation's first political parties.

In 1800, the Republicans elected Thomas Jefferson. His presidency was a period of growth and expansion. The Louisiana Purchase nearly doubled the size of the United States. Then Britain and France caused problems on the high seas. To protect American rights, James Madison led the country to war. This was a difficult time for the young republic.

President George Washington inaugurated
1789

Bank of the United States chartered
1791

Jay's Treaty
1794

Battle of Fallen Timbers
1794

Whiskey Rebellion
1794

John Adams elected president
1796

Alien and Sedition Acts
1798

168

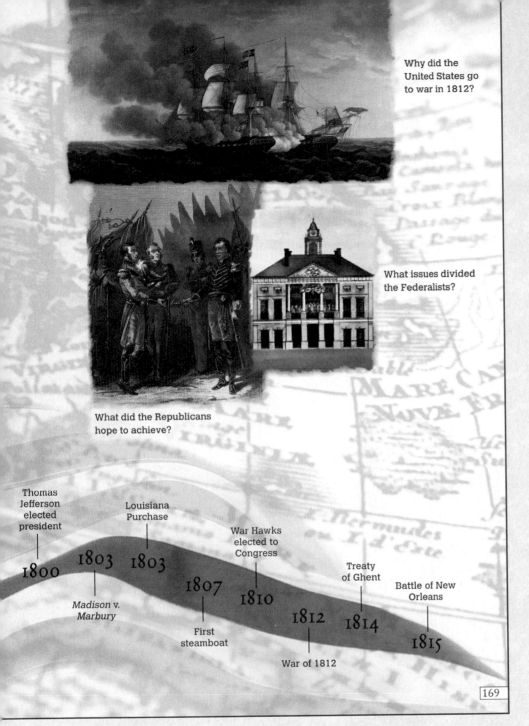

Why did the
United States go
to war in 1812?

What issues divided
the Federalists?

What did the Republicans
hope to achieve?

Thomas
Jefferson
elected
president

Louisiana
Purchase

War Hawks
elected to
Congress

Treaty
of Ghent

Battle of New
Orleans

1800 **1803** **1803** **1807** **1810** **1812** **1814** **1815**

*Madison v.
Marbury*

First
steamboat

War of 1812

Collage Answers

1 The United States went to war in 1812 to protect its rights as a neutral nation. Western settlers also accused Britain of arming Native Americans in the Ohio Valley.

2 The Republicans hoped to cut back the role of the federal government and maintain peace with foreign governments.

3 The Federalists were divided over issues related to Alexander Hamilton's financial plan for the nation and the Bank of the United States.

Collage Extension

Use the images and questions on page 169 to preview the unit. Discuss how the questions relate to the word *republic*.

Measuring Time

Explain to students that the first page of the timeline focuses on events described in Chapter 11. The second page highlights events discussed in Chapter 12.

Timeline Extension

Have students copy the timeline into their notebooks and write down information about each event as they read. Their notes might include the following details about each event:

• What happened?

• Who was involved?

• Where did it happen?

• Why was it important?

Chapter 11
THE FEDERALISTS IN POWER

Getting Focused

Skim this chapter to predict what you will be learning.

- Read the lesson titles and subheadings.
- Look at the illustrations and read the captions.
- Examine the maps.
- Review the vocabulary words and terms.

As you review the chapter, look for the basic features of the new government. Create questions that you expect the chapter to answer.

Pre-Reading Discussion

1 Ask students to read aloud the chapter title and review the meaning of the word *federalist*. Explain that once the Constitution was ratified, the word increasingly referred to a *political party*—a group of people with similar ideas about how the country should be run and who have organized to influence or run the government. What do the lesson titles and the pictures in this chapter suggest about which Americans considered themselves Federalists?

2 After students complete each bulleted direction on page 170, ask them to read aloud the last paragraph on page 170 and then identify the basic features of the new government. Have students record their questions and then read to find answers to those questions.

Creating a New Government

Thinking on Your Own

Read the Focus Your Reading questions. Create a two-column chart in your notebook. Label the first column "Important Facts" and the second column "Connections." As you read, note the important facts in the first column. In the other column, write connections between these facts and the people or events in the chapter.

In 1789, the United States faced a major task. It had to fill in the details for the new government created by the outline in the Constitution. The American people had to elect a new president. The president had to appoint executive officials and federal judges. The new Congress had to solve a variety of problems.

focus your reading

What executive departments did Congress create?

Whom did President Washington appoint to these offices?

What was Alexander Hamilton's financial plan?

vocabulary

inauguration   bonds
tariff duties

The New Government Takes Shape

In early April 1789, Congress met in New York City, then the nation's capital. After counting the electoral votes, the Senate declared George Washington president. The new vice president was John Adams. He had received the second highest number of votes.

George Washington decided not to wear his military uniform to his **inauguration**, or swearing in ceremony. He wore a plain, brown suit instead. He wanted people to see the president as an ordinary citizen. Some proposed that the president be called "His Excellency" or "His Highness." Washington asked to be called simply "Mr. President."

Extension

Electors from ten states unanimously elected George Washington president. Rhode Island and North Carolina did not vote, because they had not yet ratified the Constitution. New York had ratified the Constitution by 1789 but was unable to participate in the Electoral College because of internal problems. Have students turn to the Constitution (page 330) and find the clause that describes the way the Electoral College works. (Article II, Section 1)

Lesson Vocabulary

Each of the vocabulary words in this lesson relates to the new United States government. *Inauguration* is the process of swearing a public official into office. Explain that *tariff duties* are taxes on imports—goods shipped to the United States from another country.

Explain that *bonds* are certificates of indebtedness issued by a government in return for money it has borrowed. The certificates promise to pay a specified sum of money at a fixed time in the future along with a set amount of interest. (Interest is the cost of borrowing money.)

Lesson Summary

George Washington was elected president of the United States in 1789. That year, Congress passed a number of laws that filled in the outline for a new government created by the Constitution. One of those laws was a Tariff Act that established taxes to pay most of the government's expenses. Alexander Hamilton suggested that Congress assume debts the states incurred in wartime as well as those of the nation and pay those debts by issuing bonds. He also proposed a national bank.

Lesson Objective

Students will learn about how the new government, created by the Constitution, took shape under President George Washington.

Focus Your Reading Answers

1 Congress created the Department of State, the Treasury Department, and the War Department.

2 Washington appointed Thomas Jefferson Secretary of State, Alexander Hamilton Secretary of the Treasury, and Henry Knox Secretary of War.

3 Alexander Hamilton's financial plan called for exchanging debts incurred during the Revolutionary War for bonds that earned interest. He also wanted Congress to pay loans owed by the states and create a Bank of the United States.

George Washington was inaugurated for a second term on March 4, 1793.

Stop and Think

The second level should show the departments of state, treasury, and war. The Department of State handled relations with other nations and was headed by Thomas Jefferson of Virginia; the Treasury Department handled the nation's finances and was headed by Alexander Hamilton of New York; and the War Department was in charge of the nation's defense and was headed by Henry Knox of Massachusetts.

Picturing History

The drawing at the top of page 172 shows Washington's second inauguration—the ceremony that marked the beginning of his second term in office. Ask students to study the drawing carefully. What does it suggest about the nation's leaders? Notice the president and other officials standing on the balcony of Federal Hall in New York. Ask students who may be watching the ceremony in the street below.

Congress created the first three executive departments. It set up the Department of State to deal with other nations. Congress created the Treasury Department to look after finances and the War Department to defend the nation. It also set up the offices of attorney general and postmaster general.

Thomas Jefferson

With the Senate's approval, President Washington appointed the heads of the departments and the justices of the Supreme Court. He appointed Thomas Jefferson as Secretary of State. Alexander Hamilton became the first Secretary of the Treasury. Henry Knox was the new Secretary of War. The Chief Justice of the Supreme Court was John Jay.

To provide money to operate the government, Congress passed the Tariff Act of 1789. Thereafter, **tariff duties**, or taxes collected on imports, paid most of the government's expenses. Congress

stop and think

Create a four-level concept graph with "Executive Departments" on the top. On the second level, create three circles each with one of the executive departments in them. Underneath the circles, write a brief description of the departments. On the fourth level, write the names of the heads of the departments under each description.

Picturing History

At the time Washington appointed Thomas Jefferson Secretary of State, he had been serving as the American minister to France for five years. Discuss with students how Jefferson's role as the American minister to France may have prepared him for his new position.

Extension

In 1790, the Department of State consisted of four clerks and a messenger. Clerks wrote messages and letters to the nation's two ministers (ambassadors) and ten consuls. (A consul is a diplomat appointed to protect the nation's trade and help its citizens in a foreign country.)

Have students find out how many people work for the State Department today. In how many countries does the nation have ambassadors or consuls? Encourage students to share their findings by creating a poster showing the work of the Department of State in 1793 and today.

also passed the Judiciary Act of 1801, which created a new system of federal courts. It also sent the Bill of Rights to the states for ratification.

George Washington with his cabinet

Putting It All Together

Answers will vary, but paragraphs should include Hamilton's plans to pay off not only the nation's wartime debts but also those of the states. Paragraphs should also discuss why Hamilton wanted Congress to create a national bank.

Hamilton's Financial Plan

In 1790, Secretary of the Treasury Hamilton turned his attention to the nation's finances. During the war, Congress had borrowed about $42 million from the American people. It gave the lenders loan certificates, or IOUs, that it promised someday to repay in hard cash. Hamilton asked Congress to exchange these IOUs for **bonds**, or certificates, that earned interest. He also proposed that Congress pay the $25 million in loans owed by the states. Finally, Hamilton asked Congress to create a Bank of the United States. He said that a bank was needed to collect taxes and circulate money.

Putting It All Together

Discuss with a partner the significant points of Hamilton's financial plan. Write them in your notebook. Then write a paragraph explaining his plan.

Picturing History

Pictured on page 173, from left to right, are George Washington, Henry Knox, Edmund Randolph of Virginia (the attorney general), Thomas Jefferson, and Alexander Hamilton. By 1793, these department heads were beginning to be known as Washington's *cabinet*—the name the British used to describe those who advised the king. Although the Constitution does not specifically mention a cabinet, it soon became an important part of government. Have students think about why the positions have become so necessary to the workings of government.

1 Hamilton thought the nation needed farmers (cultivators), skilled workers, and merchants.

2 Hamilton thought that a country that has both manufacturing and farming will have the most trade.

3 Manufacturing is related to national security in that a strong nation should produce the "essentials of national supply."

Read a Primary Source

Alexander Hamilton on the Importance of Manufacturing

In his *Report on Manufacturers*, Alexander Hamilton explained the benefits of manufacturing for the United States. He also called upon Congress to pass laws to support manufacturing.

reading for understanding

What kind of occupations did Hamilton think a nation needed?

What kind of country did he think would have the most trade?

How is manufacturing related to national security?

"The spirit of enterprise . . . must necessarily be . . . less in a nation of mere cultivators than in a nation of cultivators and merchants; less in a nation of cultivators and merchants than in a nation of cultivators, [skilled workers], and merchants. . . .

"There seems to be a moral certainty that the trade of a country which is both manufacturing and agricultural will be more lucrative and prosperous than that of a country which is merely agricultural.

"Not only the wealth, but the independence and security of a country . . . connected with the prosperity of manufacturers. Every nation . . . ought to endeavor to possess within itself all the essentials of national supply. These comprise the means of subsistence, habitation, clothing, and defense. . . ."

Reports of the Secretary of the Treasury of the United States (Washington, D. C., 1897).

174

Extension

Encourage students to find out more about Alexander Hamilton's contributions to the nation. Encourage them to use the biography of Hamilton on page 179 as well as information found in the library or on the Internet. Have students create a poster that highlights their findings.

Federalists Disagree

Thinking on Your Own

Read the Focus Your Reading questions and the vocabulary. Write the vocabulary words in your notebook. As you read their definitions, write a sentence for each word that includes the definition.

In 1789, the Federalists were united in support of the Constitution. They all wanted a national government stronger than the one provided by the Articles of Confederation. But once in office, the Federalists began to disagree among themselves.

Debate over Hamilton's Plan

Several congressmen opposed Hamilton's financial plan. The group's leader was Congressman James Madison of Virginia. Madison thought the plan favored **speculators**, or men who hoped to profit from the wartime loan certificates. Many of the original lenders had sold these IOUs for as little as 25 cents on the dollar. Under Hamilton's plan, the people who bought them could exchange the certificates for bonds at face value.

Madison also opposed having the federal government take over the states' debts. Virginia and several southern states had already paid off their wartime loans. They did not want to have to pay the debts of other states.

---

focus your reading

Why did some congressmen oppose Hamilton's financial plan?

Why did Thomas Jefferson oppose the Bank of the United States?

What problems did the United States have with other nations?

vocabulary

speculators
excise tax
Whiskey Rebellion
strict interpretation
broad interpretation

Congressman James Madison

The Federalists in Power 175

Lesson Vocabulary

Introduce each vocabulary word. Explain that to *speculate* is to invest at a risk. A *speculator* is someone who risks losses for the possibility of financial gain. An *excise tax* is a tax on a particular good or service. In 1794, farmers in western Pennsylvania refused to pay the excise tax on whiskey. Their stand is known as the *Whiskey Rebellion*.

Explain that an *interpretation* is an explanation of what something means. *Strict interpretation* of the Constitution means that the explanation is based solely on what is actually stated in the document. *Broad interpretation* is often based on the "necessary and proper clause" (Article I, Section 8), which gives Congress the power to stretch its powers to deal with situations the Founders could not have anticipated.

Lesson Summary

After 1789, the Federalists began to disagree with one another. Several opposed Hamilton's plan because it favored speculators. Hamilton's supporters in Congress passed an excise tax on whiskey to pay the interest on the new bonds. The result was a Whiskey Rebellion in Pennsylvania. Jefferson was Hamilton's main opponent. He argued against a national bank because he believed that the Constitution did not give Congress the power to create one. Hamilton disagreed.

Lesson Objective

Students will learn about disagreements among the Federalists over a variety of issues that Americans faced in the late 1700s.

Focus Your Reading Answers

1 Some Congressmen opposed Hamilton's financial plan because they thought it favored speculators. They also opposed the idea of the federal government taking over the states' wartime debts. Some states had paid off their loans and did not want to pay the loans of other states.

2 Thomas Jefferson opposed a national bank because he insisted that Congress lacked the power to charter a bank.

3 The problems the U.S. had with other countries included a lack of respect for American neutrality during the wars between Britain and France, the failure of Britain to remove soldiers from frontier forts, and a desire to open the Spanish port of New Orleans to American trade.

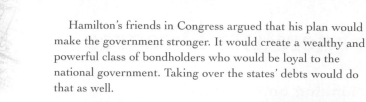

Hamilton's friends in Congress argued that his plan would make the government stronger. It would create a wealthy and powerful class of bondholders who would be loyal to the national government. Taking over the states' debts would do that as well.

Hamilton finally won enough southern votes in Congress to get his plan approved. He did this by promising northern support for a bill the South wanted. That bill would move the nation's capital from New York City to a new federal city on the banks of the Potomac River. Both bills passed in July 1790.

To pay the interest on the new bonds, Congress placed an **excise tax** on whiskey. This tax hurt many western farmers. Distilling their corn into whiskey was the cheapest way for them to ship it to market. In 1794, farmers in western Pennsylvania refused to pay the tax. President Washington sent 13,000 militia troops to Pennsylvania to put down the **Whiskey Rebellion**.

The Whiskey Rebellion focused attention on new taxes passed by Congress.

The Bank of the United States in Philadelphia remains the oldest bank building in the country.

The Bank of the United States

Federalists also disagreed about Hamilton's plan for a Bank of the United States. Secretary of State Thomas Jefferson led the opposition. He believed that a federal bank was unnecessary. It would only benefit the rich people who owned stock in the bank. Using a **strict interpretation** of the Constitution, he insisted that Congress lacked the power to charter a bank. Hamilton argued that the "necessary and proper" clause gave Congress that power. This was a loose interpretation, or **broad interpretation**, of the Constitution. In 1791, Congress passed the bank bill.

European and Native American Problems

Issues concerning relations with Europe also divided the Federalists. In 1793, France and Britain went to war. The South mainly supported France, the United States' old ally. Southerners accused Britain of taking sailors off American ships. The British also had not withdrawn their soldiers from frontier forts. Northern merchants favored Britain. They wanted closer relations and expanded trade with the British.

Jay's Treaty of 1794 was not popular and he was burned in effigy.

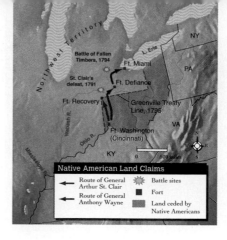

President Washington managed to ease relations with Britain. He sent John Jay to London to negotiate a treaty. In Jay's Treaty (1794), Britain agreed to remove its soldiers from American forts.

The Republicans attacked the treaty, which failed to settle other issues. Spain was concerned about Jay's Treaty and how it would impact Spanish territory in North America. Thomas Pinckney's treaty with Spain (1795) settled the issue by opening the Mississippi River and New Orleans to American trade.

General Anthony Wayne led the victory at the Battle of Fallen Timbers.

Tecumseh

The government also faced a Native American crisis. Tecumseh, a Shawnee leader, tried to unite the Ohio Valley tribes against the settlers there. The United States army put down this uprising at the Battle of Fallen Timbers (1794). Defeated, the Native Americans signed the Treaty of Greenville (1795), in which they agreed to leave the Ohio Valley.

Putting It All Together

In your notebook, write the following statement: "Hamilton's financial plan was good for the United States." Under the statement write "True" on one side and "False" on the other. Choose a position on this issue. Find facts from the lesson to support your position and list them under one of the above columns. Discuss your position with a partner.

Biography

Alexander Hamilton (1755–1804)

In December 1791, Secretary of the Treasury Alexander Hamilton sent his *Report on Manufacturers* to Congress. It presented his vision of a powerful nation bound together by a strong economy. The rural South and Middle Atlantic states would provide the nation with food and raw materials. The Northeast would produce its manufactured goods. Hamilton looked forward to an America of cities, factories, and workshops as well as plantations, farms, and villages. More than most Americans of his time, he had a national perspective.

A broad, national view came easily for Hamilton. As a recent immigrant, he had few local or regional loyalties. Born in the British West Indies in 1755, he grew up on the Dutch island of St. Croix. He arrived in New York City in 1772, at age seventeen. When the War for Independence began, Hamilton joined the patriots as captain of a New York artillery company.

In 1776, Hamilton's company joined George Washington's army in its retreat through New Jersey. Washington liked the young man and appointed him to his headquarters staff. Hamilton spent the war years as a lieutenant-colonel in the Continental Army. That also helped give him a national point of view.

After the war, Hamilton served in Congress. There he saw firsthand the need for a stronger national government. Unable to raise money, Congress could not pay its debts. In 1786, Hamilton, James Madison, and others called for a Constitutional Convention. He attended the Philadelphia convention as a New York delegate. With Madison and John Jay, he wrote the *Federalist* essays to win support for the new constitution.

In 1789, President Washington appointed his former aide de camp as secretary of the treasury. That gave Hamilton an opportunity to develop national policies. Congress approved his plans to pay off the nation's debts and to create the Bank of the United States. It also passed laws to support manufacturing, as he had called for in his *Report* in 1791. He returned to private life in 1795, having helped create a new national government and a stronger nation.

Alexander Hamilton was killed in a duel with former vice president Aaron Burr. He died on July 11, 1804, at age forty-nine.

179

Bio Facts

- Born on January 11, 1755, (or 1757, by some accounts) in Charleston on the West Indies island of Nevis.

- Moved to New York City in 1773 and entered Kings College (now known as Columbia University) in 1774.

- Commanded artillery troops during the Revolutionary War and served from 1777 to 1781 as Washington's personal assistant.

- Married New Yorker Elizabeth Schuyler in 1780; the couple had eight children.

- Served in the New York state legislature and the Continental Congress.

- Participated in the Constitutional Convention of 1787 and led the successful campaign for ratification of the Constitution in New York by authoring many of *The Federalist Papers*.

- Appointed secretary of the treasury in 1789.

- Returned to private life in 1795. Hamilton practiced law and helped found the Bank of New York. He also became a leader of the Federalists.

- Died in 1804 as the result of a duel with Aaron Burr, who served as vice president under Thomas Jefferson.

Extension

Alexander Hamilton played a key role in the 1800 presidential election. Ask students to find out more about his role in that election. They might focus on the consequences of the choices he made in that election, Jefferson becoming president, the Twelfth Amendment to the Constitution, or his duel with Aaron Burr. Ask students to present their findings to the class by using the Student Presentation Builder on the student DVD.

Lesson Summary

When George Washington left office in 1797, he warned Americans against the danger of factions. After the election of John Adams, the nation almost went to war with France. The French government insulted the United States in the XYZ Affair. The Federalists in Congress passed the Alien and Sedition Acts that banned newspapers from printing articles critical of the Federalists. The Republicans responded by passing the Kentucky and Virginia Resolutions, which threatened to nullify these acts of Congress.

Lesson Objective

Students will learn how and why factions turned into political parties between 1796 and 1800.

Focus Your Reading Answers

1 The United States almost went to war with France over an insult. The French minister said he would not meet with American diplomats until they paid a bribe of $250,000.

2 The Federalists tried to silence their opponents by passing the Alien and Sedition Acts.

3 Republicans in 1800 opposed the Alien and Sedition Acts.

Federalists vs. Republicans

Thinking on Your Own

Read the Focus Your Reading questions and the vocabulary words. In your notebook, write "America's Difficulties with France." As you read, write a bulleted note of any fact that relates to that statement.

I n his farewell address in 1796, President Washington warned Americans against the danger of **factions**. Factions are opposing groups within a political party. Washington saw the factions that had developed among the Federalists as a threat to national unity.

Why did the United States almost go to war with France?

How did the Federalists try to silence their opponents?

What did the Republicans stand for in 1800?

factions	sedition
XYZ Affair	nullify
alien	

Adams Elected President

In 1796, each faction had its own candidate for president. The Federalists nominated John Adams. The Republicans supported Thomas Jefferson. Adams won the election. The new president faced a crisis in foreign affairs. France had stepped up attacks against American shipping. It had captured 300 American ships by the time Adams took office. Hamilton and other Federalists called for war against France. The Republicans opposed going to war.

President Adams sent diplomats to talk with the French government. The French foreign

President John Adams

Lesson Vocabulary

Explain each vocabulary word in this lesson. The word *faction* refers to a group within an organization (often a political party) that has different goals than those of the party as a whole. Those who were against the ideas of Alexander Hamilton were originally a *faction* within the Federalist Party. In time, they began to meet separately from the Federalists and call themselves Democratic-Republicans or just Republicans. Later, they began to choose candidates to run for public offices. These steps turned a *faction* within the Federalist Party into a separate political party.

The *XYZ Affair* refers to a meeting in France between three American diplomats and three French spokespeople, known only as "X," "Y," and "Z." They asked the Americans to pay them a bribe. In return, they would make it easier to reopen discussions between the two nations. Americans were outraged by what became known as the *XYZ Affair*.

minister announced that he would not meet with them until they paid him $250,000. News of this insult, called the **XYZ Affair**, produced still louder cries for war.

The Alien and Sedition Acts

President Adams was concerned about the tension with France. He thought that French citizens living in the United States might side with France if a conflict began. The Federalists in Congress used this crisis to crack down on their Republican opponents. In 1798, they passed laws known as the **Alien** and **Sedition** Acts. These acts gave the president the power to expel or jail any alien, or non-citizen. They also gave the government the power to charge people with sedition, or rebellious acts.

stop and think

In your notebook, write a bulleted list of issues that faced President Adams. Then work with a partner and write how Adams solved each issue.

A fight in Congress, and later a letter to the editor, led to sedition charges against Matthew Lyons.

One of the Alien Acts increased the time a foreigner had to live in the United States before he could become a citizen. The time increased from five to fourteen years. Another of the Alien Acts allowed the president to deport any foreigner he thought was "dangerous to the peace and safety of the United States." At the time, new immigrants were usually Republicans.

The Federalists in Power 181

Lesson Vocabulary, continued

An *alien* is a person from a foreign country who is not yet a citizen of the country in which he or she now lives. The word *sedition* refers to the act of organizing or encouraging efforts to overthrow the government. Ask students to use the two definitions to explain the purpose of the Alien and Sedition Acts. To *nullify* a law is to officially state that it does not have to be obeyed. State legislators in Virginia and Kentucky *nullified* the Alien and Sedition Acts.

Stop and Think

Lists will vary, but should include attacks against American shipping, possible war with France, and the Alien and Sedition Acts.

Picturing History

In January of 1798, a heated debate raged in the House of Representatives over the best way to deal with the French. On January 30, the debate became personal, when Roger Griswold, a Federalist from Connecticut, made insulting remarks about the war record of Representative Matthew Lyons of Vermont during a debate. At first Lyons ignored the remark, but when Griswold repeated it, Lyons spit a stream of tobacco juice in Griswold's face. Griswold tried but failed to get the House to punish Lyons.

Two weeks later, the incident shown in the drawing on page 181 took place. Griswold walked up to Lyons's desk and began beating him with a heavy stick. Lyons is shown fending off Griswold with tongs from a nearby fireplace. How does the artist seem to view the incident? How does the incident help us understand why Washington saw factions as a threat to national unity?

The goal of the Sedition Act was to prevent people from speaking out against the government. The act also made it a crime to "impede the operation of any law." It provided fines and jail terms for anyone guilty of sedition, or stirring up of discontent. The Federalists used the law against Republican newspapers. The law banned articles that could damage the reputation of a government official. Twenty-five Republican editors and printers were jailed under this act.

The Kentucky and Virginia Resolutions

The Republicans fought back. Jefferson and Madison wrote resolutions declaring that the Alien and Sedition Acts violated the Constitution. The Kentucky and Virginia legislatures adopted these resolutions. Kentucky even claimed that states had a right to **nullify**, or strike down, an act of Congress.

In the meantime, President Adams sent a new set of delegates to France. They signed an agreement in which the French government agreed to protect American rights. This prevented a war with France, which was President Adams's greatest achievement. It displeased many Federalists, who wanted a war with France.

In 1800, the Republicans nominated Thomas Jefferson and Aaron Burr for president and vice president. They ran against the Federalists John Adams and Charles C. Pinckney. The Republicans

Thomas Jefferson was often criticized by the Federalists for his foreign policy.

THE PROVIDENTIAL DETECTION

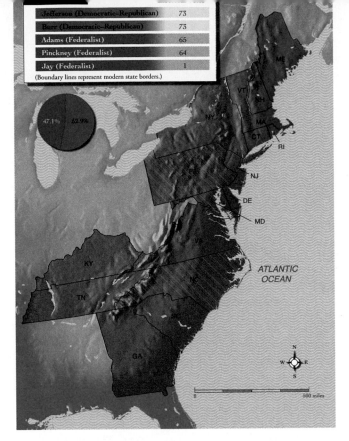

Jefferson (Democratic-Republican)	73
Burr (Democratic-Republican)	73
Adams (Federalist)	65
Pinckney (Federalist)	64
Jay (Federalist)	1

(Boundary lines represent modern state borders.)

47.1% 52.9%

ATLANTIC OCEAN

0   500 miles

Map Extension

Ask students to use the map on page 183 to answer the following questions:

- What states did the Federalists carry? (New England states, Delaware, and New Jersey)

- What states did the Democratic-Republicans carry? (New York, Virginia, South Carolina, Kentucky, Tennessee, and Georgia)

- What states were divided between the two parties? (Pennsylvania, Maryland, and North Carolina)

Putting It All Together

The list should include the XYZ Affair, the Alien and Sedition Acts, and the Virginia and Kentucky Resolutions.

campaigned against the unpopular Alien and Sedition Acts. Jefferson and Burr won, but both received the same number of votes. This electoral tie threw the election into the Federalist House of Representatives. After 36 ballots, the House finally elected Jefferson president. This led to the Twelfth Amendment, which prevented such ties in the future.

Putting It All Together

List the major events that led to Thomas Jefferson's election as president. Write them in your notebook. Then write a short paragraph about the events.

The Federalists in Power 183

Extension

Ask students to read the Twelfth Amendment to the U.S. Constitution (pages 340–341). Then have them draw a diagram explaining how it would prevent election ties like the one between Jefferson and Burr.

Chapter Review

1 Letters will vary but should reflect an understanding that Hamilton believed in a strong central government and a broad interpretation of the Constitution. Madison thought Hamilton's plan favored speculators. He also did not want the federal government to pay the wartime debts of the states. Madison favored a strict interpretation of the Constitution.

2 Answers will vary, but the paragraph should use the vocabulary terms correctly.

3 Answers will vary, but the brochure should refer to the insult to the United States implicit in the XYZ Affair and the threat posed by French citizens living in the United States.

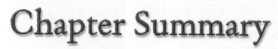

Chapter Summary

In 1789, George Washington was **inaugurated** as president of the United States. Congress passed several laws, including the Tariff Act of 1789. Thereafter, **tariff duties** paid most of the government's expenses. In 1790, Secretary Hamilton proposed that Congress pay its debts with **bonds**.

After 1789, the Federalists began to disagree. Several congressmen opposed Hamilton's plan. They thought it favored **speculators**. Hamilton's friends in Congress enacted the plan into law. To pay the interest on the new bonds, Congress placed an **excise tax** on whiskey. This produced a **Whiskey Rebellion** in Pennsylvania. Using a **strict interpretation** of the Constitution, Jefferson argued that Congress lacked the power to create a bank. Hamilton, using a **broad interpretation**, said that the Constitution's phrase "necessary and proper" gave Congress the right to start the Bank of the United States.

President Washington warned Americans against the danger of **factions**. President Adams almost got involved in a war with France. The French government had insulted the United States in the **XYZ Affair**. The Federalists in Congress passed **alien** and **sedition** acts that banned newspaper articles critical of the Federalists. The Republicans passed the Kentucky and Virginia Resolutions, which threatened to **nullify** these acts of Congress.

Chapter Review

1 Write a letter either to Hamilton or Madison asking for a job as his public relations person. Include in your letter the viewpoints you share with the person you choose.

2 Use this chapter's vocabulary words in a first-draft paragraph to summarize what you have learned about the Federalists in power. Compare your paragraph with that of a partner. Then write a final draft.

3 Create a war brochure that a Federalist may have written calling for war against France. Include the reasons for wanting a war.

Novel Connections

Below is a list of books that relate to the time period covered in this chapter. The numbers in parentheses indicate the related Thematic Strands of the National Council for the Social Studies (NCSS).

Patricia Calvert. *Great Lives: The American Frontier.* Atheneum, 1997. (II, III)

Lynn Curlee. *Capital.* Atheneum Books, 2003. (III, X)

David Rubel. *Scholastic Encyclopedia of Presidents and Their Times.* (rev. ed.) Scholastic, 2001. (II, IV, VI)

Sarah L. Thomson. *Stars and Stripes: The Story of the American Flag.* HarperCollins, 2003. (II, X)

Robert Young. *A Personal Tour of Monticello.* Lerner, 1999. (I, II)

Skill Builder

Understanding Cause and Effect

Looking for cause and effect is one way to answer "why" questions.

1. Why were you late to school? Because you overslept.
2. Why did you oversleep? Because you forgot to set the alarm.
3. Why did you forget to set the alarm? Because you had other things on your mind.

Think of each of the above questions as an effect. Each effect had at least one cause. As you can see, some events also can be both effects and causes.

Looking for cause and effect helps us understand history. We can better understand why something happened in the past (effect) if we know what other people, conditions, or events helped make it happen (cause). George Washington's service to the nation during the American Revolution (cause) helps to explain his being elected president in 1789 (effect).

By 1796, the Federalists had divided into two factions. The majority of Federalists looked to John Adams and Alexander Hamilton for leadership. A group that called themselves Republicans rallied around Thomas Jefferson and James Madison.

In your notebook, make a "Cause and Effect Chart" like the one below. Reread Lesson 2 and identify at least three causes that help explain the emergence of factions. Then reread Lesson 3. Examine how those factions acted as a cause that had at least three other effects. Write the causes and effects in your chart.

Skill Builder

1 Causes of Factions: disagreements over Hamilton's plan, including exchanging loan certificates for bonds, paying state debts, and establishing a national bank; arguments over relations with Europe; and conflicts over Jay's Treaty.

2 Effects of Factions: Alien and Sedition Acts and their use to ban Republican newspapers; Kentucky and Virginia Resolutions; the tie in the electoral college in the 1800 presidential election.

Classroom Discussion

Discuss with students some of the broader topics covered in this chapter.

- What was the attitude of the Federalists toward the Constitution? What was the attitude of Republicans? What similarities do you notice between the two parties? How important are the differences?

- What attitudes and values were reflected in the Alien and Sedition Acts? What threat to the young republic did these laws pose?

- What attitudes and values were reflected in the Virginia and Kentucky Resolutions? What threat to the republic did these resolutions pose?

- Why did events like the XYZ Affair stir up such strong feelings in the nation?

Chapter Summary

Refer to page 198 in the student book for a summary of Chapter 12.

Related Transparencies

T-11 The Louisiana Purchase

T-12 The War of 1812

T-18 T-Chart

Key Blacklines

Biography
Eli Whitney

Primary Source
Thomas Jefferson on Good Government

DVD Extension

Encourage students to use the reading comprehension, vocabulary reinforcement, and interactive timeline activities on the student DVD.

Picturing History

The drawing on page 186 shows Americans at war. Ask students what country may have been the enemy. Have them check their ideas by previewing lesson titles and subheadings as well as the illustrations and their captions.

Chapter 12 THE REPUBLICAN ERA

Getting Focused

Skim this chapter to predict what you will be learning.

- Read the lesson titles and subheadings.
- Look at the illustrations and read the captions.
- Examine the maps.
- Review the vocabulary words and terms.

Many changes took place in the United States during the early 1800s. After reviewing the chapter, make a bulleted list of changes. Add to your list as you read.

Pre-Reading Discussion

1 Have students complete each bulleted direction on page 186. Remind them that Chapter 11 focused on the administrations of George Washington and John Adams, the two Federalist presidents. Chapter 12 focuses on the administrations of Thomas Jefferson and James Madison, the first Republican presidents.

2 Ask students to look over major headings, tables, and charts in this chapter for clues to the main accomplishments and challenges of the two administrations highlighted in this chapter. Have students record their ideas in their journals and then revise their answers as they read the chapter.

The Republicans in Power

Thinking on Your Own

Write the Focus Your Reading questions in your notebook on the left side of a two-column chart. When you come to the answers to the questions, write them in the right column of the chart.

Thomas Jefferson saw his election as the beginning of a new era. He looked forward to a time of "**republican** simplicity" in American life. He wanted to bring republican, or more democratic, values to public life. Presidents Washington and Adams rode to their inaugurations in carriages. Jefferson, the first president to be inaugurated at the capitol in Washington, D.C., walked to the ceremony. He spent the next eight years trying to simplify and reduce the size of government.

focus your reading

How did Jefferson cut back the role of government?

What power did the *Marbury v. Madison* decision give the Supreme Court?

Why did Jefferson think twice about purchasing Louisiana?

vocabulary

republican
midnight appointees
Louisiana Purchase
Lewis and Clark Expedition

Republican Government

Jefferson and the Republicans in Congress moved quickly to cut back the role of the federal government. Congress let the hated Alien and Sedition Acts expire. It repealed the Naturalization Act. Jefferson persuaded Congress to cut military spending. It also shrank the size of the navy from 25 to 7 ships. Jefferson closed nearly half of the American embassies in Europe.

These savings allowed Congress to remove all excise taxes. With no taxes to collect, it abolished the internal

Thomas Jefferson

Lesson Vocabulary

Review the definition of the word *republic*. (A *republic* is a government that gets its power from the people.) Then ask students what the word *republican* means. As an adjective, *republican* indicates support for a government that gets its power from the people. As a noun, it refers to an individual who supports such a government.

Explain to students that *midnight* is sometimes used as an adjective to describe a last-minute activity. The term *midnight appointees* refers to the judges and other court officials President John Adams appointed during his final hours in office.

The *Louisiana Purchase* is the name given to the land the United States bought from France in 1803. Have students trace the area on the map on page 189. The *Lewis and Clark Expedition* is the group President Jefferson sent to explore the new territory. Meriwether Lewis and William Clark led the expedition.

Lesson Summary

Jefferson's election marked the start of a new era. He wanted to bring more democratic values to public life by cutting back on the role of the federal government and letting the Alien and Sedition Acts expire. He and Congress also repealed the Naturalization Act and cut military spending.

Jefferson refused to allow his secretary of state to deliver papers confirming Adams's last-minute appointment of judges and other court officials. Several sued and the Supreme Court ruled for the first time that a federal law was unconstitutional. In 1803, Jefferson completed the Louisiana Purchase, nearly doubling the size of the nation.

Lesson Objective

Students will learn how Jefferson tried to make the federal government more democratic.

Focus Your Reading Answers

1 Jefferson cut back the role of the government by urging Congress to let the Alien and Sedition Acts expire, repeal the Naturalization Act, and cut military spending. The savings allowed Congress to remove all excise taxes.

2 The *Marbury* v. *Madison* decision established the right of the Supreme Court to declare a law unconstitutional.

3 Jefferson thought twice about purchasing Louisiana because the Constitution said nothing about the nation buying new territory.

Stop and Think

Questions will vary. Have students verify their answers before sharing their questions and answers with a partner.

Picturing History

In 1801, John Adams named John Marshall, a Federalist from Virginia, chief justice of the U.S. Supreme Court. Marshall served on the court for 34 years. As chief justice, he did more than any other American to define the role and responsibilities of the judicial branch of the federal government. One of his most significant decisions was in the case of *Marbury* v. *Madison*. It declared that Article III of the Constitution does not allow Congress or state legislatures to pass laws that are in conflict with the Constitution itself. Ask students to explain how that decision increased the power and authority of the Supreme Court.

revenue department. That cut another 500 federal jobs. The cutbacks allowed Jefferson to pay off the national debt more quickly than Hamilton had intended. He could not, however, change all of Hamilton's policies. The Bank of the United States had a 20-year charter. He had to live with it.

stop and think

In your notebook write two questions about Jefferson's presidency for which you know the answers. Share your questions and answers with a partner.

The Federalist Judiciary

Making the judicial system Republican was more difficult. The Republicans could not get rid of Federalist judges, because they served for life. Jefferson was able to block some new appointments. During his final hours in office, John Adams had appointed several judges and court officials. Jefferson ordered Secretary of State James Madison not to deliver the appointment papers.

William Marbury, one of the "**midnight appointees**," filed a complaint with the Supreme Court. He demanded that the Court order Madison to deliver his papers. In the case of *Marbury* v. *Madison* (1803), Chief Justice Marshall declared that Marbury had no right to appeal Madison's action. He declared unconstitutional the law that gave Marbury that right. This was a major victory for the Supreme Court. It established the Court's right to declare acts of Congress unconstitutional.

Chief Justice John Marshall

Map Extension

Ask students to use the map on page 189 to answer the following questions:

- What part of the Louisiana Purchase was in dispute? (land just east and west of the mouth of the Mississippi River)

- What nations claimed that land? (U.S. and Spain)

- What river did the Lewis and Clark Expedition follow? (Missouri River)

- What mountains did the expedition cross? (Rocky Mountains)

- What other territory did the expedition cross? (Oregon Country)

The Louisiana Purchase

In early 1803, France offered to sell Louisiana to the United States. Buying Louisiana would nearly double the nation's size. It would give western farmers the unquestioned right to ship their produce down the Mississippi River. But President Jefferson believed in a strict, or narrow, interpretation of the Constitution. That document said nothing about the U.S. buying new territory.

Despite his doubts, Jefferson agreed to the **Louisiana Purchase**. He signed a treaty with France to buy Louisiana for $15 million. In the spring of 1804, Meriwether Lewis and William Clark led an expedition to explore Louisiana. They followed the Missouri River to its source, crossed the Rocky Mountains, and reached the Pacific. The **Lewis and Clark Expedition** returned in 1806 with a wealth of information about the Far West.

Meriwether Lewis

William Clark

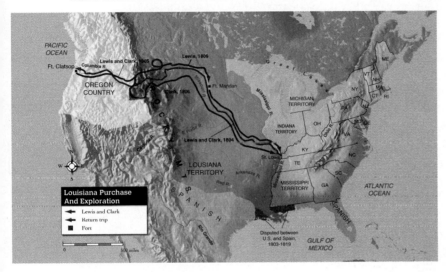

Putting It All Together

Create a web diagram in your notebook. In the middle, write the main concept, "The Republicans in Power." Go back over the section to collect facts that describe the Republicans in power. Arrange them in circles around the main concept.

Putting It All Together

The web diagram should include the expiration of the Alien and Sedition Acts, the repeal of the Naturalization Act, cuts in military spending, the removal of the excise tax, paying off the national debt, and the Louisiana Purchase.

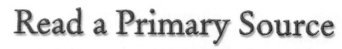

Read a Primary Source

William Clark's Journal

Both Meriwether Lewis and William Clark kept journals during their expedition to the Pacific Ocean. The following entry, with Clark's inventive spelling, is from his journal on September 26, 1804. In the entry, Clark discribes his first meeting with the Sioux.

Reading for Understanding

1 The men stopped where they did because the chiefs wanted their women and boys to see the boat.

2 The Sioux men and women wore fur robes with the flesh side out and the hairy ends turned back over their shoulders. The women also wore petticoats made of skin.

3 Clark thought that the women did all of the hard work and were slaves to their husbands who often had several wives.

> "26th of Septr Set out early and proceeded on. The river lined with Indians, [stopped] & anchored by the particular request of the Chiefs to let their Womin & Boys See the Boat. . . . Those people are Spritely . . . men particularly, they grease & Black themselves when they dress, make use of Hawks feathers about their heads, cover with a Roab. Each [has] a polecat skin to hold their Smokeables, fond of Dress, Badly armed. Ther women appear verry well, fin[e] Teeth, High Cheek [bones] Dress in Skin Peticoats, & a Roabe with the flesh Side out and harey ends turned back over their Sholders, and look well. They doe all the Laborious work, and I may say are perfect Slaves to their husbands who frequently have Several Wives."

The Journals of the Lewis & Clark Expedition
(13 vols., Lincoln, Nebraska, 1987).

reading for understanding

Why did the men stop where they did?

How did the Sioux men and women dress?

How did Clark think women were treated in Sioux society?

190

Extension

Encourage students to visit interactive Web sites that allow visitors to follow the route of Lewis and Clark. Ask students to share their discoveries with the class.

Biography

Sacagawea (c.1788–1812 or 1884)

Meriwether Lewis and William Clark met Sacagawea by accident. They did not plan to take a sixteen-year-old Shoshone woman on their journey to the Pacific, especially not one with a newborn child. She was the wife of Toussaint Charbonneau, whom the explorers hired in November 1804 as an interpreter.

The explorers, led by Lewis and Clark, stopped for the winter at the Mandan Villages in present-day South Dakota. None of them could speak the languages of the Native Americans they would meet farther west.

They hired Charbonneau, a French-speaking fur trapper, because he knew sign language. They soon learned that Sacagawea could speak Shoshone and Hidatsa.

Finding Sacagawea was a stroke of luck for Lewis and Clark. She showed the explorers how to find wild vegetables to add to their diet. When her husband's boat capsized on the Missouri River, he panicked, as he could not swim. Sacagawea saved the valuable compasses, books, and clothing that had washed overboard. Her very presence with her baby, Baptiste, proved helpful. It assured the Native Americans along the way that the explorers posed no threat. A war party would never bring along a woman with a baby.

Sacagawea was most valuable when the Lewis and Clark Expedition reached Shoshone country. She was the explorers' main interpreter with the Shoshone chiefs. Most important, she persuaded the chiefs to sell horses to Lewis and Clark. They could not have crossed the mountains in the winter without them.

Sacagawea traveled with the expedition to the Pacific Coast. On the return trip in 1806, she and Baptiste stopped off at the Mandan villages. She later took him to St. Louis, where William Clark placed Baptiste in school. Many historians believe she died of fever in December 1812, at age twenty-four, at a trading post on the Missouri River. However, there is an oral history that indicates she lived until 1884.

Sacagawea is honored by more monuments, markers, and mountain peaks than any other American woman. Her image also appears on the United States' one-dollar coin.

Bio Facts

- Born in about 1788 in a Northern Shoshone village near the Lemhi River valley in what is today eastern Idaho.

- Was captured by a raiding band of Hidatsa in about 1798 and carried to their camp near the border of North Dakota.

- Was sold to a French-Canadian fur trader named Toussaint Charbonneau.

- Met Lewis and Clark during the winter of 1804–1805 at Fort Mandan in North Dakota.

- Gave birth to her son, Jean Baptiste, on February 11, 1805, at the fort.

- When Lewis and Clark hired Charbonneau as a guide, he was told to bring Sacagawea and their baby to establish the peaceful nature of the party. They also needed a translator and negotiator with knowledge of local customs and tribes.

- Left Lewis and Clark at Fort Mandan, their starting point, on August 17, 1806, with her husband and son. Charbonneau received $500.33 for his work. Sacagawea received no payment because she was an unofficial member of the expedition.

- Took their son to St. Louis where Clark agreed to raise the boy along with his own children.

- Is believed to have died of "putrid fever" (smallpox, tuberculosis, or possibly scarlet fever) in 1812 at a trading post on the Missouri River.

Biography Extension

According to Native American accounts—especially Shoshone oral histories—Sacagawea, whom they call Porivo, did not die in 1812. They claim that she lived to the age of ninety-six, married several times over the years, and had a number of children. Those who support these stories note that Porivo met many white Americans who noted that she had intimate knowledge of the Lewis and Clark expedition, spoke French, and wore a Jefferson Medal around her neck. Dr. Charles Eastman, who had been hired by the Bureau of Indian Affairs to locate Sacagawea, believed that Porivo was Sacagawea. Others disagreed, noting that Clark believed that she was dead. Ask students to research the story further and decide which version is true.

Lesson Summary

The early 1800s was a period of economic growth in the United States. Many people moved to the Ohio Valley and the Lower South. Steamboats contributed to that growth. Manufacturing expanded in the Northeast. In 1789, Samuel Slater built the first spinning mill in the United States. Eli Whitney developed a new method of producing goods with interchangeable parts at his weapons factory in Connecticut. With the growth of farming and manufacturing, the number of American merchant ships more than doubled. As trade expanded, American shippers faced greater risks. The Barbary States of North Africa demanded tribute. In protest, Congress passed an embargo.

Lesson Objective

Students will learn how and why the nation prospered in the early 1800s.

Focus Your Reading Answers

1 The American economy expanded during the early 1800s because of the growth of farming in the West and South and of manufacturing in the Northeast.

2 During the early 1800s manufacturers used water power and new machines to produce goods. Many also used a new method of machine production known as interchangeable parts.

3 The early 1800s was a golden age of American shipping because the number of merchant ships doubled between 1793 and 1807.

Growth and Expansion

Thinking on Your Own

Read the Focus Your Reading questions and the vocabulary words. In your notebook arrange the vocabulary words into three columns: "Words I Know," "Words I Think I Know," and "Words I Do Not Know." As you read, find the definitions of the words and write them in your notebook.

The early 1800s was a period of growth and expansion for the young American nation. More settlers moved west. In cities and towns, the number of workshops and mills increased. So did American shipping and trade with other nations. Venturing out into the world brought new opportunities and new risks.

focus your reading

Why did the American economy grow during the early 1800s?

How did manufacturing change during this period?

Why was this period a golden age of American shipping?

vocabulary

spinning mill

interchangeable parts

merchant ships

tribute

neutral

embargo

Economic Growth

People continued to move west. They settled in the Ohio Valley and in the Lower

On August 14, 1807, Robert Fulton's *Clermont* made the first successful steamboat trip.

South. Northern farmers produced corn and pork, which flatboats carried down the Mississippi River to market. By 1802, more than 500 flatboats arrived each year at the Port of New Orleans. Cotton and corn were the main crops raised in the South.

Steamboats contributed greatly to the nation's economic growth. In 1807, Robert Fulton built the *Clermont*, the first workable steamboat.

Lesson Vocabulary

Several terms in this lesson are made up of familiar words. Encourage students to use those words to figure out what the new term means. A *spinning mill* is not a factory that moves in circles but one that uses machines to spin cotton into thread. The term *interchangeable parts* means exactly what it says. It is a manufacturing method in which a component of a machine, tool, or other product such as a lever in one machine can be used in another machine. As a result, even an unskilled worker can quickly put together or repair a finished product. *Merchant ships* are ships that carry goods used in trade.

The word *tribute* is one of several words in this lesson that have more than one meaning. In this lesson, *tribute* means payment by one nation for protection by another. In other words, it is protection money. *Neutral* also has many meanings. In this lesson, it refers to a nation that does not side with either party in a war or dispute. An *embargo* is a government ban on trade.

Merchant shipping increased dramatically between 1793 and 1807.

Unlike flatboats, steamboats could haul goods upriver against the current. They became widely used on the Mississippi and Ohio Rivers.

Manufacturing expanded in the Northeast. In 1789, Samuel Slater built the first thread **spinning mill** in the United States. It used water power and machines to spin cotton thread. By 1815, the northeastern states had more than 200 spinning mills.

At his firearms factory in Connecticut, Eli Whitney developed a new method of machine production. His machines replaced skilled gunsmiths. They made **interchangeable parts**, which allowed unskilled workers to assemble muskets.

The early 1800s was the golden age of American shipping. The number of American **merchant ships** on the high seas doubled between 1793 and 1807. They carried farm produce being exported to foreign markets and imported goods not manufactured in the United States. This trade provided business for ship owners and work for sailors. Experienced sailors were in great demand.

stop and think

Imagine that you lived during this period. Write a newspaper advertisement for an invention that helped make the nation prosperous. Include an illustration and a caption.

Protecting American Rights

As trade expanded, American shipping faced greater risks. The Barbary States of North Africa—Algiers, Morocco, Tripoli, and Tunis—demanded **tribute**, or protection money, from ships sailing the Mediterranean Sea. In 1801, the United States went to war with Tripoli rather than meet these demands. In 1805, negotiations ended the conflict.

The Republican Era 193

Stop and Think

The ads will vary but should include such inventions as the steamboat, the spinning mill, and interchangeable parts.

Picturing History

Steam power changed the way merchants transported goods along waterways. This illustration shows the port of New Orleans.

Extensions

1 Ask students to gather information about inventors like Henry Shreve, who improved on Fulton's steamboat. Have students present their findings to the class by using the Student Presentation Builder on the student DVD.

2 Have students gather information about Eli Whitney and his various inventions. Ask them to choose one invention and create a poster highlighting the role the invention played in American history.

Picturing History

When Robert Fulton built the *Clermont*, some people laughed at the idea of a boat that ran on steam. They called it Fulton's Folly. The *Clermont*'s journey from New York City to Albany and back proved that those critics were wrong. On the first half of the journey, the boat traveled 150 miles in 32 hours. A similar trip by flatboat or barge would have taken several days. How do you think spectators reacted to their first view of the strange-looking ship that belched a fiery shower of sparks?

The Barbary States
■ Barbary State
0   500 miles

FRANCE   EUROPE
PORTUGAL   SPAIN
ATLANTIC
OCEAN   ITALY
MOROCCO   ALGIERS   Mediterranean Sea
                              TUNIS
AFRICA   TRIPOLI

Map Extension

Have students use the map on page 194 to answer the following questions:

- Name the Barbary states. (Morocco, Algiers, Tunis, and Tripoli)

- On what continent were they located? (Africa)

- What sea lay to the north of the Barbary States? (Mediterranean Sea)

Putting It All Together

The timeline should include Fulton's steamboat voyage in 1807, the first spinning mill in 1789, Whitney's use of interchangeable parts in the late 1700s, and the golden age of American shipping in the early 1800s. Each spurred economic growth. Paragraphs should indicate the students' understanding of the timeline events and how they impacted the economy of the United States.

Stephen Decatur led a group of men who burned the *Philadelphia* in Tripoli's harbor in 1804.

Britain and France posed a greater threat. When these nations went to war in 1803, the United States declared itself a **neutral** country. By not taking sides, the United States could ship goods to both nations. However, neither nation respected the United States' neutral rights. In 1806, Britain began stopping all ships that traded with France. Some British officers also forced American sailors into the British navy. In reply, France declared British ports closed to neutral ships.

To protest against these actions, President Jefferson persuaded Congress, in 1807, to pass an Embargo Act. This **embargo** stopped American ships from leaving for any foreign ports. It was a disaster for American merchants and ship owners. Congress repealed the act in 1809, replacing it with an act that reopened trade with all nations except Britain and France.

Putting It All Together

In your notebook, make a timeline of five important events included in this lesson. Below each event explain why it was significant. Then write a paragraph explaining the timeline.

Picturing History

For hundreds of years, the leaders of the Barbary States terrorized ships on the Mediterranean Sea. In February of 1804, one group captured the U.S. frigate *Philadelphia*. Unable to recover the ship, Stephen Decatur and a small crew slipped into the harbor and burned the *Philadelphia* without the loss of a single man. On his return to the United States, at a banquet in his honor, Decatur proposed his famous toast: "Our country! In her [dealings] with foreign nations, may she always be in the right; but our country, right or wrong!" Ask students what the toast means. What point was Decatur making about his support for his country?

3 The United States Goes to War

Thinking on Your Own

Read the Focus Your Reading questions and the vocabulary words. As you read, make a list of the vocabulary words and their definitions in your notebook.

In March 1809, President James Madison asked Congress to repeal the 1809 act that restricted trade with Britain and France. It had done little to protect neutral rights. Congress opened trade with both Britain and France, but promised to cut off trade with either nation if American rights were not protected. However, many Americans were losing patience with trade restrictions. They were demanding war.

focus your reading

Why did the West and South want to go to war?

Why did the United States invade Canada?

How did Andrew Jackson defeat the British?

vocabulary

Battle of Tippecanoe

War Hawks

Treaty of Ghent

The Road to War

Support for war came mainly from the South and West. Britain's seizure of American ships brought hard times to cotton and wheat farmers. Western settlers accused Britain of arming the Native Americans in the Ohio Valley. They also had their eye on good farmland in British Canada.

In the Northwest, the Shawnee posed a serious threat to the settlers. The Shawnee leader,

British ships often stopped American merchant ships and took the crews captive.

Lesson Vocabulary

Explain that at the *Battle of Tippecanoe* a small army of about 1,000 men under the leadership of General William Henry Harrison defeated the Native Americans. The battle took place in 1811 in a wooded area about seven miles north of what is now Lafayette, Indiana.

Ask students to use what they know about *war* and *hawks* to figure out the meaning of the term *War Hawks*. (someone who promotes a policy likely to lead to war) The *Treaty of Ghent* is the agreement that ended the War of 1812. Like many European treaties, it is named for the city where the treaty was negotiated and then signed. In this case, the treaty was signed in Ghent, Belgium.

Lesson Summary

In 1809, when James Madison became president, many Americans were preparing for war. They wanted to stop Britain from interfering with their rights as a neutral nation. They were also eager to end the threat posed by Native Americans. The Battle of Tippecanoe ended the threat from the Shawnee and their allies. In 1812, Congress declared war on Britain. In 1814, the British set fire to the White House and the Capitol. General Andrew Jackson halted their attack on New Orleans. The Treaty of Ghent finally ended the war.

Lesson Objective

Students will learn why Americans went to war and what the consequences of that war were.

Focus Your Reading Answers

1 The West and South wanted to go to war because Britain's seizure of American ships hurt cotton and wheat sales abroad. Those who lived on the frontier also accused Britain of arming Native Americans in the Ohio Valley. Some also hoped to take over British Canada.

2 The United States invaded Canada because it was under British rule and many wanted farmland there.

3 Jackson defeated the British by blocking their advance with 4,500 militia lined up behind an earth barrier.

Tecumseh, tried to unite all the Ohio Valley Native American groups against the settlers. In 1811, a militia force of 1,000 men defeated the Native Americans at the **Battle of Tippecanoe**. Tecumseh and several hundred survivors escaped to Canada, where they sought British help.

stop and think

From what you have read so far, describe in your notebook the reasons America was ready for war.

In 1810, Western and Southern voters elected congressmen who shared their pro-war views. Among them were Henry Clay of Kentucky and John C. Calhoun of South Carolina. These **War Hawks**, helped persuade Congress to declare war against Britain on June 18, 1812.

Stop and Think

Answers will vary but students are likely to identify the trade restrictions, Britain's failure to show respect for the rights of Americans, and an eagerness for Canadian land.

Picturing History

The USS *Constitution* is the oldest commissioned warship afloat in the world. It was first launched in 1797 as one of six ships that George Washington ordered built to protect the nation's growing naval interests. The ship's greatest triumph came during the War of 1812, when it defeated four British frigates and earned the nickname "Old Ironsides."

The ship was supposed to be scrapped in 1830, but Oliver Wendell Holmes wrote a poem that inspired Americans to save "Old Ironsides."

Extension

Invite one or more volunteers to read aloud Oliver Wendell Holmes's poem "Old Ironsides." Discuss the meaning of the poem and why it sparked a campaign to keep the ship from being destroyed.

Canada and the Great Lakes

At first, the war did not go well for the United States. To save money, Congress slashed the size of the army. The nation had to rely on poorly trained state militia troops. They made two attempts to invade Canada but were pushed back both times. That year ended with British troops in control of American forts along the Great Lakes.

The USS *Constitution*

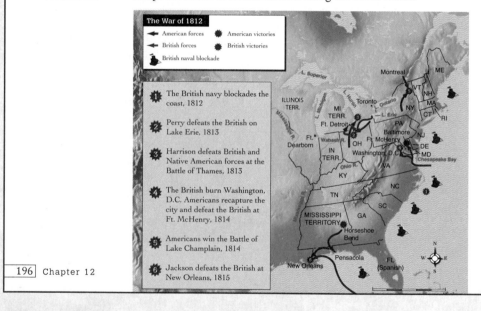

The War of 1812

◀— American forces   ⚔ American victories
◀— British forces   ⚔ British victories
🚢 British naval blockade

1. The British navy blockades the coast, 1812
2. Perry defeats the British on Lake Erie, 1813
3. Harrison defeats British and Native American forces at the Battle of Thames, 1813
4. The British burn Washington, D.C. Americans recapture the city and defeat the British at Ft. McHenry, 1814
5. Americans win the Battle of Lake Champlain, 1814
6. Jackson defeats the British at New Orleans, 1815

196   Chapter 12

Map Extension

Ask students to use the map on page 196 to answer the following questions:

- In what three parts of the United States did most of the fighting take place? (the Great Lakes, the area around Washington, D.C., and New Orleans)

- What do the ships shown off the Atlantic coast of the United States stand for? (British naval blockade)

- Name one British victory and one American victory. (British victory at Washington, D.C., and American victories at Baltimore, New Orleans, Lake Erie, York, and Thames)

Dolley Madison saved many documents during the British attack on the nation's capital.

The navy had more success. The USS *President* and the USS *Constitution* each defeated British ships in individual combat. The USS *Constitution* earned its nickname "Old Ironsides" when British cannonballs bounced off its thick oak planks. In 1813, Captain Oliver Hazard Perry defeated a fleet of British gunboats on Lake Erie.

The Chesapeake and New Orleans

In 1814, Britain attacked the United States. British ships sailed up the Chesapeake Bay, landing troops near Washington, D.C. The militia defending the city fled. The British marched into the city, setting fire to the White House and the Capitol. They tried unsuccessfully to capture Baltimore.

Andrew Jackson led the U.S. to victory at the Battle of New Orleans in 1815.

In December, Britain launched its major attack against the United States. General Sir Edward Packenham landed an army of 7,500 troops south of New Orleans. His goal was to capture the city and use it as a base to occupy the Mississippi Valley. General Andrew Jackson blocked his advance with 4,500 militia lined up behind an earth barrier. When the British attacked on January 8, 1815, Jackson's frontier hunters stopped the Redcoats. During the half-hour battle, the British suffered 2,000 casualties, including General Packenham. The survivors withdrew. Unknown to either general, the **Treaty of Ghent** (Belgium), which ended the war, had been signed two weeks earlier.

Putting It All Together

Go back to the vocabulary words in your notebook. Use the definitions that you wrote to write a sentence using each word. Make sure that your sentences relate to why the United States went to war and include facts about each event.

Chapter Review

1 Letters will vary but should show an understanding that the Embargo Act hurt New England businesses.

2 Answers will vary but possible phrases under "The Republicans in Power" may include reducing the size of government, cutting spending, midnight appointees, and the Louisiana Purchase. Under "Growth and Expansion" the list might include trade, steamboats, spinning mill, interchangeable parts, Barbary States, tributes, neutral, and embargo. The list for "The U.S. Goes to War" may include the Battle of Tippecanoe, trade restrictions, War of 1812, Lake Erie, the Battle of New Orleans, and the Treaty of Ghent.

3 Concepts will vary but should include the defining events in the Republican Era—the election of Jefferson, the Louisiana Purchase, the golden age of merchant ships, the rise of factories, the Battle of Tippecanoe, and the War of 1812.

Chapter Summary

President Thomas Jefferson wanted to make public life more **republican**. Jefferson refused to deliver appointment papers to one new Federalist judge. This "**midnight appointee**," William Marbury, complained to the Supreme Court. For the first time, the Supreme Court declared an act of Congress unconstitutional. In 1803, the **Louisiana Purchase** nearly doubled the size of the United States. Jefferson sent the **Lewis and Clark Expedition** to explore the Far West.

The early 1800s was a period of growth and expansion for the United States. Samuel Slater built the first thread **spinning mill**. Eli Whitney used machine-made **interchangeable parts** to make muskets. As trade expanded, American **merchant ships** faced greater risks. The Barbary States of North Africa demanded **tribute**. To protest against France and Britain stopping American ships, Congress declared an **embargo**.

By 1809, Americans were preparing for war. They had found no other way to stop Britain from interfering with their **neutral** rights. The **Battle of Tippecanoe** ended the Native American threat. In 1812, the **War Hawks** led the nation to war. In 1814, British troops set fire to the While House and the Capitol. The attack on New Orleans was halted by troops led by General Andrew Jackson. The **Treaty of Ghent** ended the war.

Chapter Review

1 Imagine that you are a Boston merchant during the Republican era. Write a letter to a friend in another country explaining the effect of the Embargo Act on your business.

2 Create a three-column chart with the labels "The Republicans in Power," "Growth and Expansion," and "The U.S. Goes to War." Fill in the columns with words or phrases that best describe each label. Use the information to write a short paragraph about the Republican era.

3 Choose five events about the Republican era that stand out for you. Create a concept web using the events.

Novel Connections

Below is a list of books that relate to the time period covered in this chapter. The numbers in parentheses indicate the related Thematic Strands of the National Council for the Social Studies (NCSS).

David Adler. *A Picture Book of Lewis and Clark.* Holiday House, 2003. (I, II, III)

Joseph Bruchac. *Sacajawea.* Silver Whistle, 2001. (I, II, III)

Milton Meltzer (ed.). *Hour of Freedom: American History in Poetry.* Windsong/Boyds Mills Press, 2003. (I, II, X)

Elizabeth Van Steenwyck. *My Name Is York.* Rising Moon, 2000. (I, II, III)

Robert Young. *A Personal Tour of Monticello.* (How It Was Series) Lerner, 1999. (I, II)

Skill Builder

Diaries as Primary Sources

Diaries or journals can be valuable primary sources. They often present eyewitness accounts of the events they describe. The writer usually provides a day-by-day account of what was happening. However, diaries must be used critically. A critical reader should ask the following questions of a diary entry:

- Who wrote it?
- Was the writer well informed?
- What biases did the writer display?
- What problems does the vocabulary present?
- Was it written at the time of the events described?
- Why did the author write the diary entry?

Read the entry from William Clark's journal on page 190. It is a report of this explorer's first encounter with the Sioux. Read the entry critically by asking the following questions:

1 Where and when did Clark write this entry?

2 What biases did Clark show in this entry?

3 List words he used that are unfamiliar to you and explain what they mean.

4 Why do you think Clark's spelling is not accurate?

The Republican Era 199

Skill Builder

1 Clark was on the river, and he wrote the entry on September 26, 1804.

2 Clark seems to regard Native American men as disrespectful to women.

3 Answers will vary but are likely to include *roab, smokeables, peticoats,* and *harey.*

4 Answers will vary, but students are likely to suggest that Clark was not a good speller. He had very little formal education.

Classroom Discussion

Discuss with students some of the broader topics covered in this chapter.

- Some historians speak of Jeffersonian democracy. Based on what you read in this chapter, what does the term mean in terms of his view of the role of government? the role of ordinary citizens? in terms of relations with other nations?

- What was the significance of the Louisiana Purchase? How did it change the history of the United States?

- In the early 1800s, the United States was a very new country. Name some of the ways that Americans tried to guard their independence as a nation. In your opinion, what methods were most successful?

- Some historians call the War of 1812 the Second American Revolution. What do you think they mean by that name? What does the name suggest might have happened if Britain had won the war?

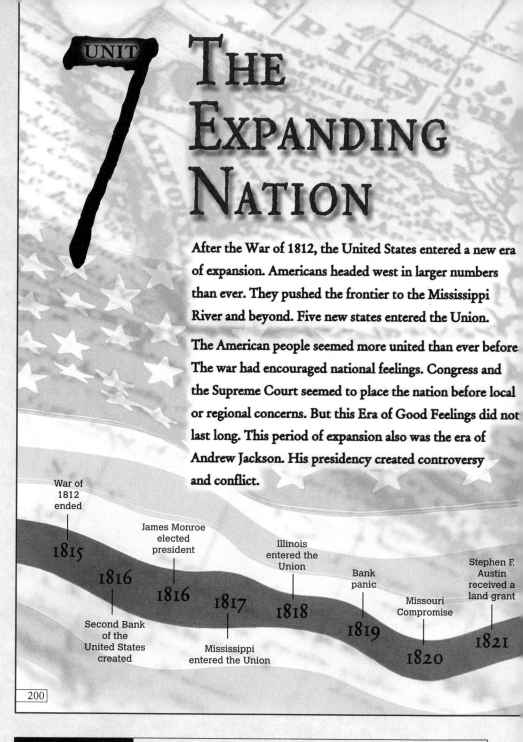

Unit Objectives

After studying this unit, students will be able to

- describe the expansion of the United States after the War of 1812

- detail the events that led to the growth of sectionalism

- explain the conflicts and controversy that marked the presidency of Andrew Jackson

Unit 7 focuses on the expansion of the United States in the years after the War of 1812.

Chapter 13, Westward Expansion, examines the causes and the effects of American expansion.

Chapter 14, The Era of Andrew Jackson, examines how the "Era of Good Feelings" was replaced by increasing regional concerns.

UNIT 7

THE EXPANDING NATION

After the War of 1812, the United States entered a new era of expansion. Americans headed west in larger numbers than ever. They pushed the frontier to the Mississippi River and beyond. Five new states entered the Union.

The American people seemed more united than ever before. The war had encouraged national feelings. Congress and the Supreme Court seemed to place the nation before local or regional concerns. But this Era of Good Feelings did not last long. This period of expansion also was the era of Andrew Jackson. His presidency created controversy and conflict.

War of 1812 ended

1815

James Monroe elected president

1816

1816

Second Bank of the United States created

1817

Mississippi entered the Union

Illinois entered the Union

1818

Bank panic

1819

Missouri Compromise

1820

Stephen F. Austin received a land grant

1821

200

Getting Started

Ask a volunteer to read aloud the two paragraphs on page 200. Discuss the meaning of the word *expand* by asking students to name synonyms. (enlarge, increase, get bigger, inflate, grow, spread out, open out, develop) Have students list some of the ways nations expand. (in area, wealth, importance, population) What do the two paragraphs suggest about the ways the United States expanded between 1815 and 1837? Ask students to examine the pictures and headings in Chapters 13 and 14. What do they add to students' understanding of the nation's expansion?

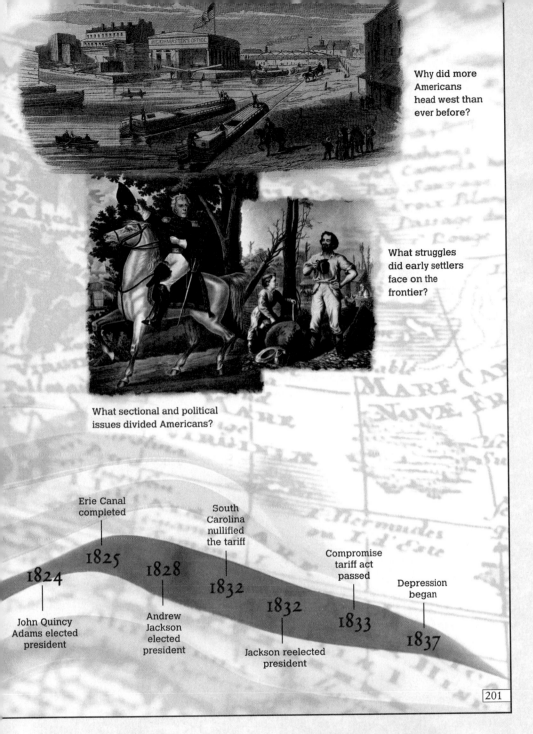

Why did more Americans head west than ever before?

What struggles did early settlers face on the frontier?

What sectional and political issues divided Americans?

Erie Canal completed

South Carolina nullified the tariff

Compromise tariff act passed

Depression began

1824

1825

1828

1832

1832

1833

1837

John Quincy Adams elected president

Andrew Jackson elected president

Jackson reelected president

201

Chapter Summary

Refer to page 214 in the student book for a summary of Chapter 13.

Related Transparencies

T-2 Land Acquisition Map

T-18 T-Chart

Key Blacklines

Biography
Abraham Lincoln

Primary Source
The Log Cabin

DVD Extension

Encourage students to use the reading comprehension, vocabulary reinforcement, and interactive timeline activities on the student DVD.

Picturing History

Ask students to describe what they see in the picture of the Erie Canal on page 202. What does the image suggest about life in the United States in the early 1800s? Encourage students to explain their answers to these questions.

Getting Focused

Skim this chapter to predict what you will be learning.

- Read the lesson titles and subheadings.
- Look at the illustrations and read the captions.
- Examine the maps.
- Review the vocabulary words and terms.

In your notebook write a sentence or two explaining what you think the chapter is about. Compare your ideas with those of a partner.

Pre-Reading Discussion

Ask students to read aloud the chapter title. Discuss the meaning of the word *frontier*. (the boundary between settled and unsettled areas) Ask students where the frontier was by

- the end of the Revolutionary War (Kentucky, Tennessee, Ohio Valley)
- 1803 (Mississippi River)

Then ask students to predict the next frontier. Have them check their predictions as they complete each bulleted direction on page 202.

Extension

Have students research the Wilderness Road, the Cumberland Road, or the Forbes Road. Ask students to present their findings to the class by using the Student Presentation Builder on the student DVD.

A People on the Move

Thinking on Your Own

Think about a time when you or someone you know moved to another area. Why did the move take place? What kind of transportation was used? Then create two columns in your notebook with the headings "Today" and "In the Past." Using the vocabulary and the Focus Your Reading questions, compare and contrast a person moving today with a person moving during the period of American expansion westward.

By 1815, Americans were a people on the move. Each summer thousands of Americans headed west. They left their homes in the eastern United States and set out for the Ohio Valley, Kentucky, and Tennessee. They went to make a better living for themselves and their families.

focus your reading

Why did people move west?

What advantages did river travel have?

What were the advantages of canal boats?

vocabulary

wagon roads   canal

flatboat

Wagon Roads

Most people traveled in wagons pulled by teams of horses or oxen. It was the cheapest way for a family to travel. The wagons carried food, clothing, and farm equipment. Adults usually walked alongside. They led the teams or herded pigs and cows. Young children rode in the wagons. "The wagons swarm with children," wrote one traveler. "I heard today of three together, which contain forty-two of these young citizens."

Travelers made use of various roads. The Wilderness Road led across Virginia to Tennessee. The Cumberland Road extended from Maryland to the Ohio River. The Forbes Road crossed Pennsylvania.

Wagon trains carried supplies and provided protection.

Westward Expansion 203

Picturing History

Teams of horses or oxen pulled the covered wagons used to transport goods from one part of the country to another. Families moving west piled their belongings onto smaller "covered wagons."

On most wagons, the bottom was bowed in the middle to keep cargo from sliding out as the wagon went up and down hills. The wheels were large so that the wagon could pass over streams without getting the cargo wet. Large wheels also allowed the wagon to pass over stumps in the roads or large rocks at a time when roads were not paved. Ask students to imagine what it would have been like to travel long distances by wagon.

Lesson Summary

By 1815, more and more people in the United States were moving west. They used three means of transportation: wagons, canal boats, and flatboats.

Lesson Objective

Students will learn the three most common modes of transportation during the early 1800s.

Focus Your Reading Answers

1 People moved west to make a better life for themselves and their families.

2 River travel was the cheapest and fastest way to travel long distances.

3 Canal boats provided shelter and hot meals for travelers.

Lesson Vocabulary

Each of the vocabulary words in this lesson relates to travel in the early 1800s. Use the illustrations in this chapter to help students visualize each term. The illustrations on pages 203 and 204 (top) show a *wagon road*. These are dirt or log roads wide enough for a wagon to pass. A *flatboat* is shown on the bottom of page 204. Ask students to explain how they think the boat got its name. A *canal* is a waterway people have dug. The illustration on page 202 shows a *canal*. Ask students to compare it to the river shown in the illustration on page 204. What similarities do students notice? What differences do they detect?

Travel by wagon was difficult and often dangerous. Most **wagon roads** in the West were only dirt paths through the forests. The worst had tree stumps standing in the middle of the road. Wagons often broke down because of these rough roads. The roads also became muddy when it rained or snowed. To avoid mud and stumps, some roads were covered with logs. These roads were called corduroy roads because they looked like corduroy fabric.

Log roads were called "corduroy roads" because of how they looked.

It was much easier to travel west by water in 1815. Most travelers who reached the Ohio River stopped to buy or build a **flatboat**. These wooden, flat-bottomed boats were easy and cheap to make. They did not run aground when the river was low. When travelers reached their destination, they took the boats apart and sold the boards for lumber.

Going down river by flatboat was the fastest way to travel. But the boats had shortcomings. People ate and slept on the open decks along with their cows and chickens. They huddled under sheets of canvas when it rained.

stop and think

Turn your book face down. In your notebook or with a partner, explain what you remember having read to this point.

Flatboats provided fast river travel.

Stop and Think

Answers will vary but should include the topics related to travel by wagon and by flatboat. Students should also include their review of the headings and pictures that they completed prior to reading the lesson.

Picturing History

People used corduroy roads in low, wet areas. They laid down the logs across the road, one after another, providing a solid but bumpy surface for horse-drawn wagons. Ask students to consider both the advantages and disadvantages of log roads during various seasons of the year.

Picturing History

When travelers in the early 1800s reached a river, they would build a flatboat, pile their wagons, horses, and other goods on it, and float downriver. Small flatboats were about 20 feet long and 10 feet wide; large ones were as much as 60 feet long and 20 feet wide. Notice how the two men in the illustration are using long poles to keep the flatboat from drifting off course.

Extension

The flatboat was not the only boat found on rivers in the early 1800s. Many people traveled by barge or on a packet. Although they resembled the flatboats in shape, they had masts, sails, and rudders. Both moved at a speed of about four miles an hour down the river and two miles an hour upstream, depending on the wind. Ask students to find out more about these boats and share their findings by creating a poster.

Canals

After 1825, people could go to the Michigan Territory, northern Ohio, Indiana, and Illinois by **canal** boat. In that year, the state of New York opened the Erie Canal between the cities of Albany and Buffalo. This canal linked the Hudson River to the Great Lakes.

Canal boats provided travelers with meals and a place to sleep.

The Erie Canal was a great success. By 1840, New York and other states had built hundreds of miles of canals.

Canal boats were the most comfortable way to travel west. Passengers sat on benches in the cabin or on top of the cabin roof. At night the benches were made into beds. The boat's crew served passengers hot meals prepared in towns along the canal.

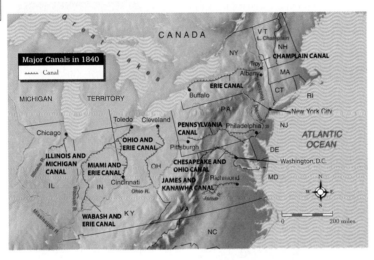

Putting It All Together

Create a newspaper advertisement for the canal boats. Persuade your audience that canal boats are the best way to travel west.

Picturing History

Compare the drawing of the canal boat on page 205 with the drawing of a flatboat on page 204. What are the main differences between the people riding on the two boats? (The people on the canal boat are dressed in fancier clothes. They are also sitting on chairs or benches.)

Putting It All Together

Although ads will vary, the following questions can be used to guide students:

- What cities and towns can be reached on the canal?

- How does the canal connect with other canals?

- How does the canal connect with major rivers?

- What attractions lie along the route of the canal?

Each ad should include details about the time period.

Map Extensions

1 Ask students to use the map on page 205 to answer the following questions:

- What canal links Philadelphia and Pittsburgh? (Pennsylvania Canal)

- What cities does the Erie Canal link? (Troy and Buffalo in New York)

- What canal is linked to the Wabash and Erie Canal? (Miami and Erie Canal)

- What parts of the country seem to have the most canals? (Northwest Territory, New York, and Pennsylvania)

2 Have students research one of the canals on the map and then draw a detailed map of the cities and towns along its route. Remind them to include a title, map key, and compass rose.

Lesson Summary

After 1815, the United States expanded to include territory up to the Mississippi River. Early settlements included towns and villages that grew to become major cities.

Lesson Objective

Students will learn about the early settlements in the West and the states added to the Union between 1803 and 1820.

Focus Your Reading Answers

1 Settlers moved to the frontier to hunt for meat and hides, which they used for food and clothing.

2 Farmers cut rings into the bark of trees to kill the trees. Then they burned them to clear land for planting.

3 Settlers needed villages and towns to provide goods and services they could not provide for themselves. These included making horseshoes and grinding flour.

Settling the Frontier

Thinking on Your Own

Before reading this section, make a three-column chart in your notebook. Give the columns these titles: "Hunters," "Farmers," and "Townspeople." Use the vocabulary and the Focus Your Reading questions to help you describe each group. Compare your descriptions with a partner.

After 1815, thousands of white settlers moved into the Ohio Valley. They pushed the frontier (the edge of settlement) west across Indiana and Illinois. South of the Ohio River, the frontier extended into Kentucky, Tennessee, Alabama, Mississippi, and Louisiana. The area beyond the frontier was still known as Indian country.

focus your reading

Why were hunters the first white settlers?

How did farmers clear the forests?

Why did newly settled areas need villages and towns?

vocabulary

lean-tos   gristmill

blacksmith

Frontier Hunters

In most areas, the first white settlers were hunters. Wild game was plentiful on the frontier. The hunters shot deer, bear, and other wild game, bringing back meat and hides. "His manners are rough," wrote one traveler. "He wears . . . a long beard . . . He carries a knife . . . and when in the woods has a rifle on his back and a pack of dogs at his heels." Women tanned and cut up the skins to make clothing for the family.

Frontier hunters lived in **lean-tos** and in small cabins. A lean-to is a shelter with a roof

Hunting on the frontier was often dangerous.

Lesson Vocabulary

Explain that a *lean-to* is a type of shelter. It resembles a roof that is propped up on the ground. Some *lean-tos* can have walls. They were used as temporary shelter.

A *smith* is someone who works with metal, often by hammering it when it is hot and soft and flexible. A *blacksmith* is a person who makes things out of a particular metal—iron. *Blacksmiths* made spikes, nails, hinges, latches, horseshoes, and wagon wheels. Discuss why their services were in great demand on the frontier.

Explain that *grist* is any grain that can be ground into flour and that a *mill* is a machine that processes raw materials by grinding them into powder or dust. Then ask students to explain what a *gristmill* is. (a machine for grinding grain into flour)

that slopes from the front to the back. It is open to the weather on the front side. Even the cabins were hastily built, as the hunters expected to move on in a short time.

The frontier was a lonely place for women and children. The men spent most of their time hunting. Bears, panthers, and wildcats made it unsafe for women and children to go very far from home. The nearest neighbors lived miles away.

Farmers were the next to arrive. They cleared the forests, chasing away the wild game. The farmers chopped down the smaller trees with axes. They killed the larger trees by cutting off a ring of bark. Then they set these dead trees on fire. The next spring they planted crops between the blackened stumps.

Farmers often burned trees to clear space for their crops.

Corn was the main crop. It provided food for the family and feed for farm animals. Corn-fattened hogs provided ham and bacon for the dinner table. Farmers traded corn and hams at the village store for things they could not make themselves.

Frontier farmers depended mostly on themselves. They raised most of their own food. The women made most of the family's clothes. Farmers did help one another. They got together to build log cabins and to have dinners and dances. They also helped one another harvest crops.

stop and think

Sketch a symbol or logo to represent each kind of settlement in the West: hunters' cabins, farms, towns.

Villages and Towns

Every settlement had at least one village. The village served the needs of the farmers who lived nearby. Most villages included a cluster of houses, a **blacksmith** shop, a **gristmill**, and a general store. The blacksmith made and repaired iron tools. The gristmill ground grain into flour. Farmers bought salt, pots and pans, and other items at the general store. They paid with hams, eggs, corn, and potatoes more often than cash.

Picturing History

Families on the frontier used a technique known as "slash and burn" farming. They cut down trees and shrubs and then burned them so they could plant their crops. The ash from the burned vegetation helped fertilize the soil. In a few years, however, the soil wore out and farmers had to clear yet another part of the forest. Discuss the advantages and disadvantages of "slash and burn" farming. How may it explain why many farmers on the frontier moved further west every few years?

Stop and Think

Symbols will vary but should be easily understood and clearly represent a hunter's cabin, a farm, and a town.

Extension

Have students research "slash and burn" farming today. It is still practiced in parts of Latin America, Africa, and Asia. Ask them to share their findings with the class.

Picturing History

Ask students to use the drawing on page 206 to answer the following questions:

- What can you learn from the picture about the land? (heavily wooded with at least one river or stream)

- What does the hunter's clothing suggest about frontier living? (His clothes are made from animal hide, suggesting that they are handmade.)

- Why do you think the hunter put a blindfold on his horse? (The blindfold kept the horse from being frightened by the fast-moving water as the pair crossed the stream.)

Picturing History

A blacksmith heats iron to the point that it can be manipulated by compressing it between two hardened surfaces— in most cases, the surface of an anvil and the face of a hammer. A forge (a contained area that allows the free and constant flow of air through the fire from the bottom up) supplies the heat. A pump keeps the air flowing. That airflow is essential to maintaining temperatures high enough to manipulate the iron. The art of blacksmithing is to keep the metal from becoming too hot or too cold. Discuss how blacksmiths may have learned their craft.

Putting It All Together

Charts will vary, but should include the key facts from this lesson and any other information students know about hunters, farmers, and townspeople.

Some small villages grew to become towns. Most towns had a doctor's office, a newspaper, and several stores. Pittsburgh became a manufacturing center. Its skilled

Towns and villages often provided farmers with a blacksmith.

workers specialized in making boats, iron tools, and glassware. Cincinnati, Louisville, and other river towns became busy port cities. Other towns also grew into cities and profited as farmers began shipping their products along the river routes.

New States

People who moved west also created new states. They wanted their own state courts, lawmakers, and governors. The new states added to the Union north of the Ohio River included Ohio (1803), Indiana (1816), and Illinois (1818). States south of the river included Louisiana (1812), Mississippi (1817), and Alabama (1819). Missouri (1820) was the first state to be added west of the Mississippi River.

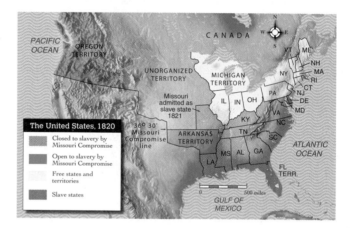

Putting It All Together

Return to your three-column chart. Based on your reading, add to your descriptions of hunters, farmers, and townspeople.

Map Extension

Use the map on page 208 to answer the following questions:

- What states in 1820 were once a part of the Northwest Territory? (Ohio, Indiana, and Illinois)

- What states were once a part of the Louisiana Purchase? (Louisiana and Missouri)

- What part of the Southeast was not yet a state? (Florida Territory)

Read a Primary Source

The Versatile Farmer

William Cobbett, a British writer and politician, lived in the United States from 1817 to 1819. During this time he lived with his family on a farm in Long Island, New York. He wrote the description below of the typical American farmer.

> " . . . Besides the great quantity of work performed by the American [farmer], his skill, the versatility of his talent, is a great thing. Every man can use an axe, a saw, and a hammer. Scarcely one who cannot do any job at rough carpentering, and mend a plough [plow] or a wagon. Very few indeed, who cannot kill and dress pigs and sheep, and many of them oxen and calves. Every farmer is a neat butcher; a butcher for market; and, of course, 'the boys' must learn. This is a great convenience. It makes you so independent as to a main part of the means of housekeeping. All are ploughmen [plowmen]. In short, a good labourer here can do anything that is to be done upon a farm . . . . "

William Cobbett, *A Year's Residence in the United States of America* (London, 1818).

reading for understanding

What does Cobbett mean by the "versatility" of the American farmer's talent?

Why would "versatility of talent" be useful to a frontier farmer?

What skills did American farmers have?

Why is the farm in the drawing surrounded by forest?

What animals were hunted by the farmers?

An early American farm

Reading for Understanding

1 Versatility relates to the ability of farmers to complete a variety of tasks.

2 Frontier farmers had to perform a variety of jobs because they often lived in remote areas without access to other people. Farms were self-sufficient, and, except for occasional trips into town, everything had to be done on the farm.

3 American farmers could use an axe, a saw, and a hammer. They could also work a plow in the fields, drive a wagon, and complete carpentry work. Farmers could also butcher many types of animals.

4 The farm in the drawing is surrounded by forest because only a small section of the land had been cleared for fields and the house.

5 Farmers hunted deer and fowl.

Extension

William Cobbett described the work of men and boys on a frontier farm. Ask students to research the work of women and girls on frontier farms. To what extent did they also display a "versatility of talent"? What did they contribute to frontier living? Ask students to present their findings to the class by using the Student Presentation Builder on the student DVD.

Biography

Bio Facts

- Born on December 24, 1809, in Kentucky.

- Worked as a saddle-maker's apprentice until the age of fourteen.

- Left home to become a trapper working as far west as California.

- Married twice to Native American women, one an Arapahoe and the other, Cheyenne.

- Guided John C. Frémont through the Rocky Mountains to Oregon and California.

- Served as federal Indian agent during the 1850s.

- Led the 1st New Mexican Volunteers during the Civil War and fought against the Navajo, Apache, and Comanche in New Mexico and Texas.

- Promoted to Brigadier General and commanded Fort Garland, Colorado.

- Died May 2, 1868, in Colorado.

Kit Carson (1809–1868)

When this notice appeared in a Missouri newspaper, Kit Carson was headed west. He had joined a wagon caravan going to Santa Fe to trade. This young apprentice, valued at one cent in Missouri, proved his true worth in the West.

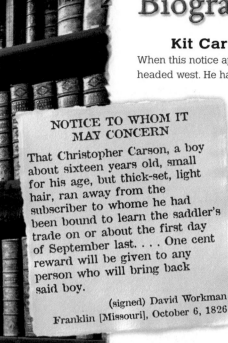

NOTICE TO WHOM IT MAY CONCERN

That Christopher Carson, a boy about sixteen years old, small for his age, but thick-set, light hair, ran away from the subscriber to whome he had been bound to learn the saddler's trade on or about the first day of September last. . . . One cent reward will be given to any person who will bring back said boy.

(signed) David Workman
Franklin [Missouri], October 6, 1826

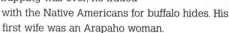

After arriving in the Mexican town of Santa Fe, Kit Carson became a trapper. For nearly fifteen years he trapped beaver in the Rocky Mountains. When beaver trapping was over, he traded with the Native Americans for buffalo hides. His first wife was an Arapaho woman.

Kit Carson knew the mountains better than most men. During the 1840s, Lieutenant John Charles Frémont hired Carson as a guide to help survey the Rocky Mountains. When the Mexican War began, Carson led General Stephen Kearney's army across the mountains to California. He fought with Kearney in California. He later fought in the Civil War as a colonel in the Union army.

After the Civil War, Kit Carson served as a government agent for the Ute and Apache People. He lived among the Native Americans and tried to keep the peace. Kit Carson died peacefully in 1868 at the age of fifty-nine. A monument in Santa Fe sums up his life in these words: "He led the way."

210

Extension

Ask students to research one of the individuals or Native American groups mentioned in the Biography. Students can present their findings to the class by using the Student Presentation Builder on the student DVD.

- John Charles Frémont

- Stephen Kearney

- Arapaho

- Ute

- Apache

Beyond the Mississippi

Thinking on Your Own

Read the vocabulary and Focus Your Reading questions. Discuss with a partner what you think are the main ideas of this section. Write your predictions in your notebook.

By the 1820s, some Americans had moved west of the Mississippi River. They settled in Texas, went to Santa Fe to trade, and trapped beaver in the Rocky Mountains.

Texas

Americans first settled in Texas in the 1820s. Texas was then part of Mexico, which had recently won its independence from Spain. In 1821, the Mexican government offered Stephen F. Austin a large **land grant**, or gift of land, if he would bring settlers to Texas. Mexico needed American settlers to help defend its Texas frontier.

Austin helped Americans settle in Mexico. At first, the settlers were happy. Each family received thousands of acres of ranch land at little cost. In time, however, they came to dislike Mexican laws and customs. They wanted to govern themselves.

In 1836, the American settlers in Texas declared their independence. General Antonio Lopez de Santa Anna, the Mexican president, led an army to put down the revolt. The Mexicans killed 187 Texans at the Alamo, including Davy Crockett and James Bowie. "Remember the Alamo" became a famous Texas battle cry. A Texas army led by General Sam Houston finally defeated the Mexicans at the Battle of San Jacinto. Texas, nicknamed the "Lone Star Republic," was independent until 1845, when it joined the Union as a state.

> **focus your reading**
>
> Why did Texas declare its independence from Mexico?
>
> Why did Missouri merchants go to Santa Fe?
>
> Who were the Mountain Men?
>
> **vocabulary**
>
> land grant   rendezvous
>
> Mountain Men

Stephen F. Austin

Picturing History

In 1821, Stephen Austin took a land grant from Mexico. He used the grant to start a colony on the Brazos River. For a number of years, he maintained good relations with Mexico and expanded the size of his colony. He also tried unsuccessfully to persuade the Mexican government to make Texas a separate state. Frustrated by his failure to do so, Austin suggested in 1833 that Texans organize a state without permission from Mexican lawmakers. The Mexican government responded by putting him in jail. After his release in 1835, he traveled to the United States to secure help for a fight for independence from Mexico. Ask students why Austin is considered the "father of Texas."

Lesson Summary

After being a part of Mexico, settlers in Texas fought for and gained independence in 1836. The Santa Fe and other trails brought new settlers to the West and provided a way of transporting furs from animals trapped by the Mountain Men.

Lesson Objective

Students will learn about the settlement of Texas and its struggle for independence from Mexico, and about the Santa Fe Trail and the role of the Mountain Men in expanding the western United States.

Focus Your Reading Answers

1 Texas declared independence from Mexico because the settlers did not like Mexican laws and customs.

2 Merchants from Missouri traveled to Santa Fe to sell goods to settlers.

3 The Mountain Men trapped animals in the Rocky Mountains and sold the furs to companies for use in clothing.

Lesson Vocabulary

Explain each vocabulary term. A *land grant* is *land* that a government gives or *grants* to a person or business. Stephen Austin received a *land grant* from Mexico in 1821.

Mountain Men were frontiersmen who trapped animals and traded for furs in the Rocky Mountain region. Every summer, they arranged a *rendezvous* to deliver their furs to market. A *rendezvous* is a French word that refers to a meeting planned for a certain time and in a certain place.

The Alamo was the site of a battle between Mexico and Texas.

Picturing History

The Spanish built the Mission San Antonio de Valero, later called the Alamo, in 1718. During the war against Mexico in 1836, it became known as the "cradle of Texas Liberty." Ask students to explain why the building earned that name. What does the picture suggest about the battle itself? Which side seems to be stronger? What is the significance of the flag that flies over the Alamo?

Extension

Encourage students to research the Battle of the Alamo. Why did Texans rally to the cry "Remember the Alamo!"? What did they want people to remember? Why did the cry rally thousands to their cause?

Santa Fe Trade

In 1821, William Becknell set out for Mexico. Becknell, a Missouri merchant, took with him packhorses loaded with cloth, hardware, and other goods. He sold these goods in the Mexican town of Santa Fe for a big profit.

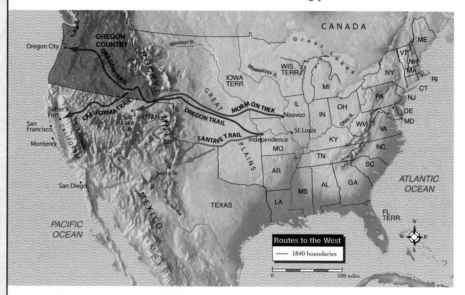

Each spring thereafter, Becknell and other merchants set out for Santa Fe in wagon caravans. They opened a new road across the plains. It was called the Santa Fe Trail. The 800-mile journey took 10 weeks. The trip was well worth the time spent. In 1824, the merchants paid $30,000 for the goods they bought in Missouri. They sold them in Santa Fe for $180,000. Many of these merchants settled in Santa Fe.

Map Extension

Use the map on page 212 and the map of the United States on page 345 to answer the following questions:

- Through what present-day states did the Oregon Trail pass? (Missouri, Kansas, Nebraska, Wyoming, Idaho, Oregon)

- What trail passed through Missouri, Kansas, Oklahoma, and New Mexico? (Santa Fe Trail)

- Through what present-day states did the California Trail pass? (Missouri, Kansas, Nebraska, Wyoming, Colorado, Idaho, Nevada, California)

- Through what present-day states did the Mormons pass? (Iowa, Nebraska, Wyoming, Utah)

stop and think

Make a Venn diagram that has three overlapping circles. Place one of the following names in each circle: Stephen F. Austin, William Becknell, and Kit Carson. Where the circles overlap, write what these men had in common. In the other parts of the circles, note how the men were different. Complete the diagram as you read this section.

The Mountain Men

In 1822, William H. Ashley advertised in a St. Louis, Missouri, newspaper for "enterprising young men" to work for him in the Rocky Mountains. The men who answered Ashley's ad were known as the **Mountain Men**. These men trapped beaver in the Rocky Mountains for Ashley's Rocky Mountain Fur Company. Beaver pelts brought high prices in eastern cities like New York and also in Europe. The pelts were used to make men's dress hats.

Fur trapping was a dangerous life. The trappers spent all winter in the mountains. They fought off grizzly bears. Hostile Native Americans attacked them. They faced harsh winter blizzards. Those who survived met during the summer at a **rendezvous** or meeting place to deliver their furs. The company paid the trappers and sold them supplies for the coming year.

Beaver trapping came to an end in the 1840s. Beaver hats fell out of fashion. Men preferred to wear silk top hats instead. Many of the Mountain Men stayed in the West. Some settled down as farmers. Kit Carson and others worked as guides. They showed explorers and settlers the way from place to place.

Mountain Men

Putting It All Together

Pretend that the year is 1817. You have moved west with your family. Write a letter to a friend back east describing your life. Include as many details from this section as you can. You may want to do some additional research.

Stop and Think

Venn diagrams will vary but should include the following:

Common characteristics: helped settle the frontier

Stephen F. Austin: founded colonies in Texas, fought Mexico

William Becknell: helped to establish the Santa Fe Trail, was a merchant, sold goods in Santa Fe

Kit Carson: trapper, Mountain Man, explorer

Putting It All Together

Letters will vary but should include information about

- reason for moving
- year and location
- the trip west
- the geography of the area settled
- dangers encountered
- people met along the route
- life after settling

Picturing History

How may drawings such as the one on page 213 have influenced people's ideas about the Mountain Men? What image do the two men project?

Chapter Review

1 Encourage students to include specific details in their drawings. They can also include a narrative or letter about the scene.

2 Students should be able to add dates, specific facts, historic places, and information about people to their original list.

3 Answers will vary, but should include the details discussed in the lesson.

Chapter Summary

By 1815, Americans were a people on the move. Most travelers set out overland by **wagon road**. Wagon travel was slow and difficult. Floating down the Ohio River on a **flatboat** was quicker. The easiest way to go was by **canal** boat.

The first people to reach the frontier were backwoods hunters who lived in **lean-tos** or rough cabins. Later, farmers moved west. They cleared the forests to make room for fields. **Blacksmiths**, storekeepers, and doctors settled in nearby villages and towns to serve the farmers' needs. Some towns grew into cities. **Gristmills** were built to grind grain into flour.

By the 1820s, settlers had crossed the Mississippi River. The government of Mexico gave Stephen F. Austin a **land grant** to help settle Texas. Texas was then the northern frontier of Mexico. In 1836, Texas won its independence when Sam Houston defeated the Mexican army at the Battle of San Jacinto. In the 1820s, merchants from Missouri opened trade with Mexico over the Santa Fe Trail. Some merchants settled down in Santa Fe. By then other Americans had reached the Rocky Mountains. The **Mountain Men** trapped beaver all winter and brought the furs to a **rendezvous** in the spring.

Chapter Review

1 Draw a picture that shows one of the following in detail:

A family going west by flatboat
A frontier farm
A Mountain Man at work

2 Look again at the prediction you made at the beginning of this chapter. You were asked what the chapter would be about. What would you add or change?

3 Pretend that you are a British visitor traveling in the American West in 1817. Using information from this chapter, write a letter home that describes what you have seen.

Novel Connections

Below is a list of books that relate to the time period covered in this chapter. The numbers in parentheses indicate the related Thematic Strands of the National Council for the Social Studies (NCSS).

Judy Alter. *Extraordinary Women of the West.* Children's Press, 1999. (II, IV)

Richard Ammon. *Conestoga Wagons.* Holiday House, 2000. (I)

Sherry Garland. *In the Shadow of the Alamo.* Gulliver Books, 2001. (I, III, IV)

_____. *Voices of the Alamo.* Pelican Publishing, 2004. (II, III)

William Loren Katz. *Black Pioneers: An Untold Story.* Atheneum, 1999. (III)

Steven Kroll. *Robert Fulton: From Submarine to Steamboat.* Holiday House, 1999. (II, IV, VIII)

Albert Marrin. *Sitting Bull and His World.* Dutton, 2000. (I, V, VI)

Mary Pope Osborne. *Adaline Falling Star.* Scholastic Books, 2002. (I, IV, V)

Skill Builder

Reading a Map

Most maps contain different kinds of information. This map of routes to the West in 1840 shows different methods of transportation. The map shows roads, canals, and rivers. These are identified on the Map Key.

Using the map, answer the following questions:

1 What roads would a traveler from Richmond, Virginia, take to get to Tennessee?

2 Which two waterways would a family use to get from New York City to Buffalo?

3 The National Road, commonly called the Cumberland Road, began in Cumberland, Maryland. Through which states did it run?

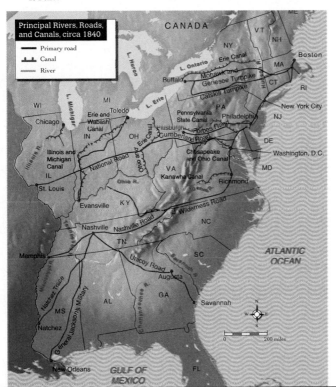

Principal Rivers, Roads, and Canals, circa 1840

— Primary road
⊥⊥⊥ Canal
— River

Skill Builder

1 Travelers could use the Wilderness Road and the Nashville Road to travel from Virginia to Tennessee.

2 People could use the Hudson River and the Erie Canal to travel from New York City to Buffalo, NY.

3 The National Road ran through Maryland, Pennsylvania, Ohio, Indiana, and Illinois.

Map Extension

The rivers, roads, and canals that crisscrossed the nation served many purposes during the early years of the United States. Assign students a canal, road, or river to research. Ask students to present their findings to the class.

Classroom Discussion

Discuss with students some of the broader topics covered in this chapter.

- How did westward expansion change the United States?

- How did the formation of the various trails help in the move west?

- What qualities did a family need to build a new life on the frontier?

- What part did improvements in transportation play in the westward movement?

Chapter Summary

Refer to page 230 in the student book for a summary of Chapter 14.

Related Transparencies

T-18 T-Chart

Key Blacklines

Biography
Sequoya

Primary Source
Jackson's Bank Veto

DVD Extension

Encourage students to use the reading comprehension, vocabulary reinforcement, and interactive timeline activities on the student DVD.

Picturing History

In 1838 and 1839, President Andrew Jackson ordered the Cherokee to give up their lands east of the Mississippi River and resettle in present-day Oklahoma. The Cherokee call their journey west the "Trail of Tears." Robert Lindneux painted *The Trail of Tears* in 1942. Ask students to examine the painting carefully and then describe the feelings it evokes. How do those feelings differ from those inspired by the pictures in Chapter 13 showing white Americans moving west?

Getting Focused

Skim this chapter to predict what you will be learning.

- Read the lesson titles and subheadings.
- Look at the illustrations and read the captions.
- Examine the maps.
- Review the vocabulary words and terms.

Recall a time when you felt content in your life. Nations, too, can have times when people feel content. With a partner, talk about what these experiences might have in common.

Pre-Reading Discussion

Have students complete each bulleted direction on page 216. Discuss the meaning of the word *content* by asking students to name synonyms. (satisfied, happy, comfortable, at ease) What does it mean for a nation to be *content*? What do the headings, maps, and illustrations in this chapter suggest about the sources of that contentment? How do pictures like the one on page 216 challenge the idea that the nation was content?

Extension

On July 12, 1817, a Boston newspaper reported on a good-will visit to the city by President James Monroe. The paper used the term "Era of Good Feelings" to describe the national mood. After reading the lesson, ask students what other terms might have been used to describe those years. What term would best describe the nation in the years just before the War of 1812? What term would best describe the nation's mood today? What events seem to shape the mood of a nation?

A Nation United

Thinking on Your Own

Read the Focus Your Reading questions. Then make a concept map with "Era of Good Feelings" in the middle. While you read, add events and situations to the concept map that would produce good feelings for the nation.

In 1816, Americans were more united than ever before. They were proud of Andrew Jackson's victory over the British at New Orleans. "The people," said Albert Gallatin, "are more American; feel and act more as a nation." Party politics no longer divided the nation. In 1816, the voters elected James Monroe, a Republican, by a landslide. It was the beginning, one newspaper reported, of "an **Era of Good Feelings**."

focus your reading

Why was this period called the Era of Good Feelings?

How did the American System strengthen the United States?

How did President Monroe's foreign policy make the country stronger?

vocabulary

Era of Good Feelings

American System

Monroe Doctrine

The American System

After the war, leaders in Congress from the North and the South agreed upon a plan to strengthen the nation's economy. They called it the **American System**.

The plan included a Bank of the United States, which Congress approved in 1816. The bank issued U.S. Bank Notes, which became the nation's new currency. Its branch banks also loaned money, which benefited farmers and merchants alike.

To help factory owners, Congress passed the Tariff of 1816. American manufacturers could not produce goods as cheaply as British factory owners. Placing a tariff or tax on imports

The Era of Andrew Jackson 217

Lesson Vocabulary

Explain each of the terms highlighted in this lesson. The *Era of Good Feelings* is a period of national unity that took place after the War of 1812. The *American System* was a congressional plan to strengthen the economy by establishing a national bank, creating a tariff that protected American factory owners, and helping states build roads and canals. How did the *American System* help to strengthen the nation?

Explain to students that a *doctrine* is a statement of policy. The *Monroe Doctrine* was a statement about American foreign policy issued by President James Monroe. He stated that the U.S. would not allow European nations to start new colonies in the Western Hemisphere—North and South America.

Lesson Summary

The years immediately after the War of 1812 are often called the Era of Good Feelings. During these years, Congress strengthened the economy and President James Monroe's foreign policy closed the Western Hemisphere to European nations eager for more colonies.

Lesson Objective

Students will learn how a strong economy and a strong foreign policy strengthened the United States in the years after the War of 1812.

Focus Your Reading Answers

1 The years after the War of 1812 were known as the Era of Good Feelings because party politics no longer divided the nation and people felt united and proud of the United States.

2 The American System strengthened the economy by setting up a national bank, passing the Tariff of 1816 to protect American-made goods, and helping states build canals and roads.

3 President Monroe's foreign policy made the country stronger by purchasing Florida from Spain, persuading the British to remove troops from the Canadian border, and issuing a policy statement that closed the Western Hemisphere to further European colonization.

Stop and Think

Answers will vary but should reflect an understanding that in a federal system, limiting the power of the states increases the power of the nation and vice versa.

Picturing History

Americans today take it for granted that the Supreme Court has the say in how the Constitution will be interpreted. John Marshall established that idea at a time when it was hotly debated. Marshall died in 1835. How did that idea strengthen the federal government?

helped them by raising the prices of those goods. In 1817, Congress agreed to provide federal funds to help states build roads and canals.

Supreme Court Decisions

During this period, the Supreme Court also helped strengthen the national government. Several court decisions, written by Chief Justice John Marshall, placed limits on the states. The Court's decision in *Dartmouth College v. Woodward* (1819) ruled that states could not overturn private business agreements. In *Gibbons v. Ogden* (1824), the Supreme Court ruled that only Congress could regulate trade between the states.

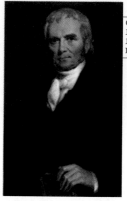

Chief Justice John Marshall

stop and think

Discuss with a partner why limiting state power would strengthen the national government. In your notebook write three ways this could happen.

Bold Foreign Policies

President James Monroe gave the United States a larger role in world affairs. He expanded the nation's boundaries by persuading Spain to sell Florida. His secretary of state, John Quincy Adams, signed a treaty with Britain that removed troops from both nations from the border with Canada. In 1823, Adams also wrote a bold policy statement for the president that closed the Western Hemisphere to future European colonization. This is known as the **Monroe Doctrine**.

President James Monroe

Picturing History

As president, James Monroe of Virginia tried to unite the country. In his inaugural address, Monroe spoke of the American people as "one great family with a common interest." How did he try as president to promote that "common interest"?

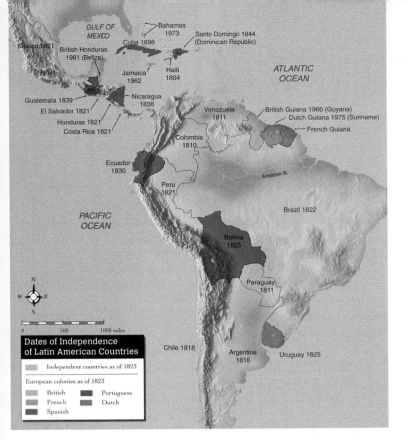

Dates of Independence
of Latin American Countries

Independent countries as of 1823

European colonies as of 1823

British
French
Spanish
Portuguese
Dutch

National Prosperity

The Era of Good Feelings was a period of prosperity. A food shortage in Europe led to high prices for American wheat, pork, and cheese. Land values rose as farmers bought more land. They also bought more plows, shovels, and farm wagons from American manufacturers.

Putting It All Together

In your notebook make a two-column chart. Label the columns "Problem" and "Solution." On the problem side, write problems that President Monroe addressed in his foreign policy. On the solution side, note how he solved the problems. Use the Internet or the library to research more about President Monroe's foreign policy and add to the chart.

Putting It All Together

Among the problems that Monroe addressed in his foreign policy were border problems with Spain, the presence of troops on the border with Canada, and European intervention in the Americas. His solutions included the purchase of Florida from Spain, a treaty with Britain to remove troops from the Canadian border, and the Monroe Doctrine, which closed the Western Hemisphere to European colonization.

Map Extensions

1 Ask students to use the map on page 219 to answer the following questions:

- What country in Latin America was the first to declare its independence? (Haiti, in 1804)

- Who declared independence first, Chile or Argentina? (Argentina, in 1816)

- Name the five countries that became independent in 1821. (Mexico, El Salvador, Honduras, Costa Rica, and Peru)

- What nation became independent in 1822? (Brazil)

2 Ask students how the events shown on the map on page 219 may have influenced the president's decision to issue the Monroe Doctrine in 1823. (The map reveals that much of Latin America became independent between 1810 and 1822. Monroe may have feared that European nations would try to take over these newly independent countries.)

Lesson Summary

The Era of Good Feelings did not last long. The panic of 1819 led to economic hard times. Northerners and Southerners quarreled over the future of slavery as one territory after another applied for statehood, beginning with Missouri in 1820. The election of 1824 caused more bad feelings. Andrew Jackson won the most votes but did not have a majority in the Electoral College. The House of Representatives decided the election in favor of John Quincy Adams.

Lesson Objective

Students will learn how and why the sectional conflicts and party politics replaced the Era of Good Feelings.

Focus Your Reading Answers

1 After the panic of 1819, factory owners demanded help from Congress. Congress helped by raising tariff rates.

2 The Missouri Compromise admitted Missouri as a slave state and Maine as a free state, thus preserving the balance in the Senate between free and slave states. It also drew a line on a map from Missouri to the Rocky Mountains at the latitude line of 36° 30'. New states north of that line would be free states and those south of it, slave states.

3 The House of Representatives decided who won the 1824 presidential election because no candidate had a majority in the Electoral College.

LESSON **2** # Sectional Conflicts and Party Battles

Thinking on Your Own

Read the Focus Your Reading questions and vocabulary. Write one sentence that predicts how the existence of slavery could threaten American unity or the union of states.

The Era of Good Feelings was short-lived. It could not survive the hard times of the 1820s. The South's efforts to admit Missouri as a slave state caused ill feelings in the North. The revival of party politics also helped divide Americans.

<table>
<tr><td>focus your reading</td></tr>
<tr><td>What demands did people make after the panic of 1819?</td></tr>
<tr><td>What was the Missouri Compromise?</td></tr>
<tr><td>Why did the House of Representatives decide who was elected president in 1824?</td></tr>
<tr><td>vocabulary</td></tr>
<tr><td>panic of 1819
Tallmadge Amendment
Missouri Compromise
Electoral College</td></tr>
</table>

Economic Hard Times

The first blow to the Era of Good Feelings was the **panic of 1819**. The Bank of the United States helped cause the panic by forcing western banks to call in their loans. Its directors were afraid the bank would lose the money it had loaned. Unable to pay back their loans, many farmers lost their farms.

The Second Bank of the United States, built in 1816, is located in Philadelphia.

As farmers placed fewer orders, factories had to close. Their owners demanded help from Congress. Congress helped them by raising tariff rates. The new Tariff of 1824 made southern planters angry. It increased the price of cloth, tools, furniture, and other items they needed. The farmers blamed northern factory owners for high prices.

Lesson Vocabulary

Ask students to define the word *panic*. (fright, terror, alarm, dread) Explain that Americans in the early 1800s used the term to describe their fear and anxiety over an event, in this case an economic downturn. The *panic of 1819* was a period when many businesses experienced hard times.

An *amendment* is an addition or change to a proposed law. In 1819, Representative James Tallmadge of New York proposed an addition to a law that would allow people in the territory of Missouri to write a state constitution. His *amendment*, known as the *Tallmadge Amendment*, would outlaw slavery in the new state.

Review the meaning of the word *compromise*. (a settlement in which each side gives up some of its demands) The *Missouri Compromise* admitted Missouri as a slave state and Maine as a free state. It also drew a line on a map that divided potential new states into free and slave states.

Remind students that the *Electoral College* is not a real college. It is a group of persons known as electors, who are chosen by voters in their states to officially elect the president and vice president. (See Article 2, Section 1, clauses 2 and 3 of the Constitution on page 334. Refer students to the Twelfth Amendment as well.)

The Missouri Crisis

In 1819, Missouri asked to be admitted to the Union as a slave state. This would destroy the balance that existed in Congress of eleven slave and eleven free states. Congressman James W. Tallmadge of New York demanded that Missouri be admitted as a free state. This led to an intense debate in and out of Congress. Most people in the North supported the **Tallmadge Amendment**. The South opposed it.

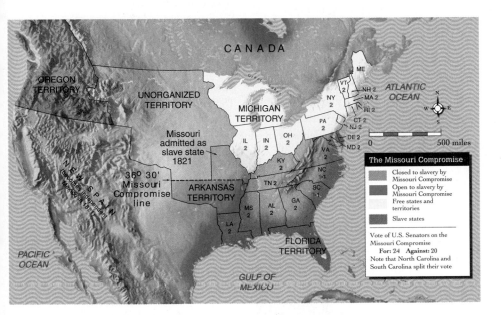

Afraid that the issue would destroy the Union, Congress agreed to a compromise. The **Missouri Compromise** (1821) admitted Missouri as a slave state. To restore the balance, it admitted Maine as a free state. To settle the question for the future, Congress drew a line on a map from Missouri to the Rocky Mountains. Any new state south of that line would be admitted as a slave state; any north of it would be a free state.

Map Extension

Ask students to use the map and its key on page 221 to answer the following questions:

- In which states did senators split their vote on the Missouri Compromise? (North Carolina and South Carolina)

- If Arkansas were to apply for statehood, would it enter the Union as a free or a slave state under the Compromise of 1820? (slave state)

- If Oregon were to apply for statehood, would it enter the Union as a free or a slave state? (free state)

- How many states were free in 1821? (12)

- How many states permitted slavery in 1821? (12)

Extension

Ask students to find out more about the way a territory becomes a state by researching one of the territories shown on the map. How many people had to live in the territory before it became a state? What other conditions did the territory have to meet? Have students create a poster to share their findings with the class.

Extension

Many Republicans questioned whether Congress had the power to create a Bank of the United States. In 1819, the Supreme Court answered that question in its decision in the case of *McCulloch* v. *Maryland*. Ask students to find out the details of the case, how a majority of the justices decided the case, what was in the case, and then share their findings with the class.

Stop and Think

Although opinions will vary, students should be required to support those opinions with facts about the Missouri and other compromises as well as reasoned arguments.

Picturing History

The campaign poster on page 222 was used in the 1824 presidential election. Ask students to study it carefully and then answer the following questions:

- What is the message of the poster?

- How did the artist use national symbols and quotations to highlight that message?

- At whom is the message aimed?

- To what emotions does it appeal?

stop and think

Was the Missouri Compromise a good way to deal with the slavery issue? Are political compromises good or bad? Debate this question with a partner. Include any other political compromises you know about.

The Democratic Spirit

By the 1820s, the United States was more democratic. The very term "democracy" had a more favorable meaning. Earlier generations viewed democracy as a threat. The Constitution had placed limits on democracy. Politicians of the 1820s put much greater trust in the people.

Politics was more democratic in many ways. At the time of the American Revolution, only property owners could vote. The new western states, added to the Union between 1810 and 1820, let every white adult male vote. The older eastern states soon dropped their property requirements as well. As a result, more people voted and took part in public life.

Andrew Jackson was popular as a "self-made man" in the 1824 elections.

Americans placed greater value on social equality. In hotels, steamboats, and marketplaces, people of all classes mixed together as equals. Inherited wealth and family name had once determined social rank. That was no longer the case. The hero of the day was the "self-made man." He was a man like Andrew Jackson, who had climbed to the top on his own.

Extension

In 1824, all of the candidates for president were Republicans, each with support in a single part of the country. None was strong enough to defeat all of his rivals. The election broke apart the Republican Party. After Adams's inauguration, some members of the party started calling themselves Democrats. Their leader was Andrew Jackson, and they spent the next four years preparing to put their candidate in the White House. Have students find out more about the beginnings of the Democratic Party. Ask them to present their findings to the class using the Student Presentation Builder on the student DVD.

Political Conflict

In 1824, the rising tide of democracy almost swept Andrew Jackson into the White House. Among the four candidates running for president, he won the most electoral and popular votes. But he did not win a majority in the **Electoral College**. In such a case, the House of Representatives must decide the election.

President John Quincy Adams

Henry Clay, one of the four candidates, persuaded his friends to vote for John Quincy Adams. Adams had come in second. Congress elected Adams, who then appointed Clay as his secretary of state.

Henry Clay

Andrew Jackson was furious. He accused Adams of defeating the will of the people by making a deal with Clay. For the next four years, Jackson's friends in Congress blocked nearly every bill that Adams wanted passed. President John Quincy Adams accomplished very little as president.

Putting It All Together

Create a two-column chart in your notebook entitled "Conflicts" and "Feelings." In the left column, list three conflicts of the period 1819–1824. Explain in the right column how these conflicts created bad feelings among Americans.

Putting It All Together

Under the heading "Conflicts," students might list the Bank of the United States, the Tariff of 1824, the Tallmadge Amendment, and the election of 1824. Each caused bad feelings by pitting the interests of one region of the country against another region.

Bio Facts

- Born on July 11, 1767, in Braintree (now Quincy), Massachusetts, the son of John Adams, the second president.

- Spent some of his early years in Europe with his father, graduated from Harvard, and entered law practice.

- Became U.S. minister to the Netherlands, the first of several diplomatic posts, in 1784.

- Married Louisa Catherine Johnson in 1797.

- Elected to the Senate in 1803.

- Appointed minister to Russia in 1809.

- Helped negotiate the Treaty of Ghent in 1814, which ended the War of 1812; became U.S. minister to London in 1815.

- Appointed secretary of state in 1817.

- Elected president by the House of Representatives in 1825; defeated for reelection by Jackson in 1828.

- Elected to the House of Representatives in 1830, served there until his death in 1848.

224

Biography

John Quincy Adams (1767–1848)

In December 1825, President John Quincy Adams delivered his first address to Congress. It called for Congress to build federal roads and canals, and establish a national university. The president also wanted a naval academy, a national observatory, a uniform system of weights and measures, and closer cooperation with Latin America. Few presidents have taken office with such a bold plan for the future.

Adams was born in Massachusetts in 1767. He was the eldest son of John and Abigail Adams. At age eleven, he went to Europe to watch his father negotiate a treaty of alliance with France. He graduated from Harvard College at age twenty, and chose to study and practice law.

John Quincy Adams gave up his law practice in 1794 to represent the United States in Europe. During the next twenty years he served as United States minister to the Netherlands, Prussia, and Great Britain. He returned home to win election to the United States Senate. In 1817, President James Monroe appointed him secretary of state. As secretary of state, he wrote the Monroe Doctrine, which warned Europe not to meddle in the affairs of the Western Hemisphere.

Despite such preparation, John Quincy Adams's presidency, from 1825–1829, was a failure. Andrew Jackson's friends in Congress blocked every measure he wanted passed. They fought him at every turn, and defeated him for reelection.

In 1830, the people of Adams's Massachusetts district elected him to Congress. He spent the next twelve and a half years serving in the House of Representatives. In Congress, he supported the Bank of the United States, fought for freedom of speech, and attempted to introduce amendments to the Constitution that would prevent any person born in the United States from being born a slave.

In 1839, fifty-three African captives aboard the *Amistad* mutinied off the coast of Cuba. They killed the captain and cook, and attempted to sail the ship back to Africa. The ship was stopped off the coast of Connecticut and the Africans arrested. Adams joined the team of lawyers who fought for the freedom of the Africans. In 1841, he argued their case before the Supreme Court. Adams's efforts helped gain the captives their freedom and eventual return to Africa. John Quincy Adams died in the Capitol Building on February 23, 1848, at age seventy-six.

Biography Extension

After his defeat for a second term as president, Adams ran for Congress from his home district. He served nine consecutive terms in the House of Representatives, earning the nickname "Old Man Eloquent" because of his speeches in opposition to slavery. Ask students to find out why Adams has won more praise for his congressional career than for his presidency. Have them share their findings with the class.

Map Extension

Ask students to use the map on page 225 to answer the following questions:

- Which parts of the country did Jackson carry in the election of 1828? (the South and the West)

- Which states were divided in the election? (New York, Maryland, and Maine)

- Why were no votes recorded for Michigan, Arkansas, or Florida? (They were territories and therefore could not participate in the election.)

The Jacksonian Democrats

Thinking on Your Own

Read the Focus Your Reading questions and vocabulary. Make a two-column chart in your notebook with the title "Andrew Jackson's Decisions." Label one column "Made National Government Stronger" and the other column "Made State Government Stronger." As you read about the decisions Jackson made as president, list them in one column or the other.

The election campaign of 1828 was hard fought. John Quincy Adams ran for reelection as the National Republican candidate. Andrew Jackson was the candidate of the new Democratic-Republican Party. The Democrats promised that Jackson would give the government back to the people. Andrew Jackson won the election with 56 percent of the popular vote.

focus your reading

What did Andrew Jackson mean by restoring government to the people?

What limits did Jackson place on states' rights?

Why was Jackson's war against the Bank of the United States good politics?

vocabulary

doctrine of nullification

trail of tears

depression of 1837

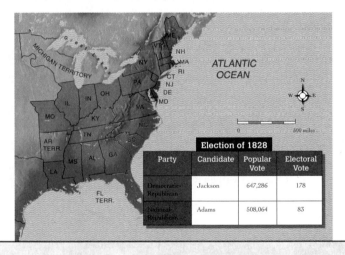

Election of 1828			
Party	Candidate	Popular Vote	Electoral Vote
Democratic-Republican	Jackson	647,286	178
National Republican	Adams	508,064	83

225

Lesson Vocabulary

Explain to students that the word *null* means "of no importance." To nullify a law is to say that the law does not have to be obeyed. Senator John C. Calhoun of South Carolina claimed that states did not have to enforce federal laws that in their opinion violated the Constitution. He called this idea the *doctrine of nullification*.

Trail of tears is the name the Cherokee gave to their forced removal from Georgia. Use the painting on page 216 to help students understand the significance of the term.

A *depression* describes an economy characterized by long-term unemployment, low prices, and low levels of trade and investment. It is a time when many businesses fail and thousands of people lose their jobs. The *depression of 1837* was such a period in American history.

226 Chapter 14

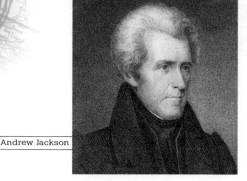
Andrew Jackson

Jacksonian Democracy

Jackson wanted the people to know that he was their president. On his first day in office, he invited everyone to the White House for refreshments. Fifteen thousand people showed up. It is the largest crowd ever to attend a White House event.

President Jackson fired many of the government clerks in Washington, D.C. He replaced them with Democrats. "Rotation in office," he said, was another way to return government to the people. It also rewarded workers of the Democratic Party.

Jackson reduced the work of the federal government. He had more faith in state governments, as they were closer to the people. In 1830, Congress passed a bill to build a national road in Kentucky. Jackson vetoed it. He thought that each state should be responsible for its own roads.

Nullification Crisis

Democrats from South Carolina had their own ideas about the rights of the states. John C. Calhoun argued that states did not have to enforce acts of Congress that they thought violated the U.S. Constitution. He called this the **doctrine of nullification**. In 1832, South Carolina refused to enforce the tariff acts of 1828 and 1832. Its leaders thought the tariffs benefited northern factory owners at the expense of the South.

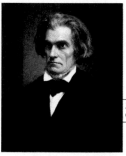
John C. Calhoun

Jackson opposed South Carolina's action. It placed the state above the federal government. He threatened to send troops to South Carolina to enforce the tariff laws. The state's leaders agreed to repeal

Picturing History

Unlike the six presidents before him, Jackson came from a poor family. At the age of thirteen, he served briefly in the Revolutionary War. After the war, Jackson headed west to Tennessee. There he became a major general in the state militia, a Superior Court judge, and Tennessee's first U.S. congressman. By the 1820s he was a wealthy plantation owner. Yet he was regarded as a "man of the people." Ask students what the phrase means and how it applied to Jackson.

Picturing History

John C. Calhoun served as vice president of the United States under both Adams and Jackson. In 1824, he ran for president along with Adams, Jackson, and others, but withdrew from the race to run unopposed for vice president. When Jackson supported the Tariff of 1828, Calhoun openly disagreed. He was so vehemently against the tariff that he resigned in 1832, becoming the first vice president in American history to voluntarily do so.

Extension

Jackson's inaugural celebration was a mob scene, as crowds pushed through the gates of the White House trying to catch sight of the new president. Have students compare accounts of Jackson's inauguration with the painting of Washington's inaugural on page 172. What similarities do they notice? How do they account for differences?

the acts of nullification if Congress would reduce the tariff. Congress passed a compromise tariff act in 1833 that reduced the rates. That ended the nullification crisis.

Indian Removal

Jackson did not include Native Americans in his promise to restore government to the people. When he took office, the State of Georgia was trying to force the Cherokee off their land. The Cherokee, who could read and write, knew how to protect their rights. The tribe filed suit against the state in the Supreme Court.

Andrew Jackson took Georgia's side. When the Court ruled in the Cherokee's favor in 1831, he refused to enforce its decision. Instead, he ordered the army to remove the Cherokee and other eastern people. The army relocated them to "Indian Territory" west of the Mississippi River. Thousands of Cherokee died on the forced march, or "**trail of tears**," to their new home.

stop and think

Imagine that you are a journalist writing a report on President Jackson's treatment of the Cherokee. Write the article. Include facts about the Cherokee and American state and national governments. Research to learn more about this topic.

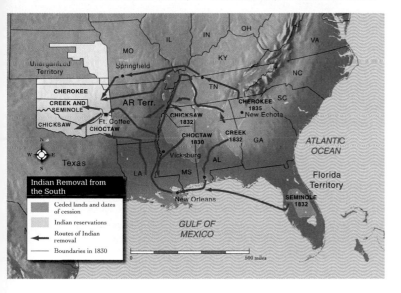

Indian Removal from the South

- Ceded lands and dates of cession
- Indian reservations
- Routes of Indian removal
- Boundaries in 1830

0   500 miles

CHEROKEE
CREEK AND SEMINOLE
CHICKSAW
CHOCTAW
Ft. Coffee
AR Terr.
Unorganized Territory
Springfield
Texas
Vicksburg
New Orleans
CHICKSAW 1832
CHOCTAW 1830
CREEK 1832
CHEROKEE 1835
New Echota
SEMINOLE 1832
Florida Territory
GULF OF MEXICO
ATLANTIC OCEAN
MO
IL
IN
OH
VA
KY
TN
NC
SC
GA
AL
MS
LA

Stop and Think
Articles will vary but students should include not only facts included in this lesson but also their research on the topic. Be sure that students identify the sources they used. Remind them to put the results of their research in their own words.

Map Extensions

1 Have students use the map on page 227 to answer the following questions:

- What groups of Native Americans were forcibly removed from the South in the 1830s? (Cherokee, Creek, Chicksaw, Choctaw, and Seminole)

- From what states were they removed? (Georgia, Alabama, Mississippi, Tennessee, Florida, and North Carolina)

- Through what states did the Cherokee travel on their journey west? (Tennessee, Kentucky, Illinois, and Missouri)

- Which Native Americans were the first to lose their lands? (Choctaw, in 1830) Which were the last? (Cherokee, in 1835)

2 Have students research the removal of one of the other groups shown on the map. How is that group's story similar to the Cherokee's? What differences seem most striking? Ask students to present their findings to the class by using the Student Presentation Builder on the student DVD.

Answers will vary but should be based on specific decisions Jackson made. Students should explain how those decisions affected their view of his presidency.

Picturing History

Use the following steps to help students analyze the cartoon:

1 Study the image carefully. Notice shapes, lines, and the position of people and/or objects.

2 Write down what you noticed without interpreting what the image means.

3 List questions you have about the picture that need to be answered before you can interpret it. (For example, what do the tall columns stand for? Why do some men look like the devil?)

4 Discuss your questions with others in the class to try to find answers.

5 What do you think the cartoonist is trying to say about Andrew Jackson and his decision to destroy the bank? Who is his intended audience?

Jackson's War Against the Bank

In 1831, Jackson declared war against the Bank of the United States. He saw the bank as a powerful institution that the people did not control. When Congress passed a bill to renew the bank's charter, Jackson vetoed it. He used the bank veto in the election of 1832 to win votes in the West and the South. Many voters there blamed the bank for the panic of 1819. Jackson won reelection, defeating Henry Clay.

This cartoon shows Andrew Jackson demolishing the Bank of the United States by withdrawing federal funds.

Although Jackson's veto was good politics, it was bad for the economy. Jackson moved the U.S. Treasury's money to state banks. They loaned it out to land buyers. Many farmers lost their farms when they could not repay the loans. Destroying the bank helped bring about the **depression of 1837**, another period of hard times. By then Jackson's second term as president was over.

Putting It All Together

Review the Thinking on Your Own chart you have kept while reading this section. On the basis of Jackson's decisions during his first four years in office, would you have voted to reelect him as president in 1832?

Extension

Ask students to create a cartoon that gives their opinion of Jackson's decision to destroy the Bank of the United States. Have students organize the cartoons into two categories (approval and disapproval) before posting them in the classroom.

Read a Primary Source

The Trail of Tears

Groups of Cherokee set out on the "trail of tears" to Indian Territory late in September 1838. In the following account, a traveler from Maine described the condition of the Cherokee when they passed through Kentucky.

reading for understanding

What season of the year did the Cherokee's journey take place?

How were they dressed?

What was the condition of their health?

"We met several detachments [of Cherokee] in the southern part of Kentucky on the 4th, 5th, and 6th of December. . . . The sick and feeble were carried in wagons . . . a great many ride on horseback and multitudes go on foot—even aged females, apparently nearly ready to drop into the grave, were traveling with heavy burdens attached to the back—on the sometimes frozen ground, and sometimes muddy streets, with no covering for the feet except what nature had given them. . . . We learned from the inhabitants on the road where the Indians passed, that they buried fourteen or fifteen at every stopping place."

Quoted in John Ehle, *Trail of Tears: The Rise and Fall of the Cherokee Nation* (New York: Doubleday, 1988).

Reading for Understanding

1 The journey took place in winter. The traveler described seeing detachments in December.

2 The traveler noted that many had no shoes.

3 The Cherokee were described as exhausted, cold, and feeble. The traveler noted that as many as 14 or 15 people were buried at every stopping place.

Extension

Ask students to compare the paintings on pages 216 and 229 with the written account. What similarities do they notice? How do they account for differences?

Chapter Review

1 Paragraphs will vary, but should indicate that the Era of Good Feelings was based in part on wartime patriotism, the American System, and Monroe's foreign policy successes. It did not survive the hard economic times of the 1820s.

2 Letters will vary, but students should show an understanding that nullification undermines the power of the nation to carry out its duties.

3 Questions will vary, but should reflect an understanding of life in the United States during the 1820s and 1830s.

Chapter Summary

The War of 1812 helped to unite Americans. The result was an **Era of Good Feelings**. During this period, Congress developed a plan called the **American System** to strengthen the economy. It included a national bank, higher tariffs, and federal funds to build roads and canals. The **Monroe Doctrine** closed the Western Hemisphere to future European colonies.

The **panic of 1819** led to economic hard times. Missouri's request to be admitted as a slave state caused ill will between the North and the South. The North supported the **Tallmadge Amendment,** which would admit Missouri as a free state. The South opposed it. The **Missouri Compromise** settled the issue. The election of 1824 created still more bad feelings. Andrew Jackson won the most votes, but he did not have a majority in the **Electoral College**. The House of Representatives decided the election in favor of John Quincy Adams.

In the presidential election of 1828, Andrew Jackson defeated John Quincy Adams. Jackson forced South Carolina to back down from its **doctrine of nullification**. Jackson supported Georgia's effort to remove the Cherokee from the state. Thousands of Cherokee died on the "**trail of tears**."

In 1831, Jackson vetoed a bill to continue the Bank of the United States. Destroying the bank helped bring on the **depression of 1837**.

Chapter Review

1 Use information from the chapter and additional research to write a paragraph about the Era of Good Feelings.

2 Review the section on the doctrine of nullification. If a state today tried to nullify a federal law, how would you respond? Write a letter to the editor of a newspaper explaining your position.

3 Suppose you could interview any person in this chapter. Who would you choose? Why? Write a series of questions you would ask during the interview. Include questions about economics, geography, society, technology, politics, and culture.

Novel Connections

Below is a list of books that relate to the time period covered in this chapter. The numbers in parentheses indicate the related Thematic Strands of the National Council for the Social Studies (NCSS).

Cornelia Cornelissen. *Soft Rain: A Story of the Cherokee Trail of Tears.* Delacorte, 2003. (II, III)

David Rubel. *Scholastic Encyclopedia of Presidents and Their Times.* Rev. ed. Scholastic, 2001. (II, IV, VI)

Skill Builder

Analyzing Political Cartoons

Political cartoons have a long history in America. In 1747, Benjamin Franklin published the first political cartoon to appear in an American newspaper. In the 1830s, newspapers often used political cartoons to attack politicians. Some cartoons focused on President Andrew Jackson. The anti-Jackson cartoon below appeared during the 1832 presidential contest.

To understand political cartoons, the reader must identify the character, the topic, and the opinion of the artist. As you examine the cartoon, discuss these three items with a partner.

This cartoon shows Andrew Jackson with a "veto" message in his right hand. On the floor are scraps of paper identified as "Constitution of the United States of America" and a tattered copy of a book entitled "Judiciary of the U States."

Examine the cartoon and use information from the lesson to answer these questions:

1 How does the cartoon present Jackson as a monarch or despot?

2 What veto by President Jackson is the cartoon most likely attacking?

3 How does the cartoon show Jackson's disregard of Supreme Court decisions?

4 To which Supreme Court decision is the cartoon most likely referring?

5 Identify the character, topic, and opinion of this cartoon.

Skill Builder

1 The cartoon shows Jackson as an absolute monarch. He has a crown, scepter, and ornate robe. He is shown as having ripped up the Constitution.

2 The cartoon is attacking Jackson's veto of the Bank of the United States.

3 Jackson is shown trampling Supreme Court decisions.

4 The cartoon may be referring to Jackson's disregard of the Supreme Court's support for the rights of the Cherokee.

5 The character in the cartoon is Jackson, and the topic is his use of power. The cartoonist believes that Jackson is abusing his power as president by disregarding the Supreme Court and trampling on the Constitution.

Classroom Discussion

Discuss with students some of the broader topics covered in this chapter.

- How did the American System help to unite the American people? What other innovations, events, or individuals helped unite Americans in the 1820s and 1830s? What innovations, events, or individuals divided Americans?

- Compare the elections of 1800 and 1828. What are the similarities between them? How do you explain the outcome of each?

- In what ways did American democracy change between Washington's time and Jackson's? How has it changed since Jackson's time?

- How did the efforts of Latin Americans to build independent nations in the early 1800s shape American foreign policy?

Unit Objectives

After studying this unit, students will be able to

- describe the impact of cotton as a cash crop on life in the South
- explain how slavery shaped Southern life in the early 1800s
- describe efforts to reform the nation and how those efforts encouraged many individuals to find their voice

Unit 8 focuses on the ways regional differences shaped the United States in the early 1800s.

- **Chapter 15, The Slave South**, examines the effects of slavery on black and white Southerners.
- **Chapter 16, Toward a More Perfect Society**, describes the effects of religious revivals and the reform movement on American life.

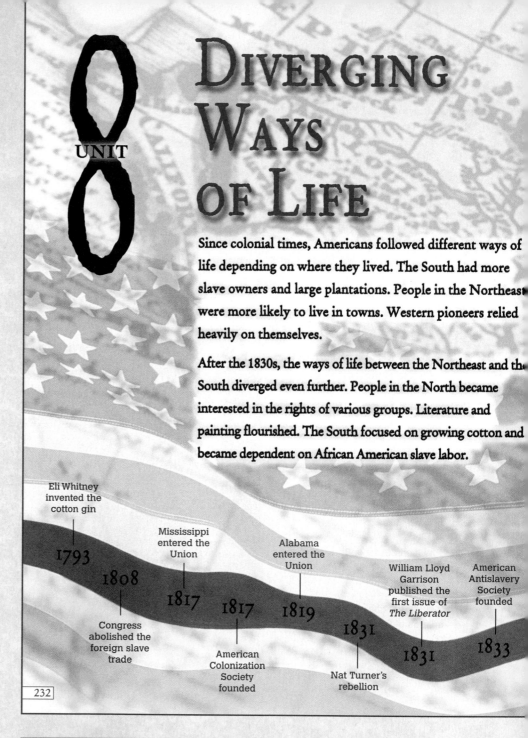

UNIT 8
DIVERGING WAYS OF LIFE

Since colonial times, Americans followed different ways of life depending on where they lived. The South had more slave owners and large plantations. People in the Northeast were more likely to live in towns. Western pioneers relied heavily on themselves.

After the 1830s, the ways of life between the Northeast and the South diverged even further. People in the North became interested in the rights of various groups. Literature and painting flourished. The South focused on growing cotton and became dependent on African American slave labor.

Eli Whitney invented the cotton gin
1793

1808
Congress abolished the foreign slave trade

Mississippi entered the Union
1817

1817
American Colonization Society founded

Alabama entered the Union
1819

1831
Nat Turner's rebellion

William Lloyd Garrison published the first issue of *The Liberator*
1831

American Antislavery Society founded
1833

232

Getting Started

After students have read the two paragraphs on page 232, discuss the meaning of the word *diverge*. When paths *diverge*, they move in different directions from a common point. Have students skim the chapter and lesson titles and scan the illustrations for examples of the way that life in the United States was diverging in the mid-1800s. Ask students to write a bulleted list of examples, then revise and expand their lists as they read Chapters 15 and 16.

Why did the South focus on growing cotton?

How did the abolitionist movement relate to the women's rights movement?

What contributed to the increased interest in the arts?

Collage Answers

1 The South focused on growing cotton, because it brought higher returns than wheat, tobacco, or other cash crops.

2 The abolitionist movement inspired some Americans to organize a women's rights movement.

3 The reform movement inspired people in the arts to declare their intellectual independence from Europe. They began to express American values and experiences in their work.

Collage Extension

Use the images and questions on page 233 to preview the unit. Discuss how the questions and images relate to the idea of *diverging ways of life*.

Florida entered the Union

First women's rights convention held at Seneca Falls

Walt Whitman published *Leaves of Grass*

1836

1843

1845

1845

1848

1851

1855

Arkansas entered the Union

Dorothea Dix reported on the mentally ill in Massachusetts

Henry David Thoreau published *Walden*

Sojourner Truth spoke at Ohio Women's Rights Convention

233

Measuring Time

Explain to students that the timeline relates to both Chapters 15 and 16.

Timeline Extension

Encourage students to use the timeline to preview the unit. What does it suggest about "diverging ways of life"? What clues does it provide to life in "the slave South"? (Some events seem to indicate the growth of slavery, while others show opposition to it.) What does it suggest about the ways Americans tried to move "toward a more perfect society"? (A number of events indicate efforts to improve American life.)

Related Transparencies

T-17 Concept Web

Key Blacklines

Biography
William and Ellen Craft

Primary Source
Cotton Picking Season

DVD Extension

Encourage students to use the reading comprehension, vocabulary reinforcement, and interactive timeline activities on the student DVD.

Picturing History

Ask students to describe what they see in the photograph on page 234. Explain that the people in the photograph are slaves. What can we learn about these individuals and their lives from the photograph? Encourage students to compare the picture with other images of slaves and slavery in the chapter. How are they similar? In what respects is the photograph on page 234 unique?

Chapter 15
THE SLAVE SOUTH

Getting Focused

Skim this chapter to predict what you will be learning.

- Read the lesson titles and subheadings.
- Look at the illustrations and read the captions.
- Examine the maps.
- Review the vocabulary words and terms.

What do you already know about the slave South? Discuss your ideas with a partner. Write a couple of sentences in your notebook that sum up your ideas.

Pre-Reading Discussion

Ask students to read aloud the chapter title. Discuss the meaning of the word *slave*. (a person owned by another person) In what sense did slavery affect everyone in the South—black and white, rich and poor, enslaved and free? Have students check their ideas as they complete each bulleted direction on page 234.

The Cotton South

Thinking on Your Own

In your notebook, create a concept map with a circle in the center. Write the word "Cotton" in the circle. Read the Focus Your Reading questions and the vocabulary. Then, with a partner, brainstorm ideas related to growing cotton and arrange them on lines connected to the circle.

In 1793, Eli Whitney invented the **cotton gin**. It was a simple machine that removed the seeds from raw cotton. The amazing thing was that it did the work fifty times faster than by hand. Besides that, a gin was cheap and easy to make. This machine changed the South and its way of life.

Eli Whitney

focus your reading

What was the cotton gin?

How did the cotton gin affect the South?

What impact did cotton growing have on southern society?

vocabulary

cotton gin   lower South

The Cotton Gin's Impact on the South

The cotton gin gave the South a new cash crop. Cotton brought much higher returns than tobacco or wheat. W. S. Hyland, who owned a large plantation in Mississippi, made $6,500 to $10,000 per year growing cotton. At that time, a New England factory worker earned about $300 a year.

The promise of getting rich growing cotton helped settle the lower South. Farmers headed west to buy land to grow cotton. They helped add new states to the Union, including Mississippi (1817), Alabama (1819), Arkansas (1836), and Florida (1845). Native American tribes that stood in the way were quickly removed.

Eli Whitney received a patent for the cotton gin in 1793.

The Slave South   235

Picturing History

Before the invention of the cotton gin, it took a worker an entire day to prepare one or two pounds of cotton for market. With a cotton gin, that same worker could clean 50 pounds a day.

Lesson Summary

In 1793, Eli Whitney invented the cotton gin. With the help of this new machine, cotton became the South's leading cash crop. It made thousands of plantation owners rich. It also sped up the settlement of the lower South. The value of cotton as a crop affected every part of the region.

Lesson Objective

Students will learn how cotton became the South's leading crop and its effects on life in the region.

Focus Your Reading Answers

1 A cotton gin was a simple machine that removed the seeds from raw cotton.

2 The cotton gin gave the South a valuable new cash crop.

3 Cotton growing had a huge impact on Southern society. It created a society headed by large, powerful plantation owners and supported by the work of enslaved people.

Lesson Vocabulary

A *cotton gin* is a machine that removes seeds from cotton.

Have students use the map on page 236 to define the *lower South*. It is the part of the South where cotton was grown, and it stretched from the Atlantic coast in the east to Louisiana and Arkansas in the west.

Map Extensions

1 Ask students to use the map on page 236 to answer the following questions:

- What states produced up to 45 bales of cotton per square mile in 1820? (Virginia, North Carolina, South Carolina, Georgia, Tennessee, Alabama, Mississippi, and Louisiana)

- What states produced up to 45 bales of cotton per square mile in 1860? (North Carolina, South Carolina, Georgia, Florida, Tennessee, Alabama, Mississippi, Louisiana, and Arkansas)

- What states produced more than 45 bales per square mile in 1860? (Louisiana, Arkansas, Mississippi, Alabama, Georgia, and Tennessee)

2 Have students use the map and their answers to the questions to write a sentence summarizing what happened to cotton production between 1820 and 1860. (*Sample answer:* Although production increased throughout the lower South, the increases were greatest in the new states west of the Appalachian Mountains.)

Stop and Think

Answers will vary but should include expansion of cotton farming to the newer states such as Mississippi, Alabama, Arkansas, and Florida; increased demand for slaves; and growth in the power of plantation owners.

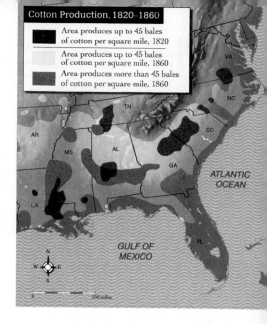

Cotton gave slavery a new lease on life. In the 1790s, slavery seemed to be dying out in the South. Farmers were planting less tobacco and more wheat, a crop that required less manual labor. Cotton made owning slaves profitable again.

Cotton also helped keep the South a rural society. While the North invested in factories and shops, the South put its money into cotton land. The only cities to rise in the South were seaports that shipped farm products to market.

> **stop and think**
>
> Write a bulleted list of ways that the cotton gin changed the South.

Cotton Reshaped Southern Society

Cotton growing and slavery created a new kind of society in the South. The most powerful families were the big plantation owners. They were the upper class, along with the merchants who bought and sold their cotton. Wealthy planters like W. S. Hyland owned thousands of acres. They had hundreds of slaves who worked under an overseer. The planters lived in big plantation houses filled with fine furniture.

Owners of larger plantations built large mansions on their estates.

Picturing History

Large plantations with hundreds of slaves were relatively rare. Most whites in Southern states never owned slaves, and those who did usually owned fewer than ten slaves. Yet even today, when many people think of the South, they picture homes like the one shown in the drawing on page 236. How do such pictures portray life in the South?

Extension

Ask students to turn the following information from the U.S. Census into a circle graph. In 1860,

- 75 percent of all free Southerners owned no slaves

- 17 percent owned at least 1 slave but no more than 9

- 7 percent owned at least 10 slaves but no more than 50

- 1 percent owned over 50 slaves

The majority of the whites in the South were middle-class farmers. They owned small farms and perhaps a slave or two. These farmers worked alongside their slaves in the cotton field. They owned modest farm houses.

The white lower class consisted of poor farmers. They owned neither slaves nor land. Most worked as hired farm laborers. Competing with cheap slave labor kept them in poverty. These "poor whites" lived in tumbledown cabins.

Cotton plantations could be thousands of acres in size.

"Free people of color" occupied the bottom rung of free society in the South. They were African Americans who had gained their freedom. The shacks in which they lived were only a little better than slave shacks.

African American slaves were at the very bottom of southern society. The majority worked on plantations and farms in the **lower South**, the major cotton-growing region. They lived in crowded slave shacks. By 1860, they made up more than one-third of the population of the South.

Putting It All Together

Return to your concept map about cotton. Add as many new lines as you can with information you have read in this section. Use the information from your concept map and your bulleted list to write a paragraph about the cotton South.

Picturing History

The picture on page 237 is a Currier & Ives print entitled "Cotton Plantation on the Mississippi." How does the artist portray plantation life? (an idyllic place where slaves and slave owners work together) Compare this image of slavery with the ones on pages 233, 234, 238, and 239. What differences seem to be most striking? Ask students to account for the differences.

Putting It All Together

Paragraphs will vary but should include information about the impact of the cotton gin and the way cotton growing encouraged the settlement of new states and reshaped Southern society.

Extension

Between 1834 and 1907, Currier & Ives, the firm owned by Nathaniel Currier and James Merritt Ives, produced over one million impressions of more than 7,000 images of American life. Historians believe that Currier & Ives created about 95 percent of all prints sold during those years. Ask students to search the Internet for other prints of Southern life created by the company. How realistic are these pictures? How do you think they shaped the way Americans viewed the South? What impact may these images have had on the way many people viewed slavery?

Slave Labor

Lesson Summary

Most slaves in the South worked in the fields from before sunup to after dark. An overseer supervised their work and disciplined them if they did not obey orders. About one out of every four slaves worked in the plantation owner's house. These slaves cooked, cleaned, and did laundry. They also helped rear the planter's children. Slaves found ways to resist by slowing the pace of work or pretending to be sick. Some ran away and, occasionally, slaves rebelled. In 1831, Nat Turner led a slave rebellion in which more than 60 white Southerners were killed.

Lesson Objective

Students will learn about the work of slaves in the South.

Focus Your Reading Answers

1 Cotton was well suited to slave labor because it required a lot of handwork.

2 A slave's workday began at dawn and, with a brief midday break, continued until dark. The work itself varied with the season. There was no slack time.

3 Slaves resisted by slowing the pace of work, pretending to be sick, breaking tools, damaging crops, running away, and occasionally rebelling.

Picturing History

The drawing on page 238 shows slaves returning from a day in the fields. Ask students to describe what they see. Discuss what the picture tells us about who worked as field hands and the kinds of the work they did.

Thinking on Your Own

Read the Focus Your Reading questions and the vocabulary. In your notebook list all the words that you associate with the concept of slave labor. Then arrange the words in categories. Discuss the categories with a partner.

Cotton was an ideal crop for slave labor. It required a lot of handwork. Planters used groups of slaves to cut the weeds out of cotton fields with hoes. The slaves slowly advanced through a field using their hoes to till the soil. In the fall, picking cotton required still more hand labor.

focus your reading

Why was cotton well suited to slave labor?

What was a slave's workday like?

How did slaves resist?

vocabulary

overseer	house slaves
field slaves	slave rebellion

Work in Cotton Fields

Slaves on large cotton plantations worked under an **overseer**. This man was hired to supervise the slaves' work. He also disciplined them. Overseers whipped slaves for getting to the field late, not picking enough cotton, not obeying orders quickly enough, and for talking back. One Alabama overseer regularly whipped the last slave to get up each morning.

Life as a field slave was difficult.

Field slaves had long workdays. They were in the field each morning at dawn. After a brief midday break they worked until dark. Sundays, Christmas, and the Fourth of July usually were their only days off.

Lesson Vocabulary

Encourage students to look for words they know to help them figure out the meaning of each vocabulary term. For example, an *overseer* is someone who directs, or *sees over*, the work of others. On plantations, *overseers* supervised the work of slaves.

Ask students to figure out the difference between a *field slave* and a *house slave*. (The difference was in where they worked. *Field slaves* worked in the cotton fields and *house slaves*, in the planter's home.)

Remind students that a *rebellion* is an armed, organized resistance to authority. What then is a *slave rebellion*? (armed organized resistance to slavery)

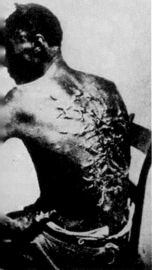

This slave is showing scars from the overseer's violence.

Other Work

Field slaves' work varied with the season. In the fall, they picked and shucked corn, dug sweet potatoes, and brought in pumpkins. They mended fences and repaired buildings during the winter. Planters also kept slaves busy clearing new cotton land. A well-managed plantation had no "slack" time, a time when no work took place.

About one out of four slaves were **house slaves.** That is, they worked in the plantation owner's house instead of in the fields. House slaves cooked, did kitchen chores, cleaned the house, and did laundry. They also helped raise the planter's children. This was easier than fieldwork. However, being a house slave had disadvantages. House servants had little privacy and little time of their own. They were always working, even on Sunday.

stop and think

Make three columns in your notebook. Label them "Overseer," "Field Slave," and "House Slave." Under each heading write descriptions of these workers.

Work as a house slave was less strenuous than work in the fields.

Picturing History

What does the photograph at the top of page 239 suggest about the violence associated with slavery? How does it challenge the view of slavery suggested by the picture on page 237?

Stop and Think

Overseer: supervised slaves' work and disciplined them; *field slave*: work varied with seasons; *house slave*: cooked, cleaned, did laundry, helped rear planter's children

Picturing History

The work of house slaves was only marginally easier than the work of field slaves. A former slave from Alabama said of his mother, "Her task was too hard for any one person. She had to serve as a maid to Mr. White's daughter, cook for all the hands, spin and card four cuts of thread a day [each cut contained 144 threads], and then do the wash. If she didn't get all this done, she got fifty lashes that night." (Quoted in *Roll, Jordan, Roll: The World the Slaves Made*, by Eugene D. Genovese. Pantheon Books, 1972, 1974, p. 335.) Ask students what his account adds to our understanding of the slave shown in the picture at the bottom of page 239.

Nat Turner led a slave rebellion in Southampton, Virginia.

Slave Resistance

Slaves did not always follow the orders of their overseers and masters. Slaves found ways to resist the overseer's demands. They deliberately slowed down the pace of work. Slaves also avoided work by pretending to be sick. They got back at the overseer by breaking tools and damaging crops. Sometimes they ran away, although most were soon caught and severely beaten.

On rare occasions, slaves rebelled. In 1800, Gabriel Prosser tried to organize a **slave rebellion** in Virginia. The plan was discovered, and he was executed. Nat Turner did lead a slave uprising in 1831. He and forty other slaves killed more than sixty white people. The revolt was put down. Turner was tried and hanged. About fifteen other slaves were also killed.

Putting It All Together

Imagine that you are a newspaper reporter at Nat Turner's trial. Write a short article about slavery and the trial. Include the words you listed at the beginning of the Lesson and the descriptions from the Stop and Think.

Extension

As a result of Nat Turner's revolt, many states throughout the South strengthened the so-called "Black Codes"—laws that applied only to slaves. Under these laws, slaves could not assemble in groups of more than five, own property, testify in court, strike a white person, learn to read or write, buy or sell goods, conduct a religious service without a white person present, or even beat drums. Ask students to find out more about the black codes. What do they reveal about the fears of white Southerners in the mid-1800s?

Biography

Nat Turner (1800–1831)

In 1800, the slave Nat Turner was born on a plantation in Virginia. He was a bright young man. By the age of five or six, he had learned to read the Bible. His master regularly took him to prayer meetings. There the slave boy impressed everyone by reciting Bible stories. His mother said that someday he would become a prophet, a holy man. Even his master, Benjamin Turner, said he was too smart to be a field slave.

At age twelve, Turner's world turned upside down. This was the age at which all young slaves were put to work. Turner was certain he would be made a house slave. Maybe he would even be freed. However, by this time his old master had died. His new owner sent him to work in the cotton fields. Being made a field slave was a terrible experience for Turner.

As he grew older, Turner turned inward. He spent more time reading the Bible. He read about Moses, who had led his people out of slavery. Turner also had many visions. In one vision he watched a great battle

between masters and slaves. He believed that his mission in life was to lead a rebellion against the slave owners of Virginia.

Before dawn on August 22, 1831, Nat Turner began his rebellion. He set out with six loyal followers. They went from farm to farm butchering whites with axes and knives. By the end of the day, the number of slaves in the rebellion had increased to forty. They had killed about sixty whites. The next day, planters armed with muskets ended the rebellion. Nat Turner and fifteen other slaves were arrested, convicted of murder, and hanged.

Nat Turner's rebellion sent a shock wave through the South. Slave owners would never again feel safe. They looked for someone to blame for Nat Turner's anger. They did not blame themselves. Instead, they linked Turner's uprising to the abolitionist movement that had started in the North.

241

Biography Extension

Nat Turner's rebellion was not the first slave rebellion in the South, or the last. Some historians estimate that there were more than 200 slave revolts and conspiracies from the 1600s to the end of the Civil War in 1865. Ask students to find out more about one of the following revolts and compare it to Nat Turner's rebellion:

- Gabriel Prosser's Rebellion (Virginia, 1800)
- Slave rebellion in St. John the Baptist Parish (Louisiana, January 8–10, 1811)
- Denmark Vesey's Uprising (South Carolina, 1822)

Ask students to present their findings to the class by using the Student Presentation Builder on the student DVD.

Bio Facts

- Born in Southampton, Virginia, on October 2, 1800, to parents who were slaves.
- Was the property of Benjamin Turner, a prosperous plantation owner.
- Developed deep religious beliefs and became a preacher.
- Ran away in 1821, but returned after 30 days as a result of a vision.
- After two more visions, came to believe that God had chosen him to lead his people out of slavery.
- Sold to Joseph Travis in 1831.
- Convinced that a solar eclipse in February 1831 was a sign from God to start a rebellion.
- Launched his rebellion by killing Travis and his family with the help of seven other slaves on August 21, 1831.
- Expected his action would trigger a massive slave uprising, but only 75 slaves joined the rebellion.
- Rebellion was ended by army of 3,000 state militiamen.
- Went into hiding but was captured six weeks later on October 30, 1831.
- Interviewed by Thomas Gray, his court-appointed attorney. The interview, as reported by Gray, was recorded as *The Confessions of Nat Turner*. Much of what is known about Turner comes from *The Confessions,* which is said to be a blend of fact and fiction.
- Was executed on November 11, 1831.

Lesson Summary

Some slaves started families. In fact, many slave owners encouraged their slaves to have children, mainly because planters needed more workers. The greatest threat to family life was the slave trade. Planters often broke up families by selling one or both parents or their children to the highest bidder at auction.

Lesson Objective

Students will learn about life in the slave quarters and the threat posed by the slave trade.

Focus Your Reading Answers

1 Slave families lived in small and crowded shacks with six to eight slaves sharing a single room. Many planters kept their slaves near starvation.

2 Profits from the slave trade encouraged planters to break up families by selling enslaved parents or their children.

3 People in the slave quarters formed a tightly knit community. They tried to take care of one another.

Picturing History

Ask students to imagine six or eight slaves sharing a single room in a cabin like the one shown in the drawing on page 242.

LESSON **3** # The Slave Community

Thinking on Your Own

Read the vocabulary and the Focus Your Reading questions. What mental pictures do you have about the slave community? In your notebook, sketch or describe one or two scenes that come to mind. Compare your sketches with those of a partner.

Most slaves had families. They tried their best to create a loving and caring home life. Planters did not object to slaves having a family. Most slave owners encouraged slaves to have more children to give their owners more slaves and more workers. They knew that slaves with spouses and children were less likely to run away. The greatest threat to the family was the possibility of a parent or child being sold and taken away to another plantation.

focus your reading

How well did slave families live?

Why was the slave trade a threat to African American families?

What kind of community life did slaves have?

vocabulary

slave quarters

slave trade

slave auction

Slave quarters were often one room.

Slave Family Life

Family life took place in the **slave quarters**. These were clusters of shacks where slaves ate, slept, and lived when not working in the fields. The shacks were small and crowded, with six to eight slaves sharing a single room.

Most planters allowed their slaves to plant gardens next to the cabin. Fresh vegetables were a welcomed addition to the salt pork and cornmeal

Lesson Vocabulary

Tell students that if a term consists of two words and they know both words, they can often figure out the meaning of the new term. Review the meaning of the word *slave*. (a person who is owned by another person) Define *quarters* as housing or a place where people live. *Trade* is the business of buying and selling. An *auction* is a public sale to the highest bidder.

Then ask students to define each of the following terms:

- *slave quarters* (the cluster of shacks where slaves lived on a plantation)

- *slave trade* (the buying and selling of slaves)

- *slave auction* (the public sale of slaves to the highest bidder)

stop and think

As you read, write bulleted notes about slave life. Be sure to include the vocabulary words and other key terms.

the planters provided. However, some planters believed that well-fed slaves would not work, so they kept their slaves near starvation.

Slave Trade

The **slave trade**, the buying and selling of slaves, was a profitable business. Traders often bought slaves in Virginia or Maryland, states that had a surplus. The slaves were then marched in groups to the cotton states of Alabama and Mississippi. The trip was long and difficult, and many slaves died during the ordeal.

After they arrived, the traders sold the slaves at a **slave auction**. That is, the slaves were put on display and sold to the highest bidder. To make sure the slaves were healthy, buyers inspected their skin and teeth—just as they would animals. Then they bid on those they wanted.

Slave sales were heartbreaking scenes. Bidders often bought only one member of a family. One observer saw a woman sold who had two children. "She begged and implored her new master on her knees to buy her children also, but . . . he would not do it. She then begged him to buy her little girl (about 5 years old) but all to no purpose."

It was common for newspapers to advertise upcoming slave auctions.

TO BE SOLD on board the Ship *Bance-Island*, on tuesday the 6th of *May* next, at *Ashley-Ferry*; a choice cargo of about 250 fine healthy NEGROES, just arrived from the Windward & Rice Coaſt. —The utmoſt care has already been taken, and ſhall be continued, to keep them free from the leaſt danger of being infected with the SMALL-POX, no boat having been on board, and all other communication with people from *Charles-Town* prevented. *Auſtin, Laurens, & Appleby.* N. B. Full one Half of the above Negroes have had the SMALL-POX in their own Country.

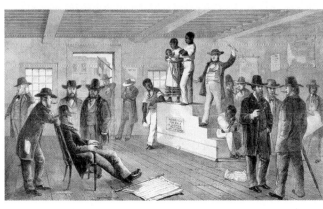

Family members were often separated on the auction block.

Stop and Think
Bulleted notes should include

- threat of family being divided as a result of someone being sold at a slave auction
- living in small shacks in slave quarters
- gardens to supplement food supply
- rarely enough to eat on many plantations

Picturing History

The advertisement on page 243 announces an upcoming sale of 250 Africans. Why was the health of slaves watched so closely?

This ad and others like it appeared in Southern newspapers in the mid-1700s. Similar ads could be found until 1808, when Congress outlawed the importation of slaves from abroad. In its place, a new trade developed. Planters in need of cash would auction off some of their slaves, as shown in the picture at the bottom of page 243.

Picturing History

Ask students to describe the people at the auction as shown on page 243. Who are the buyers? Who is being sold? A former slave from Maryland recalled:

"My brothers and sisters were sold off first, and one by one, while my mother held me by the hand. Her turn came and she was bought by Isaac Riley of Montgomery County. Then I was offered to the assembled purchasers." (From *The Life and Adventures of Henry Bibb*, by Henry Bibb, 1849)

The child's mother threw herself at Riley's feet and asked him to allow her to keep at least one of her children. He responded by kicking her out of his way. What does the story add to our understanding of the scene shown in the picture? What does the primary source on page 245 add to our understanding?

Although laws prohibited slaves from legally marrying, family bonds were strong.

The Slave Community

Slaves who lived in the slave quarters formed a tightly knit community. They tried to take care of one another. Slaves without families had "aunts," "uncles," or other stand-in relatives to help them. They helped each other through injuries, sickness, childbirth, and family deaths.

If a slave wanted to see his wife or children on another plantation, he required a written pass from his owner. Anyone caught outside the plantation without such a pass was punished—often with a severe beating. However, slaves sometimes visited after dark without anyone knowing.

In the autumn, plantation owners brought their slaves together for "shucking parties." These were working parties. While they stripped the husks from corn, slaves exchanged family information and news.

Putting It All Together

Use your bulleted notes to write a paragraph about slave life. Review the notes or sketch you made at the beginning of this Lesson and your bulleted notes if you need ideas.

Read a Primary Source

Sold at Auction: Louis Hughes

As a boy, Louis Hughes was sold to a Mississippi cotton planter. Working as a house slave, he waited on the table at meals, dusted the furniture, and swept the yard. Life as a house slave was somewhat easier than working in the fields. Read Hughes's description of how he was sold.

reading for understanding

Why did Hughes's previous owner want to sell him?

Why was he worth less than other slaves?

Based on the tone of the narrative, how do you think Hughes felt about being a Christmas gift?

> "I was sick a great deal—in fact, I had suffered with chills and fever ever since Mr. Reid bought me. He, therefore, concluded to sell me, and, in November, 1844, he took me back to Richmond, placing me in the Exchange building, or auction rooms, for the sale of slaves.
>
> "When I was placed upon the block, a Mr. McGee came up and felt of me and asked what I could do. . . . The bidding commenced, and I remember well when the auctioneer said: 'Three hundred eighty dollars—once, twice and sold to Mr. Edward McGee' As near as I can recollect, I was not more than twelve years of age, so did not sell for very much. Servant women sold for $500 to $700. . . . Good blacksmiths sold for $1,600 to $1,800.
>
> "At length, after a long and wearisome journey, we reached Pontotoc, McGee's home, on Christmas eve. Boss took me into the house and into the sitting room, where all the family were assembled, and presented me as a Christmas gift to the madam, his wife."

From *Thirty Years a Slave: The Autobiography of Louis Hughes.* (New York: Negro Universities Press, 1970).

Reading for Understanding

1 Hughes's previous owner wanted to sell him because he was sick a great deal.

2 He was worth less than other slaves because he was only twelve years old.

3 The tone suggests that Hughes did not appreciate being anyone's Christmas present.

Chapter Review

1 The songs may reflect the slaves' lack of freedom, hard life, or threats to their family; they might also focus on hopes for freedom, the rhythm of the workday, or dreams of a better life.

2 The letters will vary but should indicate the power of a large plantation owner, his concern for his slaves, and his hopes for financial success.

3 The posters will vary but should reflect information provided in the chapter.

Chapter Summary

In 1793, Eli Whitney invented the **cotton gin**. This machine allowed the South to grow more cotton, which became the South's new cash crop. Men who owned large plantations got rich growing it. Cotton also speeded up the settlement of the **lower South**. Cotton growing kept the South rural, since rich people spent their money on land and slaves, not on building factories.

Most slaves in the South worked in cotton fields. White men called **overseers** forced them to work hard. **Field slaves** often worked from before sunup until after dark. About one out of four slaves were **house slaves** who worked in the plantation owner's house. They did kitchen work, cleaned the house, and helped raise the planter's children.

Slaves found ways to resist, such as working more slowly than they could have. Some slaves ran away, but if they were caught, they were whipped severely. In 1831, Nat Turner led a **slave rebellion** in which more than sixty white people were killed.

Some slaves had a family life. They and their children lived in small, crowded cabins called **slave quarters**. The biggest danger to family life was the **slave trade**. Planters often broke up families by selling only the husband or some of the children. These slaves were sold again at a **slave auction** to whoever offered the most money.

Chapter Review

1 Slaves often sang as they worked to give themselves courage and to forget how hard the work was. Write the words to a song that you think a field slave might have composed.

2 Imagine that you are W. S. Hyland, the plantation owner. Write a letter to relatives in the North describing a day in your life.

3 Create a poster that shows one aspect of life in the South from each of the lessons in this chapter. Include plantations, slave labor, and the slave community.

Novel Connections

Below is a list of books that relate to the time period covered in this chapter. The numbers in parentheses indicate the related Thematic Strands of the National Council for the Social Studies (NCSS).

Linda Jacobs Altman. *Slavery and Abolition in American History.* (*In America* series) Enslow, 1999. (III)

Richard Bial. *The Strength of These Arms: Life in the Slave Quarters.* Houghton Mifflin, 1997. (V)

Sylviane A. Diouf. *Growing Up in Slavery.* Milbrook Press, 2001. (I, II, III)

Paul Erickson. *Daily Life on a Southern Plantation, 1853.* Puffin Books, 2000. (III)

Jennifer Fleischner. *I Was Born a Slave: The Story of Harriet Jacobs.* Sagebrush Education Resources, 2000. (V, X)

Richard Watkins. *Slavery: Bondage Through History.* Houghton Mifflin, 2001. (I, II, III)

William Loren Katz. *Black Pioneers: An Untold Story.* Atheneum, 1999. (III)

Skill Builder

Reading Graphs

Graphs are useful tools that can present a large amount of information in a small space. Graphs usually present information vertically on the left side of the graph and horizontally across the bottom.

In the graphs below, the columns at the left represent numbers of cotton bales and number of slaves. The note "in thousands" means that three zeros have been left off the numbers. The dates at the bottom represent periods of time. The dots and lines on the graphs show how the two kinds of information are related.

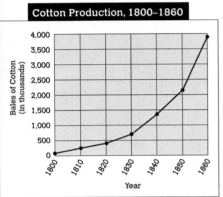

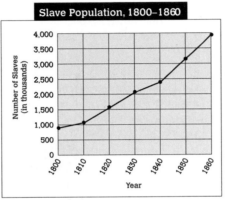

Use the graphs above to answer these questions:

1 In what year did the South produce the smallest number of cotton bales?

2 In what year did the South produce the largest number of bales?

3 About how many bales did the South produce in 1830?

4 In what year did the South have 2,000,000 slaves?

5 How long did it take the South to double the number of slaves it had in 1830?

Classroom Discussion

Discuss with students some of the broader topics covered in this chapter.

• How did the South change between 1790 and 1850? What prompted those changes?

• How do you think slavery influenced the way both black and white Southerners viewed the world around them?

• What qualities did a person need to survive slavery?

• How might life in the South have been different if Eli Whitney had not invented the cotton gin?

Chapter Summary

Refer to page 260 in the student book for a summary of Chapter 16.

Related Transparencies

T-17 Concept Web

T-18 T-Chart

Key Blacklines

Biography
William Lloyd Garrison

Primary Source
Sojourner Truth: "Ar'n't I a Woman?"

DVD Extension

Encourage students to use the reading comprehension, vocabulary reinforcement, and interactive timeline activities on the student DVD.

Pre-Reading Discussion

Have students complete each bulleted direction on page 248. Then focus on the title of the chapter. Who leads such an effort? What prompts them to do so? What kinds of changes do they want to bring about? What does it mean to work "toward a more perfect society"? Why did they try to build a perfect society?

Getting Focused

Skim this chapter to predict what you will be learning.

• Read the lesson titles and subheadings.

• Look at the illustrations and read the captions.

• Examine the maps.

• Review the vocabulary words and terms.

Read the chapter title and lesson headings. In two or three sentences, explain how the title and the headings might be related.

Picturing History

Explain to students that in the early 1800s, American women could not vote, hold elective office, or attend college. Most professions were closed to them. If they married, they could not make legal contracts, divorce an abusive husband, or gain custody of their children. Women like those in the photograph on page 248 led the fight not only for women's rights but also for other causes that would lead to a "more perfect society." Ask students to use the headings in this chapter to identify the reforms these and other Americans championed in the mid-1800s.

Religion and Reform

Thinking on Your Own

Look at the vocabulary and the Focus Your Reading questions. What do they tell you about how preachers reached people spread out over a wide country? Write two ideas in your notebook. Compare your ideas with those of a partner.

I n the early 1800s, Americans had a renewed interest in religion. To save their own souls, they flocked to religious meetings called **revivals**. These revivals are called the **Second Great Awakening**. It is called the "second" because an earlier religious awakening had taken place during the 1740s. Many people decided to make life better for others as well as themselves. They set out to **reform**, or improve, society.

focus your reading

Why were revival meetings popular?

What social reforms did people propose?

What new communities were founded?

vocabulary

revivals

Second Great Awakening

reform

An early revival meeting

249

Lesson Vocabulary

Explain each of the terms highlighted in this lesson. Ask students to define the word *reform* by examining the two parts of the word. The prefix *re-* means "again." What does the word *form* mean? (to shape or mold) Explain that *to reform* is to reshape society in order to remove abuses or end injustices.

Point out the prefix *re-* in the word *revival*. Tell students that to *revive* something is to bring it back to life. A *revival* is a meeting held by Protestants to reawaken interest in their faith. Not surprisingly, a series of *revivals* in the early 1800s were known as the *Second Great Awakening*. The first took place in the 1740s. (See Chapter 6.)

Lesson Summary

In the early 1800s, many Americans went to revival meetings where preachers urged them to lead better lives. A new interest in religion encouraged many people to improve American life by stopping the sale of liquor, providing free public schools, building better prisons, and improving the conditions of the mentally ill.

Lesson Objective

Students will learn the causes and the consequences of efforts to reform American society in the mid-1800s.

Focus Your Reading Answers

1 Revival meetings were popular because many Americans were eager to save their souls.

2 People proposed such social reforms as banning the sale of liquor, free public schools, better prisons, and hospitals for the mentally ill.

3 Reformers set up new communities like Brook Farm in Massachusetts, where people shared farm labor, and the Oneida community in New York, where a group known as the Shakers shared everything they owned.

Picturing History

Ask students to imagine that they are in the crowd at the revival meeting shown on page 249. What do they think the man standing at the center of the picture is saying? What kinds of people make up his audience? How do they seem to be responding to his speech?

The Second Great Awakening

The revivals began during the 1790s in the West. Church leaders worried about people who lived in Kentucky and the Ohio River valley. Few churches existed in that newly settled area. Preachers were sent to save the souls of people on the frontier. A minister would find a clearing in the woods, stand on a stump, and begin preaching. Settlers came from miles around. They pitched their tents, visited, and listened to the preacher.

Charles G. Finney

The preachers had a powerful message: If people did not change their ways, they would be destined to burn forever and not go to heaven. Preachers like Charles G. Finney could make people tremble from fear. Determined to lead better lives, many people felt "born again" as Christians.

From the frontier, the revivals spread to the East. Ministers in eastern cities invited preachers to hold revivals at their churches. Few church members had ever heard such preaching before. They liked it and kept coming back for more.

The Second Great Awakening made revivals popular. It gave many Americans a deeper religious faith. The awakening also brought more people to church more often.

Reforming Society

For many Americans, saving their own souls was not enough. They wanted to reform, or uplift, American society as well. By the 1830s, many thought that liquor was evil. They worked to end the sale of whiskey, beer, and wine. Others wanted free public schools. Still others set out to build better prisons and to open hospitals for the mentally ill. Dorothea Dix was shocked at how mentally ill people were treated. She found them locked up in "cages, closets, cellars, stalls, pens!" She worked to create asylums for those suffering from mental illness.

Reformers also set up new communities. "We are all a little wild here with . . . projects of social reform," wrote Ralph Waldo Emerson in 1840. "Not a reading man but has a draft of a new community in his waistcoat pocket." The group known as the Shakers led strict, religious lives. The Oneida, New York, group did away with private property, choosing to share everything they owned. People at Brook Farm, Massachusetts, shared all the farm labor. Few of these new communities lasted long.

A Shaker community

Putting It All Together

Imagine that you have just returned from a revival. In your notebook, write a letter to a friend describing this event. Explain who was there, what happened, and why people went to revivals.

Reading for Understanding

1 Dix wanted lawmakers to feel they had a duty to stop the outrages she had witnessed.

2 Mentally ill people were kept in prisons and homes for the poor.

3 Mentally ill people were confined in cages, closets, cellars, stalls, and pens. They were chained naked and beaten with rods and lashes.

Extension

Ask students to learn more about Dorothea Dix's efforts to create special hospitals for the mentally ill. They should find out

- how she became interested in the plight of the mentally ill

- what research she conducted before preparing a report to the Massachusetts legislature

- how she took her crusade to other states

Have students summarize the challenges she faced and her successes by creating a poster.

Read a Primary Source

The Claims of Suffering Humanity: Dorothea Dix

In 1843, Dorothea Dix made a report to the Massachusetts legislature. In it she described how mentally ill people were treated in that state. The following is an excerpt from her report.

"I tell you what I have seen— painful and shocking as the details often are—that from them you may feel more deeply [your] obligation . . . to prevent . . . a repetition . . . . of such outrages upon humanity. . . .

I come to present the strong claims of suffering humanity. I come to place before the Legislature of Massachusetts the condition of the miserable, the desolate, the outcast. I come as the advocate of helpless, forgotten, insane, and idiotic men and women; of beings sunk to a condition from which the most unconcerned would start with real horror; of being wretched in our prisons, and more wretched in our almshouses [homes for the poor]. . . .

I proceed, gentlemen, briefly to call your attention to the present state of insane persons, confined within this Commonwealth, in cages, closets, cellars, stalls, pens! Chained, naked, beaten with rods, and lashed into obedience."

From Dorothea L. Dix, "Memorial to the Legislature of Massachusetts, 1843," *Old South Leaflets* (Boston, 1904).

Dorothea Dix

252

Picturing History

Frederick Douglass, shown on page 253, who escaped from slavery and later became a leader in the movement to end slavery, defined a slave as "a human being who has been stripped of all rights. . . . In law, the slave has no wife, no children, no country, and no home. He can own nothing, possess nothing, acquire nothing. Everything must belong to someone else." Given this view of slavery, ask students how they think Douglass regarded gradual emancipation. (opposed it; wanted slavery abolished immediately, not when someone considered it convenient) How did he view efforts to send freed slaves to Africa? (opposed them; he believed that he and other African Americans were Americans)

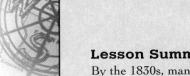

Antislavery and Women's Rights

Thinking on Your Own

"Equal rights for women is as important as freedom for slaves!" Write this statement in your notebook. Below it, make two columns and label them "I Agree" and "I Disagree." Write the thoughts that you have under each heading. Discuss your conclusions with a partner.

By the 1830s, more people opposed slavery than ever before. Revival preachers denounced slave owning as a sin. Quakers had always said it was wrong to own slaves. Many reformers opposed slavery. They saw that it violated the Declaration of Independence, which stated, "We hold these truths to be self-evident, that all men are created equal . . ." Many people thought that the Declaration applied to women as well as men. Those who opposed slavery often worked for women's rights too.

focus your reading

What method of freeing slaves did whites first propose?

How did the abolitionist movement lead to the women's rights movement?

What did William Lloyd Garrison propose?

vocabulary

gradual emancipation
abolitionists
crusade

Emancipation and Abolition

By the 1820s, most reformers called for the **gradual emancipation** of slaves. They encouraged owners to free their slaves as soon as they could. However, they did not expect freed slaves to remain in the United States. The American Colonization Society, established in 1816 by Robert Finley and other notable Americans, worked to send freed slaves to Liberia, a colony in Africa. Free blacks in northern cities had a different point of view.

Frederick Douglass

Lesson Summary

By the 1830s, many Americans were against slavery. Most wanted to gradually free the slaves. A group known as the abolitionists disagreed with that idea. They wanted all enslaved people to be freed immediately. Former slaves like Frederick Douglass and Sojourner Truth were abolitionists. The fight against slavery also inspired a movement for women's rights.

Lesson Objective

Students will learn how and why many Americans opposed slavery and why some also called for women's rights.

Focus Your Reading Answers

1 Some white Americans first proposed a gradual freeing of slaves.

2 Participation in the abolitionist movement gave many women a better understanding of their own lack of rights.

3 William Lloyd Garrison proposed that all slaves be freed immediately.

Extension

Frederick Douglass told the story of his life as a slave in his autobiography, which was first published as an abolitionist pamphlet. After reading it, many people understood the injustices of slavery for the first time. Ask students to gather more information about Douglass's work as a speaker and a writer and share their findings with the class.

Lesson Vocabulary

The word *emancipation* means "freedom." What, then, is *gradual emancipation*? (a slow process of freedom; slaves are not freed all at once)

Ask students to define the word *abolish*. (to end or stop) The suffix *-ist* refers to someone who favors an action. What action did *abolitionists* favor? (an end to slavery)

The word *crusade* originally referred to a military expedition by Christians to recapture the Holy Land from the Muslims between the 11th century and the 13th century. Today it refers to any war or campaign that advances a cause or belief.

William
Lloyd
Garrison

Picturing History

William Lloyd Garrison, shown in the photo at the top of page 254, often sounded like a preacher. He and other abolitionists attacked slavery not only because it contradicted American principles but also because they considered it a sin. Ask students how that point of view may have affected the way abolitionists regarded white Southerners. How might it have shaped the way white Southerners viewed abolitionists?

Stop and Think

Answers will vary but should be supported by information provided in this lesson.

They wanted slavery to be abolished immediately. **Abolitionists**, people who wanted to abolish slavery, opposed sending freed slaves to Africa. Among them were Frederick Douglass and Sojourner Truth, both freed slaves. They gave speeches, wrote books against slavery, and fought for all slaves to be set free.

In January 1831, the abolitionists found a new voice. William Lloyd Garrison, a white newspaper editor in Boston, published the first issue of *The Liberator*. The newspaper demanded that all slaves be freed immediately. Garrison denounced slavery as sinful. He attacked slavery like a revival preacher. Black abolitionists supported him, as did many white reform leaders who saw slavery as the greatest evil of all. In 1833, Garrison and other abolitionists met in Philadelphia to found the American Antislavery Society. The goal of the group was the complete abolition of slavery.

The Liberator was a popular abolitionist newspaper.

Many women also supported abolition. They attended meetings, helped raise money, and signed antislavery petitions. A few brave women stood up to speak at public meetings. Angelina and Sarah Grimke became well-known public speakers. Their father was a South Carolina slave owner. The Grimke sisters shocked listeners with their

stop and think

Imagine that you are a young woman living during this period. What reforms would interest you? Which would you feel threatened by?

Picturing History

The Liberator was a small newspaper with few readers. In its first year, the four-page weekly had six subscribers. At the height of its influence, its circulation was about 5,000. Yet its influence stretched far beyond its circulation. Ask students what its masthead suggests about the paper. How is it different from newspapers today?

The Seneca Falls Convention of 1848

firsthand accounts of the evils of slavery. New England ministers scolded Angelina Grimke for lecturing in public.

The women abolitionists shocked many men. Women in the 1830s lacked many of the rights that men enjoyed. It was believed that a woman's place was in the home. Women could not vote or hold public office. Even a married woman's property belonged to her husband. Women factory workers earned only one-third to one-half as much as men.

The abolitionist **crusade** paved the way for equal rights for women. "The investigation of the rights of the slave has led me to a better understanding of my own," Angelina Grimke wrote. Two female abolitionists organized the first national women's rights convention in the United States. They were Lucretia Mott and Elizabeth Cady Stanton. The meeting took place in 1848 in Seneca Falls, New York. It called for equal rights for women, including the right to vote.

Elizabeth Cady Stanton and Susan B. Anthony fought for women's right to vote.

The Seneca Falls Convention attracted nearly 300 women and forty men. This was the start of the women's rights movement. The organizers of the meeting wrote a "Declaration of Sentiments" that they modeled after the Declaration of Independence. This declaration stated, "We hold these truths to be self-evident: that all men and women are created equal." Just as the Declaration of Independence listed the colonists' grievances with Great Britain, the Declaration of Sentiments listed grievances against men. They included denying women the right to vote and limiting education for women.

Putting It All Together

Make a T-chart in your notebook. On one side write the names of people or groups involved in reform. On the other side briefly describe their work. Compare your list with that of a partner.

Bio Facts

- Born to enslaved parents in 1797 in Ulster County, a Dutch settlement in upstate New York. Her given name was Isabella Baumfree.

- One of 13 children in the family.

- Spoke only Dutch until sold from her family at the age of eleven.

- Learned to speak English quickly but spoke with a Dutch accent for the rest of her life.

- While living with her third master, John Dumont, married an older slave named Thomas. They had five children.

- Ran away with her infant son when Dumont reneged on his promise to free her.

- Eventually settled in New York City, working as a domestic for several religious communities.

- In 1843, inspired by a spiritual revelation, changed her name to Sojourner Truth.

- Walked through Long Island and Connecticut, preaching "God's truth and plan for salvation."

- After months of travel, arrived in Northampton, Massachusetts, and joined the utopian community, "The Northampton Association for Education and Industry," where she met abolitionists such as William Lloyd Garrison and Frederick Douglass.

- Published her dictated memoirs in 1850 as *The Narrative of Sojourner Truth: A Northern Slave.*

- Gave speeches around the country on abolitionism and women's suffrage.

Biography

Sojourner Truth (1797? – 1883)

Sojourner Truth was a forceful public speaker. Her speeches urged Congress to free the slaves and give women equal rights. The crowds that came to hear this African American woman were not always friendly. Men often hissed at her. "I am sorry to see them so short

minded," she said at a speech in New York City. "But we'll have our rights; see if we don't; and you can't stop us from them; see if you can. You may hiss as much as you like, but it is comin'." No one could stop her from speaking her mind.

Sojourner Truth drew on her own experience. She was born in the 1790s as a slave in rural New York State. Her slave name was Isabella Baumfree. She grew up being whipped and abused by her white owners. Baumfree married another slave named Thomas, and they had five children. She lost two children to slave traders. Baumfree was a slave until 1826, when New York freed its slaves.

Once free, she made herself into a new person. She went to Methodist revival meetings, where she was "born again" as a Christian. She found she could preach and became a traveling preacher. Then she changed her name to Sojourner Truth. *To sojourn* means to not stay in one place very long. The name fit her, as she was always on the move. She also told the truth exactly as she saw it.

In the 1840s, Truth lived in a commune near Boston. There she met William Lloyd Garrison and Frederick Douglass. They asked her to travel with them, giving speeches opposing slavery. Women she met at these speeches invited her to women's rights meetings. In 1851, she spoke at the Ohio Woman's Rights Convention. After that, she traveled throughout the North speaking against slavery and for women's rights.

In 1864, Sojourner Truth visited President Abraham Lincoln at the White House in Washington, D.C. She asked President Lincoln to free the slaves. The president asked her to remain in Washington, D.C., to work as a counselor to freed slaves.

Sojourner Truth died in 1883 at about eighty-six years of age. She had lived to see half of her goal accomplished. The Thirteenth Amendment (1865) abolished slavery. Securing equal rights for women remained in the future.

Bio Facts, continued

- Tried to petition Congress to give the ex-slaves land in the "new West."

- Died in November 1883, in Battle Creek, Michigan.

Picturing History

The cover of *Walden* is shown on page 257. In 1845, Emerson gave Henry Thoreau permission to use a piece land that Emerson owned on Walden Pond near Concord Massachusetts. Thoreau built a small cabin there, movin in on the Fourth of July. Thoreau stayed at Walden Pon for two years. Why did he live there? "I went to the woods," he wrote, "because I wished to live deliberately, confront only the essential facts of life, and see if I could not learn what it had to teach, and not, when I came to c discover that I had not lived." Ask students to compare h reasons for going to Walden with Emerson's words quot previously.

LESSON 3 Literature and the Arts

Thinking on Your Own

Read the vocabulary and the Focus Your Reading questions for clues. What themes do you think American artists and writers explored during this period? Discuss the themes with a partner. Write two or three ideas in your notebook.

In the 1830s, American writers and artists also wanted reform. Until then, they had mainly used European ideas in their literature and art. It was time, said Ralph Waldo Emerson, for them to declare their **"intellectual independence."** This feeling was widely shared. The result was a flood of truly American essays, books, and paintings.

Ralph Waldo Emerson

focus your reading

How did the spirit of reform influence writers and artists?

What American themes did writers explore?

What American scenes did painters include in their work?

vocabulary

intellectual independence

American Renaissance

Hudson River School

A New American Literature

Ralph Waldo Emerson of Concord, Massachusetts, took the lead. He wrote essays and gave lectures on the importance of the individual. People, he thought, should stand on their own feet. They should think for themselves and decide what is right. They should solve their own problems. Emerson saw these as American values.

Henry David Thoreau, Emerson's friend, did not just reject Europe. He declared

WALDEN;
OR,
LIFE IN THE WOODS.

BY HENRY D. THOREAU,
AUTHOR OF "A WEEK ON THE CONCORD AND MERRIMACK RIVERS."

BOSTON:
TICKNOR AND FIELDS.
M DCCC LIV.

Walden was published by Henry David Thoreau in 1854.

Henry David Thoreau

independence from modern society. "Nature is sufficient," he said. He lived alone in a cabin for two years. His book about those years, *Walden* (1854), is widely read today. Thoreau had his own ideas about politics, as well. He criticized the government for protecting slavery. Once, he went to jail for refusing to pay a poll tax.

The writer Walt Whitman best reflected the spirit of American democracy. His book, *Leaves of Grass* (1855), praised the diversity of American life. "Here is not merely a nation but a teeming nation of nations," he wrote.

Nathaniel Hawthorne (*The Scarlet Letter*, 1850) and Herman Melville (*Moby Dick*, 1851) also used American themes and settings in their writings. Edgar Allen Poe was an exception. Many of his tales were set in Europe. This period produced so many good writers that it is sometimes called the **American Renaissance**.

Picturing History

Henry David Thoreau had a reason for refusing to pay his taxes. In a book titled *Civil Disobedience*, he explained: "How does it become a man to behave toward the American government today? I answer, that he cannot without disgrace be associated with it. I cannot for an instant recognize that political organization as my government which is the slave's government also." Why did Thoreau refuse to pay his taxes? How did his views on slavery shape his decision to disobey the government?

stop and think

In your notebook identify two American authors and explain what they wrote about.

Walt Whitman

Picturing History

Walt Whitman published *Leaves of Grass* on the Fourth of July, 1855. The poetry in the book was a response to Ralph Waldo Emerson's 1843 essay, "The Poet." In it, Emerson called for a truly original national poet, one who would sing of the new country in a new voice.

Extension

Ask students to read aloud some of the poems included in *Leaves of Grass*. Then discuss whether Whitman was the poet Emerson was calling for. Encourage students to cite specific examples to support their ideas.

The Notch of the White Mountains, by Thomas Cole (1839)

American Art

Painters had already started to paint American scenes. A group called the **Hudson River School** specialized in painting scenes along that river. They tried to show the beauty of the American landscape. The best-known painters were Thomas Cole, Thomas Doughty, and Asher Durand.

George Caleb Bingham painted pictures of the American West. He knew the West firsthand. He grew up in Missouri when it was being settled. Among his paintings are *Fur Traders Descending the Missouri, Jolly Flatboat Men,* and *Daniel Boone Coming through Cumberland Gap.*

George Catlin also painted about the West from personal experience. His subjects were Native Americans. He traveled through the Great Plains in the 1830s, painting portraits of Native Americans. His paintings now are important historical documents. They show what Native Americans wore and how they decorated themselves.

Putting It All Together

Create a concept web. In the center circle write "Writers and Artists." On lines coming from the circle, write the names of writers and artists of this period. On lines below their names, write the titles of their works.

Chapter Review

1 The posters will vary but should reflect the strong opposition to slavery that characterized the American Antislavery Society.

2 Dialogues will vary but should show an understanding of both men's beliefs.

3 Answers will vary but should reflect an understanding of the spirit of reform that marked American life in the mid-1800s.

Chapter Summary

In the early 1800s, thousands of Americans went to **revival** meetings where preachers told them to lead better lives. These meetings were part of the **Second Great Awakening** of religion in the United States. This new interest in religion began on the western frontier, but soon reached cities of the East. Many religious men and women also wanted to **reform** American society by stopping the sale of liquor, building better prisons, and improving conditions for the mentally ill.

By the 1830s, many Americans also opposed slavery. Most called for the **gradual emancipation** of slaves. However, **abolitionists** wanted all slaves to be freed immediately, without delay. Freed slaves like Sojourner Truth and Frederick Douglass were abolitionists. The abolitionist **crusade** paved the way for women's rights.

In the 1830s, American writers and artists also called for reform. They declared their **intellectual independence** from Europe. They began to write books and to paint pictures with American themes. The period 1830 to 1860 is sometimes called the **American Renaissance** because it produced so many good writers and painters. Among them were the **Hudson River School** artists, who painted scenes along that river.

Chapter Review

1 Garrison and other abolitionists created the American Antislavery Society. Create a poster for the American Antislavery Society.

2 Imagine that you are listening to a conversation between Ralph Waldo Emerson and Henry David Thoreau. Write the dialogue that you would expect to hear.

3 Now that you have finished the chapter, reread the chapter title and lesson headings. Now how do you think the title and headings are related?

Novel Connections

Below is a list of books that relate to the time period covered in this chapter. The numbers in parentheses indicate the related Thematic Strands of the National Council for the Social Studies (NCSS).

Peter Burchard. *Frederick Douglass: For the Great Family of Man.* Atheneum Books, 2003. (II, V, VI)

Jeri Chase Ferris. *Demanding Justice: A Story About Mary Ann Shadd Cary.* (*Creative Minds Biography* series) Carolrhoda Books/Lerner Publishing, 2003. (II, III, VI)

Hariet Siegerman. *Elizabeth Cady Stanton: The Right Is Ours.* Oxford University Press, 2001. (I, VI, X)

Grant Wacker. *Religion in Nineteenth Century America.* (*Religion in American Life* series) Oxford University Press, 2000. (I, III, V)

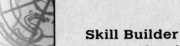

Skill Builder

Critically Reading Primary Sources

Primary sources are powerful documents. They include letters, diaries, and newspaper articles written by people from that time period. Many were written by eyewitnesses. However, this does not mean they are always accurate.

The accuracy of Sojourner Truth's 1851 "Ar'n't I a Woman?" speech is one primary source that has been questioned. Did she actually say the famous phrase "Ar'n't I a woman?" Historian Nell Irvin Painter has her doubts. The account of the speech was published in the *New York Independent* in April 1863. The author, Frances Dana Gage, attended the convention and listened to the speech.

To understand why Professor Painter has doubts, compare the date of the speech and the published account.

- What was the date of the speech?
- What was the date of the published account?

You will see that Gage published her account of the speech twelve years after the event. Would she have remembered the speech word for word after that much time had passed?

Painter's doubts led her to look for accounts closer to the time of the convention. *The Salem* (New York) *Anti-Slavery Bugle* reported the speech in June 1851. *The Bugle*'s editor took notes as he listened. The main points in his account are the same as Gage's. But the wording is different. Gage mentions the "Ar'n't I a woman?" phrase four times. *The Bugle* account does not mention it once. Surely the editor would have reported such a memorable phrase.

When you read a primary source, be sure to ask:

- How close to the time of the event was it written?
- Was the author biased in any way?
- Can I check it against other accounts?
- Could one account be more reliable than another?

Classroom Discussion

Discuss with students some of the broader topics covered in this chapter.

- Why do you think reformers became particularly active during the 1830s and 1840s? How did they affect American life?

- The roles women played in the reform movement disturbed many American men. Why do you think they disapproved of the work the women did in the reform movement? How did that work challenge the way many people at the time regarded women?

- How did American values and beliefs shape the work of writers and artists? How do those values shape the work of writers and artists today?

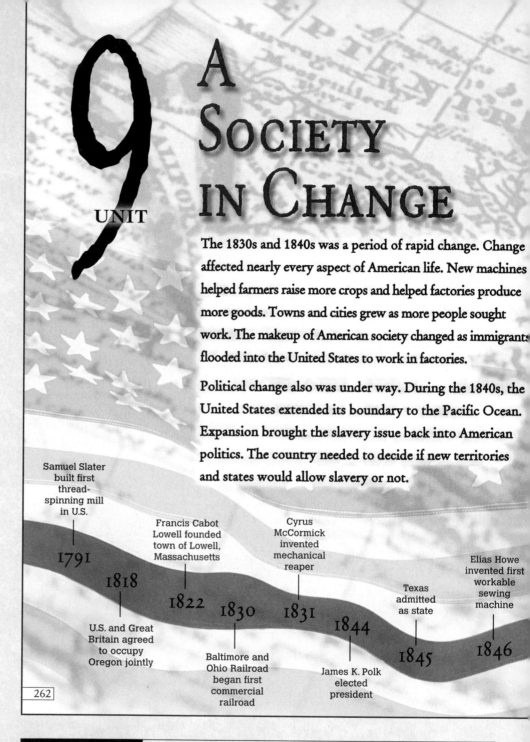

9 UNIT

A SOCIETY IN CHANGE

The 1830s and 1840s was a period of rapid change. Change affected nearly every aspect of American life. New machines helped farmers raise more crops and helped factories produce more goods. Towns and cities grew as more people sought work. The makeup of American society changed as immigrants flooded into the United States to work in factories.

Political change also was under way. During the 1840s, the United States extended its boundary to the Pacific Ocean. Expansion brought the slavery issue back into American politics. The country needed to decide if new territories and states would allow slavery or not.

Samuel Slater built first thread-spinning mill in U.S.

1791

U.S. and Great Britain agreed to occupy Oregon jointly

1818

Francis Cabot Lowell founded town of Lowell, Massachusetts

1822

Baltimore and Ohio Railroad began first commercial railroad

1830

Cyrus McCormick invented mechanical reaper

1831

James K. Polk elected president

1844

Texas admitted as state

1845

Elias Howe invented first workable sewing machine

1846

262

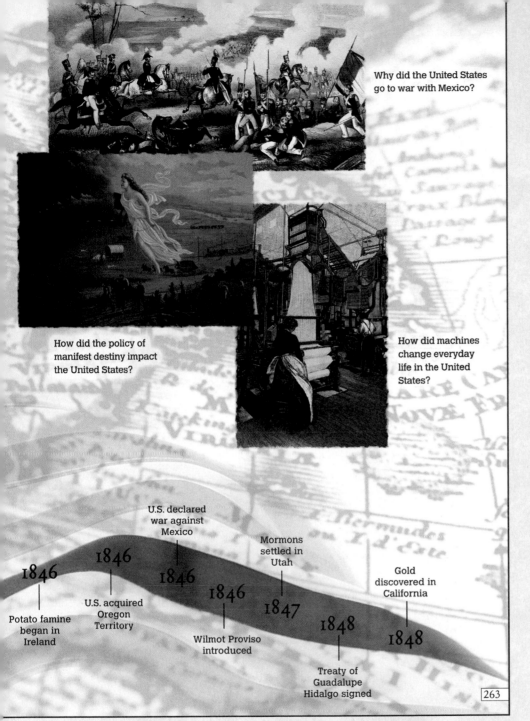

Why did the United States go to war with Mexico?

How did the policy of manifest destiny impact the United States?

How did machines change everyday life in the United States?

Collage Answers

1 The United States went to war with Mexico over the U.S. annexation of Texas and the failure of the two nations to agree on a boundary between Texas and Mexico.

2 The policy of manifest destiny encouraged Americans to add new territories to the United States.

3 Machines changed everyday life in the United States by altering the way people worked, reducing the cost of some goods, and making some household chores easier.

Collage Extension

Use the images and questions on page 263 to preview the unit. Discuss the changes they highlight.

Timeline

- 1846 — Potato famine began in Ireland
- 1846 — U.S. acquired Oregon Territory
- 1846 — U.S. declared war against Mexico
- 1846 — Wilmot Proviso introduced
- 1847 — Mormons settled in Utah
- 1848 — Treaty of Guadalupe Hidalgo signed
- 1848 — Gold discovered in California

Measuring Time

Explain to students that the timeline relates to both Chapters 17 and 18.

Timeline Extension

Encourage students to use the timeline to preview the unit. What does it suggest about the way American life was changing? (Some events seem to indicate changes in work while others relate to changes in the size of the nation.)

A Society in Change   263

Chapter Summary

Refer to page 276 in the student book for a summary of Chapter 17.

Related Transparencies

T-17 Concept Web

Key Blacklines

Biography
Elias Howe and Isaac Singer

Primary Source
Michael Chevalier: Lowell in 1834

DVD Extension

Encourage students to use the reading comprehension, vocabulary reinforcement, and interactive timeline activities on the student DVD.

Picturing History

Ask students to describe what they see in the photograph on page 264. Explain that the people in the photo are farmers. What does the photo suggest about farm life at this time in history? Ask students to identify the machine in the photo. (The photo shows a mechanical reaper used to harvest wheat.) Have students check their answers by reading Lesson 1.

Chapter 17 CHANGING TIMES

Getting Focused

Skim this chapter to predict what you will be learning.

- Read the lesson titles and subheadings.
- Look at the illustrations and read the captions.
- Examine the maps.
- Review the vocabulary words and terms.

Think about a time when you or someone you know underwent a change. How did the change affect you? What led to the change? What were some of the outcomes? Write two or three sentences about this experience in your notebook.

Pre-Reading Discussion

Have students complete each bulleted direction on page 264. Ask students what their preview of the chapter suggests about the way the nation was changing in the early 1800s. Have students relate the idea of change to their own experiences. How does one change often lead to another?

Picturing History

The men standing in the foreground in the picture on page 265 are holding scythes. The man in the background is using a cradle. It is a scythe with three to four wooden fingers attached to it. The advantage of the cradle was that by turning to the left, a farm worker could throw the grain into a swath, ready to be raked and bound into sheaves or bundles. A farmer using a cradle could harvest about two acres a day. Ask students to imagine what it must have been like to use those tools to harvest 60 acres or more.

Changes in Everyday Life

Thinking on Your Own

Examine the illustrations in this lesson. Read the section headings. What clues do they give you about the changes that occurred during the 1840s? Discuss your ideas with a classmate. Take notes in your notebook.

By the 1840s, everyday life in the United States was changing. Americans focused more on making money. The pace of life was quicker. New inventions changed the way people worked.

Rural Life

Life on American farms was changing. In 1800, most farmers raised or made most of what they used. They traded corn or pork for the salt, nails, and other things they could not make. The only farmers who depended on **cash crops** were Southern planters. By the 1840s, farmers in the North also farmed to make money. They sold most of the corn, wheat, and hemp that they raised. With the cash they bought things they had once made at home.

> **focus your reading**
>
> How did farming change between 1800 and 1840?
>
> How did farm work change?
>
> How did housework change?
>
> **vocabulary**
>
> cash crops
>
> scythe
>
> mechanical reaper

A scythe was a slow method of reaping grain.

Changing Times 265

Lesson Vocabulary

As the name suggests, a *cash crop* is a crop grown to make money. In the past, many farmers raised or grew most of what they needed. Now they bought what they needed with the money they earned by selling wheat, cotton, or other *cash crops*.

Use the picture on page 265 to help students define *scythe*. It is a long, curved single-edged blade with a long, bent handle. Farmers used it to mow grass and reap or harvest their wheat crop. Use the pictures on pages 264 and 266 to help students define *mechanical reaper*. It was a horse-drawn machine that automatically cut and bundled grain as it was pulled through a field.

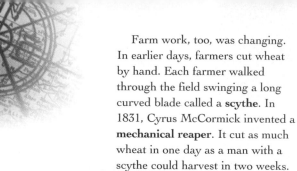
MᶜCORMICK.

Stop and Think

Answers will vary but should include the mechanical reaper, the mowing machine, the sewing machine, and/or the cast-iron cookstove.

Picturing History

The illustration at the top of page 266 is an advertisement for the mechanical reaper, used to harvest wheat. Its inventor's success was only partly due to the machine itself. Cyrus McCormick was a pioneer in business techniques. He offered farmers easy credit to buy his machines, and written guarantees that the reaper would do what he claimed it would do. He also advertised to convince farmers that they needed his machine. Ask students to identify both the positive and negative consequences of these new methods.

Farm work, too, was changing. In earlier days, farmers cut wheat by hand. Each farmer walked through the field swinging a long curved blade called a **scythe**. In 1831, Cyrus McCormick invented a **mechanical reaper**. It cut as much wheat in one day as a man with a scythe could harvest in two weeks.

stop and think

In your notebook describe two machines that created significant changes on American farms or in the home.

By the 1840s, it was in wide use. Farmers bought reapers so they could plant more wheat and make more money. They also bought mowing machines to cut hay.

The mechanical reaper made farming profitable.

Housework in the Early 1800s

Women spent much of their time making clothes for their family. They spun wool or flax into yarn and wove it into cloth. Using needle and thread, they made dresses, shirts,

266

Farmers earned money by selling their crops at market.

Picturing History

As farmers began to grow cash crops, they had to make regular trips to town to sell their crops and buy seeds, tools, and other supplies. Ask students how such trips might affect farm life. How might they also affect life in nearby cities and towns?

Elias Howe's sewing machine greatly improved women's lives.

and coats by hand. "I somehow or somewhere got the idea, when I was a small child," wrote Lucy Larcom, "that the chief end of woman was to make clothing for mankind." Cooking also was a difficult chore. To cook, women had to stoop over heavy iron pots hanging in a hot fireplace.

Women's work was changing by the 1840s. Inexpensive, factory-made cloth replaced home-woven fabric. In 1846, Elias Howe invented a sewing machine. As this machine was improved, women would spend less time sewing clothes. An invention that made cooking easier was the cast-iron cookstove. This stove had a flat, iron top that was heated from beneath by a wood fire. Because the stove top was waist high, women no longer had to bend over kettles when they cooked. They also used new, lighter-weight pots and pans that were specially made for the cookstove.

Putting It All Together

Imagine that you are a newspaper reporter in the 1840s. Write a brief article about how a typical housewife's work changed with the invention of the sewing machine and cookstove.

The cookstove changed the way people cooked at home.

Reading for Understanding

1 The family decided to leave Ireland because of a famine followed by a typhus epidemic.

2 Tilly left first so that she could find work in America and save enough money to bring over her sister.

3 The family paid for the first ticket by getting help from Squire Varney; money for the second ticket came from the money Tilly saved by working as a housekeeper.

Picturing History

Ask students how the picture on page 268 helps us understand why the ships that brought immigrants from Ireland were known as "coffin ships."

Extension

Explain to students that a famine is a severe shortage of food, in this case as the result of the failure of the potato crop. Have students find out more about the famine in Ireland in the 1840s and how it affected immigration to the United States. Ask students to share their findings with the class by creating a poster summarizing what they learned.

Read a Primary Source

An Irish Immigrant: Told by Herself

The following is an account by an Irish-American cook. She tells the story of leaving Ireland during the famine years and coming to America to find a better life.

reading for understanding

Why did this family decide to leave Ireland?

Why did Tilly leave first?

How did the family pay for the two tickets?

"Coffin ships" brought immigrants to the United States.

"What did we eat? Well, just potatoes. On Sundays, once a month, we'd maybe have a bit of flitch [salt pork]. When the potatoes rotted—that was the hard times. Oh, yes, I . . . [remember] the famine years. . . . Maria—she was one of the twins—she died the famine year of the typhus and—well, she sickened of the herbs and roots we ate—we had no potatoes. Mother said when Maria died, "there's a curse on old green Ireland and we'll get out of it." So we worked an' saved for four year an' then Squire Varney helped a bit an' we sent Tilly to America. She had always more head than me. She came to Philadelphia and got a place for general housework at Mrs. Bent's. Tilly got but two dollars a week, bein' a greenhorn. . . . She had no expenses and laid by money enough to bring me out before the year was gone. I sailed from Londonderry. . . . The passage was $12. . . . The steerage was a dirty place and we were eight weeks on the voyage—over time three weeks."

"The Life Story of an Irish Cook," Hamilton Holt, ed., *The Life Stories of Undistinguished Americans as Told by Themselves* (New York, 1906).

268

Picturing History

The picture on page 269 shows Slater's Mill. Samuel Slater built the first cotton mill in the United States in 1790 in Pawtucket, Rhode Island. Like most factories in the late 1700s and early 1800s, its machines ran on waterpower—in the case of Slater's factory, on waterpower from the Pawtucket Falls. Ask students how the need for waterpower affected where Americans could build factories in the early 1800s. (Factories had to be located on a fast-moving river or a waterfall.)

Towns, Factories, and Railroads

Thinking on Your Own

Look over the vocabulary and the Focus Your Reading questions. With a partner share what you already know about early American towns and factories. Create two questions that you think this lesson may answer. Make notes in your notebook.

By the 1840s, life was changing for Americans who lived in towns and cities. New machines and factories changed where and how people worked. The growth of factories attracted more people to the towns and cities of the Northeast.

Mills and Factories

In 1800, most skilled craftsmen worked at home or in small shops. They wove cloth or made shoes or hats with hand tools. Customers dropped by to place their orders. By the 1840s, machines were taking the place of hand tools. Machines powered by water wheels produced items faster and cheaper. The men who owned these machines put them in big shops and

---

focus your reading

Why did more Americans go to work in factories?

Why did towns and cities grow larger?

How did factories create a need for railroads?

vocabulary

spinning machines

textile mill

company town

wharves

Slater's Mill was the beginning of the cloth industry in New England.

269

Lesson Vocabulary

A *spinning machine* does what its name suggests. It is a machine that spins cotton or wool into thread. Use the drawing on page 270 to help students visualize the machine. *Spinning machines* were found in *textile mills*. The word *textile* refers to a woven or knitted fabric. A *mill* is a manufacturing plant. Ask students what a *textile mill* is. (a factory where cotton or wool is made into cloth)

A *company town* refers to a town that was built and owned by a business. The owners of a *textile mill* would often build a town near their factory for their workers.

Explain that a *wharf* is a landing place where goods are loaded onto ships or unloaded from ships. Much of the cloth produced in *textile mills* was sent to port cities like Boston or New York, where it was loaded onto ships docked at nearby *wharves*.

Lists will vary, but students should note shifts from handmade goods to machine-made goods, from work at home to work in factories, from living in small villages and towns to large cities, and from travel by wagon or boat to travel by railroad.

Spinning machines made cotton yarn or thread.

Picturing History

Spinning machines like the one shown at the top of page 270 were powered by waterwheels. The operator's job was to keep the machine running, keep it supplied with yarn, and fix it whenever a length of yarn broke or any other breakdown occurred. Ask students to imagine what it must have been like to operate a machine like this one.

factories. Skilled workers could not compete with them. They had to go to work in the factories, instead of working in small shops.

Cloth making was the first trade to move into factories. In 1791, Samuel Slater built the nation's first cotton thread-spinning mill in Rhode Island. But Slater's **spinning machines** did not weave the thread into cloth. He sent the thread to skilled weavers, who wove the cloth in their homes. In 1813, Francis Cabot Lowell built the first integrated **textile mill**. There, workers spun, wove, and dyed cloth in the same factory. His mill was a great success. It helped make New England the center of textile making in the United States.

stop and think

In your notebook list the changes in daily life that you think are especially important. Share your ideas with a partner.

Growth of Towns and Cities

The building of mills and factories spurred the growth of towns and cities. In 1822, Francis Cabot Lowell built a new factory town almost overnight. The town of Lowell, Massachusetts, was a **company town**. That is, the investors in the textile company built and owned the town. Most new factories were built in existing towns and cities. These places grew rapidly as people moved there to get jobs.

During the 1840s, the population of large American seaports also increased. In ten years, New York, Boston, and Baltimore more than doubled their populations. The tall masts of ships towered over their skylines. Their **wharves** were piled high with goods. They also became centers of manufacturing. New factories, textile mills, and locomotive works sprang up on the edges of these cities.

Lowell, Massachusetts, was a result of the textile industry.

270

Picturing History

Lowell's population exploded in the early 1800s, from just 2,500 people at the beginning of the century to over 33,000 by the 1840s. To poet John Greenleaf Whittier, Lowell was "a city springing up like the enchanted palaces of the Arabian Tales." Ask students to use the drawing to explain why visitors were so impressed with the city.

Cities such as New York grew as people began working in factories.

Peter Cooper

Expansion of Railroads

Railroads expanded rapidly during this period. The nation's first railroad, the Baltimore and Ohio, opened for business in 1830. Its cars were pulled by the *Tom Thumb*, the first steam locomotive built in the United States. Railroad companies built tracks between most cities in the Northeast during the 1840s. By 1855, railroad tracks connected New York to Chicago. The railroads provided the United States with a cheap and rapid way to transport goods and raw materials.

Peter Cooper's *Tom Thumb* was the first steam-powered locomotive.

Putting It All Together

Create two columns in your notebook. Label the first "Cause" and the second "Effect." First, list the changes (effects) in the early American workplace and living areas. Then write the cause of each change.

Factory Workers and Immigrants

Thinking on Your Own

Look at the vocabulary and the Focus Your Reading questions. What concerns would you have about children working in mills and young women living in boardinghouses? Discuss your thoughts with a classmate.

The mill and factory owners needed workers to run their machines. Most Americans lived on farms. They were busy raising crops. The owners had to look elsewhere for workers.

Child Labor

The early spinning mill companies advertised in newspapers for workers. They urged poor families to come to the mills. The entire family, they promised, would get jobs. As a result, poor families provided most of the workers in the small mills of New England. Often these were families with many children.

Children were important in mills because their small fingers could thread the machines quickly.

272

Children filled many of the jobs in spinning mills. Some became highly skilled workers. In one mill in Rhode Island, a thirteen-year-old boy was in charge of repairing

Lesson Vocabulary

Explain that one meaning of the word *board* is "food and meals." A *boardinghouse* is a place that provides paying guests with a room and meals.

Point out the word *migrant* in the word *immigrant*. A *migrant* is someone who moves from one place to another. An *immigrant* is someone who moves from one country to another to live permanently.

A *peasant farmer* is a term used in Europe to describe a small farmer (often one who rents his or her land) or a farmworker. A *famine* is a severe shortage of food for a large part of a population. Ask students what, then, a *potato famine* is. (a famine caused by the failure of the potato crop)

Lesson Summary

The new factories and mills needed workers. Many of these workers were children and young, unmarried farm women. Both the children and the "mill girls" worked long hours under poor conditions for little money. In the 1840s, factory owners found a new source of cheap labor. They hired immigrants from European countries. In time, these new workers replaced the young farm women in the textile mills.

Lesson Objective

Students will learn about the workers in the nation's first factories.

Focus Your Reading Answers

1 The early spinning mills found workers among poor New England families, particularly those with many children.

2 Young farm women worked in the large textile mills.

3 Factory owners hired immigrants because they were willing to work long hours for very low wages.

Picturing History

By 1830, 55 percent of the mill workers in Rhode Island were children. Many worked long hours for wages of less than $1 a week. Children climbed under or squeezed behind the machines to fix whatever needed fixing without stopping the machine. Why was the children's size an advantage? What were the disadvantages in hiring child workers?

the machines. The foreman of the Pawtucket Thread Company in Pawtucket, Rhode Island, was only nineteen. He had worked in textile mills for eleven years. Most children worked at machines for only a few pennies a day. Children who worked in the factories had a difficult life. Injuries, and even death, were common. Very few factory children received an education.

Weaving machines increased the speed of making cloth.

Mill Girls

The mills in Lowell, Massachusetts, and other company towns were able to find workers other than children. They brought in farm women in their late teens and twenties. The owners built **boardinghouses** for the "mill girls," as they were called. Older women looked after the young boarders. Most mill girls worked to save the money they would need to set up housekeeping once they got married. However, because of poor wages and because they had to pay for their room and board, mill girls had to work a long time to be able to save any money.

The women at Lowell worked long hours. The workday began at 5:00 A.M. At 7:00, the workers took off half an hour for breakfast. Then they worked until 12:30 P.M., when they stopped for lunch. Returning at 1:30, they labored until 7:00 P.M., which was quitting time.

> ### stop and think
>
> Imagine you are a mill girl. In your notebook, describe one day in your life.

Picturing History

In 1847, over 105,000 women and men came from Ireland to the United States. Even more arrived the following year. Have students use the drawing on this page and the primary source on page 268 to describe how the newcomers made new lives for themselves in the United States.

Putting It All Together

Charts will vary but should reflect the content of the chapter. Encourage students to use the library and the Internet to find answers to their unanswered questions.

Immigrants made up a large part of the workforce.

Immigrant Workers

In the 1840s, factory owners found a new source of cheap labor. More **immigrants** were arriving from Europe than ever before. From 1820 to 1840, 700,000 immigrants came to the United States. Between 1840 and 1860, the number jumped to 4,200,000. They came from Ireland and Germany, with large numbers also from England, the Netherlands, Norway, and Sweden. The majority of the newcomers were **peasant farmers**.

The Irish came because they were starving due to the **potato famine**. Potatoes were their principal food. In the mid-1840s, a plant disease ruined the potato crop for several years. A million Irish people died of starvation and disease. Another million and a half left the country, most coming to the United States. In Germany and elsewhere, land owners combined the peasants' small plots of land into large farms. This forced the peasants off the land. For many, their only choice was to immigrate or to starve.

American factory owners welcomed the new arrivals. Unskilled and starving, the immigrants gladly worked long hours for low wages. By 1860, immigrants had replaced most of the young farm women in the textile mills.

Putting It All Together

Where people lived and worked changed during this time in history. Create a three-column chart in your notebook. In the first column write each of these topics on a line: "Farm Machines," "Cookstoves," "Spinning Machines," "Company Towns," and "Railroads." In the next column, briefly note what you have learned about each. In the last column, write questions you still have about these topics.

Extension

Ask students to use the information below to create a bar graph showing the number of immigrants who came to the United States from Ireland between 1821 and 1860. Have students give their graphs a title.

1821–1830   50,724

1831–1840   207,381

1841–1850   780,719

1851–1860   914,119

An official report from Ireland in the mid-1800s claimed, "All who have the money are moving. Only the poorest and the weakest are left behind." How does the graph seem to support that view?

Biography

Lucy Larcom (1824–1893)

Lucy Larcom was a "mill girl." At the age of twelve, she worked in a textile mill in Lowell, Massachusetts. Her job was to remove spools of thread from a spinning machine. "We were not occupied more than half the time," she remembered. "The intervals were spent frolicking around among the spinning-frames, teasing and talking to the older girls, or entertaining ourselves with games and stories in a corner." The work was not hard, but she hated the noisy machinery. Most of all, she missed going to school.

Larcom was a quick learner. Her older sisters had taken her to school with them since she was two years old. She could read the Bible at age two and a half, and when she was five she read her first novel. She liked her teachers. She loved poetry and wrote verses. Larcom wanted to be a teacher and a poet when she grew up.

In 1835, when Larcom was eleven, her father died. With eight children to support, her mother had to go to work. She moved the children to the mill town of Lowell, Massachusetts. There she opened a boardinghouse. She did not earn enough to feed her large family. To help pay the bills, twelve-year-old Larcom went to work in the mill.

Larcom never lost her love for poetry. After work, she spent her free time reading and writing poems. She met John Greenleaf Whittier, who came to Lowell to read his poems. He encouraged her to publish her verses. Larcom published several poems in the *Lowell Offering*, a magazine produced by the mill workers. After leaving Lowell at age twenty-two, she went to school to become a teacher. She taught for several years but continued writing poetry. She published five books of poetry and her autobiography, *A New England Girlhood* (1889). Lucy Larcom died in 1893 at the age of sixty-nine.

275

Bio Facts

- Born in 1824 in Beverly, Massachusetts.

- Lost her father, a sea captain and merchant, when she was only eleven.

- Moved with her mother and sisters to Lowell, where her mother ran a boardinghouse for mill girls.

- Went to work with her sisters in the mill soon after they arrived in Lowell.

- Worked at various mill jobs for the next ten years.

- While at the mill, joined a reading and literary club formed by the mill girls and wrote essays that were read at the meetings.

- Met the poet John Greenleaf Whittier, who was editing a paper in Lowell, and became friends with his sister.

- Traveled to Illinois in 1846 with her sister Emiline.

- Taught school in Illinois for three years.

- Attended the Monticello Female Seminary in Godfrey, Illinois, from 1849–1852.

- Returned to Beverly, Massachusetts, to teach, paint, and study.

- Won a prize in 1854 for her poem "Call to Kansas."

- Taught from 1854–1862 at the Wheaton Female Seminary in Norton, Massachusetts.

- Helped edit the children's magazine *Our Young Folks* from 1865–1873.

- Published essays and poetry. Her best-known work was an autobiographical sketch, *A New England Girlhood*.

- Died in 1893.

Biography Extension

In *A New England Girlhood*, Lucy Larcom said of her years in the mills, "I know that sometimes the confinement of the mill became very wearisome to me. . . . I defied the machinery to make me a slave." In what sense were Larcom and her co-workers slaves to the machine? (The machines set the pace of the work, and the girls had to keep up with it.)

Chapter Review

1 The advertisements will vary but should highlight the main features of the mechanical reaper and should appeal to potential buyers.

2 The letters will vary but should reflect what it was like to work in a factory and live in a large city.

3 A concept web on "factory workers" should include information on child labor, the "mill girls," and immigrant workers. All three worked at machines for long hours and low pay. Their days were highly structured.

Chapter Summary

By the 1840s, everyday life in the United States was changing. Farm families who once raised most of their own food and made their own clothing were now raising **cash crops** and buying what they needed. Farmers who once cut wheat with a **scythe** now used **mechanical reapers** that could harvest more grain and make more money. Housework also was changing. Women no longer had to weave their own cloth, and the new cookstove made cooking easier.

The 1840s also saw more people living in towns and cities, especially in the Northeast. Many people moved there to work in **textile mills** and factories. In 1791, Samuel Slater built a factory to make thread with **spinning machines**. Some of the mills and factories were located in **company towns**, such as Lowell, Massachusetts. American seaports grew as shipping increased, and **wharves** were piled high with goods.

The factory and mill owners encouraged poor New England families to move to the mill towns. As a result, many of the new workers were children and teenage girls. They lived in supervised **boardinghouses**. These children and "mill girls" worked long hours under poor conditions for very little money.

Many **immigrant** workers were **peasant farmers** who fled Ireland due to the **potato famine**. Unskilled and starving, they gladly worked long hours for low wages. In time, they replaced the young farm women in the textile mills.

Chapter Review

1 Create an ad for the mechanical reaper to distribute to farmers in the 1840s.

2 Imagine that you are a young person who moved to the city in the 1840s. Write a letter to your family back on the farm about city life and work.

3 Organize a concept web with "Factory Workers" as the main topic in the center circle. In lines going out from the circle, add information related to the topic.

Novel Connections

Below is a list of books that relate to the time period covered in this chapter. The numbers in parentheses indicate the related Thematic Strands of the National Council for the Social Studies (NCSS).

Barry Denenberg. *So Far From Home: The Diary of Mary Driscoll, An Irish Mill Girl, Lowell, Massachusetts, 1847.* Scholastic, 1997. (II, V, VII)

Dorothy and Thomas Hoobler. *We Are Americans: Voices of the Immigrant Experience.* Scholastic, 2003. (II, III)

Milton Meltzer. *Bound for America: The Story of European Immigrants.* (*Great Journeys* series) Benchmark Books/Marshall Cavendish, 2001. (I, V, IX)

David L. Parker. *Stolen Dreams: Portraits of Working Children.* Lerner, 1997. (I, X)

Skill Builder

Mapping Change over Time

Maps serve different purposes. All maps show where cities, rivers, mountains, or other places are located. Maps also can show change over time.

This map shows the growth of railroads in the Northeast, Midwest, and South. Railroads that existed in 1850 are shown in purple. Those built between 1850 and 1860 are shown in orange. The locations of major cities are also shown.

Use the map to answer the following questions:

1 Which section (Northeast, Midwest, or South) had the most railroads by 1850?

2 Which section (Northeast, Midwest, or South) added the most railroads between 1850 and 1860?

3 Which section (Northeast, Midwest, or South) had the fewest railroads by 1860?

4 Which cities were major rail centers by 1860?

5 What advantage did the Northeast have by 1860?

6 Why was New Orleans at a disadvantage?

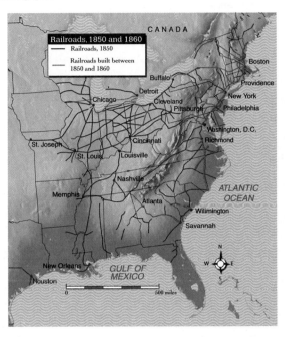

Skill Builder

1 The Northeast had the most railroads by 1850.

2 The Midwest added the most railroads between 1850 and 1860.

3 The South had the fewest railroads by 1860.

4 Cities that were major railroad centers included Boston, Providence, New York, Philadelphia, Washington, Richmond, Wilmington, Savannah, Atlanta, Nashville, St. Louis, Louisville, Cincinnati, Pittsburgh, Chicago, and St. Joseph.

5 By 1860, the Northeast had the advantage of a network of railroads linked to major seaports.

6 New Orleans was at a disadvantage because it was linked to a single railroad.

Classroom Discussion

Discuss with students some of the broader topics covered in this chapter.

- Why were the first factories in the United States in the Northeast?

- What part did inventions play in the growth of the factory system? What part did new ways of organizing work play in the growth of the factory system?

- What advantages did railroads have over travel by river and canal? What disadvantages did they have?

- How do you think the jobs held by the "mill girls" affected their lives and those of their families?

- How were the growth of factories and improvements in transportation linked? What were the links between both industries and the growth of cities?

Chapter Summary

Refer to page 290 in the student book for a summary of Chapter 18.

Related Transparencies

T-6 Growth of the United States to 1853

T-18 T-Chart

Key Blacklines

Biography
James K. Polk

Primary Source
Manifest Destiny: James K. Polk and John L. O'Sullivan

Picturing History

Ask students to describe what they see in the photograph on page 278. What seems to be the mood among the travelers? What may have motivated them to leave home and travel west?

Getting Focused

Skim this chapter to predict what you will be learning.

- Read the lesson titles and subheadings.
- Look at the illustrations and read the captions.
- Examine the maps.
- Review the vocabulary words and terms.

Use the headings to create questions about what you expect to learn from this chapter. Compare your questions with those of a partner. Write your questions in your notebook.

Pre-Reading Discussion

Ask students to complete each bulleted direction on page 278. Then focus on the title of the chapter. What is *manifest destiny*? Have students attempt a definition based on their preview of the chapter. Then explain that John L. O'Sullivan, editor of the *Democratic Review*, coined the phrase *manifest destiny* in 1845. It expressed the idea that the United States had a special destiny to overspread the entire continent of North America. That idea inspired many Americans to move to the West.

Picturing History

Ask students to use the photograph on this page and the drawing on page 279 to describe westward expansion. What do the two images have in common? How is each unique? What does each add to your understanding of the journey?

1 Westward Expansion

Thinking on Your Own

Look over the vocabulary and the Focus Your Reading questions. Write three predictions about the topic "Westward Expansion" in your notebook. Compare your predictions with a partner's.

By 1840, the line of settlement had reached the edge of the woodland and prairies. People settled as far west as Missouri and Arkansas. Beyond were the Great Plains and the Rocky Mountains. The next wave of settlement would be different from any that had gone before. This time farmers did not gradually push the frontier line west. Rather, they leapfrogged over the plains and mountains. They used Native American trails and mountain passes as highways to the Pacific Coast.

focus your reading

Why were settlers attracted to Oregon?

What religious group settled in Utah?

What did the expansionists want?

vocabulary

missionaries

Oregon fever

expansionists

manifest destiny

Oregon Fever

An important area of settlement was the Oregon Country. This area extended from the Columbia River in Oregon north into Canada. In 1840, both Great Britain and the United States claimed this territory.

A variety of covered wagons were used for the trip west.

Manifest Destiny 279

Lesson Summary
Missionaries were the first Americans to settle in the Oregon Country. After reading their glowing accounts of the region, many Americans headed west for Oregon. The Mormons settled at the Great Salt Lake in Utah. In the 1840s, many Americans were eager to add not only these territories but also Texas and California to the United States. In 1845, Texas became a state. The following year, the British signed a treaty that gave the United States what is now the states of Oregon and Washington.

Lesson Objective
Students will learn why Americans were eager to expand their borders in the 1840s.

Focus Your Reading Answers
1 Settlers were attracted to Oregon's rich farmland.

2 The Mormons were the religious group that settled in Utah.

3 Expansionists wanted to add Texas, Oregon, and California to the United States.

DVD Extension
Encourage students to use the reading comprehension, vocabulary reinforcement, and interactive timeline activities on the student DVD.

Lesson Vocabulary

Review the meaning of the word *missionary*. (a person who tries to convert others to the Christian religion) Ask students to define the term *Oregon fever* by examining the two words that make up the term. The word *fever* refers to not only a rise in body temperature but also intense anticipation. *Oregon fever* described an intense desire to settle in Oregon Country. Based on their knowledge of the word *expand*, ask students to define the word *expansionists*. Remind students that *manifest destiny* was the belief that the United States had a God-given right to extend its borders to the Pacific Ocean.

Ask students to write a sentence that explains how the following terms are linked:

• missionaries and Oregon fever

• expansionists and manifest destiny

Map Extension

Ask students to use the map on page 280 to answer the following questions:

- What does the treaty line of 1846 stand for? (indicates the division of Oregon Country between the United States and Great Britain)

- Who controls the land south of the treaty line? (the United States)

- What river did the Oregon Trail follow through what is now Idaho and Washington? (Snake River)

- The richest land in Oregon is in the Willamette Valley. How might a wagon train reach that valley from the Oregon Trail? (by heading south from Fort Vancouver along the Willamette River)

Picturing History

Brigham Young organized and led the Mormons through the Rocky Mountains to the Great Salt Lake region. Young founded Salt Lake City and built a series of prosperous colonies throughout what is now the state of Utah and the neighboring states of Arizona, California, Nevada, and Idaho. Ask students what skills Young and other pioneers needed to not only survive but also prosper in the West. What character traits did such men and women have?

The first Americans to settle in Oregon were **missionaries**. In the 1830s, preachers went there to convert Native Americans to the Christian faith. They were not very successful. Their letters home, however, contained glowing accounts of Oregon's rich farmland.

Oregon's fertile land drew settlers like a magnet. "Whoo ha! Go it, boys! We're in a perfect **Oregon fever**," exclaimed a Missouri newspaper editor. The fever spread. The Oregon Trail became the key route to the Oregon Country. By the end of 1843, more than 1,500 settlers had arrived. The number climbed to 9,000 by 1849.

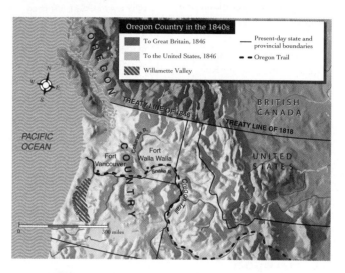

Utah

The people known as Mormons did not go all the way to Oregon. They stopped at the Great Salt Lake in Utah. The Mormons belonged to the Church of Jesus Christ of Latter-day Saints. Joseph Smith had founded this religion in New York in 1830. Harassed by their neighbors, the Mormons left New York and settled in Nauvoo, Illinois. There an anti-Mormon mob murdered Smith. In 1847, Brigham Young led the Mormons to Utah. It was then Mexican territory. They settled on farmland and built a town called Salt Lake City.

Brigham Young

Extension

Explain to students that every spring, hundreds of families headed west along the Oregon Trail. By the 1850s, travelers found not only a well-worn path to Oregon but also thousands of traveling companions. In 1852, for example, 10,000 people headed for Oregon and 50,000 for California. Wagons were reported to be traveling twelve abreast. Have students find out more about the trail and what it was like to make the journey in a covered wagon. Ask them to present their findings to the class by using the Student Presentation Builder on the student DVD.

The Mormon trek to Utah

Acquiring New Territory

In the 1840s, many Americans wanted to acquire new territory. The **expansionists** wanted to add Texas and Oregon to the United States. They also had their eyes on California, which was still Mexican

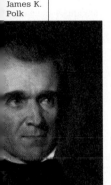
President James K. Polk

territory. Extending the nation's boundaries to the Pacific Ocean was, they said, our "**manifest destiny**," or God-given right.

In 1844, James K. Polk, an expansionist Democrat, was elected president. The Democrats called the election a vote for expansion. In February 1845, Congress admitted Texas as a state. The next year Polk threatened a war with Great Britain over Oregon. The British agreed to sign a treaty that gave the United States most of what it wanted. It included the area that is now the states of Oregon and Washington.

stop and think

"Whoo ha! Go it, boys!" was the slogan used by people moving to Oregon. Design another slogan that reflects the mood of the times about westward expansion.

Putting It All Together

Write the statement "America has a God-given right to extend her boundaries" in your notebook. Under it make two columns labeled "Agree" and "Disagree." In one column or the other, explain why you either agree or disagree. Compare your reasons with those of a partner.

Manifest Destiny 281

1 The American reporter describes the U.S. soldiers as having been ordered to treat the Mexicans as friends. The Mexicans are described as eyeing the Americans as "beings of another world."

2 The account by the Mexican merchant differs in that it describes the suffering of the Mexican people as a result of the blowing up of houses and confusion within the city.

3 Answers will vary, but students are likely to suggest the differences are due to the fact that one was an American and the other a Mexican.

Extension

Ask students to compare the views of two American military leaders, one a general and the other a young officer. Ask students to account for the differences in their points of view.

General Winfield Scott described the victory in an official report. He wrote that his small army has "beaten . . . in view of their capital, the whole Mexican army, of (at the beginning) thirty-odd thousand men — posted, always, in chosen positions, behind entrenchments, or more formidable defenses of nature and art; killed or wounded, of that number, more than 7,000 officers and men; taken 3,730 prisoners, one-seventh officers, including 13 generals, of whom three have been presidents of this republic."

Read a Primary Source

The Fall of Mexico City: Two Accounts

Below are two accounts of the capture of Mexico City at the end of the Mexican War. The first is by an American reporter, and the second is by a Mexican merchant. The American army, led by General Winfield Scott, occupied the city in September 1847.

"At 7 o'clock this morning Gen. Scott, with his staff, rode in and took quarters in the national palace, on the top of which the regimental flag of the gallant rifles and the stars and stripes were already flying, and an immense crowd [of Mexicans] . . . were congregated in the plaza as the commander-in-chief entered it. They pressed our soldiers, and eyed them as though they were beings of another world. . . . They [the soldiers] were told, however, not to injure or harm a man in the mob—as they were all our friends."

George W. Kendall, newspaper reporter for the
New Orleans Picayune, September 14, 1847.

"Seeing further resistance useless, our [Mexican] soldiers ceased firing, and on the 16th of September (sad day!) the enemy was in possession of the Mexican capital. Though we inflicted havoc and death upon the Yankees, we suffered greatly ourselves. Many were killed by the blowing up of the houses, many by the bombardment, but more by the confusion which prevailed in the city, and altogether we cannot count our killed, wounded and missing since the actions commenced yesterday at less than 4,000 among whom are many women and children. . . . What a calamity!"

Anonymous Mexican merchant, September 16, 1847, quoted in George W. Smith and Charles Judah, eds., *Chronicles of the Gringos: The U.S. Army in the Mexican War, 1846-1848* (Albuquerque: University of New Mexico).

282

Extension, continued

Ulysses S. Grant, then a young American officer, saw the victory differently. "In our army," he wrote, "every officer, from the highest to the lowest, was educated in his profession, not at West Point necessarily, but in the camp, in garrison, and many of them in Indian wars. The Mexican army of that day was hardly an army. . . . The private was picked up . . . when wanted; his consent was not asked; he was poorly clothed, worse fed, and seldom paid. . . . With all this I have seen as brave stands made by some of these as I have ever seen made."

War with Mexico

Thinking on Your Own

Look over the vocabulary and the Focus Your Reading questions. Think of a time when you or someone you know disagreed about who owned something. What created the problem? How did you resolve the issue?

In 1845, Mexico and the United States were headed for war. Mexico refused to accept the U.S. **annexation** of Texas. The two nations also could not agree on the boundary between Texas and Mexico. Thousands of square miles of land were in dispute. President James K. Polk wanted to buy New Mexico and California. Mexico refused to sell.

focus your reading

On what issues did the United States and Mexico not agree?

Why did the United States and Mexico go to war?

What did the United States get from the war?

vocabulary

annexation

disputed zone

negotiate

Treaty of Guadalupe Hidalgo

Going to War

In January 1846, President Polk was ready for war. He ordered General Zachary Taylor's army into the **disputed zone**. Mexico, in turn, sent in its troops. A clash was only a matter of time. In April, the Mexicans attacked Taylor's army, killing eleven American soldiers. When the news reached Washington, Polk sent a message to Congress. "Mexico . . . has invaded our territory and shed American blood on the American soil," he wrote. "War exists . . . by the act of Mexico herself." He did not mention that the attack took place in a zone claimed by both nations. On May 13, 1846, Congress declared war.

General Zachary Taylor

Manifest Destiny 283

Lesson Summary

In 1845, the United States and Mexico quarreled over the American annexation of Texas. Fighting broke out when President James K. Polk sent troops into an area claimed by both nations. Congress declared war on May 13, 1846. In 1848, the war ended with the Treaty of Guadalupe Hidalgo, in which Mexico agreed to sell to the United States all of its land north of the Rio Grande.

Lesson Objective

Students will learn why Mexico and the United States went to war in 1846 and the outcome of that war.

Focus Your Reading Answers

1 The United States and Mexico did not agree on the U.S. annexation of Texas and on a boundary between Texas and Mexico.

2 The United States went to war after the American and Mexican armies clashed in the disputed zone, resulting in the deaths of 11 American soldiers.

3 The United States got the Mexicans out of Texas and gained control of New Mexico and California.

Extension

Have students research the Battle of Buena Vista. Ask them to create a poster that shows why the victory turned Zachary Taylor into a national hero.

Lesson Vocabulary

Remind students that the word *annexation* refers to the process of adding land to a nation, state, or other territory. Some of the land the United States added was in a *disputed zone*. If a dispute is a disagreement, what then is a *disputed zone*? (an area claimed by two or more groups)

To *negotiate* is to work out the terms of an agreement with the other party or parties to the agreement. Every *treaty* is *negotiated*. A treaty is a written agreement between two or more nations. The *Treaty of Guadalupe Hidalgo* ended the war between Mexico and the United States. It was signed at Guadalupe Hidalgo, a small town outside Mexico City.

Captain Frémont fighting at Monterey

Picturing History

The painting at the top of page 284 shows John C. Frémont leading an American army against the Mexican army at Monterey, California. The artist, W.H.D. Koerner, was a magazine illustrator who was born 30 years after the war ended. How does the artist seem to view Fremont and his role in the battle? What feelings do the painting inspire?

Extension

Have students find out more about the battle for Monterey. What does their research suggest about the accuracy of the painting?

The Mexican War

The United States quickly got the territory it wanted. General Taylor's army drove the Mexicans out of Texas. A second army occupied New Mexico. When news of the war reached California, Americans there revolted against Mexico. Sailors stationed in California on American ships joined the revolt. Captain John C. Frémont, who was surveying in California, also sent troops. After a month of fighting, California was in American hands.

Having got what he wanted, Polk tried to end the war. But the Mexicans would not **negotiate**. The United States had to

General Winfield Scott entered Mexico City on September 14, 1847.

Picturing History

Ask students to compare the painting on page 284 of General Winfield Scott entering Mexico City with the two descriptions on page 282. How are the accounts similar? What differences seem most striking? Have students decide whether the artist was an American or a Mexican. Be sure they point to details in the painting in support of their answers.

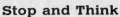

force Mexico to the peace table. In March 1847, an American army invaded Mexico. Led by General Winfield Scott, the troops fought their way into Mexico City. The fighting finally ended in September 1847.

The Peace Treaty

President Polk finally got the peace treaty he wanted. The treaty was signed on February 2, 1848. In the **Treaty of Guadalupe Hidalgo**, Mexico agreed to sell to the United States approximately 529,000 square miles of territory. This area now consists of California, Nevada, Arizona, and the western parts of New Mexico and Colorado. In return, the United States agreed to pay Mexico $15 million. That was about five cents per acre.

The United States won the Battle of Buena Vista.

Putting It All Together

In your notebook design a timeline of events that led to the annexation of Texas, New Mexico, and California. Add information you find from your own research.

Lesson Summary

As the United States acquired new territories, the issue of slavery became the subject of debate with almost every request for statehood. The Missouri Compromise of 1820 was supposed to have put the issue to rest. When it did not, the House of Representatives passed a gag rule in 1836 that banned any discussion of slavery. Then in 1846, Congressman David Wilmot proposed that slavery be banned from any territory acquired from Mexico. During the presidential election of 1848, the Whigs and the Democrats ignored the issue, so those who opposed slavery formed the Free-Soil Party. Although the party did not carry a single state, it showed the importance of the issue. When gold was discovered in California in 1848, the question of whether California would enter the Union as a free state or slave state triggered a crisis.

Lesson Objective

Students will learn how the issue of slavery affected the admission of new states to the United States.

Focus Your Reading Answers

1 Congress tried to avoid the slavery issue because it threatened to destroy the Union.

2 The Wilmot Proviso brought the issue of slavery back to Congress by trying to ban slavery from any territory acquired from Mexico.

3 Miners in California made up their own rules because the territory had no government.

LESSON **3** # The Slavery Issue

Thinking on Your Own

Read the vocabulary and the Focus Your Reading questions. Draw three columns in your notebook. In the first column, on separate lines, write "The Slavery Issue," "The Wilmot Proviso," and "Miners' Law in California." In the second column, write what you already know about these topics. In the third column, write questions you have about each topic.

The slavery issue divided Americans along sectional lines. Many realized that it could destroy the Union. Leaders in the House of Representatives and the Senate had tried to keep the issue out of Congress. The Missouri Compromise had put the issue of slavery to rest in the Louisiana Territory. In 1820, Congress agreed to the Missouri Compromise, which banned slavery from the area north of the 36° 30' line of latitude. It allowed slavery in any territories created below that line, but not in any areas north of the line. In 1836, the House of Representatives passed a **gag rule** that banned the discussion of slavery in its debates.

focus your reading

Why did Congress try to avoid the slavery issue?

How did the Wilmot Proviso bring the issue back into Congress?

Why did the miners in California make up their own rules?

vocabulary

gag rule

Wilmot Proviso

Free-Soil Party

Revival of the Slavery Issue

The Mexican War renewed interest in the slavery issue. Many antislavery people in the North had opposed the war. President Polk, they argued, went to war only to add new slave territory to the Union.

In August 1846, Congressman David Wilmot of Pennsylvania brought the issue back into Congress.

David

Lesson Vocabulary

Explain that a *gag rule* is a rule that allows lawmakers to kill or shorten a debate. The House of Representatives had a *gag rule* from 1836 to 1844 to avoid debates over slavery.

A *proviso* is a condition or clause that establishes an exception to a rule. The *Wilmot Proviso* was supposed to establish an exception to the Missouri Compromise by banning slavery in all territory acquired from Mexico—even in territories south of latitude 36° 30'.

The *Free-Soil Party* was a political party formed because of growing opposition to the extension of slavery into territories newly acquired from Mexico.

He introduced a resolution that banned slavery from any territory acquired from Mexico. The **Wilmot Proviso**, as it was called, passed in the House in 1846 and 1847, but the Senate never voted on it.

stop and think

In your notebook write two ways in which the Mexican War revived the slavery issue.

The Wilmot Proviso showed once again the power of the slavery issue to divide the nation along sectional lines. Northern Democrats and Whigs voted in favor of it. All but three of the sixty-four congressmen from the South voted against it.

Deadlock over Slavery

In the presidential election of 1848, the candidates avoided the issue. Whig candidate Zachary Taylor and Democrat Lewis Cass knew they would lose votes in the North or the South if they took a stand on slavery. Taylor, a slave owner, ignored the issue. Cass said he would let the people of a territory decide for themselves.

Some of the antislavery people formed a third party, the **Free-Soil Party**. Their candidate was former president Martin Van Buren. Van Buren was president from 1837 to 1841. While the new party did not carry a single state, it did send a warning: Avoiding the slavery issue could destroy the existing two-party political system.

Slavery was avoided during the election of 1848.

Gold in California

The discovery of gold in California brought the slavery issue to a crisis. In early 1848, James W. Marshall found gold deposits at Sutter's Mill along the American River. By May, word of the gold strike had reached San Francisco. Within a month, the city was virtually a ghost town. Everyone rushed to the gold diggings. In December, President Polk reported the discovery in his annual message to Congress. That helped trigger the great California gold rush.

Manifest Destiny 287

Stop and Think

Many people in the North had opposed the war with Mexico because they believed Polk went to war only to add new slave territories. When the war ended, antislavery groups tried to ban slavery from any territory acquired from Mexico.

Extension

Ask students to find out more about the election of 1848. Who were the candidates? What stand did each take on the slavery issue? What message did the Free-Soil Party send? Have students create a poster summarizing their findings.

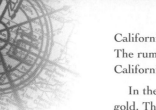

Picturing History

Gold was discovered on January 24, 1848, at Sutter's Mill in California. By August, $600,000 worth of gold had been taken from the mines in northern California. That year nearly 100,000 gold seekers arrived in California. Ask students to imagine that they are reporters in California during the gold rush. How would they describe the scene shown on page 288 to their readers? Who in the picture on page 288 would they like to interview? What questions would they like to ask him?

Putting It All Together

Answers will vary but should include the need to protect claims and the lack of a government capable of making and enforcing laws.

California "gold fever" infected thousands of Americans. The rumor was that anyone could make $1,000 a day in the California foothills.

In the spring of 1849, some 80,000 people set out to find gold. These people became knows as "forty-niners" because they moved to California in 1849. Most people went by wagon across the plains or by ship around Cape Horn. Upon arriving in California, they staked out mining claims.

Thousands of miners searched for gold in 1849

Very few of the newcomers knew anything about gold mining. They dug gravel and sand from streambeds and swirled it in shallow pans filled with water. The sand and pebbles washed out, leaving the heavier gold in the bottom of the pan. They also used boxes mounted on rockers and long wooden troughs called sluices for this purpose. California miners took out more than $81 million in gold by using these simple techniques.

By the winter of 1849, the residents of California faced a crisis. They realized that they needed a government that could make real laws, but Congress could not act. It could not agree on the status of slavery in the territory of California.

Putting It All Together

Take turns with a partner naming the issues that a miner living in California during 1848 to 1849 had to face. Write the issues in your notebook.

Extension

People from all over the world flocked to California for the gold rush. Ask students to create a world map showing where gold seekers came from. Who were among the first to arrive? What groups came later? Be sure that students include a legend, or key, to their map.

Biography

James W. Marshall (1812–1885)

On the morning of January 24, 1848, James W. Marshall walked along the millrace of the sawmill he was building. The race, or canal, brought water from the American River to power the mill. In the sand at the bottom, Marshall saw the glint of a gold nugget. To make sure it was gold, he weighed it. It was heavier than silver. He bit it and made a dent in the metal. It flattened out when he pounded it with a rock. Then he rushed off to tell John Sutter, his partner, that he had discovered gold.

James W. Marshall was born in 1812 in New Jersey. When he was twenty-one, Marshall moved to Missouri to farm. Looking for better land, he left for Oregon in 1844. He settled in California in 1845 near a trading post called Sutter's Fort.

John Sutter's trading post was the center of American settlement in California. Sutter sold farmland to the new settlers. He also hired men to make shoes, saddles, and farm tools, which he sold to the newcomers. In 1847, John Marshall agreed to help Sutter build a sawmill. They could make money selling lumber to the settlers.

When Marshall found gold, Sutter made him promise not to tell anyone about the nugget. Sutter was afraid his shoe and saddle makers would quit work to look for gold. The word of the gold discovery got out anyway. Sutter's workers took off for the hills. During the next year, more than 80,000 gold seekers rushed to California.

Neither Sutter nor Marshall benefited from the gold discovery. Without workers, Sutter's businesses failed. Hundreds of gold seekers settled on his land but refused to pay him for it. Claim jumpers took over Marshall's mining claims. They tore down the sawmill to build cabins with the lumber. Marshall spent the rest of his life cleaning out wells, making gardens, and doing odd jobs. He died a poor man in 1885 at age seventy-three.

289

Bio Facts

- Born in Lambertsville, New Jersey, on October 8, 1810.

- Left home for good at the age of twenty-four to farm in Missouri.

- Joined an emigrant train on its way to the Oregon Country in 1844.

- Left Oregon Country and headed for California in 1845; was hired as a handyman by John Sutter.

- Bought a ranch on Butte Creek but continued to work for Sutter.

- Served with John Frémont's California Volunteers during the Mexican War.

- Returned to Sutter's Fort in 1847 and was sent in September to build a sawmill on the American River.

- After finding gold, tried to hold onto his land, but was soon pushed off by hordes of miners.

- In 1857, returned to the valley where he found gold and started a vineyard.

- Lost his business by the end of the 1860s and turned to prospecting.

- Became a partner in a mine near Kelsey, California. The mine was a bust, and it left Marshall penniless.

- Died in Kelsey in 1885.

Biography Extension

Ask students to reenact the moment Marshall found gold. He wrote of the moment, "I reached my hand down and picked it up; it made my heart thump, for I was certain it was gold. The piece was about half the size and shape of a pea. Then I saw another." Have students imagine how Marshall must have felt when he realized what he had found. Why was it impossible to keep the discovery a secret?

Chapter Review

1 Journal entries will vary but should reflect the hardships of life on the Oregon Trail.

2 The Mexican position was that Americans entered Mexican territory and refused to leave. The American position was that the land belonged to the United States and the nation had a right to expand across the continent.

3 Editorials will vary, but students should state their position in their opening sentence and then use arguments and information from the chapter to support that position.

Chapter Summary

The first Americans to settle in the Oregon Territory were **missionaries**. People in the eastern United States read the glowing accounts of the region and became so excited that newspapers said they had caught **Oregon fever**. After the United States annexed Texas in 1845, **expansionists** wanted to buy California from Mexico or take it by force, if necessary. They said it was our "**manifest destiny**" to extend our country to the Pacific Ocean.

In 1845, the United States and Mexico were headed for war because Mexico opposed the **annexation** of Texas. Fighting broke out when President James K. Polk sent troops into the **disputed zone**, and Congress declared war on May 13, 1846. In 1848, the United States **negotiated** the **Treaty of Guadalupe Hidalgo** in which Mexico agreed to sell to the United States all the land it owned north of the Rio Grande.

The issue of slavery almost destroyed the Union in 1820 when Missouri was admitted as a slave state. Congress passed a **gag rule** in 1836 to keep the issue from being debated. In August 1846, Congressman David Wilmot proposed the **Wilmot Proviso**, which stated that slavery would be banned from any territory acquired from Mexico. During the presidential election of 1848 the **Free-Soil Party** ran an antislavery candidate. The discovery of gold in California in 1848 brought the slavery issue to a new crisis as gold miners wanted to make California a free territory.

Chapter Review

1 Imagine that you are a farmer traveling west to Oregon. Write a journal entry explaining your experiences along the trail.

2 Make a cartoon sketch of two characters debating. One argues the Mexican position about the Mexican War. The other takes the American position. Include facts from the text.

3 Write a newspaper editorial arguing for California either to be a free state or a slave state. Include information from your own research.

Novel Connections

Below is a list of books that relate to the time period covered in this chapter. The numbers in parentheses indicate the related Thematic Strands of the National Council for the Social Studies (NCSS).

Richard Ammon. *Conestoga Wagons.* Holiday House, 2000. (II, VII, VIII)

Laurie Carlson. *Boss of the Plains: The Hat that Won the West.* DK Ink, 1998. (III, IV)

Marissa Moss. *Rachel's Journal: The Story of a Pioneer Girl.* Harcourt Brace/Silver Whistle, 2001. (II, III, IV)

Jerry Stanley. *Hurry Freedom: African Americans in Gold Rush California.* Crown, 2000. (III)

Mike Stotter. *Wild West.* Kingfisher, 1999. (I, II)

Ann Turner. *Mississippi Mud: Three Prairie Journals.* HarperCollins, 1997. (II, III, IV)

Skill Builder

Mapping Movement

As you have learned, maps can serve many purposes. The railroad map in Chapter 17 presented change over time. Maps can also show locations of places and movement.

The map below shows the movement of armies during the Mexican War. The lines in red represent the Mexican army. The blue lines are the movements of United States troops. This map also shows which side won each major battle. Study the Map Key carefully. What other information does this map include?

Use the map to answer the following questions.

1 How many battles did General Taylor fight after leaving Corpus Christi?

2 Approximately how many miles did General Kearny travel to reach San Gabriel in California?

3 Which general led United States troops to Mexico City?

4 How many Mexican victories were there? How many American victories?

5 How did this war affect the size of the United States?

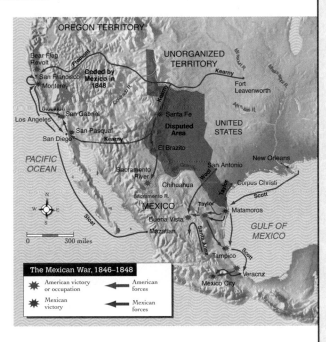

The Mexican War, 1846–1848

✹ American victory or occupation ⬅ American forces

✹ Mexican victory ⬅ Mexican forces

Skill Builder

1 Three—General Taylor fought battles at Matamoros, Buena Vista, and Tampico after leaving Corpus Christi.

2 General Kearney traveled approximately 1,500 miles from Fort Leavenworth.

3 General Scott led troops to Mexico City.

4 The map shows two Mexican victories and 12 American victories.

5 The war added over 500,000 square miles of land to the United States.

Classroom Discussion

Discuss with students some of the broader topics covered in this chapter.

- Why do you think the idea of Manifest Destiny appealed to many Americans?

- How did the issue of slavery affect the way Americans regarded both the war with Mexico and the territories the United States gained in that war?

- What events helped to speed the settlement of newly acquired western lands by people from the United States? How do you think such rapid settlement affected people already living in those areas?

- Compare and contrast the ways in which Americans settled Oregon, Utah, and California. What similarities do you notice? What are the main differences?

Unit 10 focuses on the divisions in the United States that ultimately led to civil war.

Chapter 19, The Sectional Crisis, describes efforts to avoid a confrontation over the future of slavery in the territories.

Chapter 20, The Civil War, describes the war and its immediate aftermath.

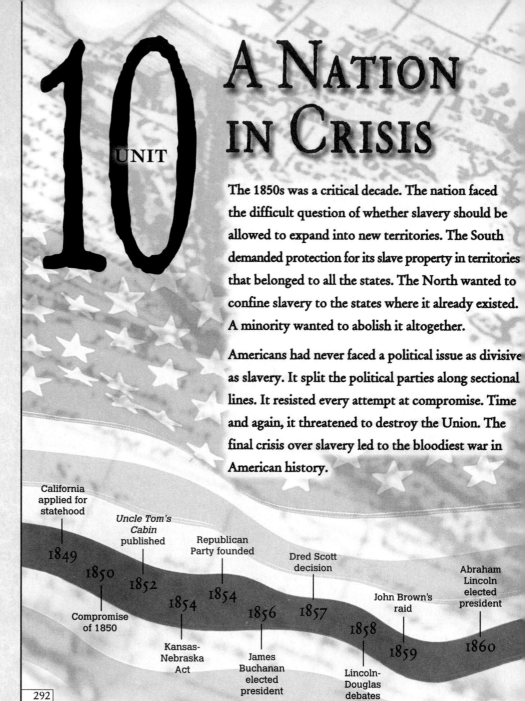

A NATION IN CRISIS

UNIT 10

The 1850s was a critical decade. The nation faced the difficult question of whether slavery should be allowed to expand into new territories. The South demanded protection for its slave property in territories that belonged to all the states. The North wanted to confine slavery to the states where it already existed. A minority wanted to abolish it altogether.

Americans had never faced a political issue as divisive as slavery. It split the political parties along sectional lines. It resisted every attempt at compromise. Time and again, it threatened to destroy the Union. The final crisis over slavery led to the bloodiest war in American history.

California applied for statehood

Uncle Tom's Cabin published

Republican Party founded

Dred Scott decision

Abraham Lincoln elected president

1849

1850

1852

1854

1854

1856

1857

1858

1859

1860

Compromise of 1850

Kansas-Nebraska Act

James Buchanan elected president

Lincoln-Douglas debates

John Brown's raid

292

Getting Started

After students have read the two paragraphs on page 292, ask them to define the word *crisis*. A *crisis* is a crucial stage in a series of events. The decisions made at this point have a direct effect on events that follow. Have students describe the crisis in the 1850s in their own words. What did Americans fear? How did they try to address those fears? What successes and failures marked their efforts to deal with the issue? Explain to students that Chapters 19 and 20 will help them find and deepen their answers to these questions.

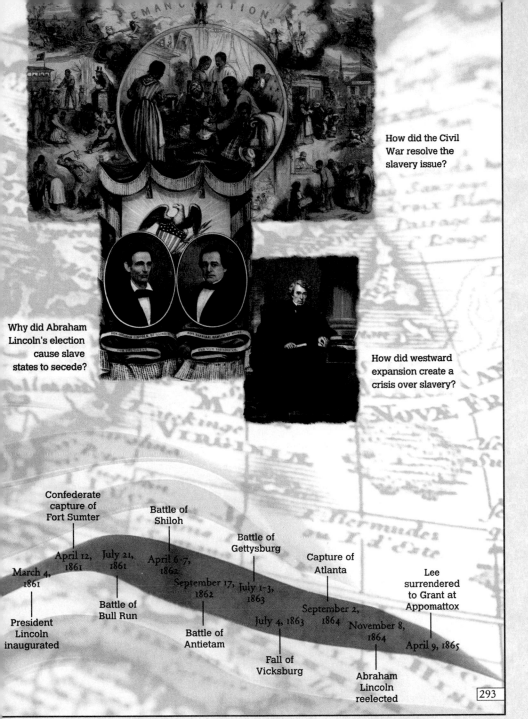

How did the Civil War resolve the slavery issue?

Why did Abraham Lincoln's election cause slave states to secede?

How did westward expansion create a crisis over slavery?

Confederate capture of Fort Sumter

Battle of Shiloh

Battle of Gettysburg

Capture of Atlanta

April 12, 1861

July 21, 1861

April 6-7, 1862

March 4, 1861

September 17, 1862

July 1-3, 1863

Lee surrendered to Grant at Appomattox

September 2, 1864

President Lincoln inaugurated

Battle of Bull Run

July 4, 1863

November 8, 1864

Battle of Antietam

Fall of Vicksburg

April 9, 1865

Abraham Lincoln reelected

1 During the war, the Union freed all slaves behind Confederate lines. After the war, the nation passed the Thirteenth Amendment to the Constitution ending slavery throughout the United States.

2 Slave states seceded from the Union after Lincoln's election because they felt the election revealed that they had become a powerless minority section.

3 Westward expansion created a crisis over slavery because Southern leaders feared that upsetting the balance of power in Congress would mean that the North could abolish slavery.

Collage Extension

Use the images and questions on page 293 to preview the unit and identify which aspects of the crisis they highlight.

Measuring Time

Explain to students that the first page of the timeline relates to Chapter 19 and the second page to Chapter 20.

Timeline Extension

Have students use the timeline to guide their reading. Ask them to copy the timeline into a notebook and then add information about each event as they read. Their notes might include the following details about each event:

- What happened?
- Who was involved?
- Where did it happen?
- Why was it important?

Explain that students can also use the timeline to review the unit. Have them identify the events that were turning points—events that marked a unique or important change of direction. For example, the election of Abraham Lincoln was a turning point in Chapter 19. In Chapter 20, the events of 1863 marked a turning point because they helped determine the outcome of the war.

T-6 Growth of the United States to 1853

T-17 Concept Web

Key Blacklines

Biography
Harriet Beecher Stowe

Primary Source
Frederick Douglass: The Dred Scott Decision

Pre-Reading Discussion

Have students complete each bulleted direction on page 294. Ask students what their preview of the chapter suggests about the crisis over slavery. Have students relate the divisions within the nation to their own experiences with disagreements. Encourage students to identify times when compromise was possible and times when it was not. Based on their own experiences, when is it easy to compromise? When is it difficult or even impossible to reach a compromise?

Chapter 19 THE SECTIONAL CRISIS

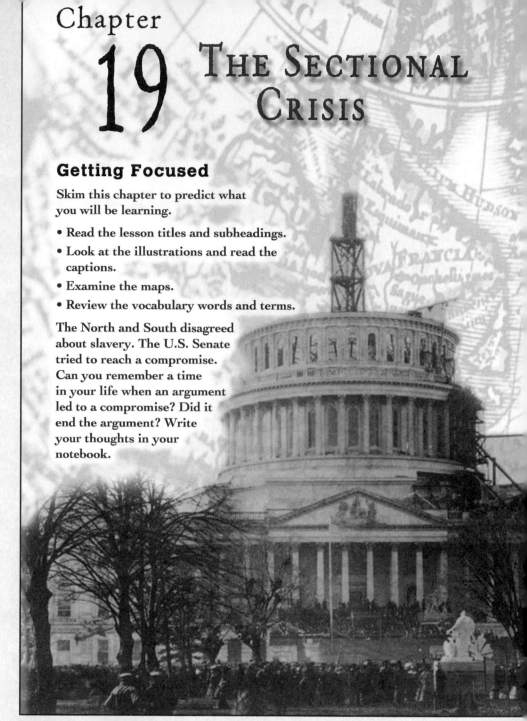

Getting Focused

Skim this chapter to predict what you will be learning.

- Read the lesson titles and subheadings.
- Look at the illustrations and read the captions.
- Examine the maps.
- Review the vocabulary words and terms.

The North and South disagreed about slavery. The U.S. Senate tried to reach a compromise. Can you remember a time in your life when an argument led to a compromise? Did it end the argument? Write your thoughts in your notebook.

Picturing History

The photograph on page 294 shows the inauguration of President Abraham Lincoln on March 4, 1861. Just a few weeks earlier, the seven Southern states that left the Union when Lincoln was elected held an inauguration for Jefferson Davis, the first president of the Confederate States of America.

Lincoln's inauguration took place at the east entrance to the unfinished Capitol building. Point out the riflemen perched in the windows. Ask students why the event may have required such tight security. Then have students describe what they see in the photograph, including its mood. How did this inauguration differ from Washington's, shown on page 172? How does it differ from modern inaugurations?

1 # Compromise of 1850

Thinking on Your Own

As you read, pay attention to the vocabulary words in the lesson. In your notebook, use each word in a sentence to show how it relates to the North-South conflict and to the compromise over slavery.

In 1849, Congress was deadlocked over the slavery issue. The people of California had asked to be admitted as a free territory. Congress responded along sectional lines. Northern congressmen favored the request. The South was solidly opposed. The result was a **sectional crisis** that threatened to destroy the Union.

The Crisis over California

To break the deadlock, President Zachary Taylor urged Californians to skip the **territorial stage**—one step in the process of a region being added to the United States. He asked them to organize a state government. No one questioned the right of a state to decide the issue of slavery for itself. They took Taylor's advice and drew up a state constitution. Taylor urged Congress to admit California as a free state.

Southern leaders in Congress were furious. They called Taylor a traitor to the South. They were afraid that all the new land acquired from Mexico would be carved up into free states. Upsetting the balance of power in Congress might mean that the North could abolish slavery. The most extreme proslavery men called for the South to **secede** from the Union.

> **focus your reading**
>
> Why were Southern congressmen angry at President Taylor?
>
> What was the Compromise of 1850?
>
> Why was the Fugitive Slave Law unpopular in the North?
>
> **vocabulary**
>
> sectional crisis
> territorial stage
> secede
> compromise
> Fugitive Slave Law
> personal liberty laws

The Sectional Crisis ⏐ 295

Lesson Vocabulary

Review the meaning of the word *crisis*. Then ask students what a *sectional crisis* is. (a condition or situation that threatens a nation by dividing it into two opposing sections) The *territorial stage* is a step in the process that results in a region becoming a state. How did the fact that California skipped the *territorial stage* lead to a *sectional crisis*?

Review the meaning of the words *secede* (to break away) and *compromise* (the settlement of a difference of opinion by having both sides agree to give up some demands). How did calls for the South to *secede* lead to a *compromise*?

Explain that the word *fugitive* refers to someone who is trying to escape justice or is being sought by officers of the law. The *Fugitive Slave Law* was supposed to help slave owners recover runaway slaves. *Personal liberty laws* were state laws that tried to prevent slave owners from reclaiming runaway slaves. Have students explain the connection between the two laws.

Lesson Summary

California skipped the territorial stage and asked to be admitted as a free state in 1850. Its admission would give the North control not only of the House of Representatives but also the Senate. Therefore some Southern leaders threatened to secede from the Union if California became a state. The Compromise of 1850 tried to resolve the impasse. California would be a free state and the rest of the land acquired from Mexico would be open to slavery. Congress also passed the Fugitive Slave Act, which made it easier for slave owners to recover runaway slaves.

Lesson Objective

Students will learn how the United States tried to avoid a crisis over slavery in 1850.

Focus Your Reading Answers

1 Southern congressmen were angry at President Taylor because he urged Californians to skip the territorial stage and organize a state government. They drew up a state constitution that banned slavery.

2 The Compromise of 1850 admitted California as a free state, organized the rest of the land acquired from Mexico into territories with no restrictions on slavery, outlawed the buying and selling of slaves in Washington, D.C., and passed a new law to help owners recover their runaway slaves.

3 The Fugitive Slave Law was unpopular in the North because U.S. marshals were required to return runaway slaves to their owners.

Answers will vary but should include the gold rush, the value of California to the nation, and the search for a compromise on the territory's future.

Ask students to use the map on page 296 to answer the following questions:

- How many free states did the nation have before California entered the Union? (15)

- How many slave states did the nation have? (15)

- How did the admission of California upset the balance of power in Congress? (With California's admission, those who opposed slavery had a majority in the Senate.)

- Based on the map, how likely were Southerners to restore the balance of power in the Senate? (unlikely, as there was a potential for more free states than for slave states)

Encourage students to use the reading comprehension, vocabulary reinforcement, and interactive timeline activities on the student DVD.

The Compromise of 1850

Both sides looked for a way out. In January 1850, Senator Henry Clay of Kentucky proposed a **compromise**. His set of proposals gave the North and the South part of what each wanted. It included:

1 admitting California as a free state

2 organizing the remainder of the land acquired from Mexico as territories with no restrictions on slavery

3 outlawing the buying and selling of slaves in the District of Columbia

4 passing a new federal law to help slave owners recover runaway or fugitive slaves

The compromise also included two less important measures that settled Texas's boundary dispute with New Mexico and paid Texas's $10 million debt. Together, these proposals were known as the Compromise of 1850.

Henry Clay

Imagine that you and your friends are creating a documentary film about California in 1849. From what you have read so far, write the film's main idea in your notebook and suggest a title for the film. As you read, note facts to include in the film.

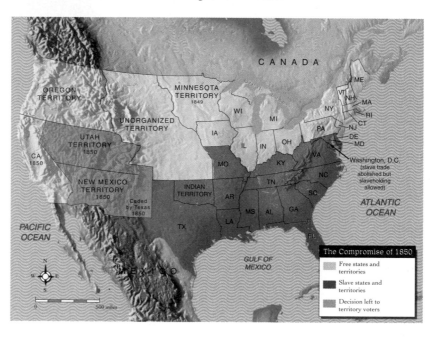

Henry Clay, shown on page 296, served his country in many capacities—as a congressman, senator, and vice president. He was known as the Great Compromiser. Have students find out how he earned that nickname.

Reaction to the Compromise of 1850

The Compromise of 1850 led to a heated debate in Congress. Henry Clay defended his proposals. John C. Calhoun of South Carolina opposed the compromise. He wanted the compromise to state that there would be no restrictions on slavery in any of the territories. Daniel Webster of Massachusetts urged both sections to compromise. Otherwise, he warned, the slavery issue would destroy the Union. The compromise finally passed in September 1850.

John C. Calhoun

Daniel Webster

The **Fugitive Slave Law** caused an uproar in the North. The law required U.S. marshals in the North to help catch runaway slaves. It filled free blacks throughout the North with terror. When an ex-slave named Shadrack was arrested in Boston, a mob broke into the jail. They freed Shadrack and sent him to Canada. Nine northern states passed **personal liberty laws** that prevented local officials from capturing ex-slaves.

The Compromise of 1850 settled the slavery issue in Congress. It did not remove it from the minds of the people.

CAUTION!!
COLORED PEOPLE
OF BOSTON, ONE & ALL,

You are hereby respectfully CAUTIONED and advised, to avoid conversing with the

Watchmen and Police Officers of Boston,

For since the recent ORDER OF THE MAYOR & ALDERMEN, they are empowered to act as

KIDNAPPERS
AND
Slave Catchers,

And they have already been actually employed in KIDNAPPING, CATCHING, AND KEEPING SLAVES. Therefore, if you value your LIBERTY, and the *Welfare of the Fugitives* among you, *Shun* them in every possible manner, as so many *HOUNDS* on the track of the most unfortunate of your race.

Keep a Sharp Look Out for
KIDNAPPERS, and have
TOP EYE open.
APRIL 24, 1851.

Northern abolitionists posted signs to warn freed slaves of the Fugitive Slave Law.

The Sectional Crisis 297

Putting It All Together

For the South, the main effects of the Compromise of 1850 renewed hope that slavery would be permitted in land acquired from Mexico, other than California. The South also won federal recognition of the rights of slave owners under the Fugitive Slave Act. For the North, the main effect was discomfort over the government's enforcement of the Fugitive Slave Act.

Eliza and her child being chased when she tried to escape

In 1852, Harriet Beecher Stowe published *Uncle Tom's Cabin*, a novel that described the evils of slavery. The novel told the story of a fictitious slave family. For the first time slave life was explained in human terms. It sold one million copies in its first two years and was turned into a play. The issue of slavery was on the minds of many and could not be avoided by Congress for long.

Harriet Beecher Stowe

In 1854, Boston abolitionists tried to rescue Anthony Burns, a runaway slave from Virginia. They were turned away by marshals after breaking down the courthouse door. The next day Burns was put on a ship and returned to Virginia.

Anthony Burns and Thomas Sims

Putting It All Together

Create a concept map in your notebook with "Compromise of 1850" in the middle circle. Add circles on the right and left, one for "North" and one for "South." Discuss the effects of the compromise for each section and list them in smaller circles under "North" and "South."

Picturing History

Anthony Burns was the second fugitive slave captured in Boston. He was arrested in 1854, three years after Thomas Sims was returned to slavery. (see page 297) Burns was twenty when he was arrested and held without bail at the request of his owner. After Burns's conviction, an estimated 50,000 citizens lined the streets of Boston to watch Burns walk in shackles toward the waterfront and a waiting ship. An African-American church in the city raised $1,300 to purchase Burns's freedom, but the marshals would not let the owner accept the money. They wanted to use Burns to set an example. To what extent did their efforts to punish him backfire? How did seeing young people like Burns or Sims in shackles make slavery personal? How did such sights prompt some people to feel they had a responsibility to take action?

Kansas and Nebraska

Thinking on Your Own

Look over the Focus Your Reading questions. As you read the lesson, take notes on how free-soilers may have reacted to Douglas's bill. How might the bill have affected their attitudes toward political parties? Discuss your notes with a partner. Write your thoughts in your notebook.

In 1854, a new crisis erupted over slavery. As before, the issue involved slavery in the territories. Senator Stephen A. Douglas of Illinois introduced a bill to create the Kansas and Nebraska Territories. Organizing that area for settlement would benefit Chicago, Douglas's hometown. This time, Northern antislavery people were angry. Once again, the issue threatened to tear the Union apart.

focus your reading

Why did Senator Douglas's bill open Kansas and Nebraska to slavery?

Who opposed the Kansas-Nebraska bill?

What impact did the Kansas-Nebraska Act have on the political parties?

vocabulary

popular sovereignty

free-soilers

Kansas-Nebraska Act

The Kansas-Nebraska Bill

Senator Douglas proposed to carve the Kansas and Nebraska Territories out of the northern part of the Louisiana Purchase. The Missouri Compromise already had outlawed slavery there. Douglas needed Southern votes in Congress for his bill. He also knew that no Southern congressman would vote to admit free territories. So he agreed to open these territories to slavery if the people there voted for it. He called this the principle of **popular sovereignty**.

Douglas knew that most of the settlers in Kansas and Nebraska would be farmers from free states. They would vote against slavery when the issue came to a vote.

Stephen A. Douglas introduced the Kansas-Nebraska Bill in 1854.

Lesson Vocabulary

The term *popular sovereignty* literally means "rule by the people." Senator Stephen A. Douglas used the term to describe the right of the people in a territory to decide whether they wanted slavery or not.

Remind students that a *bill* is a proposed law. A *bill* becomes a law after it has been passed by both houses of Congress and signed by the president. The *Kansas-Nebraska Act* created two states from the northern part of the Louisiana Purchase. Both would be open to slavery if people there voted for it.

Free-soilers were people who opposed the expansion of slavery to the territories.

Picturing History

Stephen A. Douglas shown at the bottom of page 299, believed that his principle of popular sovereignty would keep the issue of slavery from tearing apart the nation. Ask students why they think it had the opposite effect.

Lesson Summary

In 1854, Americans faced a new crisis over slavery. The Kansas-Nebraska Act let territories decide whether or not they wanted to allow slavery. The act outraged many Northerners who believed that the Missouri Compromise had already excluded slavery from the area. The law divided the Whig party, as Northern Whigs denounced the law and Southern Whigs supported it. In the summer of 1854, a new party emerged—the Republican Party. In 1856, the Republicans nominated John C. Frémont as their candidate for president. He carried 11 states, all in the North.

Lesson Objective

Students will learn how the Kansas-Nebraska Act led to new political turmoil over the issue of slavery in the territories.

Focus Your Reading Answers

1 Senator Douglas's bill opened Kansas and Nebraska to slavery because it allowed popular sovereignty—or the right for settlers to decide the issue of slavery for themselves.

2 People known as free-soilers opposed the Kansas-Nebraska bill.

3 The Kansas-Nebraska Act resulted in the collapse of the Whig Party; many Northern Democrats also left their party in protest.

Stop and Think

Answers will vary, but students should give at least three reasons in support of their argument.

Map Extension

Ask students to use the map on page 300 to answer the following questions:

- Which territories were not open to slavery after the Compromise of 1850? (Minnesota Territory, the Unorganized Territory, and Oregon Territory)

- Which territories were not open to slavery after the Kansas-Nebraska Act of 1854? (Minnesota, Washington, and Oregon Territories)

- Where and when did violence break out over the slavery issue? (Kansas Territory, after passage of the Kansas-Nebraska Act in 1854)

Reaction to the Kansas-Nebraska Bill

The Kansas-Nebraska bill created a furor. Its opponents held protest meetings throughout the North. They denounced the bill as "a gross violation of a sacred pledge [the Missouri Compromise], a criminal betrayal of precious rights." Douglas was surprised that so many people in the North opposed the bill.

Most of the bill's opponents were known as **free-soilers**. They did not intend to abolish slavery, but they strongly opposed its expansion westward. They did not think that free farmers could compete with slave labor.

stop and think

Senator Douglas's principle of popular sovereignty appeared to be fair to the North and the South. Was it really? In your notebook, argue either in favor of popular sovereignty or against it. Support your argument with three reasons.

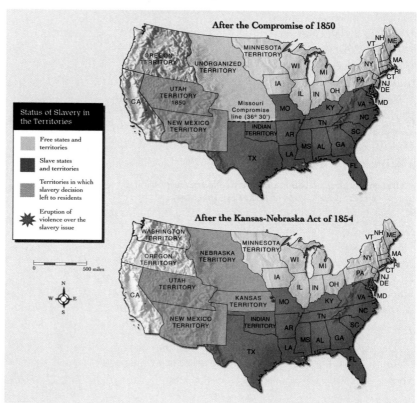

After the Compromise of 1850

Status of Slavery in the Territories

- Free states and territories
- Slave states and territories
- Territories in which slavery decision left to residents
- Eruption of violence over the slavery issue

0   500 miles

After the Kansas-Nebraska Act of 1854

Extension

Have students find out more about the violence that erupted in Kansas after passage of the Kansas-Nebraska Act. Ask them to research the event and share their findings with the class in a brief news report in the form a TV broadcast.

Proslavery people from Missouri, known as border ruffians, attacked free-soilers in Kansas.

Putting It All Together
The campaign slogans should reflect the reasons the Republican Party was founded. Remind students that slogans are brief, to the point, and memorable.

After three months of angry debate, the Kansas-Nebraska bill was passed by Congress. It became the **Kansas-Nebraska Act**. It was signed into law in May 1854.

A Time of Political Upheaval

The Kansas-Nebraska Act tore the Whig Party apart. Northern or "Conscience" Whigs denounced it. Southern or "Cotton" Whigs supported it. The party soon collapsed. Many northern Democrats also left their party in protest.

In the summer of 1854, a new anti-Nebraska party had emerged. It was called the Republican Party. That fall, it ran candidates for the House of Representatives. In 1856, the Republicans nominated John C. Frémont as their candidate for president. Although defeated by Democrat James Buchanan, Frémont carried eleven northern states. Most of Buchanan's votes came from the South. The slavery question again had divided the nation along sectional lines.

Putting It All Together

Imagine that you have joined the new Republican Party in the summer of 1854. After researching the founding of the party, design a campaign slogan for the party.

The Sectional Crisis 301

Picturing History

Ask students to study the drawing on page 301. What does it suggest about the violence in Kansas after passage of the Kansas-Nebraska Act? Who are the attackers? (proslavery people from Missouri) How does the artist portray them? (He shows them shooting people on the street.) How does the picture explain why people in the 1850s referred to the territory as "bleeding Kansas"? (Blood is being shed as a result of the violence.)

1 According to Douglas, the Kansas-Nebraska bill rests upon the principle of self-government.

2 Douglas thinks that slavery will not expand to the two territories because their climate and crops are not suited to slave labor.

3 Parker opposes the bill on moral grounds. He views slavery as immoral.

Extension

In 1858, Stephen A. Douglas campaigned for reelection to the Senate. His opponent was Abraham Lincoln. The two men engaged in a series of formal political debates. Among the issues they addressed was Douglas's idea of popular sovereignty. Have students work with a partner to find one of the debates online and reenact part of it for the class. Although Lincoln lost the election, the debates helped him become a national figure.

Read a Primary Source

The Kansas-Nebraska Debate

In January 1854, Senator Stephen A. Douglas introduced the Kansas-Nebraska bill. To attract southern support, Douglas agreed to let the people in these new territories vote on whether to allow slavery. That, in effect, repealed the Missouri Compromise.

reading for understanding

What principle does the Kansas-Nebraska bill rest upon, according to Douglas?

Why does Douglas think slavery will not expand to these territories?

On what grounds does Theodore Parker oppose the bill?

Senator Stephen A. Douglas Supports the Bill

In the following letter to a newspaper in February 1854, Senator Stephen A. Douglas defended his bill.

❝The [Kansas-Nebraska] bill rests upon . . . the great fundamental principle of self-government. . . . It does not propose to legislate slavery into the Territories, nor out of the Territories. . . . The bill, therefore, does not introduce slavery; does not revive it; does not establish it; does not contain any clause designed to produce that result. . . . All candid men who understand the subject admit that the laws of climate, and production, and of physical geography . . . have excluded slavery from that country. . . . Mr. Badger of North Carolina [declared] . . . that he and his southern friends did not expect that slavery would go there; that the climate and productions were not adapted to slave labor . . . but they insisted upon [the right of the settlers to vote for or against it] as a matter of principle, and of principle alone.❞

—From Robert W. Johannsen, ed., *The Letters of Stephen A. Douglas.*

Theodore Parker Opposes the Bill

Theodore Parker, a Congregational minister in Boston, spoke out against the bill on February 12, 1854. The following is an excerpt from his sermon.

❝So the question is, shall we let Slavery into the two great territories Kansas and Nebraska? . . . Shall men work with poor industrial tools, or with good ones? Shall they have the varied industry of New England and the North, or the Slave labor of Virginia and Carolina? Shall their land be worth five dollars and eight cents an acre, as in South Carolina, or thirty dollars and a half as in Connecticut? Shall the people all be comfortable, engaged in honest work . . . or shall a part be the poorest of the world that a few may be idle and rich?

"It is a question of political morality. Shall the Government be a commonwealth where all are citizens, or an aristocracy where man owns his brother man?❞

—From *The Nebraska Question. Some Thoughts upon Freedom in America*, by Theodore Parker.

302

Picturing History

On May 22, 1856, a member of the House of Representatives entered the Senate and beat a senator over the head with a cane until he lost consciousness. The picture on page 303 shows this violence.

Representative Preston Brooks was outraged by a speech Charles Sumner gave a few days earlier, particularly his remarks about one of Brooks's relatives—Senator Andrew Butler of South Carolina. So Brooks entered the Senate and hit Sumner in the head with a metal-topped cane. Overnight, both men became heroes in their respective regions. What did the violence suggest about the deep divisions within the nation? Why did many Americans see it as a troubling sign for the nation's future?

3 National Crisis

Thinking on Your Own

Read the Focus Your Reading questions. Make three columns in your notebook with the headings "Dred Scott," "John Brown," and "Abraham Lincoln." As you read the lesson, take notes about how each person was involved in a national crisis.

In 1856, civil war broke out in Kansas. Settlers from free and slave states chose sides on the slavery issue. Proslavery men set fire to Lawrence, Kansas, a free-soil town. In response, a free-soil fanatic named John Brown killed five proslavery settlers.

In May 1856, the violence spread to Washington, D.C. There, Senator Charles Sumner of Massachusetts gave a speech entitled "The Crime Against Kansas." He was attacked and beaten on the floor of the Senate by Congressman Preston Brooks of South Carolina.

focus your reading

Why did the slave Dred Scott claim to be a free person?

Why did John Brown raid the federal arsenal?

Why was the South shocked by Abraham Lincoln's election?

vocabulary

chief justice

annals

federal arsenal

uprising

Rep. Brooks attacks Senator Sumner in 1856.

303

Lesson Vocabulary

Explain each vocabulary term.

A *chief justice* is the judge who presides over a supreme court.

The word *annals* refers to events in the history of a nation.

An *arsenal* is a place where guns and other weapons are stored. Ask students to describe a *federal arsenal*. (a place where the federal government stores its guns and other weapons) Ask students to identify synonyms for the word *uprising*. (revolution, revolt, mutiny, rebellion)

Lesson Summary

Between 1854 and 1860, the issue of slavery increasingly divided Americans. In 1857, Chief Justice Roger B. Taney wrote that Congress could not exclude slavery from any territory. Abolitionists were outraged. In 1859, an abolitionist named John Brown led a raid on a federal arsenal to steal weapons for a slave uprising. Soon after Abraham Lincoln, a Republican, was elected president in 1860, seven Southern states left the Union.

Lesson Objective

Students will learn how divisions over slavery increasingly divided the nation and ultimately led seven states to leave the Union.

Focus Your Reading Answers

1 Dred Scott claimed to be a free person because his owner had taken him to live in Illinois, and later, Wisconsin Territory. Illinois was a free state and Wisconsin a free territory.

2 John Brown raided the federal arsenal to get weapons to arm slaves for an uprising.

3 The South was shocked by Lincoln's election because their only hope of maintaining their power in the federal government was to elect a proslavery president. Instead, Republicans, who opposed the expansion of slavery, won the election.

Stop and Think

In completing the three columns, students should indicate:

- What happened?
- When did it happen?
- Why did it happen?
- What were the consequences of the event?

Picturing History

The pictures on page 304 show Dred Scott, his wife Harriet, and their daughters Eliza and Lizzie. Ask students what the pictures suggest about Dred Scott and his family.

The Dred Scott Decision

In March 1857, the Supreme Court ruled on the slavery issue in the Dred Scott case. Dred Scott, a slave, sued for his freedom because his owner had once taken him to live in Illinois and then to Wisconsin Territory. He claimed that residence in a free state and a free territory made him a free person.

The Supreme Court ruled against Scott. The decision, written by **Chief Justice** Roger B. Taney, said that Scott was still a slave. It also ruled that Scott should not have gone to court, as slaves had no legal rights. Finally, the Supreme Court struck down the Missouri Compromise. It ruled that Congress had no right to exclude slavery from any territory.

The Dred Scott decision drove another wedge between the North and the South. The South applauded it. Republican leaders in the North called the decision "the greatest crime in the **annals** of the republic."

In 1858, the decision was the focus of a senatorial debate in Illinois between Senator Stephen A. Douglas and Abraham Lincoln. Douglas, who defended the decision, defeated Lincoln and won reelection to the Senate. Although he lost the election, Lincoln's opposition to the court decision made him a leader of the Republican Party.

The Dred Scott case highlighted the issue of slavery.

stop and think

Add new information to the three columns you made for Thinking on Your Own. Update the columns as you continue reading.

Extension

Have students find out more about how Americans responded to the Dred Scott decision. Ask students to present their findings to the class by using the Student Presentation Builder on the student DVD.

John Brown's capture after his raid on Harper's Ferry

John Brown's Raid

In October 1859, the South got shocking news. John Brown, a militant abolitionist, and eighteen men had attacked the **federal arsenal** at Harper's Ferry, Virginia. They tried to get weapons from the arsenal to arm the slaves for a massive **uprising**. A slave uprising was the slave owners' worst nightmare. They also were shocked when northern abolitionists made a hero of John Brown. Although Brown was captured, tried, and hanged, the raid drove the wedge between the sections ever deeper.

John Brown being led to his execution

Picturing History

Have students compare and contrast the two views of John Brown on page 305. The one at the top of the page is a drawing of his capture, and the one at the bottom of the page is a photograph of Brown being led to his execution. What do the two pictures suggest about the man? What do they suggest about the way many Americans viewed him?

Extension

The headlines listed below covered the front page of the *New York Herald* on the morning of October 18, 1859. Ask students to use the account in their text and additional research to determine what parts of the headlines were true and what parts were rumors. What fears do the headlines reveal? What do they suggest about the depth of the divisions over slavery?

- Fearful and Exciting Intelligence

- Negro Insurrection at Harpers Ferry

- Extensive Negro Conspiracy in Virginia and Maryland

- Seizure of the United States Arsenal by the Insurrectionists

- Arms Taken and Sent into the Interior

- The Bridge Fortified and Defended by Cannon

- Trains Fired into and Stopped — Several Persons Killed — Telegraph Wires Cut — Contributions Levied on the Citizens

Putting It All Together

The South did not have a majority in the House of Representatives or the Senate. The election of a Republican president left the region without a base of power in the federal government. The 1860 election had four candidates running for president. This split the votes four ways.

In 1858, Lincoln and Douglas debated at Knox College in Galesburg, Illinois.

The Election of 1860

In 1860, the future looked bleak for the South. Three new western states (California, 1850; Minnesota, 1858; and Oregon, 1859) gave the North a majority in the Senate.

Free-soil states also had a majority in the House of Representatives. The South's only hope was to elect a proslavery president. In November 1860, that hope also vanished.

The election of 1860 was a four-way contest. Stephen A. Douglas ran as the Democratic Party candidate. The Southern Democrats chose John C. Breckinridge from Kentucky as their proslavery candidate. The Republicans nominated Abraham Lincoln. The Constitutional Union Party, made up of former Whigs, made John C. Bell their candidate.

Abraham Lincoln

The Republicans won the election. Lincoln got more electoral votes than all of his opponents combined. He also received more popular votes than any other candidate. With Lincoln's victory, the South had become a powerless, minority section. That winter, seven slave states seceded from the Union.

Putting It All Together

Design a triangle with "Loss of Southern Power" in the middle. On each point of the triangle include one fact that indicates how the South lost power.

Biography

Dred Scott (1795?–1858)

Dred Scott was born a slave in Virginia about 1795. His owner, Peter Blow, was a cotton planter. Scott probably worked as a field slave. In 1830, the Blow family quit farming and moved to St. Louis, Missouri, taking Dred Scott with them.

As a "city slave," he was hired to work for wages. Scott worked on steamboats traveling up and down the Mississippi River. In 1832, Peter Blow sold Scott to John Emerson, a U.S. Army doctor.

In 1833, the army sent Dr. Emerson to Fort Armstrong in northern Illinois. He took Scott along. Three years later, Emerson was assigned to Fort Snelling in Wisconsin Territory. During the seven years Scott spent there, he married Harriet Robinson, a slave woman. In 1840, Emerson

was transferred to a fort in Florida. On his way south, he left Dred and Harriet Scott with his wife Irene in St. Louis. When Dr. Emerson died in 1843, Scott became Irene Emerson's slave.

In 1846, Dred Scott sued in a Missouri court for his freedom. He claimed that living on free soil in Illinois and Wisconsin Territory made him a free man. He also asked for the freedom of his wife and their children, Eliza and Lizzie. When the state court ruled in their favor, Irene Emerson appealed to the Missouri Supreme Court. It reversed the lower court's decision. In the meantime, she had sold the Scotts to her brother, John Sanford of New York.

Dred Scott sued again. As residents of two states were now involved, he could sue in a federal court. He lost again. With the help of a St. Louis lawyer, Roswell M. Field, Scott appealed to the United States Supreme Court.

On March 6, 1857, the Supreme Court ruled that the Scotts were still slaves. It also said that as a slave, Dred Scott had no right to sue in the courts. It held, finally, that Congress had no right to ban slavery from a territory.

Although they lost in the courts, the Scotts did gain their freedom. Irene Emerson married Calvin Chaffee, an antislavery congressman who objected to his wife owning slaves. In May 1858, Emerson gave the Scott family to Taylor Blow, the son of Peter Blow, Dred Scott's first owner. He freed the Scotts and helped them pay their legal bills.

Dred Scott died a free man on September 17, 1858.

307

Bio Facts

- Born about 1795 in Southhampton, Virginia. His original name was Sam.

- Worked as a farmhand, handyman, and stevedore.

- Moved with his owner, Peter Blow, to Huntsville, Alabama, in 1830, and later to St. Louis, Missouri.

- Was purchased after Blow's death in 1831 by John Emerson, a surgeon in the U.S. Army, and brought to Illinois.

- In the spring of 1836, accompanied Emerson to a fort in the Wisconsin Territory. There Scott met and married Harriet Robinson, a slave owned by a local justice of the peace. Ownership of Harriet was transferred to Emerson.

- After Emerson's death in 1843, tried to purchase his freedom from the widow, Irene Emerson, but she refused.

- Obtained the assistance of two attorneys who helped him sue for his freedom in county court. Lost the case on a technicality, but the verdict was set aside.

- In 1847, won a second trial on the grounds that he was free upon entering a free state.

- By 1848 had changed his name to Dred Scott.

- Received financial backing and legal representation from the sons of Peter Blow, Irene Emerson's brother John Sanford, and her second husband, Calvin Chaffee.

Biography Extension

The Supreme Court ruled that Scott was African American and that African Americans could not be citizens according to the Constitution. Have students find out more about the consequences of that ruling. How did it affect free African Americans? How did it affect the future of slavery not only in the territories but also in free states? Ask students to present their findings to the class by using the Student Presentation Builder on the student DVD.

Bio Facts, continued

- After the U.S. Supreme Court ruled against Scott in 1857, Irene Emerson sold the Scotts to the sons of Peter Blow, who freed the family. Scott died nine months later in 1858.

Chapter Review

1 Lists will vary but should reflect the strong feelings both for and against slavery. Students should also take into account the importance of obeying the law.

2 Covers will vary but should show an understanding of the way Stowe tried to portray slaves as human beings with names, faces, and identities.

3 Boxes will vary, but the definitions and the sentences should reflect the way the term is used in the chapter.

Chapter Summary

In 1849, to avoid the slavery issue, California skipped the **territorial stage** and asked to be admitted as a free state. Congress was facing a **sectional crisis** over the issue. Some Southern leaders even threatened to **secede** from the Union. The matter was settled when the **Compromise** of 1850 admitted California as a free state. The rest of the land acquired from Mexico would become slave territories. **Fugitive Slave Laws** made it easier for slave owners to recover runaway slaves, while **personal liberty laws** prevented officials from capturing ex-slaves.

The **Kansas-Nebraska Act** let territories decide the slavery issue for themselves. This was called the principle of **popular sovereignty**. Northern **free-soilers** were angry, as the Missouri Compromise had already excluded slavery from that area.

During the next four years, the issue of slavery split the nation apart. In 1857, **Chief Justice** Tanney wrote that Congress could not exclude slavery from any territory. Antislavery people in the North believed it was "the greatest crime in the **annals** of the republic." The South was alarmed in 1859 by John Brown's raid on a **federal arsenal**. He tried to steal weapons for a slave **uprising**. Realizing they were now a minority, seven Southern states seceded from the Union before Lincoln took office.

Chapter Review

1 Imagine that you are a Kansas farmer. Your neighbor wants you to join a raid against settlers in another county who favor slavery. Make a list of reasons for and against the raid.

2 In her novel *Uncle Tom's Cabin*, Harriet Beecher Stowe described how slaves suffered. If you could design a cover for the book, what pictures would you include?

3 Choose six vocabulary words from the chapter. Draw a box for each word and divide it into three parts. In the parts, write 1) the word, 2) its definition, and 3) a sentence that includes the word.

Novel Connections

Below is a list of books that relate to the time period covered in this chapter. The numbers in parentheses indicate the related Thematic Strands of the National Council for the Social Studies (NCSS).

Linda Jacobs Altman. *Slavery and Abolition in American History.* (*In America* series) Enslow, 1999. (III)

Katherine Ayres. *North by Night: A Story of the Underground Railroad.* Yearling, 2000. (III, IV, V)

Clinton Cox. *Fiery Vision: The Life and Death of John Brown.* Scholastic, 1997. (IV, X)

Jeri Chase Ferris. *Demanding Justice: A Story About Mary Ann Shadd Cary.* Carolrhoda Books/Lerner, 2003. (II, III, VI)

Dennis Brindell Fradin. *Bound for the North Star: True Stories of Fugitive Slaves.* Clarion, 2000. (I, V, VI)

Gena K. Gorrell and Rosemary Brown. *North Star to Freedom: The Story of the Underground Railroad.* Delacorte, 1997. (III)

George Sullivan. *Picturing Lincoln.* Clarion, 2000. (III)

Skill Builder

Reading a Presidential Election Map

In a presidential election in the United States, electoral votes are awarded by state. The party that has the most votes in each state wins all of its electoral votes. The results usually are presented on a map by showing the states, in different colors, that each party won.

The map below shows the results of the presidential election of 1860. The key in the center identifies the color used for each party and its candidate. It also indicates the total number of electoral and popular votes that each candidate received. The circle graphs at the bottom show the percentage of the total votes that each candidate won.

Use the map to answer the following questions:

1 Which party carried the largest number of free states?

2 Which candidate won the most slave states?

3 Which parties carried at least one slave state?

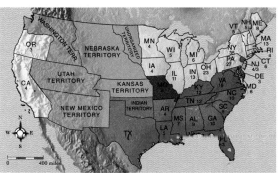

Election of 1860

	Electoral Votes	Popular Votes
Lincoln (Republican)	180	1,865,593
Breckinridge (S. Democratic)	72	848,356
Bell (Constitutional Union)	39	592,906
Douglas (Democratic)	12	1,382,713

Voter Turnout 81.2%

Electoral Votes 12.9%, 4%, 23.7%, 59.4%

Popular Votes 29.5%, 39.8%, 12.6%, 18.1%

1 The Republicans carried the largest number of free states.

2 Breckinridge won the most slave states.

3 The Constitutional Union, the Southern Democratic, and the Democratic parties carried at least one slave state.

Map Extension

Ask students to use both the map and the graphs to answer the following questions:

- Which candidate came in second in the popular vote but last in the electoral vote? (Douglas)

- If the Democratic, Southern Democratic, and Constitutional Union parties had united, which party would have won the election? (Republicans, because Lincoln had more votes in the electoral college than the other three candidates combined)

- Why might a Southerner conclude, after studying the map, that the South had become a sectional minority? (Lincoln easily won the election without carrying a single Southern state.)

Classroom Discussion

Discuss with students some of the broader topics covered in this chapter.

- Explain the Compromise of 1850. How did it benefit each region of the country? How did it benefit the nation as a whole? What problems did it leave unsolved?

- In what ways did slavery isolate the people of the South from the rest of the country? How had life there grown in different directions from life in the North and West?

- Why do you think that *Uncle Tom's Cabin* became such a bestseller? How do you think it influenced the way Americans viewed slavery?

- Why did Stephen Douglas's idea of popular sovereignty fail to resolve the issue of slavery? How did it deepen the division within the nation?

Chapter Summary

Refer to page 324 in the student book for a summary of Chapter 20.

Related Transparencies

T-3 The Civil War

T-18 T-Chart

Key Blacklines

Biography
Clara Barton

Primary Source
Home Front Patriotism

Picturing History

The Civil War was the first war that Americans photographed. Photographers like Mathew Brady took pictures of nearly every phase of the war. For the first time, Americans could see for themselves what war was like. No photographer was able to take pictures of battles, because cameras were unable to capture movement. As a result, Civil War photos show portraits of people, camp life, battle preparations, and the aftermaths of battles. What does the photo on page 310 suggest about the war? How does it differ from paintings of the Revolutionary War, the War of 1812, or the Mexican War?

Chapter 20 THE CIVIL WAR

Getting Focused

Skim this chapter to predict what you will be learning.

- Read the lesson titles and subheadings.
- Look at the illustrations and read the captions.
- Examine the maps.
- Review the vocabulary words and terms.

During the Civil War, the Union lost more than 360,000 soldiers. The Confederacy lost approximately 260,000 soldiers. Why do you think the mortality rate was so high? Write your prediction in your notebook.

Pre-Reading Discussion

Have students complete each bulleted direction on page 310. Then focus on the title of the chapter. What is a *civil war*? How is it like other wars? How does it differ from other wars? Have students record their ideas and then check them as they read the chapter.

DVD Extension

Encourage students to use the reading comprehension, vocabulary reinforcement, and interactive timeline activities on the student DVD.

The War Begins

Thinking on Your Own

Use the Glossary at the end of the book to find the definitions of the vocabulary words. Then work with a partner to use the words in sentences. Each sentence should show the meaning of the word.

In the spring of 1861, seven states in the Lower South (Alabama, Florida, Georgia, Louisiana, Mississippi, South Carolina, and Texas) seceded from the Union. They formed the new Confederate States of America, with Jefferson Davis as their president. Eight slave states in the Upper South remained in the Union. They waited to see what Abraham Lincoln would do about the slavery issue.

Abraham Lincoln

focus your reading

Why did Union troops try to capture Richmond?

Why did the North lose the Battle of Bull Run?

What did Ulysses S. Grant do in 1862?

vocabulary

inaugural address

militia

gunboats

blockade

In his **inaugural address** on March 4, 1861, President Lincoln said that he would not abolish slavery, but he would defend the Union. He stated that he would not strike the first blow: "In your hands, my dissatisfied fellow-countrymen, and not in mine, is the momentous issue of civil war." Lincoln was afraid the states of the Upper South would secede if the North attacked first.

Jefferson Davis

The Civil War 311

Lesson Vocabulary

Remind students that the word *address* has more than one meaning. In this lesson, it refers to a speech. The word *inaugural* refers to a ceremony marking the beginning of a president's term in office. What then is an *inaugural address*? (a speech to mark the beginning of a president's term in office) Have students follow a similar procedure to define the term *gunboat*. (a small boat carrying mounted guns)

Review the meaning of the word *militia*. (a group of civilian soldiers enrolled for military service) Point out the word *block* in *blockade*. Ask students to use that word to figure out what a *blockade* is. (a military effort to block off or close a place in order to control who may enter or exit)

The War Begins

On the morning of April 12, 1861, Jefferson Davis's government took action. Confederate guns fired on Fort Sumter, a federal fort in the harbor of Charleston, South Carolina. The fort surrendered the next afternoon. With the outbreak of war, Virginia, North Carolina, Tennessee, and Arkansas decided to join the Confederacy. Four border states—Missouri, Kentucky,

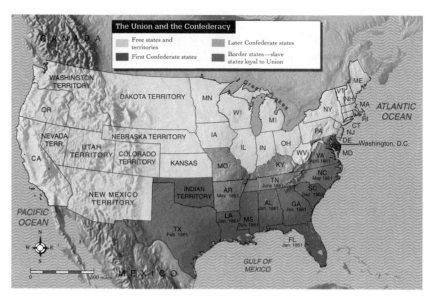

The Union and the Confederacy

Free states and territories
First Confederate states
Later Confederate states
Border states—slave states loyal to Union

Maryland, and Delaware—remained in the Union. The western counties of Virginia also remained loyal. In 1863, they joined the Union as the state of West Virginia.

The Battle of Bull Run

President Lincoln prepared the North for war. He asked the loyal states for 75,000 state **militia** troops. That spring trainloads of volunteers arrived in Washington, D.C. They were young men with little or no military experience. Lincoln hoped they could end the war quickly by capturing the Confederate capital of Richmond, Virginia.

Union soldier

Picturing History

Have students look at the pictures on page 311. A few weeks before Lincoln's inauguration, Jefferson Davis became the first president of the Confederate States of America. The two men had much in common.

Lincoln was born in 1809 in Hardin County, Kentucky, and Davis, in 1808 in what is now Todd County, Kentucky. Both men fought in the Black Hawk War. Both also served in Congress. Ask students to find out more about not only their similarities but also their differences. Have them present their findings to the class by using the Student Presentation Builder on the student DVD.

Map Extension

Ask students to use the map on page 312 to answer the following questions:

- Which state was the first to join the Confederacy? (South Carolina in December 1860)

- Which state was the last to join the Confederacy? (Tennessee in June 1861)

- Which side did the territories support during the Civil War? (Union)

- What do Missouri, Kentucky, Maryland, and Delaware have in common? (All were slave states that remained loyal to the Union.)

Picturing History

Have students study the photo on page 312 and describe what they see. What do portraits like this one or the one on page 313 tell viewers about the men who fought in the Civil War?

Extension

During the Civil War, taking pictures was complicated and time-consuming. Two photographers were needed—one to mix the chemicals and the other to position and focus the camera. Ask students to find out more about Civil War photography by researching the techniques used in the 1860s and the work of such noted Civil War photographers as Mathew Brady and Thomas Nast. Have students present their findings to the class by using the Student Presentation Builder on the student DVD.

The Battle
of Bull Run

Picturing History

The painting at the top of page 313 shows the Battle of Bull Run. Early in the battle, Confederate General P.G.T. Beauregard could not tell whether the soldiers moving onto the battlefield were Confederate reinforcements or Union soldiers. Only when he saw the Confederate flag at the head of the column did he realize that they were his own men.

Union commander Irvin McDowell also had difficulty figuring out what was happening. He described the Union retreat as a "rout" that "soon degenerated into a panic." Ask students how the artist captures that confusion in his painting.

"Forward to Richmond!" Northern newspapers cried out. Marching toward Richmond, the Union troops were defeated by a Confederate army at the Battle of Bull Run on July 21, 1861. This battle was a shock to the North and taught them a serious lesson. They would need a large and well-trained army to defeat the Confederates.

The War in 1862

In 1862, Union troops again tried to take Richmond. This time, Lincoln sent General George B. McClellan with a well-trained army. A Confederate army led by General Robert E. Lee stopped McClellan's advance. After a seven-day battle, the Union army withdrew. The North had again failed to defeat the Confederates.

In September, General Lee tried to invade the North. He attacked Union troops in Maryland. This battle was the bloodiest one-day battle of the Civil War. At the Battle of Antietam, 4,800 men were killed and 18,550 were wounded.

Union forces did, however, make headway in the West. A Union army captured the state capital at Nashville. General Ulysses S. Grant captured two Confederate forts in Tennessee. The Confederates finally stopped Grant at the bloody Battle of

Confederate
soldier

stop and think

With a partner, role-play a conversation between two people in Virginia. One supports the Confederates; the other is loyal to the Union. They know they soon may face each other as enemy soldiers. Write the most important facts for each side in your notebook.

Stop and Think
Discussions will vary but should include not only facts from this lesson but also background information from Chapter 19.

The Civil War | 313

Picturing History

The average Confederate soldier was a young man in his early 20s. The same was true of the average Union soldier. If students could meet the Confederate soldier shown on page 313 or the Union soldier on page 312, what questions might they ask him? Compile those questions into a list and help students use them to guide their reading of the chapter or to choose various research projects.

The War in the East:
1861–1863
✳ Battle site
← Union forces
← Confederate forces

Map Extension

Ask students to use the map on page 314 to answer the following questions:

- The Seven Days Battles were a series of small battles. Near what city were they fought? (Richmond)

- Was McClellan's advance from Washington, D.C., to the places where the Seven Days Battles were fought by land or by water? (by water)

- What two generals met at Antietam? (McClellan and Lee)

Putting It All Together

Battles in 1862 include USS *Monitor* vs. CSS *Virginia* (March), Battle of Shiloh (April), Seven Days Battles (June), Second Battle of Bull Run (August), Battle of Antietam (September).

Shiloh on April 6 and 7, 1862. By the end of that summer, Union **gunboats** also controlled most of the Mississippi River.

Along the Atlantic and Gulf coasts, the Union navy blockaded Confederate ports. It wanted to keep the Confederates from getting supplies from Europe. The Confederate navy sent out an ironclad ship, the CSS *Virginia*, to break the **blockade**. The USS *Monitor*, a Union ironclad, attacked the *Virginia*. This first battle ever of ironclad ships ended in a draw.

The CSS *Virginia* and the USS *Monitor* battle along the coast of Virginia.

Putting It All Together

Several battles took place in 1862. Create a timeline that places them in the sequence in which they occurred. Use the map if you need help.

Picturing History

The 1862 battle between the USS *Monitor* and the CSS *Virginia*, formerly the USS *Merrimack*, is the first battle in history between two ironclad ships. Have students imagine that they are standing on one of the wooden ships in the background. Ask them to describe the battle. What would they see? hear? smell?

Extension

Ask students to find out more about the battle or the two ironclads. Have them share their findings with the class by creating a poster that summarizes what they have learned.

Biography

Kate Cumming (1835–1909)

Kate Cumming was born in Scotland in 1835. Her family moved to Canada and then to Mobile, Alabama, when she was a child. When the Civil War began, she was twenty-six and a true daughter of the Confederacy. At first she kept busy helping to put on concerts and plays to raise money for the troops. The advancing Union army soon brought that happy and patriotic time to an end.

In April 1862, Union and Confederate troops clashed near the village of Shiloh, Tennessee. The Confederate army needed volunteers to care for the wounded. On April 7, 1862, Cumming and other women from Mobile left for Corinth, Mississippi, where the Confederates had set up a hospital. The town was twenty miles south of the battlefield at Shiloh.

Cumming was totally unprepared for what she found at Corinth. "Nothing that I had ever heard or read had given me the faintest idea of the horrors witnessed here," she wrote in her diary. "Gray-haired men—men in the pride of manhood—beardless boys—Federals and all, mutilated in every imaginable way, lying on the floor . . . so close together it was almost impossible to walk without stepping on them."

Cumming was surprised at how quickly she got used to the horror. "The foul air from this mass of human beings at first made me giddy and sick, but I soon got over it. We have to walk, and when we give the men anything, kneel in blood and water; but we think nothing of it at all." Nearly all of the seriously wounded men died within a day or two. The nurses bathed the men's wounds, gave them bread and crackers, and helped them write their last letters home.

For the next three years, Cumming journeyed from one Confederate hospital to another. After leaving the hospital at Corinth, she wrote in her diary, "I shall ever look back on these two months with sincere gratification, and feel that I have lived for something."

At the end of the war, Cumming returned to Mobile, Alabama. There she published her diary, *A Journal of Hospital Life in the Confederate Army* (1866). Afterward she moved to Birmingham, Alabama, where she taught school and music. Cumming never married. She died in June 1909 at the age of seventy-four.

Bio Facts

- Born in Edinburgh, Scotland, in 1835.
- As a child, moved with her family to Montreal, Canada, and then to Mobile, Alabama.
- Volunteered as a nurse after hearing a minister encourage women to volunteer in Confederate hospitals.
- Against the wishes of her family, left for the front lines in April 1862 with 40 other women.
- Arrived outside the battlefield of Shiloh while the fighting was still in progress.
- Remained in nearby Corinth and Okalona, Mississippi, until June 1862.
- Spent two months in Mobile, Alabama, and then volunteered to work at Newsome Hospital, in Chattanooga, Tennessee, and remained in Tennessee until the summer of 1863, when the city was evacuated.
- From 1863 to the end of the war, worked in mobile field hospitals in Georgia.
- In 1866, published *A Journal of Hospital Life in the Confederate Army*.
- Taught school after moving to Birmingham, Alabama, with her father in 1874.
- Died in Birmingham in 1909.

Biography Extension

About 2,000 women in the North and South served as volunteer nurses in military hospitals during the Civil War. Only a few recorded their experiences. Among them were not only Kate Cumming but also Louisa May Alcott, Jane Stuart Woolsey, and Katharine Prescott Wormeley.

In the North, Dorothea Dix and Clara Barton led national efforts to organize a nursing corps to care for the sick and the wounded. Dix recruited women to serve as nurses for the Army Medical Bureau. Clara Barton did similar work but was independent of the military. Barton simply loaded a wagon with medical supplies and brought them to the front lines, giving help wherever it was needed. After the war, she helped create an American branch of the International Red Cross.

Have students find out more about Dorothea Dix and Clara Barton. How were their experiences similar to those of Kate Cumming? What differences seem most striking? Have students share their findings by creating a poster that highlights the work of the woman they researched.

Reading for Understanding

1 The horrors of war changed the way these men viewed it.

2 They were both "heartily sick" of war because of the suffering of the dying and wounded.

3 Neither seemed to feel much zeal or patriotism after their experiences in battle.

Extension

In 1862, photographer Mathew Brady shocked Northerners by displaying photographs of battlefield corpses at Antietam. His exhibition marked the first time visitors witnessed the horrors of war. The *New York Times* said that Brady had brought "home to us the terrible reality and earnestness of war." Ask students to find out why Brady thought it was important for people to see what war was like. Would the soldiers quoted in the two primary sources agree?

Read a Primary Source

Front-Line Realities

Young men marched off to the Civil War glad to do their patriotic duty. Many soldiers changed their view of the war after fighting on the battlefield. The following excerpts are examples of Confederate and Union soldiers whose perspectives had changed.

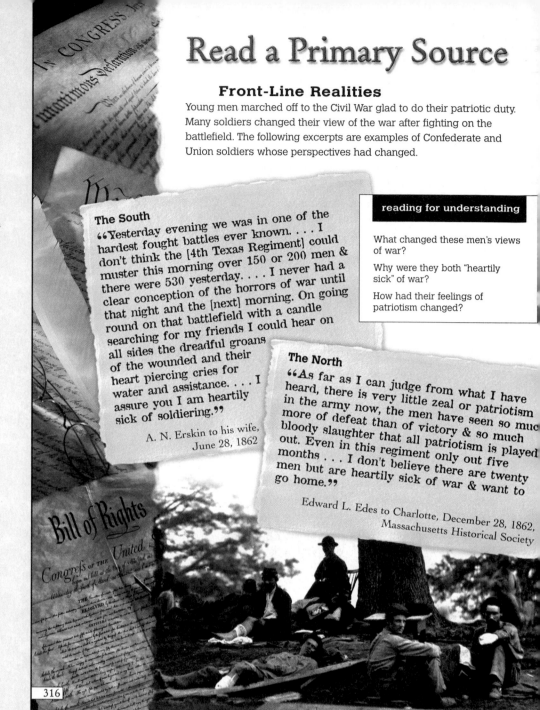

The South

"Yesterday evening we was in one of the hardest fought battles ever known. . . . I don't think the [4th Texas Regiment] could muster this morning over 150 or 200 men & there were 530 yesterday. . . . I never had a clear conception of the horrors of war until that night and the [next] morning. On going round on that battlefield with a candle searching for my friends I could hear on all sides the dreadful groans of the wounded and their heart piercing cries for water and assistance. . . . I assure you I am heartily sick of soldiering."

A. N. Erskin to his wife, June 28, 1862

The North

"As far as I can judge from what I have heard, there is very little zeal or patriotism in the army now, the men have seen so much more of defeat than of victory & so much bloody slaughter that all patriotism is played out. Even in this regiment only out five months . . . I don't believe there are twenty men but are heartily sick of war & want to go home."

Edward L. Edes to Charlotte, December 28, 1862, Massachusetts Historical Society

reading for understanding

What changed these men's views of war?

Why were they both "heartily sick" of war?

How had their feelings of patriotism changed?

316

Picturing History

The drawing on page 317 shows an iron foundry—a place where iron is melted and molded into various items. Have students study the drawing and describe what they see. What do students think it would be like to work in a foundry? How difficult is the work? How much strength does it seem to require? Ask students to brainstorm a list of war-related goods that might be produced at foundries like the one shown in the picture.

Behind the Lines

Thinking on Your Own

Read the paragraph below. What is a thimble? How much blood can one hold? In your notebook, explain the meaning of the quotation about a thimble.

In 1861 most Americans thought the Civil War would be over quickly. "A lady's **thimble** will hold all the blood that will be shed," one Confederate said. The fighting in 1862 shattered that hope. Leaders on both sides realized that the war would be long and costly. The question was which side would best be able to fight such a war.

> ### focus your reading
>
> What advantages did the North have in the Civil War?
>
> What were the South's main advantages?
>
> How did women contribute to the war effort?
>
> ### vocabulary
>
> thimble   enlisted
>
> stalemate   military hospitals

Iron foundries added to the strength of the North.

Lesson Vocabulary

Explain that a *thimble* is a small metal cap that protects one's finger while sewing. If possible, bring one to class and demonstrate how it is used.

To *enlist* is to join, sign up, or enroll. Thousands of Northerners and Southerners *enlisted* in the army. Those who were injured in battle were often sent to *military hospitals*. Ask students how a *military hospital* differs from other hospitals.

In chess, a *stalemate* is a situation in which a player has no legal moves. In a conflict, it is a situation in which neither side can win.

Lesson Summary

By 1862, leaders on both sides realized that the war would be long and costly. In a long drawn-out war, the North had the advantage of more factories, railroads, banks, and men of military age.

The South also had advantages. Many believed that having slaves to do the work at home would free more white men to fight. Also, Southerners understood that they did not have to defeat the North to win. They just had to wear down the North. So many men enlisted in the two armies that both sides had a shortage of workers on the home front. As a result, many women took on new jobs and assumed new roles.

Lesson Objective

Students will learn how the home front contributed to the war effort.

Focus Your Reading Answers

1 The North's advantages included more factories, railroads, banks, and men of military age.

2 The South's main advantages were that they had slaves who could keep the plantations running while their owners went to war. Southerners were also fighting on familiar ground, and they did not have to defeat the North to win—just wear it down.

3 Women contributed to the war effort by farming, working in factories, and taking over men's jobs in government and schools. They also volunteered to collect food and medical supplies. Some served as nurses, spies, and even soldiers.

Stop and Think

Answers will vary but Northern soldiers might point out that they had more equipment, men, railroads, banks, and factories. Southern soldiers might note that they were fighting in familiar territory, often in places close to home. They could also rely on slaves to take over their work while they were at war. Soldiers on both sides might note what they were fighting for—an end to slavery, the defense of their state, or a way of life.

Railroads allowed goods to be shipped to Northern troops.

The Two Sides Compared

In a drawn-out war, the North had several advantages. It had more factories and workshops to produce weapons and clothing for its soldiers. The Union army was very well supplied. The North also had more railroads, banks, and men of military age—those between eighteen and forty-five years old. The Confederate army never had enough tents, blankets, and uniforms. Its soldiers often fought barefoot.

stop and think

With a partner, play the roles of a Northern and a Southern soldier. What arguments could each of you make that your side probably would win the war? Add to your list from the Stop and Think in Lesson 1.

The South also had advantages. It could free more white men to fight because it had slaves to do part of the work at home or on the farm. As most of the battles took place in the South, the Confederates fought on familiar ground. They knew back roads that did not appear on the Union army's maps. They also knew that they did not have to defeat the North to win. The Confederate states could gain their independence by wearing down the North. A **stalemate**, or draw, was as good as a victory.

The War on the Home Front

The war reached into every home in America. More than 1.5 million husbands, fathers, and sons joined the Union army. Over 1 million **enlisted** on the Confederate side. This created a labor shortage that made life difficult for those at home. In 1863, the South also faced a shortage of food. Women in Richmond rioted in the streets to get bread for their families.

Picturing History

Ask students to compare the information provided in the photograph at the top of page 318 with the map of railroads in the United States on page 277. What advantages did the North have over the South in terms of rail lines? How important were railroads to the war effort?

Women supported the war by working in factories.

The war gave women new roles. They had to plant and harvest crops as well as take care of the home. "I met more women driving teams [of horses] on the road and saw more at work in the fields than men," wrote a traveler in Iowa in 1862. More women in the North worked in factories than before. In the South, planters' wives had to learn how to raise cotton. Southern women also took over men's jobs in government and as schoolteachers.

Women also contributed directly to the war effort. Many volunteered their time to collect food and medical supplies. Women served as nurses in **military hospitals**. Dozens of women also served as Union and Confederate spies and scouts. Several hundred fought on battlefields disguised as men.

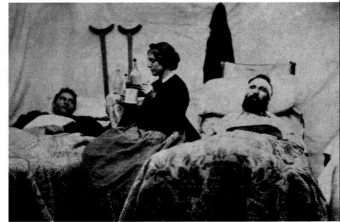

Nurses played an important role at military hospitals.

Putting It All Together

Create a T-chart. Label it "Women during the Civil War." Under the label write "Advantages" on one side and "Disadvantages" on the other side. List what you think belongs under each heading. Compare your ideas with a partner's.

Putting It All Together
Advantages
- new occupations such as nurses and factory workers
- became school teachers and held government jobs
- volunteered to collect food and medical supplies

Disadvantages
- heavy work on plantations and farms
- fought for food in the South to feed families

Extension

Dr. Mary Edwards Walker is the only woman awarded the Congressional Medal of Honor for her service in any war. She was also one of the first women to become a physician in the United States. When she tried to enlist as a Union physician, she was turned down but allowed to serve as a nurse on a voluntary basis. She eventually worked as a field surgeon near the Union front lines before being appointed an assistant surgeon to the 52nd Ohio Infantry. She also spent four months in a Confederate prison in Richmond.

Have students find out more about her life and her work. What do her experiences suggest about the difficulties women encountered in serving their country during the Civil War? What do her experiences suggest about the opportunities they had? Have students share their findings by creating a poster that highlights Walker's contributions to the war effort.

Turning of the Tide

Lesson Summary

The turning point in the Civil War came in 1863. It was the year that Abraham Lincoln issued the Emancipation Proclamation. It was also the year the Union stopped a Confederate advance into the North at Gettysburg. And 1863 was also the year that the Union took complete control of the Mississippi River after defeating the Confederates at Vicksburg. The war dragged on, however, until 1865, when Confederate General Robert E. Lee surrendered to Union General Ulysses S. Grant on April 9.

Lesson Objective

Students will learn why 1863 was a turning point in the war and how the events of that year contributed to the Union victory.

Focus Your Reading Answers

1 Lincoln emancipated the slaves because he did not think he could win the war without doing so. In his view, freeing the slaves would drain the Confederates' labor supply and also provide the Union Army with additional troops.

2 The Battle of Gettysburg was a turning point because it stopped a Confederate advance into Union territory. The Battle of Vicksburg gave the North complete control of the Mississippi River.

3 Sherman's victory in Atlanta affected the 1864 presidential election by restoring confidence in Lincoln and his ability to win the war.

Thinking on Your Own

Read over the Focus Your Reading questions. Make predictions about what this lesson will include. Write three predictions in your notebook.

For the North, the year 1863 was a turning point in the Civil War. Until then the North had fought to save the Union, not to **abolish** slavery. On January 1, 1863, President Abraham Lincoln added a new purpose—freeing the slaves. Union generals also had more success on the battlefield that year. The war was far from over, but the North could finally see a ray of hope.

Ulysses S. Grant

focus your reading

Why did President Lincoln emancipate the slaves?

Why are the battles at Gettysburg and Vicksburg called turning points?

How did Sherman's victory affect the 1864 presidential election?

vocabulary

abolish

Emancipation Proclamation

ratified

surrendered

Emancipating the Slaves

In 1862, President Lincoln concluded that the North could not win the war without freeing the slaves. Promising them freedom would encourage slaves to leave their plantations. That would drain the Confederates' labor supply. It also would provide the Union army with additional troops.

On January 1, 1863, Lincoln issued the **Emancipation Proclamation**. It freed all the slaves behind the Confederate lines. Many slaves living in the border states would not be freed until the Thirteenth Amendment was **ratified** in 1865. The proclamation helped the Union cause. Slaves who were freed as the troops advanced into the South did join the Union army. More than 130,000 black soldiers and sailors fought on the Union side.

Lesson Vocabulary

Remind students that the word *abolish* means "to end." *Abolitionists* wanted to *abolish*, or end, slavery. To *emancipate* means "to set free." A *proclamation* is an official order. Ask students how the *Emancipation Proclamation* abolished slavery in the Confederacy.

To *ratify* means "to approve." Before slavery could be *abolished* throughout the nation, the states had to *ratify* the Thirteenth Amendment. The Civil War ended when the South *surrendered*, or admitted defeat and laid down their weapons.

Robert
E. Lee

Gettysburg and Vicksburg

In the summer of 1863, General Robert E. Lee led a Confederate army north from Richmond. Union armies tried to stop him at Fredericksburg and Chancellorsville, Virginia. They lost both battles. Then Lee invaded Pennsylvania hoping to break the North's will to fight. General George G. Meade met him at the town of Gettysburg with a Union army. After three days of hard fighting, from July 1 to 3, Meade stopped the Confederates, who suffered heavy losses. But Meade let Lee's army get away.

The next day, General Ulysses S. Grant won a victory at Vicksburg. The Confederates had approximately 30,000 troops dug in on the bluffs overlooking the Mississippi River at Vicksburg, Mississippi. Every Union attack had failed. Grant finally surrounded the city, cutting it off from its supply lines. On July 4, 1863, the Confederates surrendered. Vicksburg fell, giving the North control of the Mississippi River.

President Lincoln liked Grant. He won battles. In the fall of 1863, Lincoln placed Grant in command of the Union army in Virginia. General Grant, he believed, could defeat General Lee.

The Final Year

Despite the victories of 1863, the war dragged on. The North grew weary. In 1864, Abraham Lincoln doubted that he would be reelected. The Democrats ran General George B. McClellan as their candidate.

The War in the West: 1862–1863

Battle site
Union forces
Confederate forces

St. Louis
Ohio R.
Louisville
KENTUCKY
Paducah
Ft. Donelson
Pea Ridge
Ft. Henry
Nashville
Murfreesboro
ARKANSAS
TENNESSEE
Memphis
Shiloh
Chattanooga
Little Rock
Corinth
A.S. Johnston
MISSISSIPPI
ALABAMA
Vicksburg
Jackson
LOUISIANA
Montgomery
Port Hudson
Mobile
FLORIDA
New Orleans
Farragut

0   100 miles

The Civil War   321

Picturing History

Like Ulysses S. Grant, Robert E. Lee, pictured at the top of page 321, was a graduate of West Point and a veteran of the war with Mexico. Have students find out why Lee gave up his commission in the United States army to join the Confederacy, even though he had freed his own slaves long before the war began and strongly opposed secession. Have students create a poster that explains why Lee made the choices he did.

Map Extension

Ask students to use the map on page 321 to answer the following questions:

- Who led the Confederate army at Shiloh? (A.S. Johnston)

- Where did Grant lead his army after his victory at Shiloh? (Corinth and then south along the Mississippi to Vicksburg)

- How did Grant's victory at Vicksburg cut the Confederacy in half? (By controlling the Mississippi, he cut off Texas, Arkansas, and Louisiana from the rest of the South.)

- In which state were most of the battles in the West fought? (Tennessee)

Picturing History

Ulysses S. Grant, pictured on page 320, was the general who won a costly victory at Shiloh in April 1862. Grant lost 13,000 of the 63,000 men that he commanded there. When critics suggested that Lincoln replace Grant, the president disagreed. "I can't spare this man—he fights." Ask students what Lincoln's comment suggests about Grant. What does it suggest about Lincoln?

Extension

At the start of the war, the Union army turned away thousands of African Americans eager to volunteer. Lincoln needed the support of whites in the border states and they were strongly opposed to arming African Americans. When the president changed his stand, an estimated 120,000 blacks volunteered. Most fought in all-black units under white officers. Blacks also aided the Confederacy. As early as 1861, Tennessee allowed free blacks to join its state militia. Have students find out more about the record of African Americans in both armies during the Civil War. Have them present their findings to the class by using the Student Presentation Builder on the student DVD.

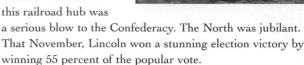

Picturing History

On July 1, 2, and 3, 1863, more men fought and more men died at Gettysburg than at any battle before or since on North American soil. Ask students to study the painting at the top of page 322. How does the artist view the battle?

Stop and Think

Arguments will vary but should reflect the debate over the future of slavery during the Civil War.

Picturing History

Ask students to describe what they see in the photograph on page 322. What does the photograph suggest about the devastation of war? How is it similar to the account below of the Battle of Gettysburg written by Alfred Carpenter? How does it differ?

Extension

A few weeks after the battle, Alfred P. Carpenter, an eighteen-year-old soldier who fought at Gettysburg, wrote a letter describing his experiences. Although wounded twice at Gettysburg, Carpenter survived the battle, but not the war. He died in 1864. Ask students to compare and contrast his view of the fighting with the images shown in the painting.

They promised to negotiate a peace if McClellan won. The Union cause was in trouble.

In early September 1864, General William T. Sherman captured Atlanta. The loss of this railroad hub was a serious blow to the Confederacy. The North was jubilant. That November, Lincoln won a stunning election victory by winning 55 percent of the popular vote.

After taking Atlanta, Sherman's army marched through Georgia to the sea. It destroyed everything in its path including railroads, farms, and cities. Then Sherman turned north to take the war into the Carolinas.

General Grant spent the year 1864 hammering away at Robert E. Lee's army. He fought Lee at the Battles of The Wilderness and at Cold Harbor. He lost more men than Lee, but that did not matter. Grant was determined to wear Lee down. In early April 1865, Grant's army finally surrounded Lee's troops in western Virginia. On April 9, 1865, General Lee **surrendered** to General Grant at Appomattox Court House, Virginia. The Civil War had finally ended, and the United States of America had been preserved.

Roughly 46,000 Americans died at the Battle of Gettysburg, a turning point in the war.

Atlanta was destroyed during Sherman's march through Georgia.

stop and think

Imagine that you are an advisor to President Lincoln. You want to persuade him to free the slaves. What arguments would you make? Discuss your arguments with a partner and include them in your notebook.

322 | Chapter 20

Extension, continued

"The hill must be held at all hazards. We advanced down the slope . . . with a rush and a yell we went. Bullets whistled past us; shells screeched over us; canister and grape fell about us; comrade after comrade dropped from the ranks; but on the line went. No one took a second look at his fallen companion. We had no time to weep.

"We were nearing the Rebel line, and in a moment more we would have been at it hand to hand . . . forward we went again and the Rebs were routed, and the bloody field was in our possession; but at what a cost!

"The ground was strewed with dead and dying, whose groans and prayers and cries for help and water rent the air. The sun had gone down and in the darkness we hurried, stumbled over the field in search of our fallen companions, and when the living were cared for, laid ourselves down on the ground to gain a little rest, for the morrow bid far more stern and bloody work, the living sleeping side by side with the dead. . . . Scarcely a hundred men were left out of the three hundred and more who were with us in the morning. Two out of every three had fallen."

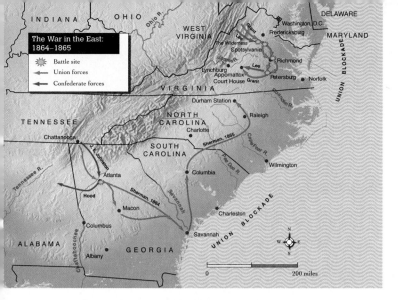

The War in the East: 1864–1865

- ☀ Battle site
- ← Union forces
- ← Confederate forces

The Civil War was the bloodiest and most costly war in American history. It took the lives of 360,000 Union and 260,000 Confederate soldiers at a cost of $20 billion. The South lost two-thirds of its wealth in property, half of its farm equipment, and two-fifths of its livestock. It paid dearly for its attempt to secede from the Union.

Robert E. Lee surrendered to Ulysses S. Grant at Appomattox Court House, Virginia.

Putting It All Together

Work with a partner. Imagine that the date is late April 1865, and you have just attended a funeral of a Union soldier. Explain to a partner what might have been said in the funeral sermon. Have your partner explain what might have been said at a Confederate soldier's funeral. Include information about the battles where they fought and other information you learned about the Civil War.

The Civil War 323

Picturing History

General Grant later wrote of his meeting with Lee at Appomattox Court House:

"I said that his army should lay down their arms. I said further I took it that most of the men in the ranks were small farmers. It was doubtful whether they would be able to put in a crop without the aid of the horses they were then riding. Therefore, I instructed the officers to let every man of the Confederate army who claimed to own a horse or mule to take the animal to his home. . . .

"General Lee remarked that his men had been living for some days on parched corn. I told him to send to Appomattox where he could have all the provisions wanted."

Grant had discussed the terms of surrender with Lincoln. What do the terms suggest about the way Grant and Lincoln regarded Southerners? What do the terms suggest about the way they viewed the future?

Chapter Review

1 Articles will vary but should show that students have consulted several sources. A good news story answers the following questions:

- Who was involved?

- What happened?

- Where did it happen?

- When did it happen?

- Why did it happen?

2 The editorials will vary but each should begin by expressing the writer's point of view and then providing information or arguments in support of that opinion.

3 Answers will vary but students should provide additional details to deepen or enrich their answers.

Chapter Summary

In 1861, eleven slave states seceded from the Union. President Abraham Lincoln said in his **inaugural address** that he would fight to preserve the Union. When the Confederates attacked Fort Sumter in South Carolina, Lincoln asked the loyal states for 75,000 **militia** troops. The Union army failed to capture the Confederate capital at Richmond, Virginia, in 1861 and again in 1862. More than a **thimble** of blood was shed.

Union **gunboats** gained control of most of the Mississippi River in 1862. The Union navy **blockaded** Southern ports. The Confederates tried to break the blockade. The attempt failed when the USS *Monitor* stopped the CSS *Virginia*.

Both the North and the South had their own advantages. However, the South believed that a **stalemate** was as good as a victory. The war created new roles for women, and many served as nurses in **military hospitals**. So many men **enlisted** in the two armies that a labor shortage existed at home.

The year 1863 was a turning point in the Civil War. President Lincoln's **Emancipation Proclamation** made it a war to free the slaves. Slavery, however, would not be **abolished** in all states until the Thirteenth Amendment was **ratified**.

Confederate General Robert E. Lee finally **surrendered** to General Ulysses S. Grant on April 9, 1865.

Chapter Review

1 Civil War armies brought supplies to their soldiers in horse-drawn wagons. Research the conditions of delivering these supplies and write a newspaper article about the Confederate supply wagons at Vicksburg.

2 Write an editorial for either a Union or Confederate newspaper that explains why your side won or lost the war. Include as many of the vocabulary words as you can.

3 Look over the Focus Your Reading questions. Choose one that you would like to answer in more detail. Find additional information about the question in a library or on a Web site.

Novel Connections

Below is a list of books that relate to the time period covered in this chapter. The numbers in parentheses indicate the related Thematic Strands of the National Council for the Social Studies (NCSS).

Catherine Clinton. *The Black Soldier: 1492 to the Present.* Houghton Mifflin, 2000. (II)

Wilma King. *Children of the Emancipation.* (Picture the American Past series) Millbrook, 2000. (V)

Jim Murphy. *The Journal of James Edmond Pease, a Civil War Union Soldier.* (*My Name Is America* series) Scholastic, 1998. (IV, V)

Gary Paulsen. *Soldier's Heart: A Novel of the Civil War.* Delacorte, 1998. (II, IV, V)

Carolyn Reeder. *Across the Lines.* Atheneum, 1998. (IV, V)

G. Clifton Wisler. *When Johnny Went Marching: Young Americans Fight the Civil War.* HarperCollins, 2001. (II, IV)

Karen Zeinert. *Those Courageous Women of the Civil War.* Milbrook, 1998. (II, V, X)

Skill Builder

Interpreting Multiple Graphs

Most graphs focus on one topic. However, sometimes multiple graphs are shown together.

The graphs below present advantages the Union had over the Confederacy. The topic of each is listed along the top of the graph. The values of each are presented in each graph.

Use the graph to answer the following questions:

1 In what area did the North have the greatest advantage?

2 In what area was the South most nearly equal?

3 How does the information in this graph help explain which side won the Civil War?

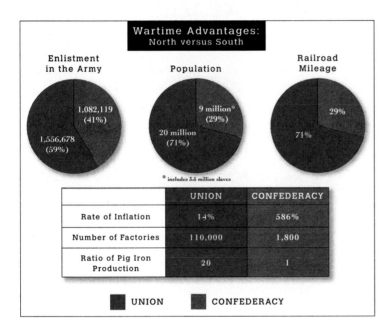

The Civil War 325

The Civil War 325

Skill Builder

1 The North had the greatest advantage over the South in the number of factories it had.

2 The South was nearly equal to the North in army enlistment.

3 The graphs and table show that the North had all of the wartime advantages over the South. The North had great advantage over the south in many areas: population, railroad mileage, rate of inflation, number of factories, and ratio of pig iron production.

Classroom Discussion

Discuss with students some of the broader topics covered in this chapter.

- Many Northerners came to believe that the chief aim of the war was to free the slaves. Did Lincoln agree? If not, what did he see as the purpose of the war?

- To what extent did the war change the role women played in American life?

- Why do you think the Civil War was fought in the South instead of in the North?

- Why was 1863 the turning point in the war?

- How is a civil war like other wars you have studied? In what ways is it unique?

- How does a nation recover from a civil war? How does it reunite a divided people?

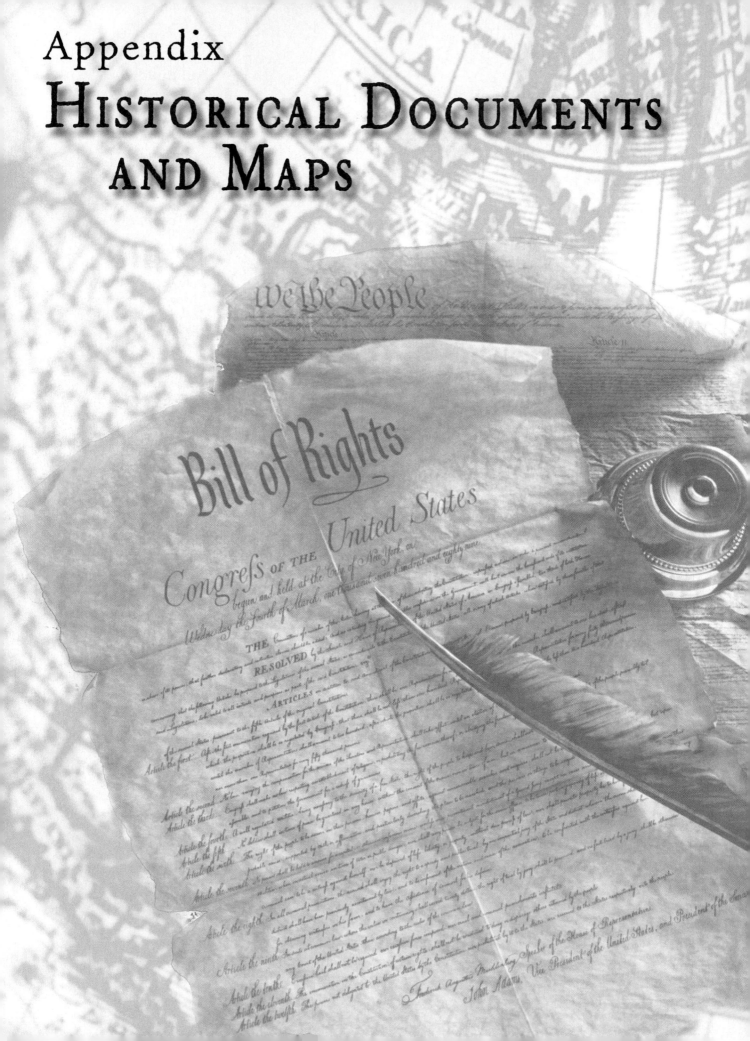

Appendix
Historical Documents and Maps

The Declaration of Independence

Action of Second Continental Congress, July 4, 1776

The unanimous Declaration of the thirteen United States of America

WHEN in the Course of human Events, it becomes necessary for one People to dissolve the Political Bands which have connected them with another, and to assume among the Powers of the Earth, the separate and equal Station to which the Laws of Nature and of Nature's God entitle them, a decent Respect to the Opinions of Mankind requires that they should declare the causes which impel them to the Separation.

WE hold these Truths to be self-evident, that all Men are created equal, that they are endowed by their Creator with certain unalienable Rights, that among these are Life, Liberty and the Pursuit of Happiness — That to secure these Rights, Governments are instituted among Men, deriving their just Powers from the Consent of the Governed, that whenever any Form of Government becomes destructive of these Ends, it is the Right of the People to alter or to abolish it, and to institute new Government, laying its Foundation on such Principles, and organizing its Powers in such Form, as to them shall seem most likely to effect their Safety and Happiness. Prudence, indeed, will dictate that Governments long established should not be changed for light and transient Causes; and accordingly all Experience hath shewn, that Mankind are more disposed to suffer, while Evils are sufferable, than to right themselves by abolishing the Forms to which they are accustomed. But when a long Train of Abuses and Usurpations, pursuing invariably the same Object, evinces a Design to reduce them under absolute Despotism, it is their Right, it is their Duty, to throw off such Government, and to provide new Guards for their future Security. Such has been the patient Sufferance of these Colonies; and such is now the Necessity which constrains them to alter their former Systems of Government. The History of the present King of Great- Britain is a History of repeated Injuries and Usurpations, all having in direct Object the Establishment of an absolute Tyranny over these States. To prove this, let Facts be submitted to a candid World.

HE has refused his Assent to Laws, the most wholesome and necessary for the public Good.

HE has forbidden his Governors to pass Laws of immediate and pressing Importance, unless suspended in their Operation till his Assent should be obtained; and when so suspended, he has utterly neglected to attend to them.

HE has refused to pass other Laws for the Accommodation of large Districts of People, unless those People would relinquish the Right of Representation in the Legislature, a Right inestimable to them, and formidable to Tyrants only.

HE has called together Legislative Bodies at Places unusual, uncomfortable, and distant from the Depository of their public Records, for the sole Purpose of fatiguing them into Compliance with his Measures.

HE has dissolved Representative Houses repeatedly, for opposing with manly Firmness his Invasions on the Rights of the People.

HE has refused for a long Time, after such Dissolutions, to cause others to be elected; whereby the Legislative Powers, incapable of the Annihilation, have returned to the People at large for their exercise; the State remaining in the mean time exposed to all the Dangers of Invasion from without, and the Convulsions within.

HE has endeavoured to prevent the Population of these States; for that Purpose obstructing the Laws for Naturalization of Foreigners; refusing to pass others to encourage their Migrations hither, and raising the Conditions of new Appropriations of Lands.

HE has obstructed the Administration of Justice, by refusing his Assent to Laws for establishing Judiciary Powers.

HE has made Judges dependent on his Will alone, for the Tenure of their Offices, and the Amount and Payment of their Salaries.

HE has erected a Multitude of new Offices, and sent hither Swarms of Officers to harrass our People, and eat out their Substance.

HE has kept among us, in Times of Peace, Standing Armies, without the consent of our Legislatures.

HE has affected to render the Military independent of and superior to the Civil Power.

HE has combined with others to subject us to a Jurisdiction foreign to our Constitution, and unacknowledged by our Laws; giving his Assent to their Acts of pretended Legislation:

FOR quartering large Bodies of Armed Troops among us;

FOR protecting them, by a mock Trial, from Punishment for any Murders which they should commit on the Inhabitants of these States:

FOR cutting off our Trade with all Parts of the World:

FOR imposing Taxes on us without our Consent:

FOR depriving us, in many Cases, of the Benefits of Trial by Jury:

FOR transporting us beyond Seas to be tried for pretended Offences:

FOR abolishing the free System of English Laws in a neighbouring Province, establishing therein an arbitrary Government, and enlarging its Boundaries, so as to render it at once an Example and fit Instrument for introducing the same absolute Rules into these Colonies:

FOR taking away our Charters, abolishing our most valuable Laws, and altering fundamentally the Forms of our Governments:

FOR suspending our own Legislatures, and declaring themselves invested with Power to legislate for us in all Cases whatsoever.

HE has abdicated Government here, by declaring us out of his Protection and waging War against us.

HE has plundered our Seas, ravaged our Coasts, burnt our Towns, and destroyed the Lives of our People.

HE is, at this Time, transporting large Armies of foreign Mercenaries to compleat the Works of Death, Desolation, and Tyranny, already begun with circumstances of Cruelty and Perfidy, scarcely paralleled in the most barbarous Ages, and totally unworthy the Head of a civilized Nation.

HE has constrained our fellow Citizens taken Captive on the high Seas to bear Arms against their Country, to become the Executioners of their Friends and Brethren, or to fall themselves by their Hands.

HE has excited domestic Insurrections amongst us, and has endeavoured to bring on the Inhabitants of our Frontiers, the merciless Indian Savages, whose known Rule of Warfare, is an undistinguished Destruction, of all Ages, Sexes and Conditions.

IN every stage of these Oppressions we have Petitioned for Redress in the most humble Terms: Our repeated Petitions have been answered only by repeated Injury. A Prince, whose Character is thus marked by every act which may define a Tyrant, is unfit to be the Ruler of a free People.

NOR have we been wanting in Attentions to our British Brethren. We have warned them from Time to Time of Attempts by their Legislature to extend an unwarrantable Jurisdiction over us. We have reminded them of the Circumstances of our Emigration and Settlement here. We have appealed to their native Justice and Magnanimity, and we have conjured them by the Ties of our common Kindred to disavow these Usurpations, which, would inevitably interrupt our Connections and Correspondence. They too have been deaf to the Voice of Justice and of Consanguinity. We must, therefore, acquiesce in the Necessity, which denounces our Separation, and hold them, as we hold the rest of Mankind, Enemies in War, in Peace, Friends.

WE, therefore, the Representatives of the UNITED STATES OF AMERICA, in GENERAL CONGRESS, Assembled, appealing to the Supreme Judge of the World for the Rectitude of our Intentions, do, in the Name, and by Authority of the good People of these Colonies, solemnly Publish and Declare, That these United Colonies are, and of Right ought to be, FREE AND INDEPENDENT STATES; that they are absolved from all Allegiance to the British Crown, and that all political Connection between them and the State of Great-Britain, is and ought to be totally dissolved; and that as FREE AND INDEPENDENT STATES, they have full Power to levy War, conclude Peace, contract Alliances, establish Commerce, and to do all other Acts and Things which INDEPENDENT STATES may of right do. And for the support of this Declaration, with a firm Reliance on the Protection of divine Providence, we mutually pledge to each other our Lives, our Fortunes, and our sacred Honor.

John Hancock	Charles Carroll	Geo. Taylor	Josiah Bartlett
Button Gwinnett	Of Carrollton	James Wilson	Wm. Whipple
Lyman Hall	George Wythe	Geo. Ross	Saml Adams
Geo Walton	Richard Henry Lee	Caesar Rodney	John Adams
Wm Hooper	Th Jefferson	Geo Read	Robt Treat Paine
Joseph Hewes	Benja Harrison	Tho M. Kean	Elbridge Gerry
John Penn	Thos Nelson Jr.	Wm Floyd	Step Hopkins
Edward Rutledge	Francis Lightfoot Lee	Phil. Livingston	William Ellery
Thos Heyward Junr.	Carter Braxton	Frans. Lewis	Roger Sherman
Thomas Lynch Junr.	Robt Morris	Lewis Morris	Samel Huntington
Arthur Middleton	Benjamin Rush	Richd. Stockton	Wm. Williams
Samuel Chase	Benja. Franklin	Jno Witherspoon	Oliver Wolcott
Wm. Paca	John Morton	Fras. Hopkinson	Matthew Thornton
Thos. Stone	Geo Clymer	John Hart	
	Jas. Smith	Abra Clark	

The United States Constitution

The pages that follow contain the original text of the United States Constitution. Sections that are no longer enforced have been crossed out. The spelling and punctuation of the document remain in their original format. The headings are not part of the original Constitution.

We the People of the United States, in Order to form a more perfect Union, establish Justice, insure domestic Tranquility, provide for the common defence, promote the general Welfare, and secure the Blessings of Liberty to ourselves and our Posterity, do ordain and establish this Constitution for the United States of America.

Article I
Legislative Branch

Section 1
Congress

All legislative Powers herein granted shall be vested in a Congress of the United States, which shall consist of a Senate and House of Representatives.

Section 2
House of Representatives

Clause 1: The House of Representatives shall be composed of Members chosen every second Year by the People of the several States, and the Electors in each State shall have the Qualifications requisite for Electors of the most numerous Branch of the State Legislature.

Clause 2: No Person shall be a Representative who shall not have attained to the Age of twenty five Years, and been seven Years a Citizen of the United States, and who shall not, when elected, be an Inhabitant of that State in which he shall be chosen.

Clause 3: Representatives and direct Taxes shall be apportioned among the several States which may be included within this Union, according to their respective Numbers, ~~which shall be determined by adding to the whole Number of free Persons, including those bound to Service for a Term of Years, and excluding Indians not taxed, three fifths of all other Persons.~~

The actual Enumeration shall be made within three Years after the first Meeting of the Congress of the United States, and within every subsequent Term of ten Years, in such Manner as they shall by Law direct.

The Number of Representatives shall not exceed one for every thirty Thousand, but each State shall have at Least one Representative; ~~and until such enumeration shall be made, the State of New Hampshire shall be entitled to chuse three, Massachusetts eight, Rhode-Island and Providence Plantations one, Connecticut five, New-York six, New Jersey four, Pennsylvania eight, Delaware one, Maryland six, Virginia ten, North Carolina five, South Carolina five, and Georgia three.~~

Clause 4: When vacancies happen in the Representation from any State, the Executive Authority thereof shall issue Writs of Election to fill such Vacancies.

Clause 5: The House of Representatives shall chuse their Speaker and other Officers; and shall have the sole Power of Impeachment.

Section 3
Senate

Clause 1: The Senate of the United States shall be composed of two Senators from each State, chosen by the Legislature thereof, for six Years; and each Senator shall have one Vote.

Clause 2: Immediately after they shall be assembled in Consequence of the first Election, they shall be divided as equally as may be into three Classes. The Seats of the Senators of the first Class shall be vacated at the Expiration of the second Year, of the second Class at the Expiration of the fourth Year, and of the third Class at the Expiration of the sixth Year, so that one third may be chosen every second Year; and if Vacancies happen by Resignation, or otherwise, during the Recess of the Legislature of any State, the Executive thereof may make temporary Appointments until the next Meeting of the Legislature, which shall then fill such Vacancies.

Clause 3: No Person shall be a Senator who shall not have attained to the Age of thirty Years, and been nine Years a Citizen of the United States, and who shall not, when elected, be an Inhabitant of that State for which he shall be chosen.

Clause 4: The Vice President of the United States shall be President of the Senate, but shall have no Vote, unless they be equally divided.

Clause 5: The Senate shall chuse their other Officers, and also a President pro tempore, in the Absence of the Vice President, or when he shall exercise the Office of President of the United States.

Clause 6: The Senate shall have the sole Power to try all Impeachments. When sitting for that Purpose, they shall be on Oath or Affirmation. When the President of the United States is tried, the Chief Justice shall preside: And no Person shall be convicted without the Concurrence of two thirds of the Members present.

Clause 7: Judgment in Cases of Impeachment shall not extend further than to removal from Office, and disqualification to hold and enjoy any Office of honor, Trust or Profit under the United States: but the Party convicted shall nevertheless be liable and subject to Indictment, Trial, Judgment and Punishment, according to Law.

Section 4
Elections and Meetings

Clause 1: The Times, Places and Manner of holding Elections for Senators and Representatives, shall be prescribed in each State by the Legislature thereof; but the Congress may at any time by Law make or alter such Regulations, except as to the Places of chusing Senators.

Clause 2: The Congress shall assemble at least once in every Year, and such Meeting shall be on the first Monday in December, unless they shall by Law appoint a different Day.

Section 5
Rules of Procedure

Clause 1: Each House shall be the Judge of the Elections, Returns and Qualifications of its own Members, and a Majority of each shall constitute a Quorum to do Business; but a smaller Number may adjourn from day to day, and may be authorized to compel the Attendance of absent Members, in such Manner, and under such Penalties as each House may provide.

Clause 2: Each House may determine the Rules of its Proceedings, punish its Members for disorderly Behaviour, and, with the Concurrence of two thirds, expel a Member.

Clause 3: Each House shall keep a Journal of its Proceedings, and from time to time publish the same, excepting such Parts as may in their Judgment require Secrecy; and the Yeas and

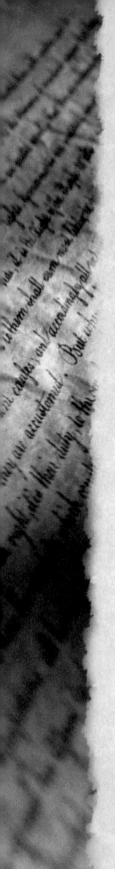

Nays of the Members of either House on any question shall, at the Desire of one fifth of those Present, be entered on the Journal.

Clause 4: Neither House, during the Session of Congress, shall, without the Consent of the other, adjourn for more than three days, nor to any other Place than that in which the two Houses shall be sitting.

Section 6
Privileges and Restrictions

Clause 1: The Senators and Representatives shall receive a Compensation for their Services, to be ascertained by Law, and paid out of the Treasury of the United States. They shall in all Cases, except Treason, Felony and Breach of the Peace, be privileged from Arrest during their Attendance at the Session of their respective Houses, and in going to and returning from the same; and for any Speech or Debate in either House, they shall not be questioned in any other Place.

Clause 2: No Senator or Representative shall, during the Time for which he was elected, be appointed to any civil Office under the Authority of the United States, which shall have been created, or the Emoluments whereof shall have been encreased during such time; and no Person holding any Office under the United States, shall be a Member of either House during his Continuance in Office.

Section 7
How Bills Become Laws

Clause 1: All Bills for raising Revenue shall originate in the House of Representatives; but the Senate may propose or concur with Amendments as on other Bills.

Clause 2: Every Bill which shall have passed the House of Representatives and the Senate, shall, before it become a Law, be presented to the President of the United States; If he approve he shall sign it, but if not he shall return it, with his Objections to that House

in which it shall have originated, who shall enter the Objections at large on their Journal, and proceed to reconsider it. If after such Reconsideration two thirds of that House shall agree to pass the Bill, it shall be sent, together with the Objections, to the other House, by which it shall likewise be reconsidered, and if approved by two thirds of that House, it shall become a Law. But in all such Cases the Votes of both Houses shall be determined by yeas and Nays, and the Names of the Persons voting for and against the Bill shall be entered on the Journal of each House respectively.

If any Bill shall not be returned by the President within ten Days (Sundays excepted) after it shall have been presented to him, the Same shall be a Law, in like Manner as if he had signed it, unless the Congress by their Adjournment prevent its Return, in which Case it shall not be a Law.

Clause 3: Every Order, Resolution, or Vote to which the Concurrence of the Senate and House of Representatives may be necessary (except on a question of Adjournment) shall be presented to the President of the United States; and before the Same shall take Effect, shall be approved by him, or being disapproved by him, shall be repassed by two thirds of the Senate and House of Representatives, according to the Rules and Limitations prescribed in the Case of a Bill.

Section 8
Powers of Congress

Clause 1: The Congress shall have Power To lay and collect Taxes, Duties, Imposts and Excises, to pay the Debts and provide for the common Defence and general Welfare of the United States; but all Duties, Imposts and Excises shall be uniform throughout the United States;

Clause 2: To borrow Money on the credit of the United States;

Clause 3: To regulate Commerce with foreign Nations, and among the several States, and with the Indian Tribes;

Clause 4: To establish an uniform Rule of Naturalization, and uniform Laws on the subject of Bankruptcies throughout the United States;

Clause 5: To coin Money, regulate the Value thereof, and of foreign Coin, and fix the Standard of Weights and Measures;

Clause 6: To provide for the Punishment of counterfeiting the Securities and current Coin of the United States;

Clause 7: To establish Post Offices and post Roads;

Clause 8: To promote the Progress of Science and useful Arts, by securing for limited Times to Authors and Inventors the exclusive Right to their respective Writings and Discoveries;

Clause 9: To constitute Tribunals inferior to the supreme Court;

Clause 10: To define and punish Piracies and Felonies committed on the high Seas, and Offences against the Law of Nations;

Clause 11: To declare War, grant Letters of Marque and Reprisal, and make Rules concerning Captures on Land and Water;

Clause 12: To raise and support Armies, but no Appropriation of Money to that Use shall be for a longer Term than two Years;

Clause 13: To provide and maintain a Navy;

Clause 14: To make Rules for the Government and Regulation of the land and naval Forces;

Clause 15: To provide for calling forth the Militia to execute the Laws of the Union, suppress Insurrections and repel Invasions;

Clause 16: To provide for organizing, arming, and disciplining, the Militia, and for governing such Part of them as may be employed in the Service of the United

States, reserving to the States respectively, the Appointment of the Officers, and the Authority of training the Militia according to the discipline prescribed by Congress;

Clause 17: To exercise exclusive Legislation in all Cases whatsoever, over such District (not exceeding ten Miles square) as may, by Cession of particular States, and the Acceptance of Congress, become the Seat of the Government of the United States, and to exercise like Authority over all Places purchased by the Consent of the Legislature of the State in which the Same shall be, for the Erection of Forts, Magazines, Arsenals, dock-Yards, and other needful Buildings;—And

Clause 18: To make all Laws which shall be necessary and proper for carrying into Execution the foregoing Powers, and all other Powers vested by this Constitution in the Government of the United States, or in any Department or Officer thereof.

Section 9
Powers Denied to the Federal Government

Clause 1: ~~The Migration or Importation of such Persons as any of the States now existing shall think proper to admit, shall not be prohibited by the Congress prior to the Year one thousand eight hundred and eight, but a Tax or duty may be imposed on such Importation, not exceeding ten dollars for each Person.~~

Clause 2: The Privilege of the Writ of Habeas Corpus shall not be suspended, unless when in Cases of Rebellion or Invasion the public Safety may require it.

Clause 3: No Bill of Attainder or ex post facto Law shall be passed.

Clause 4: No Capitation, or other direct, Tax shall be laid, unless in Proportion to the Census or Enumeration herein before directed to be taken.

Clause 5: No Tax or Duty shall be laid on Articles exported from any State.

Clause 6: No Preference shall be given by any Regulation of Commerce or Revenue to the Ports of one State over those of another: nor shall Vessels bound to, or from, one State, be obliged to enter, clear, or pay Duties in another.

Clause 7: No Money shall be drawn from the Treasury, but in Consequence of Appropriations made by Law; and a regular Statement and Account of the Receipts and Expenditures of all public Money shall be published from time to time.

Clause 8: No Title of Nobility shall be granted by the United States: And no Person holding any Office of Profit or Trust under them, shall, without the Consent of the Congress, accept of any present, Emolument, Office, or Title, of any kind whatever, from any King, Prince, or foreign State.

Section 10
Powers Denied to the States

Clause 1: No State shall enter into any Treaty, Alliance, or Confederation; grant Letters of Marque and Reprisal; coin Money; emit Bills of Credit; make any Thing but gold and silver Coin a Tender in Payment of Debts; pass any Bill of Attainder, ex post facto Law, or Law impairing the Obligation of Contracts, or grant any Title of Nobility.

Clause 2: No State shall, without the Consent of the Congress, lay any Imposts or Duties on Imports or Exports, except what may be absolutely necessary for executing it's inspection Laws: and the net Produce of all Duties and Imposts, laid by any State on Imports or Exports, shall be for the Use of the Treasury of the United States; and all such Laws shall be subject to the Revision and Controul of the Congress.

Clause 3: No State shall, without the Consent of Congress, lay any Duty of Tonnage, keep Troops, or Ships of War in time of Peace, enter into any Agreement or Compact with another State, or with a

foreign Power, or engage in War, unless actually invaded, or in such imminent Danger as will not admit of delay.

Article II Executive Branch

Section 1
President and Vice-President

Clause 1: The executive Power shall be vested in a President of the United States of America. He shall hold his Office during the Term of four Years, and, together with the Vice President, chosen for the same Term, be elected, as follows

Clause 2: Each State shall appoint, in such Manner as the Legislature thereof may direct, a Number of Electors, equal to the whole Number of Senators and Representatives to which the State may be entitled in the Congress: but no Senator or Representative, or Person holding an Office of Trust or Profit under the United States, shall be appointed an Elector.

Clause 3: ~~The Electors shall meet in their respective States, and vote by Ballot for two Persons, of whom one at least shall not be an Inhabitant of the same State with themselves. And they shall make a List of all the Persons voted for, and of the Number of Votes for each; which List they shall sign and certify, and transmit sealed to the Seat of the Government of the United States, directed to the President of the Senate. The President of the Senate shall, in the Presence of the Senate and House of Representatives, open all the Certificates, and the Votes shall then be counted. The Person having the greatest Number of Votes shall be the President, if such Number be a Majority of the whole Number of Electors appointed; and if there be more than one who have such Majority, and have an equal Number of Votes, then the House of Representatives shall immediately chuse by Ballot one of them for President; and if no Person have a Majority, then from the five highest on the~~

List the said House shall in like Manner chuse the President. But in chusing the President, the Votes shall be taken by States, the Representation from each State having one Vote; A quorum for this Purpose shall consist of a Member or Members from two thirds of the States, and a Majority of all the States shall be necessary to a Choice. In every Case, after the Choice of the President, the Person having the greatest Number of Votes of the Electors shall be the Vice President. But if there should remain two or more who have equal Votes, the Senate shall chuse from them by Ballot the Vice President.

Clause 4: The Congress may determine the Time of chusing the Electors, and the Day on which they shall give their Votes; which Day shall be the same throughout the United States.

Clause 5: No Person except a natural born Citizen, or a Citizen of the United States, at the time of the Adoption of this Constitution, shall be eligible to the Office of President; neither shall any Person be eligible to that Office who shall not have attained to the Age of thirty five Years, and been fourteen Years a Resident within the United States.

Clause 6: In Case of the Removal of the President from Office, or of his Death, Resignation, or Inability to discharge the Powers and Duties of the said Office, the Same shall devolve on the Vice President, and the Congress may by Law provide for the Case of Removal, Death, Resignation or Inability, both of the President and Vice President, declaring what Officer shall then act as President, and such Officer shall act accordingly, until the Disability be removed, or a President shall be elected.

Clause 7: The President shall, at stated Times, receive for his Services, a Compensation, which shall neither be encreased nor diminished during the Period for which he shall have been elected, and he shall not receive within that Period any other Emolument from the United States, or any of them.

Clause 8: Before he enter on the Execution of his Office, he shall take the following Oath or Affirmation:—"I do solemnly swear (or affirm) that I will faithfully execute the Office of President of the United States, and will to the best of my Ability, preserve, protect and defend the Constitution of the United States."

Section 2
Powers of the President

Clause 1: The President shall be Commander in Chief of the Army and Navy of the United States, and of the Militia of the several States, when called into the actual Service of the United States; he may require the Opinion, in writing, of the principal Officer in each of the executive Departments, upon any Subject relating to the Duties of their respective Offices, and he shall have Power to grant Reprieves and Pardons for Offences against the United States, except in Cases of Impeachment.

Clause 2: He shall have Power, by and with the Advice and Consent of the Senate, to make Treaties, provided two thirds of the Senators present concur; and he shall nominate, and by and with the Advice and Consent of the Senate, shall appoint Ambassadors, other public Ministers and Consuls, Judges of the supreme Court, and all other Officers of the United States, whose Appointments are not herein otherwise provided for, and which shall be established by Law: but the Congress may by Law vest the Appointment of such inferior Officers, as they think proper, in the President alone, in the Courts of Law, or in the Heads of Departments.

Clause 3: The President shall have Power to fill up all Vacancies that may happen during the Recess of the Senate, by granting Commissions which shall expire at the End of their next Session.

Section 3
Duties of the President

He shall from time to time give to the Congress Information of the State of the Union, and recommend to their Consideration such Measures as he shall judge necessary and expedient; he may, on extraordinary Occasions, convene both Houses, or either of them, and in Case of Disagreement between them, with Respect to the Time of Adjournment, he may adjourn them to such Time as he shall think proper; he shall receive Ambassadors and other public Ministers; he shall take Care that the Laws be faithfully executed, and shall Commission all the Officers of the United States.

Section 4
Impeachment

The President, Vice President and all civil Officers of the United States, shall be removed from Office on Impeachment for, and Conviction of, Treason, Bribery, or other high Crimes and Misdemeanors.

Article III
Judicial Branch

Section 1
Federal Courts

The judicial Power of the United States, shall be vested in one supreme Court, and in such inferior Courts as the Congress may from time to time ordain and establish. The Judges, both of the supreme and inferior Courts, shall hold their Offices during good Behaviour, and shall, at stated Times, receive for their Services, a Compensation, which shall not be diminished during their Continuance in Office.

Section 2
Extent of Judicial Powers

Clause 1: The judicial Power shall extend to all Cases, in Law and Equity, arising under this Constitution, the Laws of the United States, and Treaties made, or which shall be made, under their Authority;—to all Cases affecting Ambassadors, other public Ministers and Consuls;—to all Cases of admiralty and maritime Jurisdiction;—to Controversies to which the United States shall be a Party;—to Controversies between two or more States;—between a State and Citizens of another State; —between Citizens of different States, —between Citizens of the same State claiming Lands under Grants of different States, and between a State, or the Citizens thereof, and foreign States, Citizens or Subjects.

Clause 2: In all Cases affecting Ambassadors, other public Ministers and Consuls, and those in which a State shall be Party, the supreme Court shall have original Jurisdiction. In all the other Cases before mentioned, the supreme Court shall have appellate Jurisdiction, both as to Law and Fact, with such Exceptions, and under such Regulations as the Congress shall make.

Clause 3: The Trial of all Crimes, except in Cases of Impeachment, shall be by Jury; and such Trial shall be held in the State where the said Crimes shall have been committed; but when not committed within any State, the Trial shall be at such Place or Places as the Congress may by Law have directed.

Section 3
Treason

Clause 1: Treason against the United States, shall consist only in levying War against them, or in adhering to their Enemies, giving them Aid and Comfort. No Person shall be convicted of Treason unless on the Testimony of two Witnesses to the same overt Act, or on Confession in open Court.

Clause 2: The Congress shall have Power to declare the Punishment of Treason, but no Attainder of Treason shall work Corruption of Blood, or Forfeiture except during the Life of the Person attainted.

Article IV
The States

Section 1
Recognition of Each Other's Acts

Full Faith and Credit shall be given in each State to the public Acts, Records, and judicial Proceedings of every other State. And the Congress may by general Laws prescribe the Manner in which such Acts, Records and Proceedings shall be proved, and the Effect thereof.

Section 2
Citizens' Rights in Other States

Clause 1: The Citizens of each State shall be entitled to all Privileges and Immunities of Citizens in the several States.

Clause 2: A Person charged in any State with Treason, Felony, or other Crime, who shall flee from Justice, and be found in another State, shall on Demand of the executive Authority of the State from which he fled, be delivered up, to be removed to the State having Jurisdiction of the Crime.

Clause 3: No Person held to Service or Labour in one State, under the Laws thereof, escaping into another, shall, in Consequence of any Law or Regulation therein, be discharged from such Service or Labour, but shall be delivered up on Claim of the Party to whom such Service or Labour may be due.

Section 3
New States and Territories

Clause 1: New States may be admitted by the Congress into this Union; but no new State shall be formed or erected within the Jurisdiction of any other State; nor any State be formed by the Junction of two or more States, or Parts of States, without the Consent of the Legislatures of the States concerned as well as of the Congress.

Clause 2: The Congress shall have Power to dispose of and make all needful Rules and Regulations respecting the Territory or other Property belonging to the United States; and nothing in this Constitution shall be so construed as to Prejudice any Claims of the United States, or of any particular State.

Section 4
Guarantees to the States

The United States shall guarantee to every State in this Union a Republican Form of Government, and shall protect each of them against Invasion; and on Application of the Legislature, or of the Executive (when the Legislature cannot be convened) against domestic Violence.

Article V
Amending the Constitution

The Congress, whenever two thirds of both Houses shall deem it necessary, shall propose Amendments to this Constitution, or, on the Application of the Legislatures of two thirds of the several States, shall call a Convention for proposing Amendments, which, in either Case, shall be valid to all Intents and Purposes, as Part of this Constitution, when ratified by the Legislatures of three fourths of the several States, or by Conventions in three fourths thereof, as the one or the other Mode of Ratification may be proposed by the Congress; Provided that no Amendment which may be made prior to the Year One thousand eight hundred and eight shall in any Manner affect the first and fourth Clauses in the Ninth Section of the first Article; and that no State, without its Consent, shall be deprived of its equal Suffrage in the Senate.

Article VI
National Supremacy

Clause 1: All Debts contracted and Engagements entered into, before the Adoption of this Constitution, shall be as

valid against the United States under this Constitution, as under the Confederation.

Clause 2: This Constitution, and the Laws of the United States which shall be made in Pursuance thereof; and all Treaties made, or which shall be made, under the Authority of the United States, shall be the supreme Law of the Land; and the Judges in every State shall be bound thereby, any Thing in the Constitution or Laws of any State to the Contrary notwithstanding.

Clause 3: The Senators and Representatives before mentioned, and the Members of the several State Legislatures, and all executive and judicial Officers, both of the United States and of the several States, shall be bound by Oath or Affirmation, to support this Constitution; but no religious Test shall ever be required as a Qualification to any Office or public Trust under the United States.

Article VII Ratification

The Ratification of the Conventions of nine States, shall be sufficient for the Establishment of this Constitution between the States so ratifying the Same. Done in Convention by the Unanimous Consent of the States present the Seventeenth Day of September in the Year of our Lord one thousand seven hundred and Eighty seven and of the Independence of the United States of America the Twelfth In witness whereof We have hereunto subscribed our Names,

───────────────

George Washington, President and Deputy from Virginia

Delaware
George Read
Gunning Bedford, Junior
John Dickinson
Richard Bassett
Jacob Broom

Maryland
James McHenry
Daniel of St. Thomas Jenifer
Daniel Carroll

Virginia
John Blair
James Madison, Junior

North Carolina
William Blount
Richard Dobbs Spaight
Hugh Williamson

South Carolina
John Rutledge
Charles Cotesworth Pinckney
Charles Pinckney
Pierce Butler.

Georgia
William Few
Abraham Baldwin

New Hampshire
John Langdon
Nicholas Gilman

Massachusetts
Nathaniel Gorham
Rufus King

Connecticut
William Samuel Johnson
Roger Sherman

New York
Alexander Hamilton

New Jersey
William Livingston
David Brearley
William Paterson.
Jonathan Dayton

Pennsylvania
Benjamin Franklin
Thomas Mifflin
Robert Morris
George Clymer
Thomas FitzSimons
Jared Ingersoll
James Wilson
Gouverneur Morris
Attest: William Jackson, Secretary

Amendments to the Constitution

The pages that follow contain the original text of the Amendments to the United States Constitution. Sections that are no longer enforced have been crossed out. The spelling and punctuation of the document remain in their original format. The headings are not part of the original Amendments.

Amendment 1 (1791)
Religious and Political Freedom

Congress shall make no law respecting an establishment of religion, or prohibiting the free exercise thereof; or abridging the freedom of speech, or of the press; or the right of the people peaceably to assemble, and to petition the Government for a redress of grievances.

Amendment 2 (1791)
Right to Bear Arms

A well regulated Militia, being necessary to the security of a free State, the right of the people to keep and bear Arms, shall not be infringed.

Amendment 3 (1791)
Quartering of Soldiers

No Soldier shall, in time of peace be quartered in any house, without the consent of the Owner, nor in time of war, but in a manner to be prescribed by law.

Amendment 4 (1791)
Search and Seizure

The right of the people to be secure in their persons, houses, papers, and effects, against unreasonable searches and seizures, shall not be violated, and no Warrants shall issue, but upon probable cause, supported by Oath or affirmation, and particularly describing the place to be searched, and the persons or things to be seized.

Amendment 5 (1791)
Life, Liberty, and Property

No person shall be held to answer for a capital, or otherwise infamous crime, unless on a presentment or indictment of a Grand Jury, except in cases arising in the land or naval forces, or in the Militia, when in actual service in time of War or public danger; nor shall any person be subject for the same offence to be twice put in jeopardy of life or limb; nor shall be compelled in any criminal case to be a witness against himself, nor be deprived of life, liberty, or property, without due process of law; nor shall private property be taken for public use, without just compensation.

Amendment 6 (1791)
Rights of the Accused

In all criminal prosecutions, the accused shall enjoy the right to a speedy and public trial, by an impartial jury of the State and district wherein the crime shall have been committed, which district shall have been previously ascertained by law, and to be informed of the nature and cause of the accusation; to be confronted with the witnesses against him; to have compulsory process for obtaining witnesses in his favor, and to have the Assistance of Counsel for his defence.

Amendment 7 (1791)
Right to Trial by Jury

In Suits at common law, where the value in controversy shall exceed twenty dollars, the right of trial by jury shall be preserved, and no fact tried by a jury, shall be otherwise re-examined in any Court of the United States, than according to the rules of the common law.

Amendment 8 (1791)
Bail and Punishment

Excessive bail shall not be required, nor excessive fines imposed, nor cruel and unusual punishments inflicted.

Amendment 9 (1791)
All Other Rights

The enumeration in the Constitution, of certain rights, shall not be construed to deny or disparage others retained by the people.

Amendment 10 (1791)
Rights of States and the People

The powers not delegated to the United States by the Constitution, nor prohibited by it to the States, are reserved to the States respectively, or to the people.

Amendment 11 (1795)
Suits Against a State

The Judicial power of the United States shall not be construed to extend to any suit in law or equity, commenced or prosecuted against one of the United States by Citizens of another State, or by Citizens or Subjects of any Foreign State.

Amendment 12 (1804)
Election of President

The Electors shall meet in their respective states, and vote by ballot for President and Vice-President, one of whom, at least, shall not be an inhabitant of the same state with themselves; they shall name in their ballots the person voted for as President, and in distinct ballots the person voted for as Vice-President, and they shall make distinct lists of all persons voted for as President, and of all persons voted for as Vice-President, and of the number of votes for each, which lists they shall sign and certify, and transmit sealed to the seat of the government of the United States, directed to the President of the Senate;

The President of the Senate shall, in the presence of the Senate and House of Representatives, open all the certificates and the votes shall then be counted;

The person having the greatest number of votes for President, shall be the President, if such number be a majority of the whole number of Electors appointed; and if no person have such majority, then from the persons having the highest numbers not exceeding three on the list of those voted for as President, the House of Representatives shall choose immediately, by ballot, the President. But in choosing the President, the votes shall be taken by states, the representation from each state having one vote; a quorum for this purpose shall consist of a member or members from two-thirds of the states, and a majority of all the states shall be necessary to a choice.

~~And if the House of Representatives shall not choose a President whenever the right of choice shall devolve upon them, before the fourth day of March next following, then the Vice-President shall act as President, as in the case of the death or other constitutional disability of the President.~~

The person having the greatest number of votes as Vice-President, shall be the Vice-President, if such number be a majority of the whole number of Electors appointed, and if no person have a majority, then from the two highest numbers on the list, the Senate shall choose the Vice-President; a quorum for the purpose shall consist of two-thirds of the whole number of Senators, and a majority of the whole number shall be necessary to a choice. But no person constitutionally ineligible to the office of

President shall be eligible to that of Vice-President of the United States.

Amendment 13   (1865)
Abolition of Slavery

Section 1 Neither slavery nor involuntary servitude, except as a punishment for crime whereof the party shall have been duly convicted, shall exist within the United States, or any place subject to their jurisdiction.

Section 2 Congress shall have power to enforce this article by appropriate legislation.

Amendment 14   (1868)
Civil Rights in the States

Section 1 All persons born or naturalized in the United States, and subject to the jurisdiction thereof, are citizens of the United States and of the State wherein they reside. No State shall make or enforce any law which shall abridge the privileges or immunities of citizens of the United States; nor shall any State deprive any person of life, liberty, or property, without due process of law; nor deny to any person within its jurisdiction the equal protection of the laws.

Section 2 Representatives shall be apportioned among the several States according to their respective numbers, counting the whole number of persons in each State, excluding Indians not taxed. But when the right to vote at any election for the choice of electors for President and Vice President of the United States, Representatives in Congress, the Executive and Judicial officers of a State, or the members of the Legislature thereof, is denied to any of the male inhabitants of such State, being twenty-one years of age,(See Note 15) and citizens of the United States, or in any way abridged, except for participation in rebellion, or other crime, the basis of representation therein shall be reduced in the proportion which the number of such male citizens shall bear to the whole number of male citizens twenty-one years of age in such State.

Section 3 No person shall be a Senator or Representative in Congress, or elector of President and Vice President, or hold any office, civil or military, under the United States, or under any State, who, having previously taken an oath, as a member of Congress, or as an officer of the United States, or as a member of any State legislature, or as an executive or judicial officer of any State, to support the Constitution of the United States, shall have engaged in insurrection or rebellion against the same, or given aid or comfort to the enemies thereof. But Congress may by a vote of two-thirds of each House, remove such disability.

Section 4 The validity of the public debt of the United States, authorized by law, including debts incurred for payment of pensions and bounties for services in suppressing insurrection or rebellion, shall not be questioned. But neither the United States nor any State shall assume or pay any debt or obligation incurred in aid of insurrection or rebellion against the United States, or any claim for the loss or emancipation of any slave; but all such debts, obligations and claims shall be held illegal and void.

Section 5 The Congress shall have power to enforce, by appropriate legislation, the provisions of this article.

Amendment 15   (1870)
Black Suffrage

Section 1 The right of citizens of the United States to vote shall not be denied or abridged by the United States or by any State on account of race, color, or previous condition of servitude.

Section 2 The Congress shall have power to enforce this article by appropriate legislation.

Amendment 16   (1913)
Income Tax

The Congress shall have power to lay and collect taxes on incomes, from whatever source derived, without apportionment among the several States, and without regard to any census or enumeration.

Amendment 17   (1919)
Direct Election of Senators

Section 1 The Senate of the United States shall be composed of two Senators from each State, elected by the people thereof, for six years; and each Senator shall have one vote. The electors in each State shall have the qualifications requisite for electors of the most numerous branch of the State legislatures.

Section 2 When vacancies happen in the representation of any State in the Senate, the executive authority of such State shall issue writs of election to fill such vacancies: Provided, That the legislature of any State may empower the executive thereof to make temporary appointments until the people fill the vacancies by election as the legislature may direct.

Section 3 This amendment shall not be so construed as to affect the election or term of any Senator chosen before it becomes valid as part of the Constitution.

Amendment 18   (1919)
National Prohibition

Section 1 ~~After one year from the ratification of this article the manufacture, sale, or transportation of intoxicating liquors within, the importation thereof into, or the exportation thereof from the United States and all territory subject to the jurisdiction thereof for beverage purposes is hereby prohibited.~~

Section 2 ~~The Congress and the several States shall have concurrent power to enforce this article by appropriate legislation.~~

Section 3 ~~This article shall be inoperative unless it shall have been ratified as an~~ ~~amendment to the Constitution by the legislatures of the several States, as provided in the Constitution, within seven years from the date of the submission hereof to the States by the Congress.~~

Amendment 19   (1920)
Women's Suffrage

The right of citizens of the United States to vote shall not be denied or abridged by the United States or by any State on account of sex.

Congress shall have power to enforce this article by appropriate legislation.

Amendment 20   (1933)
"Lame-Duck" Amendment

Section 1 The terms of the President and Vice President shall end at noon on the 20th day of January, and the terms of Senators and Representatives at noon on the 3d day of January, of the years in which such terms would have ended if this article had not been ratified; and the terms of their successors shall then begin.

Section 2 The Congress shall assemble at least once in every year, and such meeting shall begin at noon on the 3d day of January, unless they shall by law appoint a different day.

Section 3 If, at the time fixed for the beginning of the term of the President, the President elect shall have died, the Vice President elect shall become President. If a President shall not have been chosen before the time fixed for the beginning of his term, or if the President elect shall have failed to qualify, then the Vice President elect shall act as President until a President shall have qualified; and the Congress may by law provide for the case wherein neither a President elect nor a Vice President elect shall have qualified, declaring who shall then act as President, or the manner in which one who is to act shall be selected, and such person shall act accordingly until a President or Vice President shall have qualified.

Section 4 The Congress may by law provide for the case of the death of any of the persons from whom the House of Representatives may choose a President whenever the right of choice shall have devolved upon them, and for the case of the death of any of the persons from whom the Senate may choose a Vice President whenever the right of choice shall have devolved upon them.

Section 5 Sections 1 and 2 shall take effect on the 15th day of October following the ratification of this article.

Section 6 This article shall be inoperative unless it shall have been ratified as an amendment to the Constitution by the legislatures of three-fourths of the several States within seven years from the date of its submission.

Amendment 21 (1933)
Repeal of Prohibition

Section 1 The eighteenth article of amendment to the Constitution of the United States is hereby repealed.

Section 2 The transportation or importation into any State, Territory, or possession of the United States for delivery or use therein of intoxicating liquors, in violation of the laws thereof, is hereby prohibited.

Section 3 This article shall be inoperative unless it shall have been ratified as an amendment to the Constitution by conventions in the several States, as provided in the Constitution, within seven years from the date of the submission hereof to the States by the Congress.

Amendment 22 (1951)
Presidential Term of Office

Section 1 No person shall be elected to the office of the President more than twice, and no person who has held the office of

President, or acted as President, for more than two years of a term to which some other person was elected President shall be elected to the office of the President more than once. ~~But this article shall not apply to any person holding the office of President when this article was proposed by the Congress, and shall not prevent any person who may be holding the office of President, or acting as President, during the term within which this article becomes operative from holding the office of President or acting as President during the remainder of such term.~~

Section 2 This article shall be inoperative unless it shall have been ratified as an amendment to the Constitution by the legislatures of three-fourths of the several states within seven years from the date of its submission to the states by the Congress.

Amendment 23 (1961)
Voting in the District of Columbia

Section 1 The District constituting the seat of government of the United States shall appoint in such manner as the Congress may direct:

A number of electors of President and Vice President equal to the whole number of Senators and Representatives in Congress to which the District would be entitled if it were a state, but in no event more than the least populous state; they shall be in addition to those appointed by the states, but they shall be considered, for the purposes of the election of President and Vice President, to be electors appointed by a state; and they shall meet in the District and perform such duties as provided by the twelfth article of amendment.

Section 2 The Congress shall have power to enforce this article by appropriate legislation.

Amendment 24 (1964)
Abolition of Poll Taxes

Section 1 The right of citizens of the United States to vote in any primary or other election for President or Vice President, for

electors for President or Vice President, or for Senator or Representative in Congress, shall not be denied or abridged by the United States or any state by reason of failure to pay any poll tax or other tax.

Section 2 The Congress shall have power to enforce this article by appropriate legislation.

Amendment 25 (1967)
Presidential Disability and Succession

Section 1 In case of the removal of the President from office or of his death or resignation, the Vice President shall become President.

Section 2 Whenever there is a vacancy in the office of the Vice President, the President shall nominate a Vice President who shall take office upon confirmation by a majority vote of both Houses of Congress.

Section 3 Whenever the President transmits to the President pro tempore of the Senate and the Speaker of the House of Representatives his written declaration that he is unable to discharge the powers and duties of his office, and until he transmits to them a written declaration to the contrary, such powers and duties shall be discharged by the Vice President as Acting President.

Section 4 Whenever the Vice President and a majority of either the principal officers of the executive departments or of such other body as Congress may by law provide, transmit to the President pro tempore of the Senate and the Speaker of the House of Representatives their written declaration that the President is unable to discharge the powers and duties of his office, the Vice President shall immediately assume the powers and duties of the office as Acting President.

Thereafter, when the President transmits to the President pro tempore of the Senate and

the Speaker of the House of Representatives his written declaration that no inability exists, he shall resume the powers and duties of his office unless the Vice President and a majority of either the principal officers of the executive department or of such other body as Congress may by law provide, transmit within four days to the President pro tempore of the Senate and the Speaker of the House of Representatives their written declaration that the President is unable to discharge the powers and duties of his office. Thereupon Congress shall decide the issue, assembling within forty-eight hours for that purpose if not in session. If the Congress, within twenty-one days after receipt of the latter written declaration, or, if Congress is not in session, within twenty-one days after Congress is required to assemble, determines by two-thirds vote of both Houses that the President is unable to discharge the powers and duties of his office, the Vice President shall continue to discharge the same as Acting President; otherwise, the President shall resume the powers and duties of his office.

Amendment 26 (1971)
Eighteen-Year-Old Vote

Section 1 The right of citizens of the United States, who are 18 years of age or older, to vote, shall not be denied or abridged by the United States or any state on account of age.

Section 2 The Congress shall have the power to enforce this article by appropriate legislation.

Amendment 27 (1992)
Congressional Salaries

No law varying the compensation for the services of the Senators and Representatives shall take effect until an election of Representatives shall have intervened.

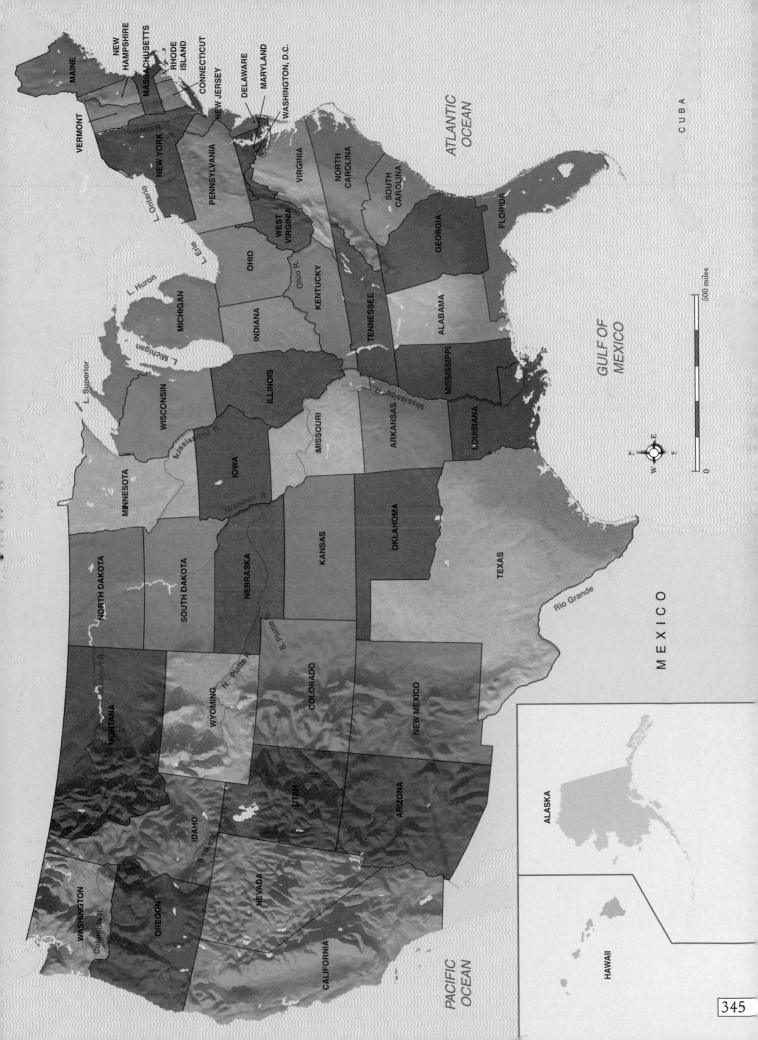

MAINE

NEW HAMPSHIRE

VERMONT

MASSACHUSETTS

RHODE ISLAND

CONNECTICUT

NEW JERSEY

DELAWARE

MARYLAND

WASHINGTON, D.C.

NEW YORK

Hudson R.

PENNSYLVANIA

L. Ontario

L. Erie

VIRGINIA

WEST VIRGINIA

NORTH CAROLINA

OHIO

Ohio R.

KENTUCKY

SOUTH CAROLINA

GEORGIA

FLORIDA

ATLANTIC OCEAN

CUBA

L. Huron

MICHIGAN

L. Michigan

INDIANA

TENNESSEE

ALABAMA

L. Superior

WISCONSIN

ILLINOIS

Mississippi R.

MISSISSIPPI

GULF OF MEXICO

500 miles

MINNESOTA

IOWA

Mississippi R.

MISSOURI

ARKANSAS

LOUISIANA

Mississippi R.

Missouri R.

NORTH DAKOTA

SOUTH DAKOTA

NEBRASKA

KANSAS

OKLAHOMA

N

W E

S

Missouri R.

S. Platte R.

N. Platte R.

TEXAS

Rio Grande

MONTANA

WYOMING

COLORADO

NEW MEXICO

MEXICO

IDAHO

UTAH

ARIZONA

Snake R.

WASHINGTON

Columbia R.

OREGON

NEVADA

CALIFORNIA

PACIFIC OCEAN

ALASKA

HAWAII

345

PACIFIC OCEAN

Tropic of Cancer

Equator

Tropic of Capricorn

NORTH ATLANTIC OCEAN

SOUTH ATLANTIC OCEAN

INDIAN OCEAN

ARCTIC OCEAN

PACIFIC OCEAN

0

2000

4000

6000

8000 miles. (at Equator)

N
W   E
S

MEXICO
UNITED STATES OF AMERICA
CANADA
GREENLAND
ICELAND

BELIZE
CUBA
HAITI
DOMINICAN REPUBLIC
PUERTO RICO
GUATEMALA
EL SALVADOR
HONDURAS
NICARAGUA
COSTA RICA
PANAMA
VENEZUELA
COLOMBIA
ECUADOR
PERU
GUYANA
SURINAM
FRENCH GUIANA
BRAZIL
BOLIVIA
CHILE
ARGENTINA
PARAGUAY
URUGUAY
FALKLAND/MALVINAS ISLANDS

ANTARCTICA

WESTERN SAHARA
MAURITANIA
SENEGAL
GAMBIA
GUINEA-BISSAU
GUINEA
SIERRA LEONE
IVORY COAST
LIBERIA
BURKINA FASO
GHANA
TOGO
BENIN
NIGERIA
MALI
NIGER
CAMEROON
EQUATORIAL GUINEA
GABON
CONGO
CHAD
LIBYA
ALGERIA
MOROCCO
SPAIN
PORTUGAL
ANDORRA
FRANCE
SWITZERLAND
AUSTRIA
LUXEMBOURG
BELGIUM
NETHERLANDS
IRELAND
UNITED KINGDOM
CZECH REP.
GERMANY
DENMARK
NORWAY
SWEDEN
FINLAND
ESTONIA
LATVIA
LITHUANIA
POLAND
SLOVENIA
CROATIA
ITALY
YUGOSLAVIA
ALBANIA
MACEDONIA
GREECE
BULGARIA
ROMANIA
MOLDOVA
UKRAINE
BELARUS
SLOVAK REP.
HUNGARY
RUSSIA
GEORGIA
ARMENIA
AZERBAIJAN
TURKEY
CYPRUS
SYRIA
LEBANON
ISRAEL
JORDAN
IRAQ
IRAN
KUWAIT
SAUDI ARABIA
QATAR
UNITED ARAB EMIRATES
OMAN
YEMEN
EGYPT
SUDAN
ERITREA
ETHIOPIA
SOMALIA
CENTRAL AFRICAN REPUBLIC
DEMOCRATIC REPUBLIC OF THE CONGO
UGANDA
KENYA
RWANDA
BURUNDI
TANZANIA
ANGOLA
ZAMBIA
MALAWI
MOZAMBIQUE
NAMIBIA
BOTSWANA
ZIMBABWE
SWAZILAND
LESOTHO
SOUTH AFRICA
MADAGASCAR
MAURITIUS

KAZAKHSTAN
KYRGYZSTAN
UZBEKISTAN
TAJIKISTAN
TURKMENISTAN
AFGHANISTAN
PAKISTAN
INDIA
NEPAL
BHUTAN
BANGLADESH
MYANMAR (BURMA)
THAILAND
CAMBODIA
LAOS
VIETNAM
MALAYSIA
BRUNEI
SRI LANKA
CHINA
MONGOLIA
RUSSIA
SOUTH KOREA
NORTH KOREA
JAPAN
TAIWAN
PHILIPPINES
INDONESIA
PAPUA NEW GUINEA
AUSTRALIA
NEW ZEALAND

Glossary/Index

Acknowledgements

Photo Credits

3 (t)©The Image Bank/Getty Images, (bl)©BP/TAXI/Getty Images, (br)©The Granger Collection; 4 (t)©PhotoDisc/Getty Images, (b)©John McAnulty/CORBIS; 6 (l)©HIP/Scala/Art Resource, NY, (r)©Ohio Historical Society; 7 ©University of Arizona; 8 ©Richard A. Cooke/CORBIS; 9 ©Courtesy the Phoebe Apperson Hearst Museum of Anthropology and the Regents of the University of California; 10 ©Mary Evans Picture Library; 11 ©North Wind Picture Archives; 13 (t)©CORBIS, (b)©North Wind Picture Archives; 14 ©CORBIS; 16 ©Geoffrey Clements/CORBIS; 17 ©North Wind Picture Archives; 20 (t)©Mary Evans Picture Library, (b)©Greg Probst/CORBIS; 21 ©Bettmann/CORBIS; 23 (t)©Mary Evans Picture Library, (b)©Bettmann/CORBIS; 24 ©Mary Evans Picture Library; 25 ©Bettmann/CORBIS; 26 ©Bettmann/CORBIS; 27 ©Mary Evans Picture Library; 28 ©Mary Evans Picture Library; 29 ©Mary Evans Picture Library; 30 ©Mary Evans Picture Library; 31 ©Mary Evans Picture Library; 32 ©Mary Evans Picture Library; 33(t)©Mary Evans Picture Library, (b)©The Granger Collection; 37 (t)©North Wind Picture Archives, (bl)©The Library of Congress, (br)©J.C. Kanny/Lorpresse/Corbis Sygma; 38 (t)©The Great North West Trading Co., (b)©Denver Public Library, Colorado Historical Society, and Denver Art Museum; 39 ©North Wind Picture Archives; 41 (t)©CORBIS, (b)©North Wind Picture Archives; 42 ©Stapleton Collection/CORBIS; 43 ©North Wind Picture Archives; 45 ©Denver Public Library, Colorado Historical Society, and Denver Art Museum; 47 (t)©Mary Evans Picture Library, (b)©North Wind Picture Archives; 48 (t)©Bettmann/CORBIS, (b)©The Granger Collection; 52 (t)©Bettmann/CORBIS, (b)©Kevin Fleming/CORBIS; 54 (t)©North Wind Picture Archives, (b)©Bettmann/CORBIS; 55 (t)©The Granger Collection, (b) ©The Granger Collection; 56 ©North Wind Picture Archives; 57 ©North Wind Picture Archives; 58 ©North Wind Picture Archives; 59 ©Bettmann/CORBIS; 60 (t)©North Wind Picture Archives, (b)©Bettmann/CORBIS; 61 (t)©Bettmann/CORBIS, (b)©Bettmann/CORBIS; 62 (t)©Bettmann/CORBIS, (b)©The Granger Collection; 63 ©North Wind Picture Archives; 64 ©Francis G. Mayer/CORBIS; 65 ©North Wind Picture Archives; 69 (t)©The Granger Collection, (bl)©Bettmann/CORBIS, (br)©The Library of Congress; 70 (t)©Jeremy Horner/CORBIS, (b)©Tony Arruza/CORBIS; 71 ©The Granger Collection; 72 (t)©The Granger Collection, (b)©Michael Freeman/CORBIS; 74 (t)©The Granger Collection, (b)©CORBIS; 78 ©Bettmann/CORBIS; 79 (t)©CORBIS, (b)©CORBIS; 82 ©The Granger Collection; 83 ©The Library of Congress; 86 (t)Morristown National Historical Society, (b)©Kevin Fleming/CORBIS; 87 ©North Wind Picture Archives; 88©Bettmann/CORBIS; 89 ©The Granger Collection; 90 (t)©Bettmann/CORBIS, (b)©Bettmann/CORBIS; 92 ©North Wind Picture Archives; 94 (t)©The Granger Collection, (b)©Philadelphia Museum of Art/CORBIS; 95 ©Bettmann/CORBIS; 96 ©The Library of Congress; 98 (t)©The Granger Collection, (b)©The Granger Collection; 99 ©North Wind Picture Archives; 103 (t)©Francis G. Mayer/CORBIS, (bl)©Bettmann/CORBIS; 104 (t)Time Life Pictures/Getty Images, (b)©Bettmann/CORBIS; 105 ©CORBIS; 106 (t)©North Wind Picture Archives, (b)©Bettmann/CORBIS; 108 (t)©North Wind Picture Archives, (b)©Bettmann/CORBIS; 110 ©Bettmann/CORBIS; 111 ©North Wind Picture Archives; 112 ©Bettmann/CORBIS; 114 ©The Library of Congress; 115 ©Bettmann/CORBIS; 116 ©Bettmann/CORBIS; 117 ©The Library of Congress; 119 ©The Library of Congress; 120 (t)©Lee Snider; Lee Snider/CORBIS, (b)©Richard T. Nowitz/CORBIS; 121 ©Bettmann/CORBIS; 122 (t)©CORBIS, (c)©David Muench/CORBIS; 122 ©The Granger Collection; 124 (t)©Francis G. Mayer/CORBIS, (b)©Bettmann/CORBIS; 126 (l)©CORBIS, (r)©The Library of Congress; 127 ©Bettmann/CORBIS; 128 (t)©Bettmann/CORBIS, (b)©Bettmann/CORBIS; 129 ©The Library of Congress; 130 (t)©North Wind Picture Archives, (b)©Bettmann/CORBIS; 132 (t)©Bettmann/CORBIS, (b)©The Granger Collection; 133 ©CORBIS; 135 ©Bettmann/CORBIS; 137 (t)©Christie's Images/CORBIS, (bl)©Bettmann/CORBIS, (br)©The Library of Congress; 138 (t)©The Library of Congress; (b)©Dennis Degnan/CORBIS; 139 ©David Muench/CORBIS; 140 ©The Library of Congress; 141 ©Bettmann/CORBIS; 144 (t)©CORBIS, (b)©National Archives; 145 ©The Granger Collection; 147 ©Photodisc/Getty Images; 148 ©Bettmann/CORBIS; 149 ©Bettmann/CORBIS; 150 (b)©The Library of Congress; 151 ©The Library of Congress; 154 (t)©National Archives, (b)©Bettmann/CORBIS; 159 ©Hulton Archive/Stringer/Getty Images; 169 (t)©Francis G. Mayer/CORBIS, (bl)©Bettmann/CORBIS, (br)©CORBIS;170 ©The Granger Collection; 172 (t)©Bettmann/CORBIS, (b)©The Library of Congress; 173 ©Bettmann/CORBIS; 175 ©Bettmann/CORBIS; 176 ©Bettmann/CORBIS; 177 (t)©CORBIS, (b)©National Archives, Courtesy of the New York State Historical Association, Cooperstown; 178 (l)©Stapleton Collection/CORBIS, (r)©Bettmann/CORBIS; 179 ©Archivo Iconografico, S.A./CORBIS; 180 ©The Library of Congress; 181 ©Bettmann/CORBIS; 182 ©The Library of Congress; 186 (t)©Bettmann/CORBIS (b)©Bettmann/CORBIS; 187 ©The Library of Congress; 188 ©The Library of Congress; 189 (l)©Bettmann/CORBIS, (r)©Bettmann/CORBIS; 191 ©Bettmann/CORBIS; 192 Time Life Pictures/Getty Images; 193 ©Bettmann/CORBIS; 194 ©Naval Historical Foundation; 195 ©The Granger Collection; 196 ©Bettmann/CORBIS; 197 (t)©Bettmann/CORBIS, (b)©Bettmann/CORBIS; 201 (t) ©CORBIS, (bl) ©Bettmann/CORBIS, (br) ©CORBIS; 202 (b)©Bettmann/CORBIS; 203 ©Shelburne Museum, Shelburne, Vermont; 204 (t)©CORBIS, (b)©Bettmann/CORBIS; 205 ©CORBIS; 206 ©Bettmann/CORBIS; 207 ©Bridgeman Art Library, Gift of Mrs D. Carnegie; 208 ©Bettmann/CORBIS; 209 ©Bettmann/CORBIS; 210 (t)©Denver Public Library, Colorado Historical Society, and Denver Art Museum, (b)©The Granger Collection; 211 ©Texas State Library and Archives Commission; 212 ©CORBIS; 213 ©Mary Evans Picture Library; 216 (t)©Bettmann/CORBIS; 218 (t)©The Library of Congress, (b)©The Library of Congress; 220 ©Lee Snider; Lee Snider/CORBIS; 222 ©The Library of Congress; 223 (t)©The Library of Congress, (b)©Bettmann/CORBIS; 224 ©Bettmann/CORBIS; 226 (t)©The Library of Congress; 228 ©Bettmann/CORBIS; 229 ©Max D. Standley; 231©Bettmann/CORBIS; 233 (t)©Bettmann/CORBIS, (bl)©Bettmann/CORBIS, (br)©Bettmann/CORBIS; 234 ©Bettmann/CORBIS; 235 (c)©Bettmann/CORBIS, (b)©Bettmann/CORBIS; 236 ©CORBIS; 237 ©CORBIS; 238 ©Bettmann/CORBIS; 239 (b)©The Granger Collection; 240 ©The Granger Collection; 241 ©The Granger Collection; 242 ©The Granger Collection; 243 (b)©Northern Illinois University; 244 ©CORBIS; 248 (t)©Rick Gayle/CORBIS, (b)©CORBIS; 249 ©Bettmann/CORBIS; 250 ©The Granger Collection; 251 ©CORBIS; 252 ©Bettmann/CORBIS; 253 ©Bettmann/CORBIS; 254 (t)©Bettmann/CORBIS; 255 (t)©Bettmann/CORBIS, (b)©Bettmann/CORBIS; 256 ©Bettmann/CORBIS; 257 (l)©Bettmann/CORBIS, (r)©CORBIS; 258 (t)©Bettmann/CORBIS, (b)©Bettmann/CORBIS; 259 ©The Granger Collection; 263 (t) ©CORBIS, (bl)©CORBIS, (br)©North Wind Picture Archives; 264 (t)©Bettmann/CORBIS, (b)©Hulton-Deutsch Collection/CORBIS; 265 ©North Wind Picture Archives; 266 (t)©Mary Evans Picture Library, (b)©North Wind Picture Archives; 267 (t)©Bettmann/CORBIS, (b)©Mary Evans Picture Library; 268©Bettmann/CORBIS; 269 ©Bettmann/CORBIS; 270 (t)©Mary Evans Picture Library, (b)©North Wind Picture Archives; 271 (t)©Museum of the City of New York/CORBIS, (c)©Francis G. Mayer/CORBIS, (b)©Underwood & Underwood/CORBIS; 272 ©Stapleton Collection/CORBIS; 273 ©North Wind Picture Archives; 274 ©CORBIS; 278 (t)©Bettmann/CORBIS, (b)©Denver Public Library, Colorado Historical Society, and Denver Art Museum; 279 ©The Granger Collection; 280 ©Bettmann/CORBIS; 281 (t)©The Granger Collection, (b)©The Corcoran Gallery of Art/CORBIS; 283 ©The Corcoran Gallery of Art/CORBIS; 284 (t)©North Wind Picture Archives, (b)©Bettmann/CORBIS; 285 Hulton Archive/Getty Images; 286 ©Bettmann/CORBIS; 287 ©David J. & Janice L. Frent Collection/CORBIS; 288 (t)©Bettmann/CORBIS, (b)©Bettmann/CORBIS; 289 ©CORBIS; 293 (t)©The Granger Collection, (bl)©Picture History LLC, (br)©Bettmann/CORBIS; 294 ©The Library of Congress; 297 (cl)©Bettmann/CORBIS, (br)©Library of Congress, Rare Book and Special Collections Division; 298 (t)©The Library of Congress, (b)©North Wind Picture Archives; 301 ©The Granger Collection; 303 ©Bettmann/CORBIS; 304 ©CORBIS; 305 (t)©CORBIS, (b)©Bettmann/CORBIS; 306 (t)©North Wind Picture Archives, (b) ©The Library of Congress; 307 ©The Granger Collection; 310 (b)©The Library of Congress; 311 (l)©The Library of Congress, (r)©The Library of Congress, 312 ©Minnesota Historical Society/CORBIS; 313 (t)©Museum of the City of New York/CORBIS, (b)©The Library of Congress; 314 ©Francis G. Mayer/CORBIS; 316 ©CORBIS; 317 ©CORBIS; 318 ©CORBIS; 319 (t) ©Bettmann/CORBIS, (b) ©CORBIS; 320 ©The Library of Congress; 321 ©CORBIS; 322 (t) ©The Library of Congress, (b) ©The Library of Congress; 323 ©Bettmann/CORBIS

(t) top, (b) bottom, (l) left, (r) right

American History, written at a 5 to 8 reading level, is an integrated series of print and electronic resources designed to provide a complete classroom solution for students who need extra support. Every chapter and lesson in the student book contains features and activities to keep students engaged in the learning process. The student DVD, the Annotated Teacher's Edition, and the Teacher's Resource Binder all provide additional materials for English Language Learners.

American History incorporates the National Council for the Social Studies (NCSS) high school thematic strands. *American History 1* covers events before 1865, ending with the Civil War and the surrender of the South. *American History 2* begins with the assassination of President Abraham Lincoln and continues through the modern era.

ANCILLARY MATERIALS

Student Edition DVD

- PDFs of all student book pages
- Audio narration of each page in the student book
- Spanish audio introduction of each key chapter concept
- Spanish audio ELL activity for each chapter
- Four interactive games per chapter
- Student Presentation Builder
- Interactive historical timeline
- Interactive Glossary

Annotated Teacher's Edition

- Reduced student pages with wrap-around teacher notes
- Teaching objectives for each lesson
- Lists of classroom materials
- Extension activities
- Vocabulary lessons
- Literary connections
- Classroom discussions

Teacher's Resource Binder

- Includes Annotated Teacher's Edition
- 160 blackline masters, eight per chapter, consisting of
  - a reading comprehension activity
  - a vocabulary reinforcement activity
  - an additional biography
  - an additional primary source document
  - a map activity
  - a chapter activity
  - a chapter review
  - a chapter quiz
- 20 overhead transparencies
- CD-ROM consisting of the following PDFs
  - entire Annotated Teacher's Edition
  - one test per unit
  - one full book assessment
  - one ELL reading activity per chapter
  - one ELL vocabulary activity per chapter
  - one puzzle per chapter

American History 1		American History 2	
Student Edition	0-07-704435-5	Student Edition	0-07-704438-X
Student Edition with DVD	0-07-704434-7	Student Edition with DVD	0-07-704437-1
Annotated Teacher's Edition	0-07-704453-3	Annotated Teacher's Edition	0-07-704454-1
Teacher's Resource Binder	0-07-704436-3	Teacher's Resource Binder	0-07-704439-8

The McGraw·Hill Companies

ISBN 0-07-704453-3

9 780077 044534

McGraw Hill **Wright Group**